Psychotherapy in a New Key

PSYCHOTHERAPY

IN A NEW KEY

A Guide to Time-Limited

Dynamic Psychotherapy

HANS H. STRUPP

JEFFREY L. BINDER

Basic Books, Inc., Publishers   New York

Library of Congress Cataloging in Publication Data

Strupp, Hans H.
  Psychotherapy in a new key.

  Bibliographic references.
  Includes index.
  1. Psychotherapy. I. Binder, Jeffrey L. II. Title.
III. Title: Time-limited dynamic psychotherapy.
RC480.5.S773 1984   616.89'14   83–46075
ISBN 0–465–06747–6

To Lottie, Karen, Barbie, and John

AND

To Vanessa and Aaron, Jane, and Marty

Contents

Foreword by Merton M. Gill, M.D.   *viii*

Preface   *xi*

Acknowledgments   *xviii*

Chapter 1
Overview and Background   *3*

Chapter 2
Patients' Problems as a Function of Disturbed
Interpersonal Relationships   *28*

Chapter 3
The Therapist's Stance   *40*

Chapter 4
Assessment   *51*

Chapter 5
The Dynamic Focus   *65*
     Thomas E. Schacht, Jeffrey L. Binder, and Hans H. Strupp

Chapter 6
Clinical Illustration of the Assessment Process and
the Development of a Focus   *110*

Chapter 7
Technique   *135*

Contents

Chapter 8
Case History Illustrating the TLDP Approach   *194*

Chapter 9
Termination   *259*

Chapter 10
Research Considerations   *267*

Chapter 11
Epilogue   *302*

References   *314*

Name Index   *325*

Subject Index   *328*

Foreword

OVER THE YEARS, Hans Strupp has demonstrated an admirable, unflagging persistence in tackling the difficulties of systematic research in psychotherapy. His work has always been psychoanalytically informed. It has remained so even through the rise, and apparent beginning subsidence of the wave, of behavior therapy and its replacement by cognitive-behavior therapy.

Psychoanalysis proper and psychoanalytic psychotherapy have always been distinguished by the systematic attention to the analysis of the transference in psychoanalysis and by the greater focus on extra-transference material in psychotherapy (with a concomitant explicit analysis of transference only if unavoidable).

The present work is no mere recapitulation of the many available descriptions of psychoanalytic psychotherapy. Indeed, its great merit lies in the fact that it shares the outlook of a beginning movement toward a greater integration of classical and interpersonal psychoanalytic theory and technique—that is, to place significantly greater stress on their dyadic aspects. One result has been a greater emphasis on the analysis of transference even when the external conditions, such as lesser frequency, sitting up, the nature of the psychopathology, and the training of the therapist are not those of psychoanalysis proper. The main reason this shift has seemed to many incompatible with conditions other than those of psychoanalysis proper is that it is not realized that it makes sense only in the context of a reconceptualization of transference and the nature of psychosocial reality. Rather than seeing psychosocial reality as dichotomized into veridical and distorted, with transference defined as a distortion, an alternate view is that psychosocial reality is multiple; it is contributed to by both participants in the psychotherapeutic interaction, with transference characterized by the rigidity with which reality is construed and constructed.

This changed model of psychosocial reality finds expression in the present work in the emphasis on attention to the clues in the patient's associations on how the interaction is being experienced; in the manner in which the therapeutic setting and interventions give plausibility to that experience; and in explicit focus on these aspects of the process.

Another way of stating this reconceptualization is that it involves a reconceptualization of countertransference as well as of transference. Instead of seeing countertransference as only an unfortunate departure from ideal neutrality, the therapist is seen as inevitably involved to a varying degree in a relationship. The therapist derives important information from his or her subjective experience and from implicit clues in the patient's associations as to the nature of the patient's experience, as well as from how the therapist's own experience and behavior have contributed to the patient's. While it is only in the unusual instance that some specific acknowledgment of the therapist's involvement is necessary or desirable, awareness of the experience plays a role in how the therapist sees the plausibility in the patient's experience. The therapist does not see the involvement as a shameful lapse, with perhaps a concomitant temptation to be blind to it, but rather sees it as the inevitable aspect of a human interaction that better enables him to carry out the primary task of understanding and helping the patient. As the therapist becomes progressively aware of involvements he or she had not recognized, the therapist will also be able to modify undesirable transference-countertransference interactions. It is worth emphasizing that this reconceptualization of transference, and its analysis as well of countertransference, significantly distinguish the therapy described here from other contemporary brief-psychodynamic therapies.

A major additional feature of the psychotherapy described here by Strupp and Binder is introduced by the limitation in time. Current socioeconomic considerations obviously play a role in this limitation. Therapists will also want to know how the changed model can be applied without this limitation, but there may be an important advantage to working first with the more readily encompassed brief therapy.

I suggest the limitation of time plays a role in the authors' proposal that the therapist should formulate and follow a focal theme (though the authors are commendably flexible on this point). I believe it remains to be seen how necessary this formulation of a focus is, even in time-limited therapy and how much of an interference it may cause in following the model of explicit attention to transference and countertransference. While I recognize that an open-ended stance may seem to court an aimless jumping about—especially unfortunate when there is a limitation of time and frequency—I think it remains to be seen whether a theme may not evolve as well or even better with greater leeway given to the patient to determine it, even with the limiting conditions.

Happily, and consistent with Strupp's devotion to research, we will learn more on these points because he and his associates will apply the model that is admirably and clearly described in this work in an extensive program of investigation. We will learn how consistently the technique can be used, how the process develops, and the outcome in patients with differing degrees of pathology. Research in psychotherapy has notoriously had little influence on practice. There is reason to hope we will see an exception to that unhappy history.

MERTON M. GILL, M.D.

Preface

THE TECHNIQUES of psychotherapy have traditionally been described in terms of broad strategies that are, in turn, anchored in general principles derived from an underlying theory. In Freud's voluminous writing, for example, one finds relatively few papers specifically devoted to techniques, and as is well known, he never published a major treatise devoted to this topic (see Strachey 1958). On the one hand, he did not want prospective patients to know too much about the modus operandi of psychoanalysis; on the other, he feared that a book on technique might be an open invitation to would-be therapists to practice "wild analysis" (without having obtained proper training). While subsequent authors (Fenichel 1945; Greenson 1967; Menninger 1958) broke with this tradition, techniques have continued to be described in fairly general terms. It was taken for granted that in order to become a therapist, one would have to undergo intensive and prolonged training of which course work, personal analysis, and supervised experience were the cornerstones. The practice of psychotherapy has always been viewed as a complex clinical art, necessitating a prolonged apprenticeship. This model, of course, continues to be valued, and there is general agreement that psychotherapeutic skills cannot be learned from a book, any more than one can become a painter, pianist, or surgeon without practice and extensive supervised training.

Training and practice aside, descriptions of psychotherapeutic techniques potentially serve other functions. For one thing, they may provide objective criteria for judging whether therapists who purport to practice a given form of therapy are adhering to its major tenets. For many years it was tacitly accepted that therapists who claimed to be practicing psychoanalysis, psychoanalytic psychotherapy, client-centered therapy, behavior therapy, or one of the many modalities that have emerged during the last several decades were, in fact, practicing that form of therapy. Furthermore, it was assumed that *all* therapists who identified themselves with a particular theoretical orientation were practicing the same form of therapy. Glover (1955), basing himself on an earlier survey of British psychoanalysts—presumably a highly homogeneous group—was among the first to cast doubts on this proposition. As new theories and techniques made their appearance, as training came to be conducted in a multitude of centers, and as therapists with widely varying backgrounds began to enter the field, the meaning of theoretical labels became increasingly elusive. The term *eclectic,* which many therapists now use to describe their orientation and practices, is so fuzzy it defies precise definition.

The latter-day insistence on more specific descriptions of treatment modalities appears to have at least three major sources. The first is traceable to the growing influence of research and the recognized need for disciplined scientific study (Strupp and Bergin 1969; Bergin and Strupp 1972). Put succinctly, the credo of all scientific endeavors is specificity. Thus, if one wishes to study phenomena and processes, one must define, and if possible quantify them. Global descriptions of psychotherapeutic techniques, therefore, will not suffice.

For example, journal editors have begun to question manuscripts in which it is asserted that, say, a sample of "neurotic" patients had been treated by "analytically oriented psychotherapy." Similarly, it cannot be assumed that a meaningful consensus has been established when techniques mentioned in a case history are described in shorthand terms. Kiesler (1966) was among the first to explode the "uniformity myth," the notion that patients, therapists, and techniques represent interchangeable units.

The second source derives from societal pressures exemplified by demands from insurance companies and governmental agencies for specifications of the treatments they are being asked to underwrite. The third refers to the qualifications of practitioners who administer a particular form of psychotherapy. For purposes of licensing and other forms of legislation it is indispensable to develop criteria by which one may judge whether a practitioner meets certain standards of competence.

The appearance of so-called treatment manuals in our time may be viewed as the clinical investigator's response to the demands for greater specificity. To illustrate, Beck, Rush, Shaw, and Emery (1978) have written a manual on cognitive behavior therapy; Klerman, Rounsaville, Chevron, and Weissman (1984) have taken a similar approach to interpersonal psychotherapy; and Luborsky (1984) has authored what may have been the first manual on psychoanalytic therapy. It is generally recognized that behavioral techniques are more amenable to this kind of specification than approaches that are based on psychodynamic conceptions; nonetheless, the task may not be insuperable. The primary use of treatment manuals thus far has been in the context of controlled research, of which the National Institute of Mental Health Collaborative Study of Depression is a major example.

The present volume likewise began as a treatment manual. As such, it grew out of the research conducted by the Vanderbilt University Psychotherapy research group (see chapter 10), and it will continue to form the basis for a systematic study of time-limited dynamic psychotherapy (TLDP) currently in progress at Vanderbilt. However, we believe that we have gone beyond codifying a traditional form of therapeutic practice. Instead we endeavored to integrate our understanding of psychoanalytic psychotherapy as it has evolved over the years and to present a contemporary model of that treatment modality. We regard this book both as a guide to a refined form of time-limited dynamic psychotherapy and as an attempt to place before the reader a blueprint of psychoanalytic psychotherapy that is broadly applicable irrespective of time limits.

As a treatment manual, the book will serve to undergird the training of therapists whose therapeutic activities will be the topic of systematic scrutiny in the current Vanderbilt study. In particular, we are interested in exploring the extent to which specialized training will have a measurable effect on the therapeutic process and its outcome. Second, we shall study the kinds of patients who can benefit from this approach as well as the limitations to which it will undoubtedly be subject. We shall investigate what therapists learn, how they apply what they learn, and what the effects of this learning on the therapeutic process and its outcome might be. In short, we shall examine, in detail and in depth, in what particular ways the systematic training of therapists makes a difference. To our knowledge, no such evidence currently exists.

With respect to the broader objective, our model of time-limited dynamic psychotherapy is an approach to individual psychotherapy that integrates clinical concepts from a variety of psychodynamic perspectives. The aim of the therapy is to help patients whose difficulties in living manifest themselves through anxiety, depression, and interpersonal difficulties which are viewed as the product of chronic maladaptations. The proposed model of time-limited dynamic psychotherapy (TLDP) is not primarily geared to the amelioration of presenting symptoms—although improvements in this domain are obviously expected. Rather, we are concerned with a more lasting modification of the patient's character structure.

We hypothesize that earlier difficulties with significant others have given rise to patterns of interpersonal relatedness that originally served a self-protective function but are now anachronistic, self-defeating, and maladaptive. Central to these problems are deficiencies in self-esteem, inability to form satisfying interpersonal relationships that gratify the person's needs for closeness, and interferences with autonomous adult functioning. To the extent that these difficulties are basic aspects of the patient's personality structure and interpersonal repertoire, they tend to come into play whenever the patient forms a relationship with a significant person, including the therapist. Although these enactments are the source of the patient's current difficulties, they also provide unique opportunities for significant corrections. The TLDP model seeks to identify these patterns as they emerge in the context of the patient-therapist relationship, and through this process, to produce therapeutic changes in the patient's cognitions, feelings, and the quality of his or her interpersonal relations. Thus, TLDP serves as a vehicle for interpersonal learning within a specialized human context—a collaborative, therapeutic relationship.

Major emphasis is placed on the contemporary transactions between patient and therapist, and the patient's increased understanding and appreciation of their role and function in his or her current life. The therapeutic relationship thus comes to serve as a laboratory for studying *in vivo* the patient's difficulties in living as well as a means for correcting them. Accordingly, to benefit from TLDP, patients must be capable of forming a collaborative relationship with the therapist.

The therapist's principal tools are empathic listening, understanding of the psychodynamics of the patient's current difficulties in terms of his or her life history, and clarification of their self-defeating character. A key issue here is the patient's resistance to change and the stratagems he or she unwittingly uses to defeat the therapeutic efforts. Consistent focus is directed to the patient's manner of construing and relating to the therapist both as a significant person in the present as well as a personification of past relationships. Furthermore, by attending closely to the patient's enactments, the therapist gains important clues from his or her own emotional reactions in the ongoing process. In other words, the patient–therapist relationship is conceived of as a dyadic system in which the behavior of both participants is continually scrutinized by the participants themselves. The overarching goal of TLDP is to mediate a constructive human experience which results in improvements in the quality of the patient's interpersonal relations.

Major theoretical antecedents of these formulations are, of course, readily apparent. Of greatest significance, clearly, are basic psychoanalytic principles pertaining to transference, countertransference, resistance, and the growing understanding of the ego's defensive functions. Woven into the approach also are newer conceptions of transference and countertransference (which will be discussed later), ideas originating in Harry Stack Sullivan's theory of interpersonal relations (Anchin and Kiesler 1982), object relations theory (Kernberg 1976), and applications of general systems theory (Bateson 1972; Haley 1973; Watzlawick 1978; Watzlawick, Weakland, and Fisch 1974).

The forward-looking ideas of Alexander and French (1946) have greatly influenced our thinking, as have the writings of specialists in time-limited dynamic psychotherapy whose contributions will be reviewed in chapter 1. Importantly, TLDP forms part of the trend in contemporary psychoanalytic theory to free clinical observations and therapeutic operations from the influence of metapsychology, whose relevance for therapeutic work has increasingly been questioned (Gill 1976, 1979; Klein 1976; Schafer 1976, 1983). Our goal is to stay close to clinical and observational data, and to avoid as much as possible higher-level inferences and complex theoretical constructions. In keeping with this emphasis, we shall also attempt to steer clear of all aspects of theory that have no apparent consequences for therapeutic activity. In the same vein, we do not view terms such as symptoms, resistance, transference, interpretations, and so on, as referring to discrete classes of phenomena; instead their meaning is defined by the operations occurring between patient and therapist and their adaptive significance for the patient.

The introduction of a "system" of psychotherapy is usually accompanied by the assertion that it is uniquely effective. The available research evidence strongly suggests (Bergin and Lambert 1978) that no form of psychotherapy is currently entitled to such claims. There is also a common misapprehension that special "techniques" might lead to superior treatment outcomes. Again, there is little evidence to support the view that techniques per se are responsible for particular treatment results. Frequently neglected in such discussions is the interpersonal context between patient and therapist in which techniques are always embedded. It must also be stressed that the patient's capacity and willingness to form a productive working relationship with the therapist is a critical determinant of treatment outcomes.

In making these observations, we do not wish to be misunderstood as taking the pessimistic but currently popular position that all techniques are basically equivalent; that the therapist's technical skills are inconsequential; and that anyone who is capable of empathy and a certain amount of warmth can function effectively in the therapeutic role. To the contrary, our approach is predicated precisely on the hypothesis—which we plan to test empirically in concurrent research—that technical operations that are grounded in a coherent theoretical framework do significantly further the therapeutic enterprise.

Obviously there are many ways in which one person can exert a therapeutic influence on the behavior of another. This fact, however, does not invalidate the development of psychotherapy as a clinical and scientific discipline, even if the outcomes (as measured by crude contemporary instruments) are seemingly identical. There appears to be a serious flaw in reasoning which often takes the following form: Since most individuals derive therapeutic benefits from conversations with a benign listener in which they feel accepted and understood; and since, particularly in short-term encounters, the results appear to be indistinguishable from those achieved by highly trained therapists, it follows that the skills of a seasoned psychotherapist are of no moment; that psychotherapy is on a par with faith healing; that little can be learned from intensive study of patient–therapist interactions; and that what we know about psychotherapy today is not palpably different from folk wisdom that has been intuitively available for millenia.

We similarly take issue with the contemporary notion that the techniques of psychotherapy are a form of health-care technology whose safety and efficacy can be established apart from the practitioner employing them and the patient to whom they are applied. Instead, we are at pains to demonstrate throughout this volume that while techniques are crucially important in psychotherapy (that is, they need to be studied, researched, taught, and refined), they are inextricably embedded in the interpersonal context (the therapeutic relationship) between patient and therapist. The competent psychotherapist, in our view, has mastered and practices complex skills; treatment outcomes, however, are at best a partial index to the value of these skills. In short, we believe it is a gross oversimplification to view psychotherapy as analogous to a drug which is so powerful that it overrides all circumstances—the patient's general state of health, chronicity, complications, and the like. If one searches for generalizations it would be more appropriate to say that psychotherapy "works" when the "right" patient forms a productive working relationship with the "right" therapist. The term *productive relationship* describes the key to the success or failure of therapeutic work. All terms in this equation are in great need of specification, as is the term *psychotherapy* itself. In this book we shall endeavor to become more specific about the kinds of problems, the kinds of persons, and the kinds of operations that are of particular interest to us.

The book seeks to provide an overview of TLDP and to illustrate the approach with clinical examples. In so doing, we hope to give the reader a clear picture of the basic ideas, principles, and recommended techniques. Our formulations have aided in, and in turn, benefited from the training of a small group of therapists who participated in our pilot study. Major anticipated users will be practicing therapists who wish to improve their skills, graduate students in clinical psychology, residents in psychiatry, and students in the other mental health professions.

Above all, we hope that the book will be a contribution to the training of *thinking* psychotherapists—clinicians who view their profession as a disciplined activity evolving from increments in clinical experience and scientific evidence. While the practice of psychotherapy is a clinical art, it should be viewed as a process susceptible to continual questioning and scientific scrutiny. In sum, we believe that in embarking on therapy with a particular patient, the journey will be greatly facilitated if the therapist makes use of a map that informs the travelers where they are, where they might be going, and how they might best get there. As every psychotherapist can testify, there is a recurrent danger of getting lost.

HANS H. STRUPP
JEFFREY L. BINDER

Acknowledgments

THE WRITING of this book was aided by the continuing support of the National Institute of Mental Health, to the Vanderbilt University Research Project, through Research Grant MH-20369 to Hans H. Strupp, Principal Investigator. In turn, numerous members of the Vanderbilt research group have contributed significantly to our efforts. We are particularly indebted to Dr. Thomas E. Schacht, Research Assistant Professor at the Vanderbilt Center for Psychotherapy Research, whose collaboration resulted in his taking major responsibility in writing chapter 5 on the dynamic focus. His tenure at Vanderbilt was made possible by Research Training Grant MH 16247 from the National Institute of Mental Health. Dr. Gloria J. Waterhouse, a former member of the Vanderbilt research team, worked closely with us on earlier versions of the manuscript and provided helpful criticisms and advice.

We wish to thank Dr. Merton M. Gill for his warm interest and support of our work. His critical comments and suggestions proved invaluable. In particular, Dr. Gill's creative writings on the role of transference and its analysis have greatly influenced our own formulations. Dr. Allen A. Bergin, an old friend, critically read the manuscript and made a number of thoughtful suggestions for improvement.

It has been a genuine pleasure to work with Ms. Judith Greissman, Senior Editor of Basic Books. We gratefully acknowledge her enthusiastic support and empathic guidance.

Our secretary, Mrs. Esther Stuart, patiently typed more drafts and revisions than any of us care to remember.

Psychotherapy in a New Key

Chapter 1

Overview and Background

SHORT-TERM PSYCHOTHERAPY is increasingly being called the wave of the future, a prediction that seems to apply primarily to outpatient mental health services (Barten 1969; Budman 1981; Budman and Gurman 1983; Small 1979). Among the reasons for this development, the following appear particularly weighty. First, regardless of therapists' theoretical predilections and their stated treatment goals, surveys consistently show that most outpatient therapies last no longer than 20 sessions, and even in private practice, treatments typically do not exceed 26 sessions (Pardes and Pincus 1981). Second, financers of psychotherapy (insurance companies), legislators, and policymakers have become increasingly concerned with the problem of controlling costs. The watchword has become *accountability*, coupled with the expectation that psychotherapists document the safety, efficacy, appropriateness, and cost-effectiveness of the various psychotherapies. Third, the changing structure of health-care delivery appears to favor systems such as health maintenance organizations, which typically put a premium on cost-effectiveness, with corresponding limits on the amount of outpatient psychotherapy they will authorize. (So far, fewer restrictions apply to inpatient psychotherapy which, of course, is considerably more expensive than outpatient therapy.*)

Fourth, in the absence of strong research evidence favoring long-term psychotherapy (including psychoanalysis), there has been a growing interest in time-limited therapy. And finally, developments within the field of short-term therapy itself have invited a more skeptical attitude toward the traditional view, according to which short-term psychotherapy is at best a poor substitute for more intensive and prolonged efforts.

The thrust of the foregoing developments is predominantly technological, economic, and political. They are not principally aimed at the advancement of knowledge, such as a better understanding of the basic ingredients in effective psychotherapy. Increments in scientific knowledge may, of course, occur as a result of improvements in technology, but they tend to be seen as secondary. Instead, the contemporary emphasis is largely pragmatic: Does it work? How much does it cost? not How does it work?

This distinction is important because it seems to be based on the assumption that available knowledge is adequate to support technological developments. One might argue, of course, that the two objectives need not be mutually exclusive, and the history of science is replete with instances where attempted solutions to practical problems have given rise to significant advances in scientific knowledge. Our concern is with the one-sided emphasis on technology, the furor with which horse races between seemingly divergent forms of psychotherapy are being advocated, and the relatively scant attention accorded the necessarily slow and painstaking efforts aimed at achieving a better understanding of the dynamic forces in psychotherapy. Modern psychotherapy, in general, and short-term or time-limited psychotherapy, in particular, are threatening to become fields in a hurry. It remains to be seen whether a more orderly, scientific development will be short-circuited or bypassed.

The present work reflects our conviction that in the long run society will benefit substantively from research aimed at a better scientific understanding of the psychological factors in psychotherapy which are, after all, its defining characteristic. If technical improvements can be made along the way, so much the better, but they should not obscure the ordinary goal

*There is evidence to show that long-term psychotherapy accounts for a large proportion of costs of outpatient psychotherapy. In one study, 75 percent of the ambulatory mental health visits were accounted for by persons who made 20 or more visits per year. In another study, the percentage was 86. On the other hand, inpatient treatment accounts for more than half, and sometimes as much as 80 percent, of the cost of mental health care for the population (McGuire and Frisman 1983).

of science. Our aim throughout this volume is to build upon existing knowledge in the hope of extending it through careful study and research. Herein, incidentally, is found another root of our interest in time-limited psychotherapy: If we can assume that the same dynamics governing long-term therapy are also at work in the shorter forms, the latter are much to be preferred because their scientific investigation is much easier and much more economical.

Does psychotherapy work? No question about this area of activity has been asked with greater interest, passion, and insistence, despite the fact that it is no more meaningful than the question: Does surgery work or does internal medicine work? Obviously, much greater specification of the terms is needed. Despite the difficulty of providing clear-cut answers, considerable headway has been made by a number of respected investigators in sifting the voluminous literature (Bergin and Lambert 1978; Luborsky, Singer, and Luborsky 1975; Meltzoff and Kornreich 1970; Smith, Glass, and Miller 1980). Their conclusions have been quite consistent, and the spirit is admirably conveyed by Smith, Glass, and Miller, whose analyses were based on 475 controlled studies of psychotherapy:

> Psychotherapy is beneficial, consistently so and in many different ways. Its benefits are on a par with other expensive and ambitious interventions, such as schooling and medicine. The benefits of psychotherapy are not permanent, but then little is.
>
> Different types of psychotherapy (verbal or behavioral; psychodynamic, client-centered, systematic desensitization) do not produce different types or degrees of benefit.
>
> Differences in how psychotherapy is conducted (whether in groups or individually, by experienced or novice therapists, for long or short periods of time, and the like) make very little difference in how beneficial it is.
>
> Psychotherapy is scarcely any less effective than drug therapy in the treatment of serious psychological disorders. When the two therapies are combined, the net benefits are less than the sum of their separate benefits (pp. 183–89).

Taken together, the results of various independent analyses lend substantial support to the field as a whole. Perhaps most impressive are the robust effects of the great diversity of operations grouped under the heading of psychotherapy. Thus, whether psychotherapy is performed expertly or imperfectly, whether patients are selected carefully or haphazardly, whether the treatment is short term or long term, the outcomes are generally favorable. As a minimum, these findings establish psychotherapy as a useful tool in treating a range of disturbances in living, all the more so since there are often no viable alternatives. A second implication is that factors common to all forms of psychotherapy appear to carry greater weight in treatment outcomes than particular techniques advocated by various schools. We shall explore this issue at greater length in chapter 10.

It is often overlooked that the majority of studies supporting the effectiveness of psychotherapy refer to treatments that most dynamically oriented practitioners would consider short term (that is, less than 50 visits and less than one year). This is no artifact; indeed, as has been noted, the bulk of outpatient psychotherapy practiced and most of the evidence documenting its effectiveness refers to time-limited treatments. Yet paradoxically, the vast majority of dynamically oriented training programs for psychiatrists and psychologists offer no systematic instruction in the short-term psychotherapies. This contradiction is apparent from the beginning of training, where students are instructed in the long-term model (usually psychoanalysis) whereas most patients are, in fact, seen on a short-term basis. The result is that most therapists struggle to develop bootstrap forms of short-term treatment, by which they seek to apply the knowledge they have acquired in formal training to the realities of practice. Most therapists seem to be quite successful in making these translations. It may also be a tribute to the sturdiness of the long-term model that it tolerates modifications of various sorts. On the other hand, it is possible that the moderate effects typically credited to psychotherapy might be significantly enhanced if there were systematic training programs based on more specific principles and more consonant with the realities of clinical practice.

Toward Shorter Forms of Psychotherapy

The literature reflects a growing interest in short-term psychotherapies over the last twenty years. However, the bulk of these writings deal with single cases or small series of cases treated for specific problems (colitis, mourning reactions, panic attacks). Crisis intervention techniques represent a related development (Bellak and Small 1978; Small 1979). While offering useful additions to the therapeutic armamentarium, these reported efforts do not provide systematic models for dealing with a variety of patients to match the more comprehensive models offered by the open-ended approaches. Furthermore, most reports of short-term techniques, including those based on the dynamic orientation, reflect a conservative view of short-term treatment. According to this view, only well-functioning individuals with recent, mild to moderate symptoms are suitable, and the goals are limited to symptom amelioration or removal (Flegenheimer 1982; Butcher and Koss 1978; Malan 1976*a*).

An alternative approach to short-term dynamic therapy is found in the radical viewpoint (Malan 1976*a*). This approach holds that with properly selected patients extensive and long-standing forms of psychopathology can be treated with results comparable to those obtainable from open-ended therapies (Flegenheimer 1982; Malan 1976*a*). The proponents of this view have presented comprehensive systems for treating patients suffering from a variety of complaints (Davanloo 1978, 1980; Malan 1976 *a;* Mann 1973; Mann and Goldman 1982; Sifneos 1979).

In general terms, advocates of short-term therapy have the following options:

1.   One can select patients whose presenting difficulties and personality makeup is such that relatively minor interventions will guarantee good therapeutic results.

2.   One can scale down therapeutic goals and declare that one will be satisfied with relatively circumscribed improvements.

3.   One can seek to improve the therapeutic technology so that therapeutic change occurs more rapidly. A distinction must be made here. A rapid improvement is not necessarily a lasting improvement. Furthermore, questions may be entertained as to whether a particular approach is humane, in keeping with the patient's best interest (however this may be defined), consonant with reasonable demands on the therapist (time, effort, commitment, and so on), and in keeping with other practical considerations.

If we examine, as we shall do next, the state of the art in time-limited dynamic psychotherapy, we find that major efforts in this arena have been directed at the foregoing issues and that solutions have been sought through a better alignment between patient selection, goals, and appropriate technology.

Following the review of historical developments, we shall sketch the manner in which TLDP resembles and diverges from other approaches. In this respect it should be emphasized that TLDP embodies the cumulative research experience of the Vanderbilt research team. The results of these investigations are described more fully in chapter 10; see particularly the section titled "The Vanderbilt I Study and Its Lessons."

Historical Background: Overview and Critique

The history of time-limited psychotherapy is closely interwoven with the history of psychoanalysis. Most of the analyses conducted by Freud in the early years would, by modern standards, be described as decidedly short term. However, beginning with the turn of the century, treatments expanded from several months to several years. It is interesting to note that Freud (1905, S.E., 7) tended to be apologetic about the length of analyses even when they lasted only a few months. By 1920, some of Freud's collaborators, notably Rank and Ferenczi, began to explore the possibility of shortening analytic treatment from the typical duration of several years. Their recommendations were set forth in a monograph which appeared in the mid-twenties (Ferenczi and Rank 1925). While initially sympathetic to these endeavors, Freud soon changed his mind and considered them ill-advised. The details of these developments have been described by numerous authors (Flegenheimer 1982; Malan 1976a; Thompson 1950) and need not be repeated. Although Ferenczi and Rank raised questions about the analyst's passive role and various theoretical issues, they reaffirmed prevailing views. Thus, the purpose of analysis was "the full re-living of the Oedipus situation in the relation of the patient to the analyst, in order to bring it, with the help of the patient's insight, to a new and more fortunate conclusion" (Ferenczi and Rank [1925] 1957: 54).

Central to these considerations, then as now, were both theoretical and practical concerns. In 1918, Freud (1918, S.E., 17) was considering ways to make psychoanalysis available to larger segments of the patient population; that is, individuals who were less affluent but who, he felt, should be equally entitled to the benefits available from psychoanalysis. His proposed solution was expressed in the famous phrase "the pure gold of analysis [might be freely alloyed] with the copper of direct suggestion" (p. 168). (A more recent anonymous observer pointed out that an alloy tends to be stronger and more lasting than pure gold!)

Breuer and Freud's ([1895] 1957) early attempts to treat hysterical patients led to the theory that strangulated affects were the driving force in neurotic symptomatology and that their patients were suffering from reminiscences; that is, traumatic memories whose accompanying affects had been repressed. Improvements were thought to result from reexperiencing these painful affects under hypnosis. Freud's subsequent work led, of course, to an increasing appreciation of childhood conflicts and the role of infantile sexuality in producing the symptoms and difficulties troubling the patients in their adult lives. Concomitantly, hypnosis was abandoned as a therapeutic technique and free association substituted. The analysis of transference and resistance, designed to uncover the infantile neurosis, became the primary strategy in therapy. The search for and reconstruction of the childhood antecedents of a patient's neurosis were important factors contributing to the increasing length of psychoanalyses. Still, affective reexperiencing of childhood conflicts in the presence of the analyst remained preeminent. Yet, as Thompson (1950) noted, Freud was recurrently dissatisfied with the therapeutic outcomes.

Freud, as his writings document, was always a conservative in appraising the therapeutic results of psychoanalysis. Indeed, it may be said that he had a lifelong ambivalence on the subject. On the positive side, he spoke proudly of psychoanalysis as "primus inter pares" (compared with other forms of psychotherapy); on the negative side, he recommended that psychoanalysis should only be undertaken as a last resort, deplored its length, the difficulties impeding therapeutic progress, and the impermanence of treatment outcomes. He was also aware that many of his famous cases were not brilliant successes. When in the latter mood (particularly toward the end of his life), he saw a greater future for psychoanalysis as an instrument for studying intrapsychic processes than as a therapeutic tool. (See Freud [1911–1915] *S.E., 12:* 89–171).

There was a long road between the therapeutic goal of recalling repressed memories and the gradually emerging emphasis on the analysis of the total personality. While the ambitions of therapists grew (beginning perhaps in the 1920s), there was no commensurate increase in the quality of the therapeutic results. Longer analyses might be more thorough but their outcomes were not necessarily superior.* It must be recognized, however, that as the years went by, analysts undertook increasingly difficult tasks. For example, the treatment of a borderline patient is undoubtedly a different challenge from the treatment of a circumscribed phobia. In any case, in making treatment decisions, careful thought must be given to (1) the nature of the problem; (2) therapeutic goals; and (3) an assessment of the circumstances. When this is done, it may turn out that longer (or more intensive) does not necessarily mean more effective, and in any case it may be undesirable to roll out a cannon to shoot a mosquito. The contemporary emphasis on ascertaining with the greatest possible precision what kinds of therapeutic results might be expected from particular therapeutic efforts with specified patients (Bergin and Strupp 1972) is a new development which will predictably have far-reaching implications for therapeutic prac-

---

*To this date we have no hard evidence to show that there is a reliable relationship between length of analysis and extent of therapeutic change.

tice in the future. We shall deal with this issue throughout this volume.

To return to our historical account, the early attempts to counter the trend toward longer analyses also reflected fundamental disagreements between Freud and his followers concerning the therapeutic ingredients in psychoanalysis. Ferenczi and Rank (1925) argued that there was no necessary connection between therapeutic change and the working through of the infantile neurosis. The latter proccess might enhance the scientific goal of understanding personality development but might not be essential to therapeutic change. Instead, they believed that all of the patient's past that was therapeutically important was concentrated in the current transference. Therefore, the essential ingredient in therapeutic change was the patient's current emotional experience of his or her childhood conflict in the patient-therapist relationship. By implication, the therapist whose behavior would contrast with that of the significant figures in the patient's past, would then be in a position to promote an emotional understanding of the patient's childhood conflicts as manifested in the present. In this way, Ferenczi and Rank restored to prominence Freud and Breuer's original emphasis on current affective experience although the theoretical context had shifted markedly. Furthermore, they recommended that the therapist adopt a more active stance in making interpretations. This would keep emotional tension high and promote expression of the patient's basic conflicts in the here and now of the transference. Finally, they advocated that the therapist be more empathic and avoid acting in ways that might confirm the patient's transference expectations.

Ferenczi and Rank's recommendations were anathema to Freud and his collaborators for several interrelated reasons. They appeared to manipulate the transference instead of letting it evolve freely; they assigned a more active role to the therapist, thus departing from the blank screen model that had been proposed by Freud; and in opposition to the classical view, they tended to make psychoanalysis a two-person encounter. There were undoubtedly other reasons; in any case, Ferenczi and Rank's proposals soon fell into disrepute.

Further work along the lines sketched above stagnated until the 1940s when a renewed impetus was provided by Alexander and French (1946). These respected analysts, like Ferenczi and Rank before them, questioned the assumption that the depth and endurance of therapeutic results were proportionate to prolonged work aimed at genetic reconstructions. They revived what might be termed the interpersonal view by asserting that therapeutic change occurs when a patient relives, in the here and now of the transference, chronic neurotic conflicts or patterns of behavior. For a neurotic conflict to be changed therapeutically, it had to be alive in the present. Consequently, only conflicts that could be revived in therapy and that were accompanied by sufficiently intense affect could become the object of analysis. Furthermore, they believed that it was essential for the therapist to adopt a role palpably different from the one assigned to him or her by the patient's transference expectations. In this way the therapist would facilitate a "corrective emotional experience," which they regarded as the therapist's primary contribution to the treatment process. For example, if the patient expected to be dominated by a punitive authority figure, the therapist should take care to act in a warm and permissive manner. Alexander and French also recognized the risk of overtreatment, particularly the danger that the patient might become overly dependent on the therapist. Accordingly, they experimented with interruptions of treatment, varied the frequency of sessions, and set termination dates.

These improvements were greeted with marked hostility by the analytic establishment which was quick to discredit the new ideas. Tampering with orthodoxy, notably manipulation of the transference, became once again the rallying ground for the opposition. However, Alexander and French's questioning of cherished psychoanalytic assumptions and their advocacy of experimentation laid the groundwork for reconceptualizations and technical changes that have characterized the therapeutic scene in more recent years. (For accounts of newer developments, see Butcher and Koss 1978; Castelnuovo-Tedesco 1975; Small 1979). Alexander and French, while remaining faithful to basic psychoanalytic insights, were vocal advocates of flexibility, and they recognized that advances in technique could come only from vigorous experimentation and challenges to prevailing practices. For a number of years, their work failed to gain widespread acceptance, although it was generally conceded that their ideas might have a certain utility.

This situation gradually changed as several groups—working independently until the 1970s—began to experiment with technical changes, particularly in the context of short-term therapy. The Tavistock group (Balint, Ornstein, and Balint 1972; Malan 1963, 1976a & b, 1979) undertook systematic studies of time-limited therapy in the 1950s. Sifneos (1972, 1979), Mann (1973), and Mann and Goldman (1982) initiated their respective approaches in the 1960s, and Davanloo (1978, 1980) followed suit shortly thereafter.* The conclusions of these relatively independent enterprises were strikingly similar:

*It would be a mistake to conclude that developments in psychoanalytic technique since Alexander and French (1946) are encompassed by the workers whose theories and techniques are described in the remainder of this chapter. On the contrary, the mainstream of psychoanalytic thought has stayed closer to the long-term, intensive model, which has retained its preeminence. By contrast, the departures emphasized in this chapter have remained on the

1. Patients suffering from *longstanding* neurotic and characterological problems could be treated with a dynamically oriented therapy in a much shorter time than had previously been believed.

2. Basic principles of psychoanalytic therapy—interpretation of transference and resistance—could be applied to time-limited therapy.

3. The results of this form of treatment could produce enduring changes in character structure.

Although the treatment models developed by the preceding groups share major therapeutic principles, they differ in a number of respects, perhaps most notably in the kinds of patients each considers suitable. At one end of the spectrum are located Sifneos's and Mann's models which are limited to relatively well-functioning, psychologically minded, and highly motivated patients. Davanloo, whose approach is geared to certain types of resistant patients, occupies the opposite extreme, with Malan holding a middle position. In order to place the TLDP approach in historical perspective, we shall next examine the contributions of these exponents in somewhat greater detail. While their efforts have been by no means the only ones, they exemplify the contemporary trend toward empirically based methods for time-limited therapy based on psychodynamic principles.

Short-Term Anxiety-Provoking Psychotherapy (STAPP)

Sifneos (1972, 1979) set out to determine whether psychoanalytically oriented methods could be adapted to a time-limited form of psychotherapy to help patients with significant neurotic problems. In keeping with psychoanalytic teachings, it had previously been assumed that short-term therapy (12 to 20 sessions) could produce symptom relief in patients suffering from acute distress but that no enduring characterological changes were to be expected. When practical necessities left no alternative, Freud (Breuer and Freud [1895] 1957) himself had occasionally used short-term

---

fringes of psychoanalytic practice. A major reason for this state of affairs is undoubtedly the enduring skepticism regarding time-limited forms of psychoanalytic therapy on the part of the analytic establishment, which particularly espouses the notion that these modalities are at best poor substitutes for more extended treatment.

Nor do we wish to convey the impression that TLDP is a direct descendant of the short-term approaches to be discussed here. In certain respects, this is true; however, as we shall attempt to make clear, our thinking has been influenced, perhaps more heavily, by theoretical developments (interpersonal theory, object relations theory, and systems theory, as well as psychoanalytic theory) that have paid little attention to time-limited treatment. Indeed, we see it as a major aim of our work to incorporate these latter developments into a time-limited approach.

methods with dramatic results, but he devalued these successes as transference cures or flights into health. Challenging this tradition, Sifneos developed an approach whose principal features include an emphasis on (1) patient selection and (2) specialized technical management.

While Sifneos is a proponent of the radical view that time-limited treatment can produce deep and enduring change, his techniques and selection criteria are conservative relative to other short-term therapists. With respect to patient selection, Sifneos carefully selects patients who despite their neurotic disturbances manifest notable ego strength. Components of the latter include: psychological mindedness; honesty; introspectiveness; curiosity; readiness to collaborate actively with the therapist; willingness to experiment with more adaptive behavior; and realistic expectations of therapy. These criteria are subsumed under the concept of motivation for change (or alternately, minimal defensiveness). Sifneos also stipulates that conflicts be limited to certain circumscribed areas of functioning (usually heterosexual relationships) and that they be susceptible to formulation in oedipal terms (a triangular relationship conflict). This condition allows the therapist to define a narrow target area of work, the oedipal focus.

Sifneos's conservative screening criteria have led to the selection of patients whose problems typically create only few or minor problems for the therapeutic relationship. Ordinarily, they are highly motivated for self-understanding and readily accept the emotionally detached, interpretive role of the therapist. Accordingly, while Sifneos alludes to the importance of countertransference issues, he states that, in fact, there are "few problems involved with countertransference" (1979: 90–92). Consistent with this conservative approach, Sifneos views countertransference as an impediment to therapy which results from the therapist's vulnerability to reenactment of his or her own oedipal conflicts in response to the patient's expression of parallel conflicts. Furthermore, Sifneos advises self-analysis or treatment whenever the therapist is in danger of deviating from his or her neutral stance.

Selection is made contingent on a detailed history (to determine the presence of oedipal issues), as well as an informal mental status examination, aimed at an evaluation of relevant personality characteristics. On the basis of this assessment, a focus for therapy is established and presented to the patient. This takes the form of an intellectual explanation of the patient's maladaptive behavior, with stress on the enduring influence of relationship patterns originating in family conflicts.

Sifneos wished to demonstrate that the foremost technique of psychoanalysis, genetic transference interpretations, could also be the technical foundation of short-term dynamic psychotherapy. Thus, having selected patients who demonstrate the highest qualifications for any form of analytic therapy, he focuses the therapeutic work on interpretations of the transference and genetic reconstructions. Correspondingly, there is less emphasis on what occurs in the therapeutic relationship, although the existence of a good working alliance is taken for granted and considered a prerequisite for the patient's ability and willingness to immerse himself or herself in therapeutic work. The curative effects of Sifneos's anxiety-provoking psychotherapy are attributed largely to correct interpretations of oedipal constellations.

Therapy usually lasts 12 to 15 sessions, and no time limits are set in advance. Sifneos reports that his patients frequently take the initiative in bringing up the issue of termination. He believes that the stringency of his selection criteria precludes the acceptance of patients who are prone to form dependent attachments. The therapist's active stance is undoubtedly another factor in decreasing the chances of this eventuality.

Sifneos has taken great pains to present his method for public scrutiny: operationalizing selection criteria, describing techniques, conducting follow-up interviews, and presenting videotapes of representative therapy sessions. Taken collectively, this constitutes reasonable evidence that certain "attractive" patients who have commonly been treated in long-term dynamic psychotherapy or psychoanalysis can be helped significantly in much shorter periods of time and that basic psychoanalytic principles need not be compromised. While this is clearly an important contribution, it has not been shown conclusively that the therapeutic results are due to the kinds of technical interventions advocated by Sifneos rather than to patients' preexisting ego resources, including their ability to form a productive working alliance with the therapist early in therapy. Given these stipulations, other kinds of therapeutic interventions might be equally effective. Sifneos's impressive clinical skills and persuasiveness are unquestionably also important factors in the reported outcomes.

Time-limited Psychotherapy: James Mann

The Boston psychoanalyst, James Mann (Mann 1973; Mann and Goldman 1982), has developed a form of time-limited psychotherapy that puts the experience and meaning of time at the center of attention. His approach has two unique features: (1) a rigid adherence to 12 sessions, conducted on a weekly basis; and (2) the issue of time limits is used to understand the entire process and progress of treatment. Mann states that other time-limited therapists have not appreciated the "ongoing dynamic significance of this kind of time-limit in the total process of treatment" (Mann and Goldman 1982). Underlying this approach is the assumption that all emotional conflicts treatable by Mann's therapy ultimately have their affective roots in the patient's struggle between unconscious wishes for endless nurturance and love versus the conscious awareness of the finiteness of time, reflecting limitations on the degree to which one's wishes can be gratified.

This form of time-limited therapy is considered suitable for a broad spectrum of psychopathology, and the central issue can range across oedipal and preoedipal conflicts. Furthermore, Mann's selection criteria do not include a broad survey of ego functions. Thus he views his criteria as more flexible than those of Sifneos or Malan. Mann believes that serious psychopathology may be treated if the patient's overall ego strengths are adequate. In a departure from the other exponents represented here, he states that if diagnostic errors are made, the treatment plan can be changed accordingly, without harm to the patient. However, the two ego functions that Mann does assess—the capacity for rapid affective involvement and the capacity for rapid affective disengagement (the capacity to tolerate loss)—may be seen as rather stringent. In fact, Mann's patients evidently demonstrate a remarkable capacity to respond positively to the kind of therapy and relationship he offers: "A rapid working alliance and positive transference appear and, in this setting, the presenting symptoms and complaints tend to disappear" (Mann and Goldman 1982: 18).

A therapeutic focus, close to the patient's subjective experience, is defined. In the first 1 to 4 interviews, Mann attempts to articulate the patient's "chronically endured pain," which reflects a rigidly fixed negative self-image. The treatment process rides a dual track: it consists of an examination of the central issue, followed later in the treatment by a thorough exploration of the patient's feelings about termination. The latter, Mann believes, inevitably combines the patient's unique problems with a negative self-image and the universal reactions to separation and loss.

Once the therapist formulates a central issue for therapy, he or she presents it to the patient, along with a description of the treatment arrangements. By the patient's explicit acceptance of these arrangements, a specific sequence of dynamic events is set in motion. The therapeutic process is roughly divided into three phases, each lasting approximately 4 interviews, characterized, respectively, by (1) initial unconscious expectations of endless nurturance; (2) disappointment and ambivalence, as the reality of inevitable separation emerges; and (3) the patient's attempt to repeat the affective reactions to his or her earliest (traumatic) separation from meaningful objects. The aim at this point is to promote a healthier separation experience. This allows for a new internalization of the lost object (the therapist) with less sadness, anger, guilt, and fear than was true of earlier figures. The tight treatment arrangements of this approach are considered an advantage, since they aid the therapist in understanding the patient, in conceptualizing the therapeutic process, and in planning interventions.

Careful patient selection and a strong therapeutic alliance carry the treatment even through periods of intense disappointment and ambivalence. Accordingly, Mann is not confronted with noticeable problems in the therapeutic relationship created by the patient's chronic problems with trust and intimacy. He is thus free to devote his attention to elaborating the self-defeating interpersonal consequences of the patient's negative self-image outside the therapy. Transference interpretations are rarely used until the termination phase, when they foster the patient's understanding of how he or she distorts the meaning of termination in terms of his or her negative self-image. Countertransference is viewed as a problem primarily in terms of the therapist's discomfort (or neurotic conflicts) about the rigid termination deadline.

Unlike the other therapists discussed here, Mann and his colleagues have not attempted empirical studies of the process and outcome of this therapy. Mann evidently believes that the method has not yet achieved a degree of conceptual specificity necessary to undertake empirical investigations (Mann and Goldman 1982).

The Tavistock Group: David Malan

In the 1950s, a group of psychoanalytically oriented therapists working in London under the leadership of Michael Balint (Balint, Ornstein, and Balint 1972) began to develop a form of time-limited psychotherapy based on psychoanalytic principles. Balint's seminal ideas were developed further by David Malan, who emerged after Balint's death as the most eloquent and influential spokesperson for this group. Malan also recognized the great importance of undergirding his clinical observations with systematic research on process and outcome, which he has pursued with great diligence and dedication over the years.

The Tavistock group initially subscribed to the then prevailing notion that short-term psychotherapy might reduce symptoms of acute neurotic conflicts in generally well-functioning individuals but that such efforts were a second-best substitute for long-term, intensive therapeutic efforts. The work, however, took a different direction when it was found that few such patients could be located among the typical applicants to the Tavistock Clinic. Instead, patients frequently manifested chronic problems and greater disturbances than seemed theoretically optimal for time-limited therapy. Bowing to this reality, the Tavistock workers chose to be flexible in their selection procedures, particularly if one of the collaborating therapists expressed a strong desire to accept a particular person for treatment. This flexibility resulted in the unexpected finding that patients showing marked deficiencies in ego strength and other criteria considered necessary for time-limited therapy could still be helped. Indeed, in numerous instances the results were quite impressive even though time-limited therapy in some cases lasted up to 40 hours. Typically, a calendar date marks the planned termination. Malan states that this procedure avoids the problem of deciding whether to make up sessions missed by the patient.

A crucial quality characterizing these patients (also stressed by Sifneos) was a positive response to interpretations in the area of the focal conflict (discussed later). Malan called this quality a "dynamic interaction." By this he meant that the patient must be appropriately responsive to the form of therapy and the kind of relationship offered by the therapist. Promising patients were those able to quickly develop trust in the therapist as evidenced by open communication of feelings which in turn allowed the therapist to arrive at a better understanding of the patient's problems and to communicate that understanding.

Diagnostic assessment plays an important part in Malan's approach. In addition to assessing the patient's background and current functioning along fairly traditional lines, the diagnostic assessments serve the twofold goal of (1) establishing a focal conflict theme and (2) forecasting what will happen when therapy gets underway. The forecasting serves additional purposes: (a) to gauge the patient's vulnerability to severe disruptions in day-to-day functioning, and (b) to predict the manner in which the focal theme will manifest itself during the course of therapy. Although Malan acknowledges the importance of balancing attention between formal history taking and fostering a therapeutic alliance, the balance seems to be skewed in the direction of diagnostic operations.

As already noted, Malan believes that the patient's responsiveness to the particular therapeutic techniques proposed in the Tavistock approach is a crucial predictor of outcome. Thus he recommends the use of trial interpretations in order to gauge the patient's willingness and ability to work in psychoanalytic therapy. One form of trial interpretation consists of interpreting the patient's resistances as soon as they are noticed. If the patient does not readily relinquish his or her resistance, particularly that occurring around the focal conflict, Malan considers his approach contraindicated.

In this form of therapy the emotional conflicts potentially included in the therapeutic focus—as is true of the approaches of Mann and Davanloo—are not limited to oedipal issues but may take other forms as long as a circumscribed area of work can be demarcated. Furthermore, it is theoretically possible to work on several foci provided they are clearly related. With regard to identifying a focus, Malan speaks of an "interpretive theme that gradually crystallizes over a few sessions."

Like Sifneos, the Tavistock workers assert that with appropriate patients genetic transference interpretations can be successfully employed in time-limited dynamic psychotherapy. Thus, interpretations connecting transference experiences with family constellations in childhood, transference-parent links (T/P links), are considered the essential therapeutic ingredient. Furthermore, all interpretive work is targeted within a circumscribed area of conflict.

It may seem that, following the traditional psychoanalytic model and reminiscent of Sifneos's priorities, Malan focuses major attention on technical problems surrounding interpretations of the transference. Correspondingly, there is less emphasis on the dyadic character of the patient-therapist relationship and the therapist's personal reactions to the patient's behavior in therapy. Patients who evoke strong (negative) reactions from the therapist are presumably judged unsuitable for Malan's approach.

Malan's research is based on extensive studies of several cohorts of patients who were followed for several years. He has also published a sizable collection of case histories. The primary source of data consists of therapists' case notes which also formed the basis for ratings of process and outcome which entered into the statistical analyses. A major conclusion drawn from the studies supports the clinical impression that appropriate patients can undergo significant personality changes in time-limited therapy. These changes appear to be as profound and enduring as those occurring in more protracted treatment modalities.

The Montreal Group: Habib Davanloo

Another approach to time-limited psychotherapy is exemplified by the work of Habib Davanloo, an analyst who received his training in Boston and spearheaded short-term therapy at Montreal General Hospital. Beginning in 1975, he organized several international conferences that brought together a number of experts, including Sifneos and Malan. Davanloo has more recently developed a close working relationship with Malan in particular. His approach is generally akin to that of Malan, and indeed it may be characterized as a logical extension of Malan's work. Distinguishing features include an emphasis on (1) selection of certain types of resistant patients, and (2) active and persistent confrontation of the patient's resistances from the beginning of therapy.

Davanloo's diagnostic assessments are essentially similar to those of Malan. He gathers extensive background information in order to gauge the patient's ego functions, and like Malan he attempts to identify a focus for therapeutic work. However, unlike Malan he actively confronts the patient's resistances even after initial trial interventions have failed to produce an impact. The immediate goal is to undercut the patient's difficulties in establishing a productive working alliance with the therapist.

Whereas Sifneos, Mann, and (to a lesser extent) Malan consider marked resistances emerging in the initial encounter as contraindications to time-limited dynamic psychotherapy, Davanloo prefers to work with patients who, while clearly possessing significant adaptive resources, manifest massive (typically intellectualizing) defenses (character armor). In Davanloo's view, these defensive operations must be identified, challenged, and defused as rapidly as possible. The therapist therefore becomes what Davanloo calls a "relentless healer" who seeks to break through the patient's barriers against human relatedness. If the effort succeeds, the patient is well on his or her way to forming a productive working alliance, and the outcome of therapy may be successful; conversely, the patient's struggle may become intensified, conceivably leading to anger and hostility directed at the therapist and/or premature termination. According to Davanloo, the latter rarely happens, but this may be a function of his having selected patients who respond positively to the therapist's challenges. At any rate, strong resistances become the principal target of trial interpretations which determine whether the patient can work within the framework of Davanloo's confrontive approach. It may also be seen that the therapist, from the beginning, creates for himself a position of dominance which the patient must accept.

Davanloo subscribes to the traditional psychoanalytic view of transference as the arena in which unconscious conflicts are being enacted. Like Malan, he endeavors to interpret transference manifestations by linking them to childhood experiences (the T/P link). The therapeutic effort, therefore, is largely encompassed by interpretations aimed at (1) eroding the patient's resistances as they manifest themselves in relation to the therapist, and (2) clarifying the nature of the patient's conflict with reference to past family constellations.

Since the kinds of patients selected by Davanloo—often individuals with entrenched obsessional trends—vigorously oppose intimacy in any form (even dominance-submission) by fighting off a therapist whose object is to penetrate their characterological defenses, countertransference reactions are more likely to occur than in any of the other approaches mentioned. Predictably, such reactions will interfere with the therapist's optimal functioning. Davanloo warns that such reactions may result in an inappropriate exclusion of patients from short-term therapy; conversely, if they are accepted, the therapist's countertransference may become a "major vehicle in the development of misalliances with the patient" (1978). Aside from this warning, Davanloo does not systematically pursue the patient's impact on the therapist's personal reactions. Instead, he takes the position that the patient's persistent failure to respond positively to the therapist's confrontations is a contraindication for this form of therapy. Although Davanloo presses the patient harder for a commitment than Sifneos, Mann, or Malan, the judgment of suitability depends markedly on the patient's receptivity to the therapist's unique approach and the role it assigns to the patient. Consequently, patients who cannot work productively within the therapist's framework are either rejected or they may withdraw on their own initiative because they find the therapy too threatening.

Davanloo's handling of termination differs markedly from that of Malan. He does not set a termination date at the beginning of treatment. Instead, he tells the patient that therapy will last "only as long as necessary to resolve the main conflicts." He tries to select patients who do not appear to have noticeable problems with dependency or separation, and his active approach is designed to counteract the patient's wishes for dependency. On the other hand, this may force the patient to adopt a submissive stance vis-à-vis the therapist's authority. Davanloo's therapies tend to last 15 to 30 sessions, although the length may be extended, if necessary. He, as the other therapists mentioned, prefers 45 to 50 minute interviews on a weekly basis.

Davanloo's approach continues the trend initiated by the Tavistock group of further extending the range of suitable patients. Although the content of their focal conflicts may be equally (or more) diverse, the approach is designed primarily for patients who are noticeably more resistant than those treated by Malan.

Davanloo has documented his work through videotapes and summary reports of several cohorts of patients. He has also reported the results of what appear to be fairly informal follow-up studies. Like Malan, he explains his results by reference to basic principles of psychoanalytic therapy, and he asserts that the patients' changes are as radical and enduring as those claimed for longer and more intensive therapies.

TLDP in Historical Context

Although the form of time-limited dynamic therapy to be described in this book shares a number of elements with other systems having similar objectives, there are also important conceptual and practical differences. The similarities include the following points:

1. *Patient selection.* A patient is assessed for his or her ability to engage in time-limited therapy in terms of features of personality organization that are considered relevant to the task required by the treatment. That is, the nature of the patient's psychopathology (symptoms, diagnostic categorization) is secondary to evidence of his or her potential to form a collaborative relationship with a psychotherapist. The primary source of this evidence is the patient's handling of trial interventions made in the first few interviews.

2. *Definition and pursuit of a central issue or dynamic focus.* Along with other workers in the area, we believe it is essential to formulate an area of work defined in terms that are specific and meaningful to therapist and patient. Our formulation of a dynamic focus, however, diverges from that of other workers. As we shall see (chapter 5), it is a heuristic device rather than a target.

3. *Transference analysis is a major area of work.* The enactment in the therapeutic relationship of the patient's emotional conflicts is considered the major goal for interpretive work. However, TLDP is unique in viewing all therapeutic transactions within a dyadic, interpersonal framework.

4. *Time limits are set.* Although fairly liberal (25 to 30 hours), time limits are set at the outset and issues surrounding termination are continually addressed throughout treatment.

Notwithstanding these broad similarities, TLDP represents a further step in the evolution of time-limited therapy, and as such, it diverges in many important respects from previous approaches. In order to accent these differences it will prove useful to enumerate the basic assumptions about psychopathology and the therapeutic processes that have shaped the conceptual framework of the major time-limited dynamic therapies. It will be seen that these assumptions represent a traditional psychoanalytic point of view:

1. Neurotic conflicts are manifested in contemporary relationships as the repetition of childhood patterns of conflict. The current versions of childhood conflict are manifested in the therapeutic relationship as transference, which is defined as "the expression of impulses, feelings, fantasies, attitudes and defenses with respect to a person in the present which do not

appropriately fit that person but are a repetition of responses originating in regard to significant persons of early childhood, unconsciously displaced on to persons in the present" (Greenson and Wexler 1969).

2.   This conception of neurotic conflict and transference represents a linear view, in which current emotional conflicts are caused by a repetition of childhood conflicts which express themselves through derivatives. The driving force for the persistence of the patient's difficulties is the repetition compulsion, a theoretical construct composed of two elements: (a) the pressure of unconscious instincts (sex, aggression) seeking expression, and (b) the ego's attempt to master old traumatic conditions or events associated with an infantile neurosis.

3.   The infantile neurosis is reconceptualized in highly circumscribed form as the nuclear conflict (Malan 1976a) or core conflict (Davanloo 1980). In terms of childhood conflict, the aim of treatment can be as ambitious as seeking its resolution (Davanloo 1980).

4.   The derivatives of the core conflict are expressed toward the therapist through the transference, which can be interpreted as early as the first interview provided (a) it is a negative transference or (b) it reflects features of the dynamic focus.

5.   The dynamic focus is a circumscribed conflict which is conceptualized in metapsychological impulse/defense terminology (for example, a patient's rigidly "nice" behavior may represent a reaction formation against anal sadistic impulses). While discussion of the conflict with a patient is usually in interpersonal terms, the method of translating the more abstract, metapsychological level of discourse to the clinical level is not clearly spelled out by proponents of time-limited therapy (although Mann has made noteworthy progress [Mann and Goldman 1982]). On a clinical level, the dynamic focus represents a circumscribed pattern of interpersonal conflict in contemporary relationships, including the patient-therapist relationship. A prerequisite for establishing a dynamic focus is the patient's ability to quickly provide historical information that allows the therapist to formulate a clear childhood pattern of conflict (the core conflict) which offers a direct genetic connection to the current problem. The dynamic focus, then, is a current, salient emotional conflict that represents a repetition of a childhood neurosis.

6.   Change is presumed to occur as a result of insight into the connection between current patterns of maladaptive behavior and their origin in childhood conflicts. Thus, the primary technical strategy is to make interpretations that link current transference enactments to their childhood precursors. These T/P links, or genetic transference interpretations, are based on data concerning childhood antecedents of current neurotic con-

flicts that are provided by the patient from the first interview and are considered factual.

7. The approach to the analysis of transference is decidedly intra-psychic, that is, the primacy of the T/P links is predicated upon the projection of transference onto a neutral therapist. The patient's resistances are regarded as defensive operations against the emergence of unconscious conflicts and associate painful affects. The therapist's role, accordingly, is largely that of a more or less uninvolved technical expert whose task (analogous to that of a surgeon) is to penetrate the defenses in order to gain access to the major conflict lying beyond. Countertransference, by this reasoning, is considered an impediment to therapy in the time-limited approaches reviewed here. (See chapter 7 for a detailed discussion of the countertransference issue.)

The foregoing principles of personality functioning and the technical strategies flowing from them form the foundation of all radical systems of time-limited therapy that have been advanced to date. The application of these principles, so familiar in long-term psychoanalytic psychotherapy, to time-limited approaches represents a notable achievement. It has allowed the use of the psychoanalytic approach with certain patients and in settings (mental health centers) where long-term treatment is neither desirable nor possible. The radical systems of time-limited therapy have combined a conservative psychoanalytic view of the therapeutic process with innovative technical applications (namely, work in a circumscribed area, the setting of time limits, and early transference interpretation). There are also far-reaching implications for the selection of patients considered suitable candidates for this form of treatment.

The major short-term approaches we have described are built upon a model of how emotional conflicts are manifested in the therapeutic situation. The patient presents his or her life story of conflict in a specific narrative form (Schafer 1983), encompassed schematically by the statement: "I am today a person in specific conflict, and this conflict is a product of clear-cut emotionally injurious parental influences on my childhood." In other words, the patient is able and willing to communicate material about current problems in his or her life in a manner that allows the therapist to formulate a circumscribed area of work. Furthermore, the patient is able to adduce childhood recollections that allow the therapist to identify a pattern of childhood conflict that can be made to coincide with the formulation of current problems. The proponents of this view explicitly assert that patients who cannot provide contemporary material and historical facts which lend themselves to organization into a dynamic focus are too characterologically disturbed to be treated by time-limited therapy. This appears to be an untested assumption, and at this juncture in the development of time-limited therapy, an unwarranted one.

An alternative view is that patients employ a variety of narrative formats in presenting their life stories (Schafer 1983), and that there is no direct correlation between a particular format and the extent of psychopathology. Stated differently, the time-limited therapists have made a point of selecting patients based on personality organization rather than psychopathology. Thus, they have defined a certain range of personality organizations that they will treat. However, it seems premature to conclude that patients who do not readily evidence these personality organizations cannot be treated by time-limited psychotherapy.

For instance, a patient may present his or her life story of conflict in the following narrative form: "I am today a person in conflict, and this conflict is the product of childhood experiences of which I have only a fuzzy understanding or of which I am unaware." In this rather common instance, the patient provides information about current conflicts in his or her life that may or may not be readily organized into a focal problem. Furthermore, his or her recollection of childhood experiences may be fuzzy or the recollections may not readily be organized into a core conflict theme.

To cite still another possibility, the patient's presentation may take the narrative form: "I am today a person in conflict, and as far as I know it has nothing to do with my childhood." In this case, whether or not the patient provides childhood recollections that lend themselves to the formulation of a dynamic focus, the patient is not moved by connections between his or her current problem and recollections of childhood experiences.

The therapist's inability to formulate a T/P link in early sessions or his or her failure to gain the patient's acceptance of such a link once it has been formulated does not necessarily prove that the patient is unsuitable for time-limited therapy. All it indicates is that the patient's conflicts cannot be understood or managed within the traditional framework used to establish a dynamic focus. However, it is conceivable that an alternative conception of the dynamic focus (and of the therapeutic process), one that allows greater flexibility in adapting to varying narrative formats for presenting one's life story, may provide a means of treating a wider range of patients than is currently thought possible. We have developed such an alternative conception of the dynamic focus which will be introduced in the next chapter and described more fully in subsequent ones.

As we have seen, the model of the therapeutic process adopted by the major time-limited dynamic systems hinges upon historical reconstruction. Therapeutic change is brought about by insight. The latter is conceived of as the affective experiencing and cognitive understanding of current maladaptive patterns of behavior that repeat childhood patterns of interpersonal conflict. This model is implemented through early and repeated interpretations of T/P links. When evidence of transference behavior appears, it is rapidly clarified and interpretively linked to parallel experiences from childhood, using historical data provided by the patient.

This process presupposes the existence of rather specific personality characteristics (ego functions): (1) As described earlier, the patient must be capable of presenting his or her life story in a manner that provides material for articulating a T/P link; (2) he or she must have ready access to feelings; and (3) he or she must have a ready appreciation of the significance of transference behavior, that is, an ability and willingness to view current conflictual experiences as a repetition of earlier patterns of conflict (i.e., he or she must have a strong observing ego). These are impressive capacities for a patient to *carry into* treatment, and they explain the common criticism that the major approaches to time-limited therapy are appropriate only for the healthiest individuals. While this criticism is often used as a flippant dismissal of psychotherapy in general, we believe that it does have a valid core.

In presenting the approach in this book and pursuing a correlated program of research, it is our aim to determine whether patients can be successfully treated by TLDP even if they are more or less deficient in the ego functions that would make them ideal candidates. To achieve this objective, the model of therapy and associated techniques must allow the therapist sufficient flexibility to deal empathically and effectively with those aspects of the patient's behavior that may have a profound impact on the course of therapy. We are thinking primarily of hostility, negativism, and similar behaviors that often prove highly frustrating to therapists and may lead to serious pitfalls.

We view our approach as a sequel to the work of Ferenczi and Rank as well as the more recent pioneer work of Alexander and French. However, we reject as a major therapeutic goal reconstructions of the past or the recall of repressed memories. In agreement with such contemporary authors as Spence (1982), we believe that the search for historical connections is neither feasible nor therapeutically promising. Instead, we assign priority to analysis of the ways in which the patient's subjective reactions to past experiences (particularly childhood experiences) continue to exert a profound influence on the relationships which he or she currently forms. From this viewpoint it is not required to reconstruct the patient's history but only to assume that current emotional disturbances and interpersonal difficulties are a product of that history. Thus, while recollections of the past are given a serious consideration in terms of placing current behavior in a historical context, we pay special attention to the patient's enactments of his or her neurotic conflicts in the therapeutic relationship which we consistently treat as a dyadic system; and we seek to clarify the manner in which anachronistic beliefs, wishes, and fantasies complicate the patient's interpersonal relations in the present.

This approach is no longer heretical. It combines traditional Freudian conceptions with more recent developments in object relations theory and neo-Freudian thinking. Readers will also discern the influence of systems theory, particularly as it has been applied in family therapy.

The foregoing developments, however, have occurred primarily within long-term intensive therapy, and often with special reference to severely disturbed (borderline) patients. We believe it is timely to apply the newer insights to time-limited dynamic therapy. In so doing we join the ranks of those contemporary theorists who have undertaken the task of freeing clinical observations and therapeutic operations from the influence of metapsychology whose clinical relevance is increasingly being questioned (Gill 1976b; Klein 1976; Schafer 1976, 1983). Throughout we have endeavored to stay close to clinical and observational data, avoiding as far as possible higher-level inferences and complex theoretical constructions. We have striven to evolve an approach that is sensible, practical, communicable, teachable, and researchable. At the same time, we wished to incorporate the best contemporary clinical insights. The lessons learned in the Vanderbilt I study (see chapter 10) have provided an invaluable empirical basis for TLDP.

Summary

We view TLDP as an approach to individual psychotherapy which integrates clinical concepts from a variety of psychodynamic perspectives and which is aimed at the achievement of circumscribed objectives in 25 to 30 sessions. It is intended for patients whose difficulties in living manifest themselves through anxiety, depression, and conflicts in interpersonal relations (inability to achieve intimacy, inhibitions, social withdrawal). Furthermore, it is considered particularly appropriate for those patients whose conflicts are enacted in the therapeutic relationship in a way that poses significant obstacles to the establishment and maintenance of a working relationship. Current interpersonal difficulties, in our view, are typically the product of chronic maladaptations. Accordingly, TLDP does not focus mainly on presenting symptoms—although improvements in the patient's feeling-state are obviously expected—but rather aims at a more lasting modification of the patient's character structure.

Major emphasis is placed on the *contemporary* transactions between patient and therapist, and the patient's increased understanding and appreciation of their role and function in his or her current life. The therapeutic relationship thus comes to serve as a laboratory for studying *in vivo* the patient's difficulties in living as well as a means for correcting them.

The therapist's principal tools are empathic listening, understanding of the psychodynamics of the patient's current difficulties as much as possible in terms of his or her life history, and clarification of their self-defeating character, particularly as they occur in the immediacy of contemporary patient–therapist transactions. The goal is to mediate a constructive experience in living which results in improvements in the patient's self-concept and the quality of interpersonal relations.

Finally, our emphasis is upon integration of theoretical and technical aspects of the therapist's work. To this end, we attempt to avoid all aspects of theory that have no apparent consequences for therapeutic activity. Thus, we hope to make psychotherapy more realistic by linking our approach to systematic investigations designed to define more stringently the limits of what therapy can accomplish with particular persons and specified investments of therapeutic time and effort. The time has come to abandon the unrealistic view that psychotherapy can be all things to all people, nor should one ordinarily expect radical changes in lifelong patterns of maladaptation in a few sessions. However, much work remains to be done to explore these potentialities and limits.

Chapter 2

Patients' Problems as a Function of Disturbed Interpersonal Relationships

AS ALREADY INDICATED, TLDP is based on psychoanalytic conceptions and their extensions and reformulations by contemporary theorists, whose work we refer to throughout this book. Equally prominent is our allegiance to an interpersonal perspective which is anchored in the theories of Harry Stack Sullivan, members of the neo-Freudian school (Horney, Erikson), and the contributions of modern interpersonal theorists (Anchin and Kiesler 1982). Our purpose is neither to construct a new theory of personality development nor to attempt a systematic integration of existing theories. Rather, we have chosen interpersonal conceptions as a framework for the proposed form of psychotherapy because of their hypothesized relevance and utility.

Accordingly, we posit that psychotherapy is basically a set of interpersonal transactions. It is a process which may become therapeutic because of the patient's unwitting tendency (which he or she shares with all human beings) to cast the therapist in the role of a significant other and to enact with him or her unconscious conflicts or maladaptive patterns of behavior rooted in unconscious conflicts. Through participant observation, the therapist provides a new model for identification. He or she attempts then to grasp latent meanings in the patient's interpersonal behavior and communicates this understanding to the patient, thereby helping the latter to assimilate aspects of his or her experience that were hitherto unrecognized or disowned (repressed).* To this end, the patient's experiences with significant others in his or her current and past life represent important sources of information which aid the therapist's understanding; however, they are secondary to the contemporary transactions between patient and therapist.

The foregoing implies that the patient's self-identity and interpersonal behavior are an important function of learning experiences during his or her formative years. The challenges facing every child in growing up are rooted in the prolonged biological and psychological dependency characterizing human development. Accordingly, interpersonal relations with significant others in early childhood prove decisive for the child's development. The family's function in child rearing, to cite one representative author (Lidz 1963), may be grouped under the following headings: (1) nurture; (2) the structuring of the offspring's personality; (3) basic socialization; (4) enculturation, including the proper guidance of language development; and (5) providing models for identification for the child to internalize. Thus, deficiencies in any of these sectors result in developmental deficits which at the adult level may be recognized as neurotic (or sometimes psychotic) disturbances. Essentially, these are forms of immaturity that interfere with the person's adaptive functioning. Because of early deprivations, traumatic experiences, and the like, the patient is unable to gain sufficient gratifications from his or her contemporary interactions

---

*The therapist creates both an interpersonal context (characterized by the qualities discussed in the following chapter) and, within that context, attempts to mediate certain learning experiences. To call the former nonspecific or common factors and the latter specific or technical, as is often done in the research literature, impresses us as an artificial distinction. In our view, therapists practice their craft with varying degrees of skill, but one cannot apply techniques in an interpersonal vacuum nor have an interpersonal context in the absence of techniques. What sets trained therapists apart from untutored individuals is not techniques in the usual sense but rather the trained therapist's understanding and grasp of interpersonal processes, psychodynamics, and the goals at which his or her activities are aimed. This understanding is greatly supported and facilitated by a theory of psychotherapy which is anchored in the research and clinical literature. For a fuller discussion, see chapter 10.

with others and lacks adequate resources (or denies their existence) to mold his or her environment in accordance with his or her legitimate wishes and needs. The patient has unrealistic expectations of himself or herself and others, and frequently feels stymied. Patterns of dealing with changing life circumstances are rigid, and although he or she may perceive their maladaptive character, the patient feels unable to change them. Chronic anxieties are a manifestation of a pervasive sense of helplessness resulting, in part, from interpersonal conflicts but also from unconscious fantasies relating to primitive sexual and aggressive impulses whose vicissitudes are of course basic to psychoanalytic thinking. In short, the patient is in a state of conflict and suffers as a result. The dilemma often takes the following form:

1. The patient does not know the nature of the problem he or she is trying to resolve, having hidden it in order to avoid painful affects.

2. Excluding the problem from awareness, however, does not result in its resolution. Instead, the person is forced to return to it because it continually interferes with current interpersonal relationships. Thus, the patient dimly recognizes that there is unfinished business with significant childhood figures, but feels unable to complete it.

3. In particular, the patient tends to cast himself or herself in the role of the helpless child vis-à-vis a powerful parent in the (futile) hope that in so doing the original problem will have a different outcome. Without realizing it, the patient continually reenacts the original problem with significant persons in his or her current life (including the therapist), and in important aspects treats them as if they were the significant others of the patient's past. However, since the clock cannot be turned back, there can be no solution.

4. Stuck in many respects at an earlier level of development, the patient is unable to take advantage of opportunities for satisfying interpersonal relationships in the present. This inability contributes to a continual state of frustration and rage. Through his or her present-day behavior the patient not only perpetuates conflicts with significant childhood figures but actively foregoes existing opportunities for gratifying relationships in current life with significant persons.

A dream by a young married woman patient who was fiercely competitive with her (aggressive) mother neatly illustrates the neurotic dilemma: The patient had to pass an oral examination in mathematics in the presence of her mother, but she failed. It may be seen that she had to fail in order to maintain her role as an obedient child who is loved by her mother; to regard herself as her mother's equal (and aggressive rival) would bring her face-to-face with her aggressive and competitive strivings which, from the young woman's perspective, had to be repressed. In her current life, the patient experienced difficulties in choosing the right job, deciding to have a child, and relating to women as equals.

The preceding restrictions refer to fantasies and affective experiences, as well as behaviors with significant others. They may also give rise to various symptoms (anxiety, depression, somatic complaints, and so on), and even more importantly they are reflected in the person's character style, that is, in his or her habitual interpersonal techniques. Examples of the latter are chronic shyness, domineering tendencies, and submissiveness. The interpersonal origin of the latter dispositions may seem obscure and difficult to trace, but they always have a learning history. In general, it may be noted that any conflict or character trend that is alive in the present (a problem that is giving rise to painful affects and is therefore bothersome to the patient) is more readily susceptible to therapeutic intervention than symptoms or dispositions that are ego syntonic (acceptable to the person).

What is the nature of the painful childhood experiences responsible for producing restrictions in the patient's ability to relate satisfyingly with significant others and which result in neurotic symptoms as well as in troublesome character styles? In most instances, they are not the aftermath of single events (the death of a parent at a vulnerable stage of the child's development, a beating by an irate father) but rather the end result of prolonged patterns of parent-child relationships which *in the aggregate* have adversely affected the child's personality development and maturation. In the final analysis, we are dealing with injuries to the child's self-esteem and his or her sense of self-worth as a human being. It is valid folk wisdom that in order to become a loving adult, one must have had the experience of being loved as a child. Conversely, any experience, particularly experiences over extended periods of time, that disturbs the child's sense of security will have more or less serious consequences for his or her personality development. Typical examples include parental attitudes of hostility, rejection, indifference, or self-absorption, the effects of which may be escalated by a parent's premature death, separation, birth of a sibling, and the like. Unless mitigated by more benign ones (a loving grandparent or a parent substitute), such experiences will lead to disturbances in the child's self-esteem and produce associated complications. As Sullivan (1955) stated, the self is essentially made up of "reflected appraisals," that is, one values oneself as one has been valued by significant others.

The child, however, is not only a passive organism on which the parental influence is stamped mechanically. Extensive research has shown that the neonate already engages in dynamic interaction with the mother which becomes intensified when the toddler begins to assert his or her own will. This may take the form of resisting the parent, creating tugs-of-war, expressing defiance by passive means, and so on.

Equally significant are the child's fantasies and the meanings he or she attributes to parental behavior. Because they antedate language development, many of these fantasies have never been verbalized. Because of the child's immaturity and limited capacity for validating experiences, the latter may represent exaggerations or distortions of adult reality, colored by primitive fantasies rooted in sexual or aggressive wishes. Thus, the parents are imbued with magical qualities which, in turn, may fill the child with great anxiety. As Freud convincingly showed, the human capacity for fantasy and symbol making becomes a powerful determinant of the child's experiences and emotional reactions to these experiences. In other words, the child is influenced not only by the parents' veridical behavior but by his or her primitive theories concerning the meaning of their behavior.

What everyone learns early in life is to avoid, as far as possible, actual or symbolic experiences that reinstate painful affects aroused by memories (as well as misconstructions) of earlier experiences. If this means avoiding intimacy in interpersonal relations or restricting them in other ways, that is the price that will have to be paid. So-called defensive operations, therefore, serve a self-protective function by shielding the person (however ineffectively) from the experience of painful affects, such as anxiety.

Restrictions in human living might be tolerable were it not for the fact that they lead to further complications. For example, a person who believes that interpersonal intimacy is dangerous will avoid it by becoming detached, aloof, disdainful, and so on. At the same time, however, since psychological needs impel the individual toward interpersonal closeness, a painful quandary arises when he or she feels unable to bring it about. As already noted, the reason the person does not know is because of the ubiquitous human tendency to hide from oneself painful experiences and their aftermath. By the same token, whenever there is the threat of such experiences being reinstated (as typically occurs in the course of psychotherapy), the patient will take measures to prevent this occurrence. Such resistances may take the form of attacking, opposing, or devaluing the therapist as he or she becomes identified with the parent who inflicted the original injury.

It is important to recognize that only *some* aspects of the patient's interpersonal relationships are contaminated and subject to the foregoing distortions. Were this not the case, psychotherapy would be impossible. In other words, the patient is usually quite capable of relating to the therapist as an adult human being and can acknowledge consciously that the therapist is not omniscient, omnipotent, or the most marvelous individual that ever lived. Furthermore, the patient realizes that the therapist does not possess the extreme negative qualities the patient periodically attributes (projects) to him or her. In short, the patient can see himself or herself as an adult engaged with another (benign) adult in a particular form of human interaction. Being capable of self-observation, the patient can also verbalize the subjective experience with the therapist as well as with other persons. The patient can take distance, as it were, from his or her feelings, affects, impulses, and so on, and examine them more or less objectively. This ability to experience and to reflect on one's experience is an essential prerequisite for psychotherapy. The patient participates and, with the therapist's help, increasingly makes use of his or her capacity for self-observation. Individuals who lack this capacity are generally poor candidates for dynamic psychotherapy.

The patient's reality orientation also permits the development of a measure of trust in the therapist, a sense that it may be all right to admit one's (real or imagined) weaknesses and shortcomings and to verbalize feelings and recollections about which the patient feels guilty or ashamed. The patient's trust in the security of the therapeutic situation is contingent upon his or her growing conviction that self-disclosure will have no adverse consequences, such as criticism, rejection, or humiliation.

The ability to trust, however circumscribed it may be by hurtful past experiences, is the basis for the therapeutic alliance. It is made possible by the patient's capacity to form a trusting relationship with another human being who provides reasonable evidence (through attitudes and behavior) that it is safe to be oneself. When this important precondition is met, the possibility for collaboration in the joint endeavor of psychotherapy has been created. It means that the patient can look upon the therapist as an ally in his or her struggles and that the therapist has an ally in the patient who, within limits determined by apprehensions present in any of his or her relationships, will endeavor to collaborate by providing honest, unedited accounts of experiences (particularly if they evoke painful affects). These accounts are the raw material, the empirical data, with which the therapist works in dynamic therapy.

Within the context of such a benign relationship, the distinctions mentioned earlier make their appearance. This discovery was one of Freud's great contributions: If a person is troubled by painful feelings which are rooted in past interpersonal experiences, the creation of a particular human situation (the therapeutic situation) invariably leads to an enactment of these experiences. Patients affectively experience the present as if it were the past, and they imbue significant persons in the present with qualities and attributes carried forward from the past. To the extent that there is a reasonable correspondence between reality and these attributions, the patient is able to relate flexibly and adaptively to persons in the present. Indeed, all of us depend on the ability to transfer from the past to the present; that is, we apply in the present what we have learned in the past. If there is a poor match between certain aspects of the past and the present, adaptation is impaired. The task of psychotherapy is to achieve a better alignment between the patient's predispositions and present-day reality. To bring about these corrections, the therapist relies heavily on the contemporary transactions between himself or herself and the patient.

Object relations theory (Allen 1977; Sandler and Sandler 1978) casts further light on these issues. Every current relationship is more or less influenced by past relationships which have become organizing themes in the personality structure and, as such, are reenacted in the present. Past relationships which are responsible for this influence embody wished-for relationships that the individual unconsciously believes will achieve security, nurturance, and well-being. The urge to reexperience these wished-for relationships is particularly strong when the person's security is threatened. In that event, the object relationship enacted in the present becomes defensively distorted in order to protect the patient from the feared vulnerability resulting from fantasies or yearnings for primitive forms of intimacy (such as total possession of or engulfment by the love object). The patient will resist awareness of these fantasies because of painful affects (loss of self-esteem) associated with them.

The patient's dilemma may be schematized as follows: On the one hand, the primitive fantasy (composed of images, wishes, fears) presses for awareness which is unconsciously equated with enactment (incorporation or destruction of the love object); on the other hand, such awareness is strenuously resisted by what Freud called the "archaic superego" which fears dire punishment for the forbidden wish. Hence the patient is left with a precious secret, the nature of which he or she cannot adequately identify or put into words. The patient wants to keep the secret (because it has a certain pleasurable value) but also wants to be rid of it because it acts like an ego-alien symptom. The problem can only be solved by the patient's learning to trust the therapist sufficiently to allow the secret to be expressed in symbolic form so that the therapist can recognize and interpret it. Thus, by naming the problem, the therapist robs the fantasy of the power it has over the patient's ego, and in effect, abolishes the patient's unconscious conflict.

In terms of object relations theory, internal object relationships are composed of self-images, images of the other, and a set of transactions that takes place between them. Associated with these transactions are a variety of feelings, wishes, thoughts, and expectancies that characterize the object relationship. It is assumed that an experience becomes meaningful when it is associated with strong affects, either pleasant or unpleasant. Consequently, an enduring internal object relationship will have a strong affective component, which lends it psychological meaning and contributes the motive force for its continued reenactment.* Internal object relationships are patterned like structured role relationships, with particular roles assigned to self and object. The tendency to actualize these structured role relationships in current interpersonal relationships leads to the unconscious assignment of certain roles to oneself and to others. There is, then, an isomorphic relationship between internal object relationships and the characteristic form taken by current conflictual interpersonal relationships.

Thus, internal object relationships which are associated with enduring strong affects may embody the patient's thwarted attempts to achieve intimacy in relationships. Accordingly, they will press for enactment in current interpersonal relationships, including the therapeutic relationship. Furthermore, the patient will unconsciously seek to draw from the therapist behaviors that reenact the role assigned to the object in the patient's enduring scenario. This process we call the patient's enactment of an anachronistic, conflictual relationship predisposition. It is our translation of the concept of transference into interpersonal terms. It emphasizes not only the patient's readiness to perceive the therapist in terms of his or her salient predisposition, but equally important, it encompasses the behavior by which the patient unconsciously attempts to manipulate the therapist into reciprocally enacting the role of the object in the patient's scenario. For the stated reasons, the interpersonal relationship between patient and therapist continually oscillates between the valid adult-adult relationship of the present and the anachronistic child-parent relationship of the past.

Essentially, the therapist uses the relationship with the patient as the medium for bringing about change. Whatever the patient learns in psychotherapy, whatever conduces to therapeutic change, is acquired exclusively in and through the dynamics of the therapeutic relationship. In other words, therapeutic learning is experiential learning. One changes as one lives through affectively painful but engrained interpersonal scenarios, and as the therapeutic relationship gives them outcomes different from those expected, anticipated, feared, and sometimes hoped for. To promote these

*See chapter 5, "The Dynamic Focus" for a discussion of the intrapersonal and interpersonal processes that perpetuate the reenactment of internal object relationships.

changes, the therapist, first, assiduously avoids engaging in activities that have the effect of perpetuating the difficulties that have resulted in the patient's interpersonal difficulties, and, second, actively promotes experiences in constructive living.

With respect to the first, the therapist remains constantly attentive to the patient's unconscious attempts to elicit reciprocal behavior that meets the patient's need (wish) for domination, control, manipulation, exploitation, punishment, criticism, and so on. Such unwitting invitations may take the form of subtle seductions, requests for advice, special attention, extra hours, and many other maneuvers to which the therapist must be alert. The only way to avoid completely the impact of the patient's transference pressures would be for the therapist to erect barriers against any empathic involvement with the patient. A more therapeutic stance is to maintain a "free floating responsiveness" (Sandler and Sandler 1978) to the patient's attempts to draw the therapist into a particular scenario. A therapist who cautiously goes along with the patient (both consciously and unconsciously) while remaining alert to his or her own reactions, can obtain invaluable information about the nature of the self- and object-representational components of the patient's relationship predispositions.

With respect to the second, the patient must come to experience the therapist as a reliable and trustworthy ally who is in the patient's corner, and who, in a fundamental sense, has the patient's best interest at heart. To that end, the patient must become convinced that the therapist has something worthwhile to offer, that he or she has a genuine commitment to the patient as a person rather than a case, and that the therapeutic experience is manifestly helpful. These are the essential ingredients of a good therapeutic alliance, the prime moving force in all forms of psychodynamic psychotherapy. Conversely, unless these conditions are met early in therapy, it is predictable that a good outcome—certainly in time-limited psychotherapy—is seriously in question (Strupp 1980a, 1980b, 1980c, 1980d).

Figure 2-1 represents a diagram of the patient–therapist relationship depicting the model of psychotherapy we are proposing in this book. The following observations are germane:

1. Patient and therapist are always engaged in a dynamic interaction, represented by the outer boundary of the figure.

2. At the same time, patient and therapist have their separate identities represented by the circles A_1 and A_2. They interact as adults in the real world and their interaction is governed by the rules of the particular psychotherapy. For example, patient and therapist participate of their own

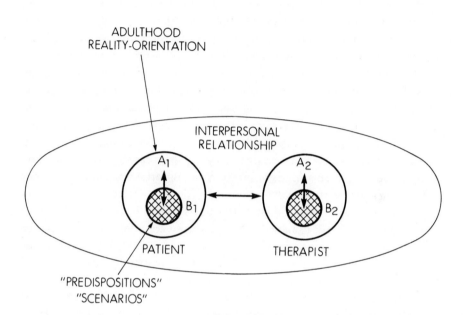

ADULTHOOD
REALITY-ORIENTATION

INTERPERSONAL
RELATIONSHIP

A₁

B₁

PATIENT

A₂

B₂

THERAPIST

"PREDISPOSITIONS"
"SCENARIOS"

FIGURE 2.1

The Therapeutic Relationship

free will, and either party can terminate the relationship at any time. Like any personal interaction, psychotherapy is both real and has an "as if" quality. It is real in the sense that the participants are engaged in a structured human relationship; and it has an as if quality in the sense that the patient tends to relate to the therapist as if he or she were a personification from the past (a powerful parent figure). An intermediate goal of therapy is to enhance the patient's ability to relate to the therapist as he or she really is, that is, as a fellow adult. The therapeutic process serves as a vehicle for achieving this end.

3. All human beings have predispositions, action tendencies, scenarios which they enact more or less automatically with significant persons in their life. An important function of these tendencies is to maintain a sense of personal integrity, to live out various unconscious fantasies, and to achieve interpersonal closeness (intimacy) while preventing separation and loss. Thus they assure the gratification of important wishes and needs which are part of the total personality. These are shown as the cross-hatched areas, B_1 and B_2. Some of these wishes are realizable in therapy; for example, the wish to have in the therapist a confidant, an understanding friend, an ally, and so on. Other wishes are not realizable; for example, the wish to control the therapist as a love object who must never leave and who should devote his or her entire life to the patient.

4. The patient's problem in living (or "illness") is an unwitting tendency to enact unrealistic scenarios with contemporaries; that is, to engage them in idiosyncratic dramas that have adverse consequences for the patient. For example: The patient may have a self-image as an unlovable person as well as one who cannot give love, and may further believe that others share this view; the patient wants closeness but can only seek it by embracing these basic assumptions; consequently, the patient will structure relationships with others so as to bring about what is both wished for and feared. If significant others can be found to enact this particular drama (which is usually not difficult because others may have their own neurotic needs), the scene is orchestrated in accordance with the predetermined scenario, with predictable results that act as a self-fulfilling prophecy to the patient. Therefore, the task of psychotherapy is (1) to create optimum (safe) conditions for the enactment of the patient's scenarios; (2) to allow them to be enacted (within limits); (3) to help the patient see what he or she is doing while doing it; and (4) to restrict the enactment of complementary roles assigned by the patient, forcing the latter to rewrite, modify, and correct the assumptions underlying his or her scenarios. This process is greatly facilitated by the therapist's consistent and reliable behavior as a fellow adult who through his or her actions disconfirms a number of the patient's

anachronistic and false assumptions about reality; that is, about the behavior, motives, and so on of others.

5. In communicating with the patient, the therapist is always addressing both parts A_1 and B_1 of the patient's personality (the converse is of course also true). That is, the therapist's messages are heard both by part A_1, which is in touch with the therapist as a fellow adult, and by part B_1, which seeks to misconstrue what is actually going on between the two participants. A_1 is always influenced by B_1, but A_1 also seeks to control B_1 which, on some level, is recognized as irrational, unrealistic, and so on. A_1 is largely identical with the observing ego which collaborates with the therapist, forms a therapeutic alliance, and in other respects desires better adjustments to reality.

The implications of these propositions will be elaborated on in subsequent chapters.

Chapter 3

The Therapist's Stance

General Considerations

The essence of psychotherapy, as stressed throughout this book, is a specialized human relationship designed to mediate an experience that brings about constructive changes in the patient's self-concept and behavior. Thus, the therapist's attitudes and behavior in relation to the patient are clearly of paramount importance. As a fellow human being, he or she is a privileged participant in the life of another person who has turned to the therapist for help. As a professional, the therapist is a trained clinical observer whose expertise is encompassed by an ability to understand the nature of the patient's difficulties and to turn this understanding to therapeutic advantage. In practice, these roles merge; however, the therapist consistently strives to adhere to his or her professional role, which is unique in human relations. It has been said that the psychotherapeutic relationship is a highly personal relationship within a highly impersonal framework. This unique structure of the relationship forms the basis of the joint therapeutic endeavor.

A great deal has been written on the subject of the therapist's role and function, and we shall assume that the reader has acquired a working knowledge of basic psychodynamic principles. In this chapter, we shall briefly restate salient ones; our primary purpose, however, is to emphasize those aspects of the therapist's behavior that are uniquely relevant to the practice of time-limited dynamic psychotherapy.

The guiding principle in all forms of dynamic psychotherapy is the therapist's ability to *listen* (Fromm-Reichmann 1950). He or she must continually ask the dual question: (1) How can I best understand the inner world of the other person, and (2) what might be the most constructive intervention at this time? In approaching this question, the therapist must be mindful of the dual goal of psychotherapy proposed in this volume: (1) to assist the patient in achieving greater independence and self-reliance, and (2) to promote greater satisfaction and intimacy in human relationships. In keeping with psychodynamic principles, we believe that these goals are best approximated by systematic efforts to enhance the patient's self-understanding.

Hidden behind the patient's anxieties and self-protective mechanisms lies the hope of a loving and supportive relationship in which one is understood. This, in turn, would alleviate the patient's suffering and state of demoralization (Frank et al. 1978). The patient is buoyed by this hope even when at times the therapist feels that his or her patience is being tried by patient provocations, hostility, or negativism. Despite appearances to the contrary, the patient is always trying to solve a problem of interpersonal relatedness—to feel loved, wanted, and accepted.

The therapist's attitude should consistently reflect interest, respect, a desire not to hurt (even when provoked), a suspension of criticism and moral judgment, and a genuine commitment to help (within the limits set by the therapeutic role and by being human). As Hill (1958) put it, the therapist should engage in activities that are maximally constructive and minimally destructive.

Most typically, this calls for receptive and quiet listening, attempting to understand, and simply being there. Often the therapist is being most helpful when he or she is receptive, silent, attuned, and trying to understand what the patient is communicating in symbolic or disguised ways. In particular, the therapist should resist the compulsion to do something, especially at those times when he or she feels under pressure from the patient (and himself or herself) to intervene, perform, reassure, and so on. Frequently underestimated is the degree to which the therapist's presence and empathic listening constitute the most powerful source of help and support one human being can provide to another.

Too often therapists feel called upon—by themselves as well as by their patients—to solve a problem, to be clever, powerful, and omniscient. Indeed, the more helpless and vulnerable the patient feels, the greater will be the need to idealize and overestimate the therapist's abilities and powers. Our culture's preoccupation with technology and the expectations of quick results further conspire to put the therapist under pressure: What should I do? Was this the right thing to do? What would have been better? Questions of this kind are frequently posed by young (as well as by more experienced) therapists. These constraints may appear intensified in time-limited therapy when termination always looms large and results are expected in relatively short order. Nonetheless, often the best thing a therapist can do is to maintain a stance of listening and trying to understand. Paradoxically, this is frequently disparaged as not "doing" very much.

The therapist's stance, in all instances, should be expectant; that is, ready not only for observing but also for experiencing, and to some degree, for becoming engaged in the interpersonal scenario enacted by the patient—the *in vivo* expression of his or her problems in relatedness. Conversely, there is nothing for the therapist to do unless and until the patient sets in motion a process to which the therapist can resonate. The therapist's resonance is largely an intuitive process that can be described only in general terms. Basic questions always include: What is the patient communicating to me, verbally as well as nonverbally? What reciprocal role does he or she assign to me? What does the patient expect me to do? What am I expected to be? What responses is he or she trying to "pull" from me? What, in broad terms, is the nature of the interpersonal drama in which I am being asked to participate?

No matter what the patient communicates directly—and even more important—indirectly, it should never be forgotten that the comments are being addressed to the therapist as a significant other. Therefore, the totality of the patient's behavior always contains comments about the therapist and the real or fantasied relationship with the therapist. This realization should be kept in the forefront of the therapist's thinking and guide listening and participation in the patient's life as it is unfolding during each therapy hour. Concomitantly, nothing about the patient's communication or the therapeutic situation is ever trivial. To be sure, the patient may be compelled by inner necessities to hide important concerns from the therapist, or to mislead or divert the therapist's attention to peripheral issues, and so on, but in all cases the question becomes: Why is the patient doing it? Why can he or she not be more direct? What feelings are being avoided? For example, patients may be intent on proving to themselves (and to the therapist) that no one understands them; or patients may be impelled to provoke the therapist in order to cling to him or her, and so on. A major challenge faced by the therapist is to grasp what the patient is communicating or enacting. This may be synchronous with what he or she is saying, but more often behavior in therapy (as well as outside) is not synchronized with what is being communicated verbally. A common hazard to which all therapists fall prey at one time or another is entrapment; that is, being manipulated by the patient who is impelled to divert attention to a side issue which would take the patient—as well as the therapist —off the hook, thereby vitiating and subverting synchronized communication.*

In a given therapy hour, the patient's initial communication (the opening move) often embodies the theme that will pervade the session; at other times, the therapist may have to listen for a time—occasionally for a long time—before becoming aware of the theme; at still others, the patient may be so defended that a theme does not emerge in verbal communications. Although these may appear to be lost hours to the patient (as well as the therapist), it is at these times that the therapist must scrutinize with particular keenness the nature of the transactions in which he or she is participating. For the affective theme is never really lost, although it may recede from the content of the patient's communications, only to reappear in subtle aspects of the patient-therapist relationship. Put another way, if the theme of the session seems to elude the therapist, it is frequently acted out in the therapeutic transactions. By the same token, therapists need to guard against the fallacy of giving undue weight to their verbalizations or to those of the patient or to look for "aha!" experiences of insight.

On the other hand, there are good hours (Auerbach and Luborsky 1968; Hoyt 1980; Strupp, Ewing, and Chassan 1966) that are experienced as such by the patient and the therapist. Characteristics of such hours are: (1) the presence of strong (and typically painful) affect which indicates that an important issue is close to the patient's awareness; (2) the affect is experienced in relation to the therapist while the patient is simultaneously recognizing that the therapist is only in part the real object toward whom the affect is directed; (3) the therapist has a clear picture of the scenario currently being enacted (that is, the patient and the therapist are on the same wavelength); and (4) by virtue of the foregoing, the therapist is able to recast (interpret) the patient's scenario within a new context. The latter should lead to a more adaptive view of adult reality.

*An entire course of therapy may proceed on the basis of such misapprehensions, and the outcome of the process may result in changes that are rated as "improvements" by the patient as well as others. The distinction between genuine improvement and what Malan (1976a) calls "false solutions" may be found only in the patient's well-being. In the case of a faulty solution, the patient may have hoodwinked the therapist (and himself or herself) into dealing with a problem that was not the real one and therapy ultimately will leave the patient disappointed and dissatisfied because, in a deeper sense, he or she will continue to feel misunderstood.

Examples of opening moves setting the stage are ubiquitous. Two may suffice: The patient sits down, states the feeling that he or she should not be here and then turns to seemingly divergent matters. As the hour unfolds, the therapist remains attuned to the opening remark and attempts to understand why the patient felt that way at the beginning, namely that he or she did not want to be with the therapist. The therapist may find corroborating material clarifying the reasons for the patient's feelings. In the second example, a female patient, whose central problem concerns hostility toward men to whom she feels compelled to submit, enters the room and asks the therapist: "Do you think that one's emotions can cause physical problems?" As the therapist learned later, the patient had developed a bladder problem prior to meeting with her lawyer for the purpose of suing her divorced husband for child support. She viewed the lawsuit as unacceptably aggressive and anticipated punishment. She also informed the therapist, almost in the same breath, that she experienced "nothing," both when meeting the lawyer as well as the therapist. The question was clearly intended to put pressure on the therapist to respond to a loaded question and to express a sense of victory at his inability to do so; thus proving to her the impotence of all men (whom, not surprisingly, she also idealized).

The therapist's powers, obviously, are always limited. They are limited not only by virtue of being human, but by the fact that on many occasions the connotative meanings of patients' communications, because of complex defensive operations, are indeed difficult to identify and to understand. Hence the therapist is often baffled. At other times, the therapist may believe that he or she understands something important about a salient aspect of the patient's conflict, but considers the time inopportune for communicating this understanding to the patient (because of the patient's resistance). At still other times, the therapist may realize that he or she is indeed powerless to help the patient deal expeditiously with a longstanding, deeply engrained character pattern, conflict, and so on. The following rules are important to keep in mind:

1. Resist the *furor sanandi* (the frenzy to cure) in all forms—to direct, persuade, coax, cajole, control, manage, and so on.

2. Resist the temptation to do something, especially when you experience a strong pull for action from the patient.

3. Resist feelings of omnipotence, grandiosity, omniscience, and the desire to impress.

4. If you are not sure of your ground for saying something, keep silent. (Recall an old Maine proverb: "One can seldom listen his way into trouble.")

5. Ascertain in advance that your evidence is reasonably adequate and consider alternative hypotheses. Favor parsimonious constructions that stay close to the clinical data. In particular, avoid clinical jargon and broad generalizations (penis envy, death wishes, and so on).

6. Make a realistic appraisal of what is likely to be the most constructive intervention at this point in time.

7. Above all, keep in mind the defining characteristic of psychotherapy as a *human relationship*. Thus, the fundamental reason for your ability to help your patients is your own humanity. You can help because as a fellow human being you can resonate to their experience and help patients understand their inner world.

The last point deserves elaboration: The therapist is able to bring about a corrective emotional experience because of skill in participating (indwelling) in the patient's experience. Further, as a professional person who understands basic principles of psychodynamics, the therapist can help the patient bring order into baffling, troublesome, and anxiety-provoking phenomena whose meaning the patient understands only inadequately. The essence of psychotherapeutic change, however, is not the patient's comprehension of some abstract principle; rather it is the result of a human *experience* in which he or she feels understood and in which this understanding is given new meanings. Therefore, what the therapist clarifies or interprets is far less important than what the patient experiences in the context of the interaction. Critical is the shared understanding of the subjective truth of the patient's experience (Schecter 1981). While composed of elements that can be dissected and described, the therapeutic experience is an entity, a Gestalt, something that is assimilated at an organismic level.

Recommended Attitudes for Therapeutic Listening

The *consistency* of the therapist's stance, as it is communicated over a period of time, is in itself a powerful therapeutic factor. The following is a concise summary of our position translated into action:

Therapist Respect for Patient

The therapist shows the utmost respect toward the patient as a fellow human being, who is basically no different from the therapist. The therapist possesses certain technical skills and enjoys the status of a professional, but this is the only "superiority" to which he or she is legitimately entitled. The therapist's stance should be that of a reasonable, mature, and trustworthy fellow adult who fosters a *symmetrical* relationship between equals. The patient should never have the experience of being treated as an object, a case, the bearer of a disorder or disease (a hysteric, a psychopath), or as an organism to be treated, modified, shaped, or manipulated.

Respect also means steadfast adherence to the professional role: The therapist grants no special favors and expects none; the patient's right and responsibility to make decisions are respected. The therapist does not take over except in dire emergencies, does not use the patient for personal purposes or gratifications except those explicitly provided for by the nature of the professional relationship (including the therapist's enjoyment of the work and being able to earn a living by it), and recognizes the patient's right to the therapist's full time and attention during each session. The therapist should rarely push, promote a course of action, or limit the patient's freedom in other ways. Moralistic behavior on the therapist's part is a sign of disrespect and should never be in evidence. By the same token, the therapist should not criticize, judge, exhort, admonish, and so on. Through attitudes and actions it should be made clear to the patient that the therapist is entitled to the same privileges, that is, the therapist's freedom of action should not be infringed upon or abridged by the patient.

An appropriately businesslike, friendly, and matter-of-fact attitude conveys proper respect. So does the consistent communication that the therapist is fully committed to the therapeutic task of being helpful to the patient—not necessarily on the patient's terms. Effusiveness, attempts to foster a buddy-buddy relationship, and insincerity should be stringently avoided. The therapist does best when being himself or herself and observing the discipline demanded by the craft. The patient should never be pampered or spoiled by being treated as special, unusual, or unique. Pomposity, arrogance, and conceit are among the greatest deterrents to a proper therapeutic attitude.

Respect is conveyed by means of all aspects of the therapist's behavior and has its basis in the therapist's self-respect. As is true of all human interactions, what is conveyed by attitude and action is far more important than the content of the message. What counts is the therapist's total demeanor and the spirit in which he or she communicates with the patient.

Empathic Listening

The therapist listens empathically. This is perhaps the most fundamental principle rightfully shared by all forms of psychotherapy and by clinicians as divergent in their views as Rogers, Fromm-Reichmann, and Kohut. It asserts the overriding importance of the therapist's continued and concentrated effort at understanding the patient—his or her feelings, anxieties, struggles, and concerns. Through empathy the therapist participates in the two-person relationship; and empathy is the single most important human and technical tool at the therapist's disposal. Listening means immersing oneself in the world of another human being; allowing oneself to resonate to the spoken and, more important, the unspoken messages; and being aware of one's own feelings, images, fantasies, and associations. It is an intuitive process which is guided by the following rules:

1.   As often as possible, leave the initiative with the patient. Allow patients to explore, pursue their own leads, and make their own discoveries. This stance, by itself, permits patients to become more independent and self-directing. Concomitantly, the maximum help you can give patients is to foster reliance on thier own resources rather than yours. This stance also shows the greatest respect for the patient as a fellow adult. It may also be a powerful contrast to attitudes the patient has become used to from parents and other significant adults.

2.   Keep listening until you have a reasonable conviction that you understand what the patient is trying to communicate. In most instances, do not interrupt patients or break into their train of thought or associations. However, when opportune, stimulate the patients' curiosity about and interest in themselves and in collaborating with you. Raise questions and wonder aloud in order to clarify and elaborate the patients' communications.

3.   Listen for the theme (or themes) of the hour. If no theme appears to emerge, attend even more keenly to clues in the relationship. If, after a while, you are still puzzled, it may be appropriate to express your puzzlement, with a view to enlisting the patient's collaboration. Do not engage in far-fetched constructions. Learn to feel comfortable in acknowledging that you are at a loss. It can be a powerful lesson in reality testing.

4.   Be task oriented but communicate a relaxed attitude. Therapy is serious business but it need not be grim business. An occasional touch of humor, such as a joke or other episode, may do much to lighten the load and help establish a collaborative atmosphere.

5.   Be sparing in your communications without being monosyllabic. Meaningful communications at relatively rare intervals have greater impact than continual chatter. Use simple, nontechnical language. Generally refrain from driving a point home by repeating your comments, which may have the effect of muddying rather than clarifying the problem under discussion.

6.   Resist the temptation to be clever or brilliant. Attempts at definitive interpretations may scuttle further inquiry and are not as helpful as interpretive pointing to topics possibly worth examining. The latter fosters a process of mutual curiosity and exploration. The best interpretations are the ones the patient gradually learns to make.

7.   Avoid making dogmatic statements; instead, emphasize tentativeness in your communications. At the same time, spare the patient your own uncertainties, ruminations, and preoccupations. If at a given time you are not getting through to the patient, desist from pushing harder. Stand back and try to understand the reasons for the patient's inattention or resistance, then try to enlist the patient's efforts in jointly examining what is happening.

8.   If you feel there is nothing to say, say nothing. This is true particularly at times when you feel under pressure from the patient to respond to a question that may be designed to sidetrack or derail the interpersonal process of therapy. If the patient persists, silence can be taken as rudeness, and it is preferable to examine together possible reasons for the patient's persistence.

9.   Steer clear of attempts on the patient's part to distract you from important therapeutic tasks. Avoid small talk, chitchat, and other maneuvers that obscure the essential legitimate purpose of the patient's being with you.

10.   Be sympathetic to the patient's difficulties, even when you feel that your patience is being tried. Patience is one of the good therapist's most important attributes.

11.   Take care to strengthen the patient's self-esteem; conversely, never make comments that may have the effect of lowering it. Be alert to those occasions when the patient may hear your communication as a criticism, rebuke, or exhortation. The patient's tendency to enact conflictual relationship themes may cause your interventions to be misunderstood or misconstrued. Try to correct misapprehensions as speedily as possible.

12.   Be alert to being drawn into power struggles, arguments, or disputes. More generally, remain alert to the tug of reciprocal roles unwittingly assigned to you by the patient (that of a punitive authority figure or an exploitative parent). As a participant observer you cannot totally avoid such role assignments, but they need to be clarified (interpreted) at the proper time (see chapter 7, "Technique").

13.   Don't compete with the patient in any area because you may unwittingly be recruited to play the role of a parent who spurs the patient (child) on to achievements, performances, and the like. Don't allow your-

self to be perceived as a love object that makes demands, tries to seduce, or otherwise fosters allegiance. Always keep in mind that therapy is not an end in itself but a means for the patient to win independence and autonomy. He or she should become capable of intimacy (relatedness) while retaining separateness.

14. Be absolutely honest at all times; never dissimulate. Because most patients have had ample experience with duplicity (double binds), they are often exceptionally sensitive in detecting such qualities in a therapist. Honesty, however, does not mean uncritical self-disclosure on the therapist's part. The therapist is entitled to privacy, as is the patient. The fact that the therapist necessarily becomes the recipient of the patient's confidences, confessions, and so on, calls for special efforts on the therapist's part to protect them. Under no circumstances should they ever be exploited.

15. Be aware of, and if the occasion arises, acknowledge your human limitations and imperfections. In all your dealings with the patient, be realistic. Convey by word and action that there are many things you cannot do and you are not interested in attempting. Patients will idealize the therapist (as a reflection of their own perceived neediness and helplessness) and then take delight in demonstrating that their idol has clay feet.

16. Convey the message that the most valuable assistance you can give is to participate in the patient's inner world, identifying scenarios he or she is enacting, and clarifying seemingly complex processes. Patients may often want more or complain that what the therapist gives is not enough. Stand your ground!

17. At the same time, be considerate of the patient's neurotic suffering. Respect it, empathize with it, but don't take the responsibility (assume guilt) for changing it, other than through legitimate therapeutic interventions. If, at a given juncture, the patient is in unusual distress and asks for an extra hour, provide it if you can; if you cannot, express your regrets. People will respect that. If you feel compelled to give something that you do not wish to give, you will resent it; therefore, don't try.

18. Under most circumstances, observe reasonably close time limits. If the patient arrives late, you are not obligated to make up the lost time. If you arrive late, you do have such an obligation. Usually it is possible to terminate an hour with a gentle "time is up" statement or something of the sort.

19. Assiduously avoid rigidity and rituals. They can become serious obstacles to progress because the patient will adjust to them and curb his or her spontaneity. It must be recognized, of course, that anything can become a ritual (regularly scheduled meetings, payment of fees, the physi-

cal arrangement of the office, and so on); try to be aware and minimize these factors.

20.   Don't apologize for your human limitations or try to live up to the patient's unrealistic wishes and expectations. Even if you could, it would be poor therapy. If you put forth your best effort and the patient is dissatisfied, he or she has no choice but to find another therapist. You should try to help the patient understand these feelings, but the desire to find someone else may win out. In that event, you may even assist the patient in identifying such a person if asked to do so.

21.   You cannot force the patient to change nor should you respond to fantasies the patient may have on this score. However, the patient is entitled to an early statement—preferably during the first hour—of the rules by which therapy is being conducted. This need not be a legalistic contract but the patient should understand in broad terms what role he or she is expected to play, the role the therapist intends to play, and how their collaboration may help. Such explanations should be simple and straightforward. It may be necessary to reiterate them later on.

22.   The therapist should never assume the role of a punitive parent or a hard taskmaster. Reality does impose limits on everyone but it is poor procedure for the therapist to rub it in.

23.   In other respects, too, it may be inviting for the therapist to exploit the "superior" role vis-à-vis the patient, particularly since the patient, by definition, feels in need of help. By acting punitive or tough, the therapist may deal with his or her own problems of impulse control. In general, beware of communications that are carried on a wave of your own strong feelings (positive or negative); chances are that such communications are self-serving.

24.   In general, scrutinize your communications and seriously try to ascertain in advance whether they are in the patient's interest or yours. If in doubt, refrain! At the same time, take care not to throttle your spontaneity. There is probably nothing worse than a "wooden" therapist or one who is experienced by the patient as a machine.

25.   If you are tired or otherwise not in best form, it may be appropriate to admit it frankly. If on occasion your attempts at clarifications become garbled or you are less concise and lucid than you might like to be, say so. These are but two examples of communicating that you are not godlike. A major principle of good psychotherapy is to observe a disciplined attitude (dictated by necessity and the nature of the craft) without letting it interfere with one's ability to be spontaneous, creative, and empathic. The patient and therapist are, first and foremost, two human beings interacting with each other.

Chapter 4

Assessment

The Assessment Process

Although the initial TLDP assessment interviews are generally more structured than subsequent sessions (in the sense that the therapist is more active in gathering pertinent information for diagnostic and prognostic purposes), therapy proper begins from the first moment the patient meets the therapist. We believe that the traditional dividing line between diagnosis and therapy is largely artificial and a vestige of the model in which a team of mental health professionals formally made a diagnosis, after which a patient was referred for therapy to another person. (For reasons of administrative convenience it may still be necessary to follow this pattern in clinics or mental health centers.) It must also be conceded that in order to determine a candidate's suitability for TLDP it is essential to make certain diagnostic assessments; that is, someone must conduct what H. S. Sullivan called a "reconnaissance."

However, while the assessment interviews are aimed at gathering a great deal of information in a brief period of time, it is important to remember that this effort is conducted in the context of a two-person relationship. Accordingly, the kind of dialogue initiated by the therapist, as well as the participants' reactions to each other, will have a powerful impact both on the kind of data that are elicited and the character of the developing therapeutic relationship. If the interview is conducted for the patient's benefit (rather than for the purpose of arriving at a formal diagnosis), it has the potential of being therapeutic. Following any therapeutic interview, the patient should leave with the feeling that he or she has benefited from the joint work (needless to say, the accompanying feelings are by no means always pleasant). This injunction also places a responsibility on the therapist to make an effort to facilitate such experiences. Accordingly, we will show how the assessment process forms a link in the therapist's overriding effort to establish a productive working alliance.

The two principal goals of the assessment process are to establish the patient's suitability for TLDP and to provide the therapist with a blueprint for the conduct of therapy. This blueprint is formulated as a dynamic focus and will be discussed at greater length in chapter 5. The present chapter concerns the process by which the therapeutic relationship is used as a medium for (1) obtaining a general picture of the patient's current disturbance; (2) gauging the patient's willingness and capacity to engage in the therapeutic tasks required by TLDP; and (3) beginning to establish a working alliance.

The patient who talks with a therapist for the first time has a story to tell—a story of problems, conflicts, and unhappiness. The patient hopes (expects, demands) relief to be forthcoming from the therapist, who is viewed as a professional helper, or healer. An immediate tension is generated between the patient's desire for relief and the therapist's sense of responsibility for providing it. The strength and quality of this tension is a function of (1) the level of the patient's felt disturbance as well as the form his or her impatience for relief takes; that is, the transference pattern that shapes it; and (2) the manner in which the therapist responds to this impatience. If the therapist feels under pressure to arrive at a quick understanding of the patient's problems—especially, to "do" something about them—the assessment process will assume an unduly narrow form.

For example, the therapist may become preoccupied with gathering facts about symptoms, current functioning, and particularly, the patient's life history. This activity may serve the purpose of rapidly generating a diagnosis and/or a psychodynamic formulation. A diagnosis or a dynamic formulation may reassure the therapist that he or she knows what troubles the patient. It may also help to clarify the problem for the patient and to recommend appropriate treatment. However, this fact-gathering or history-taking approach may result in "accumulating an assortment of descriptions of current and past events which [commonly] invite *speculation* as to how they fit together" (Shevrin and Shectman 1973; emphasis added).

Even if the therapist's speculations about the patient's psychopathology are relevant in broad terms, this is a risky method for identifying the current problem.

Experiences and events dating to childhood create lines of influence that contribute to the organization of an individual's current adaptive and maladaptive psychological functioning. However, it is impossible to be sure that any given historical factor, no matter how great its theoretical importance, is having a noteworthy influence on an individual's *current* functioning (A. Freud 1965). Alternatively, a particular experience or event may have influenced the person at some earlier time but that influence may not now be "alive."

Furthermore, historical facts recounted by patients are, to varying degrees, reworked unconsciously in line with the patients' preconscious and conscious views of themselves and their worlds; that is, memories of events and experiences are continually modified to become consonant with enduring affective themes around which an individual's character is organized (Mayman 1968). For example, as therapists we are familiar with the observation that, during the course of therapy, recollected images of parental figures from childhood change to accommodate previously hidden experiences of conflict or of closeness and tenderness.

In short, a patient's memories of personally relevant events, particularly those referring to early childhood, are often subject to a variety of reconstructions. While such information may be useful for gaining a better understanding of a patient's emotional life, it is hazardous to rely on it as a primary source for formulating the patient's current problem. It appears sounder to assign priority to evidence of maladaptive functioning manifested in the immediacy of the therapeutic relationship as well as current relationships outside of therapy. Thus, lines of influence can be identified that lead *from* maladaptive functioning in current relationships *to* recollections of earlier relationships. Such data can then be scrutinized for information relevant to the identified *current* problem.

Let us return to other problems inherent in a history-taking or fact-finding approach. While emphasizing the acquisition of "diagnostic facts," the therapist may neglect to assess the patient's willingness and capacity to engage in the treatment the therapist expects to offer.

It is not unusual to encounter the situation of having formulated a dynamic conflict that appeared to trouble a new patient, only to watch helplessly as he or she becomes disillusioned with what the therapist has offered and leaves treatment. Even if the patient remains in the therapeutic relationship, the therapist may inadvertently promote the patient's expectation that he or she is to be the passive recipient of the therapist's "treatment." Thus, the assessment process may create an iatrogenic resistance to obtaining the patient's active collaboration in therapy. Such collaboration, we reiterate, is critical for the success of TLDP. Accordingly, an assessment effort that promotes a passive role for the patient works against the therapist's major objective, namely, that of initiating an effective treatment process.

From the opening moments of the first interview, as we have suggested in chapter 1, the unfolding interaction between patient and therapist serves as a medium for enactment of those interpersonal conflicts that are currently most salient in the patient's life. Thus, the TLDP therapist is attentive to the affective impact of this new relationship upon the patient, and intervenes to clarify it. In more traditional terms, the therapist attempts to examine transference experiences and behavior whenever they seem to be present.

Equally important, the therapist must be continually alert to the affective reactions (countertransference) that the patient's maladaptive modes of relating evoke. Such subjective information provides important clues for identifying maladaptive attitudes and behaviors. Beyond that, a therapist who fails to recognize the patient's emotional impact on the therapist may mistakenly view his or her own affective reactions as objective prognostic judgments. To illustrate: In a continuing case seminar on time-limited therapy conducted by one of us, a young therapist was looking for a case to present. He dismissed as unsuitable for time-limited treatment a new patient he had seen once, because he felt that the patient would not amount to much as a therapy case. In reviewing the information obtained in the initial interview, a prominent affective theme emerged from the patient's history. It concerned vocational and social failures accompanied by a self-image, reflected in his experience of his parents' attitudes toward him, that he would not amount to much. This self-image was not only evident in his behavioral history, it affected as well his behavior toward the therapist, who had unwittingly reacted with a deprecatory attitude masked as an objective prognostic judgment. The therapist decided to see the patient in time-limited therapy, which proved quite successful.

We proceed on the working assumption that the most striking and emotionally charged transference-countertransference patterns reflect the problems that will become the focus of therapy. (This view will be presented in greater detail in chapter 6.) Concurrently, the therapist obtains information about symptoms and daily functioning, as well as about current and past relationships. However, the schema for organizing this information into a coherent diagnostic picture is developed primarily from clues obtained by careful attention to the nature of the unfolding therapeutic relationship. The content of the patient's interpersonal conflicts is reflected in his or her modes of relating to the therapist and is elaborated by reference to parallel patterns of conflict gleaned from examination of current and past relationships outside therapy. Similarly, the potential responsivity to the therapeutic tasks required by TLDP is most directly assessed by the patient's manner of interacting with the therapist and only secondarily by modes of functioning in outside relationships.

Gathering information about the patient's presenting difficulties is only one of the tasks facing the therapist. Equally, if not more important, is careful scrutiny of the emerging relationship for clues concerning the patient's suitability for TLDP. Attention to these factors also builds rapport by means of the therapist's demonstrated interest in the patient's *immediate* experience.

EXAMPLE

In the second interview a female patient expressed some uneasy feelings about continuing and questioned the therapist both about the nature of the therapy and about himself. Through careful examination of these uneasy feelings it became clear that the patient feared that the therapist would be coercive and would be angered if she resisted his directives. Further examination of her presenting difficulties revealed that this anticipation about the therapeutic relationship reflected a salient pattern of interpersonal difficulties which was to become part of the treatment focus. Thus, timely attention to the patient's apprehensions concerning the therapeutic relationship reassured her about the therapist's intentions as well as providing important diagnostic information.

Such short-term dynamic therapists as Sifneos (1979), Malan (1976a), Davanloo (1980), and Wolberg (1980) have been particularly innovative in using the initial assessment interviews as a trial run to determine whether the patient is responsive to the therapeutic tasks required by their respective approaches to treatment. These therapists have placed primary importance on the patient's responses to trial interpretations as a selection criterion; thus, if the patient rigidly resists dealing with these initial interpretive efforts, it is unlikely that short-term treatment will be offered.

It is well to remember that to varying degrees and in different forms all patients resist the impact of therapeutic interventions. The reason is that such interventions, regardless of their content, tend to promote greater interpersonal closeness (usually coupled with the activation of hidden fantasies) which the patient is impelled to fend off.

It is our impression that most short-term therapists fail to give adequate attention to the character and extent of the patient's modes of resisting so-called trial interpretations. Instead of looking upon resistances as diagnostic clues to the interpersonal problem(s) to be dealt with in therapy, there is an overreliance on the historical approach as a means of generating a dynamic formulation and a focus for therapy. This is often the case even if the contemporary transactions between therapist and patient are used to assess the patient's suitability for treatment. The emphasis on historical facts may then become a major limiting factor in deciding a patient's suitability for time-limited therapy. This is so because, as we have noted previously, in most approaches the patient is expected to provide historical data with sufficient clarity to enable the therapist to construct rapidly a dynamic formulation based on such information. In the view of most short-term therapists, this formulation must include a current conflict which can be readily linked to a nuclear conflict from childhood. If the patient is unable to supply the requisite historical information in a brief period of time, he or she may be considered unsuitable for time-limited treatment.

In our view, the contemporary transactions between patient and therapist should be used *both* to assess the patient's responsivity to the required therapeutic tasks and to identify the content of the patient's major interpersonal conflicts.

As the therapist attempts to engage the patient, the threat of intimacy implied by this effort will evoke an approach-avoidance conflict: The patient desperately wants to relate while at the same time is afraid of a relationship. Within this context, information about current relationships, as well as relationships from the recent and remote past, is obtained.

Guidelines for Assessment

Who can be treated with TLDP? In reviewing other time-limited approaches, we have seen that the range of patients thought to be treatable has been progressively extended. Indeed, some experienced clinicians (Wolberg 1980) have recommended giving *all* patients a trial of short-term therapy. However, most therapists prefer some guidelines for deciding which patients might be suitable or unsuitable candidates. The best available evidence remains clinical experience. For example, Malan (1976a) excludes patients on the basis of a set of criteria developed over a period of years at the London Clinic of Psycho-Analysis: (1) serious suicide attempts; (2) drug addiction; (3) convinced homosexuality; (4) long-term hospitalization; (5) more than one course of electroconvulsive therapy; (6) chronic alcoholism; (7) incapacitating chronic obsessional symptoms; (8) incapacitating chronic phobic symptoms; or (9) gross destructive or self-destructive acting out. While we do not recommend slavish adherence to these criteria, they are clearly useful as red flags to warn of potential difficulties in using short-term treatment. In fact, most major time-limited dynamic approaches, including ours, advocate application of these or similar criteria for excluding patients.

To varying degrees, these exclusionary criteria represent major deficits in personality or behavior that may detract from the prospective patient's ability to engage in the tasks demanded by TLDP. A diagnostic label or a dynamic formulation may refer to relevant personality strengths or weaknesses but will do so vaguely and indirectly. Recognizing this important point, we unequivocally assert that once major symptomatology is ruled out, descriptions of psychopathology, symptoms, complaints, and so on are not particularly useful in forecasting the patient's appropriateness for this form of therapy. Instead, focus rests on the assessment of those dimensions of personality functioning which clinical experience has shown to be most relevant. The following list of criteria is quite similar to those proposed by other workers in the area:

1. *Emotional discomfort.* The patient is sufficiently uncomfortable with his or her feelings and/or behavior to seek help via psychotherapy.

2. *Basic trust.* Sufficient trust and hope for relief from distress through a relationship with the therapist exists that the patient is willing and able to come regularly for appointments and to talk about his or her life.

3. *Willingness to consider conflicts in interpersonal terms.* The patient is sufficiently flexible to consider the possibility that his or her problems ultimately reflect difficulties in relating to others, problems to which, without adequately realizing it, he or she contributes.

4. *Willingness to examine feelings.* No matter how much difficulty is experienced in talking about feelings, the patient is open to considering the possibly important role that his or her emotional life plays in interpersonal difficulties. Conversely, no matter how troublesome and intense the present affects (including those that might become directed toward the therapist), the patient possesses sufficient capacity to emotionally distance from these feelings so that patient and therapist can jointly examine them.

5. *Capacity for mature relationships.* The patient evinces sufficient capacity for

relating to others as separate individuals so that identifiable relationship predispositions, no matter how painful and conflict ridden, can be enacted in the therapy relationship and then collaboratively examined. This ability is lacking in those patients who are so mistrustful and whose affects are so isolated that the therapist either cannot identify the enactment of a relationship predisposition, or even if an identification is made, the patient is unable to see anything meaningful in a collaborative examination of those patterns. Also unsuitable are those patients who lack the capacity to experience and relate to others as separate, whole persons. This may manifest itself by relentless, intractable attempts to manipulate the therapist into satisfying the patient's neurotic needs. In extreme cases, the therapist is essentially prevented from functioning in a psychotherapeutic role.

6. *Motivation for the treatment offered.* Motivation for therapy or motivation for change is commonly considered a crucial characteristic indicating a patient's suitability for time-limited treatment. In our view, motivation refers to regularities in the organization and behavioral expression of the patient's hopes, anxieties, feelings, fantasies, attitudes, and expectancies that contribute to and characterize his or her interpersonal relationships. Consequently, to the extent that patients are able to experience and relate to the therapist as a potentially helpful adult, they demonstrate an ability to achieve more stable and realistic relationships. Thus, the assessment of motivation is reflected in the judgments reflected in criteria 1 through 5.

While the personality dimensions stressed in selecting patients for TLDP are similar to those used by other time-limited approaches, we advocate greater latitude with respect to levels of functioning that others might consider too impaired. We do not require, for example, that the potential TLDP patient actually demonstrate the capacity to express feelings; however, we do look for a willingness to consider that such behavior might be a useful aim in therapy. This latitude is possible because in TLDP a "good" therapeutic relationship is not a prerequisite for treatment; rather, the *obstacles* to developing such a relationship, as they emerge in the patient–therapist interaction, are considered the primary arena of work.

The kinds of data that are obtained in a typical evaluation interview for short-term therapy usually fall into the following categories: (1) nature of the current and previous "illnesses," including details about symptoms, history of relevant "illnesses" in family members, previous treatments, and formal mental status examination; (2) history of past relationships, including a detailed family history; (3) information about current relationships; (4) observations about transactions in the therapeutic relationship. Most short-term therapists assert or imply that this information should be obtained from all candidates with equal thoroughness and that this can be accomplished in 1 to 3 interviews. We have already discussed the problems we see with this fact-finding approach. Beyond that, it is difficult to imagine that such a thorough and comprehensive effort can be accomplished with every patient. It seems more reasonable that with each patient one or more of these categories should be emphasized based on the patient's preferred manner of telling his or her story and the kinds of problems manifested.

For example, if during the initial interview there arises a question concerning serious psychopathology, the therapist must obviously gather pertinent information to test this diagnostic hypothesis.* This process may involve taking a detailed family history, medical history, formal mental status examination, referral for psychological testing, and so on. However, in the absence of evidence for specific situational problems or serious disturbance, TLDP recommends a particular set of priorities for the content areas to be examined. These include, in descending order of importance:

1. transactions in the therapeutic relationship;
2. current and recent relationships with significant others;
3. relationships with significant others in childhood.

We have not listed examination of symptoms as a separate endeavor, because we believe that this information is obtained in most useful form as part of the therapist's examination of the patient's subjective experience in various relationships.

While the primary source of observations for identifying chronic, rigid maladaptive patterns of interpersonal behavior is the evolving therapeutic relationship, the assessment interviews are also used to obtain a comprehensive picture of the kinds and qualities of interpersonal relationships the patient tends to establish with others. An overview of the patient's current and past relationships, in which both adaptive and maladaptive patterns may be in evidence, provides support for and elaboration of the hypotheses derived from observations of the therapeutic interaction. This background also provides a baseline from which to evaluate changes in the

---

*Our clinical impression, supported by research evidence (Sandifer, Horndern, and Green 1974), suggests that within the first few minutes of an assessment interview a relatively experienced therapist makes a fairly accurate intuitive judgment about a patient's severity of pathology. Similarly, the therapist rapidly forms attitudes toward a patient which may be of far-reaching significance for the formulation of the therapeutic "problem" as well as the course of therapy (Strupp 1960).

patient's functioning as therapy proceeds. Finally, information about the patient's past and current relationships is used during therapy to highlight the relevance of discoveries made about the patient's modes of relating to the therapist.

Another goal of the assessment interview(s) is to evaluate the patient's potential for communicating perceptions of and reactions to a therapist. (This capacity is relevant to one of the central tasks in TLDP, that of the patient reporting experiences in the therapeutic relationship.) Therefore, the therapist remains alert for opportunities to question the patient about his or her reactions to the therapist and to the interview situation. When an opportunity arises for drawing parallels between difficulties in the patient's current or past relationships and features of the unfolding interview relationship, or when the therapist senses the presence of affectively charged issues concerning their relationship, he or she offers pertinent observations. This provides an opportunity to evaluate how the patient handles such "process" information.

In the assessment interview the TLDP therapist should keep in mind the content areas previously enumerated. Depending on the nature of the presenting complaints and other circumstances, the therapist may rapidly form hypotheses concerning their relative importance in a given case. However, the topics may be explored in any order. To the greatest extent possible, the interview should be congruent with the topics spontaneously introduced by the patient. In this way patients are encouraged to tell their own story. Furthermore, by proceeding in this fashion, the therapist quickly learns a great deal about the patients' preferred modes of relating and about the interpersonal experiences they consider most important. The therapist must continually weigh the advantages of encouraging patients to pursue topics of their own choosing versus steering the inquiry into particular content areas. Flexibility must be the watchword in this effort, the best guide being the therapist's clinical experience and intuitive judgment. Ideally, there should be an optimal balance between following the patient's lead and directing the inquiry into areas deemed most relevant to the patient's current difficulties. Some questioning is usually necessary, and it may also communicate the therapist's interest in the unfolding account. The therapist, however, should strenuously resist the temptation to take over if the patient's communications are halting, burdened by seemingly unnecessary detail, and so on. For various and often complex reasons, patients may prefer the passive role, to which they are accustomed in medical settings. The patient should rapidly learn that the TLDP therapist's role is different from that of the physician who, having made a diagnosis, takes charge of the treatment.

The initial interview yields samples of the kinds of interactions between patient and therapist that may be expected to deepen as therapy proceeds. The therapist will typically engage in the following activities:

1. ask specific questions to clarify the patient's interpersonal behavior and subjective experiences;
2. ask open-ended questions to extend the inquiry into the patient's interpersonal behavior and subjective experiences;
3. offer clarifying and interpretive comments, including parallels between instances of maladaptive interpersonal behavior in seemingly diverse relationships or interactions.

Let us recall another central aim of the assessment interviews, that of formulating a dynamic focus, which will determine the content to be selectively attended to during therapy. This focus, as we shall see, will be formulated in interpersonal terms. Consequently, it is important for the therapist to elicit information on the extent to which the patient is able to recognize and discuss subjective experiences in interactions with significant others. In order to pursue this objective, the therapist should thoroughly examine current and past relationships, emphasizing those of greatest importance to the patient. Features of particular interest in each relationship, corresponding to the structure of the dynamic focus (see chapter 5), include: (1) the patient's view of his or her own interpersonal actions;* (2) the patient's view of another person's actions and reactions to him or her; (3) the expectations and meanings the patient attributes to transactions with the significant other; and (4) the patient's self-image and self-esteem as a result of participating in the relationship.

An Outline for Conducting the Assessment Interview

The following outline can serve as a framework, to be used flexibly, in organizing material to be developed during the assessment interviews, as well as in guiding the therapist toward particular topic areas. In each of the major topic areas the therapist should take note of the following questions:

*We define "action" in this context to include cognitions and feelings as well as overt behavior (Schafer 1983).

1. In what period(s) of the patient's life and in which kinds of relationships is there evidence of difficulties reflecting the current problems which led the patient to seek treatment?

2. In surveying the patient's interpersonal relationships over the course of his or her life, note the qualities of relations and interactions with (a) peers; (b) authority figures; (c) those perceived in subordinate roles; (d) others of the same sex as the patient; (e) others of the opposite sex.

3. In surveying the patient's interpersonal history and current relationships, note evidence of conflicts around (a) anger, aggression, and assertiveness; (b) passivity and dependence; (c) interdependence and intimacy (including separation/autonomy struggles); (d) affectionate, tender, loving feelings and yearnings; (e) playfulness and spontaneity; (f) sexual impulses and feelings; (g) pleasure and enjoyment versus constriction of impulses and feelings and/or dysphoria.

Interview Outline

I. *Presenting Problem:*
   1. What is the nature of the presenting problem? ("What brings the patient in now?")
   2. Can the patient view the problem in interpersonal terms? Who are the significant persons involved?
   3. Is there an immediately identifiable trauma or precipitant? If not, can one be found?
   4. Does the presenting problem appear to occur for the first time in the patient's life? How long has the patient been aware of it? Have there been previous episodes? If so, when and under what circumstances did they occur? How did the patient handle any previous episodes?
   5. How did the patient decide to seek therapy now? (Examining this question might involve having the patient review his or her thinking even minutes before having made the decision to contact the therapist.)
II. *Relationships:* current, recent past, adolescence/childhood.
   1. Social relationships.
   2. School and/or work relationships.
   3. Intimate and/or sexual relationships (including the patient's spouse and children).

4. Family of origin (parents, parental surrogates, siblings, relatives).
5. Leisure/recreational activities and interests.

With reference to topics listed below, the therapist should examine the situations and/or events in terms of their effects on and meanings for the patient's interpersonal relationships.

III. *Significant Losses* (Emotional and/or actual):
Separations and/or losses occurring in (1) childhood; (2) adolescence; (3) adulthood. Such losses or separations might include the following: (a) parental separation or divorce; (b) death of a parent; (c) birth of siblings; (d) frequent moves; (e) patient's own separation or divorce from a spouse; (f) death of a spouse or other loved one.
IV. *Other Significant Life Disruptions.*
Serious injury or illness to self or significant other, job or career disruptions, and so on.

Summary

The major task of assessment is not to arrive at a clinical diagnosis that neatly fits one of the traditional nosological categories but rather to determine the prospective patient's suitability for TLDP as well as a circumscribed area of work. To make this determination it is necessary to initiate an interpersonal process which in basic essentials is identical to the therapeutic process characteristic of TLDP. We are attempting to make an interpersonal diagnosis; that is, we are trying to determine whether the patient can be productively inducted into a particular psychotherapeutic relationship. In short, we are proceeding on the assumption that the patient's presenting difficulties in cognitive, emotional, and behavioral functioning are rooted in disturbed interpersonal relationships, both present and past, and that TLDP can bring about an amelioration of the effects of these disturbances.

There is no better way than to use the therapist-patient relationship, from the beginning, as a vehicle for observing the patient's interpersonal behavior. Data gathered in this way must of course be supplemented by pertinent information concerning the patient's interpersonal experience with significant others, both in the present and in the past. Last, but not least, it is necessary to apply certain exclusionary criteria which on the basis of clinical experience might argue strongly against accepting the person for TLDP.

One of the major advantages of this method of assessment is its practical utility. In other words, it provides guidelines for immediate therapeutic activity. While scientific inquiry ideally aims at complete explanation, parsimony of explanation is equally important, particularly as a guide to action. Shevrin and Shectman (1973:44) state the point well: "In clinical work explanatory economy can be defined as that extent of explanation necessary *to deal with the problem at hand*" (emphasis added). We concur and further believe that diagnostic labels and complex dynamic formulations provide little help in deciding what to do next with a particular patient who may need and desire psychotherapy. In contrast, our approach proposes a design for action. The next chapter, on the dynamic focus, provides further specification of this design.

Chapter 5

The Dynamic Focus

Thomas E. Schacht, Jeffrey L. Binder, and Hans H. Strupp

THE DYNAMIC FOCUS addresses the problem of gathering and organizing therapeutically relevant information, and of incorporating this information systematically into the therapy.

The dynamic focus as construed in TLDP is a heuristic. The focus helps therapists to generate, recognize, and organize psychotherapeutically relevant information. This active and explicit approach to discovery contrasts with the passive, broadly exploratory, and open-ended model advocated in some time-unlimited approaches. In such long-term psychotherapies, for example, it may be expected that spontaneous organizing tendencies will suffice if therapists conduct themselves properly and if patients are suited to the tasks of treatment. Thus Gill and Hoffman (1982) assert: "Presumably the analysis of transference becomes, during the course of the work, the analysis of a *more organized* set of perceptions and reactions *without any special effort* on the analyst's part to bring this about" (p. 143, emphasis added). While a few patients may do well in the absence of special effort on the therapist's part, many others do not easily accommodate to such an approach.

Historical Overview

The term *dynamic focus,* or just *focus,* has been widely associated with the central problem of maximizing therapeutic efficiency in time-limited treatments (Armstrong 1980; Bellak and Small 1978; Binder 1977; Binder and

65

Smokler 1980; Budman 1981; Davanloo 1980; Flegenheimer 1982; Malan 1976a; Mann 1973; Ryle 1979; Sifneos 1972). Indeed, several of the afore-mentioned authors claim that inability to find or maintain a focus is a fundamental contraindication for brief psychotherapy. At least one research group has honored this seminal concept by labeling its brief dynamic treatment approach "focal" psychotherapy (Balint, Ornstein, and Balint 1972). Related concepts include "nuclear conflict" (Alexander and French 1946); "core neurotic conflict" (Wallerstein and Robbins 1956); central "transference predisposition" (Racker 1968); "residual trauma" (Blos 1941; Ekstein 1956); "central issue" (Mann and Goldman 1982); and "core conflictual relationship theme" (Luborsky 1977).

A dynamic focus is commonly stated in terms of a cardinal symptom, a specific intrapsychic conflict or developmental impasse, a maladaptive conviction about the self, an essential interpretive theme, or a persistent interpersonal dilemma or pattern of maladaptive activity. The content and form of the dynamic focus may vary across theoretical orientations and from therapist to therapist. For example, a therapist may attempt to focus on dependency wishes connected with a patient's struggles during the developmental crisis of autonomy versus shame; or, a treatment might focus on unresolved aggressive feelings connected with the process of grieving for a lost object, on pervasive sexual guilt, or on unconscious castration anxiety stimulated by the oedipal implications of impending graduation from college. Although specific authors have clearly defined favorites, such as Sifneos's (1972) preference for oedipal conflicts, the psychotherapy literature offers no consensual limits to the list of potential focal topics.

Unfortunately, current clinical literature offers few explicit procedures and only a handful of general principles for identifying a dynamic focus. It is more usual to encounter the view that identifying a dynamic focus is a high-level intuitive art. Malan (1976a) for example, holds that a focus "crystallizes" in the sensitive therapist's mind. While there is agreement among students of brief psychotherapies that a dynamic focus should function as an orienting beacon or frame of reference for the therapist's interventions, there is no consensus on the specific form such a focal beacon should take (intrapsychic conflict, interpersonal dilemma, developmental impasse, persistent affective theme), nor is there agreement on how the therapist should pursue, develop, and elaborate a focal formulation (Kinston and Bentovim 1981), or even regarding how the quality of a particular focus may be evaluated. Progress toward greater conceptual specificity of the dynamic focus has occurred largely in a research context

(Gill and Hoffman 1982; Luborsky 1977; Ryle 1979; Schacht, in press). However, since research procedures are often too specialized or cumbersome for routine clinical application, therapists have little in the way of concrete guidance and must usually rely on their own inventiveness, theoretically informed intuition, and clinical experience.

Despite its theoretical centrality, practical application of the dynamic focus concept has remained vague and unfocused. The purpose of this chapter is to outline an explicit model.

Conceptual Foundations of the TLDP Focus

In TLDP a focus is not used simply to limit, constrict, circumscribe, or shorten a therapy. A focus should not hinder the patient's awareness or expression; nor should it reduce a patient's complaints to stereotyped forms. A TLDP focus is also different from a target problem (an unfortunate metaphor which implies that a therapist is some sort of marksman and that clinical techniques are weapons in a therapeutic armamentarium).

The TLDP focus should be understood as an ad hoc individualized theory which clarifies and connects behavioral and experiential phenomena that otherwise appear unrelated and discontinuous. The focus is not an absolute or final formulation (which may, in any case, be a naive and impossible goal). Rather, it is a heuristic guide to inquiry. Both the process of generating a focus, and the focus itself, help patients expand their sense of themselves, integrate bewildering experiences, and master complex problems in living. The major value of a TLDP focus rests in the way in which it may help to organize a therapeutic experience. If therapy is thereby shortened, the reduction in the time required for effective treatment is generally a byproduct of this enhanced organization. When therapy must be brief it is best shortened straightforwardly by setting time limits. A focus then becomes a tool for making efficient use of the allotted time.

Clinicians should be careful lest their focal work transform a good therapeutic environment into one in which the patient acquiesces to a domineering professional. Thus, the focus ought not be imposed by the therapist; this would contravene the basic principles of TLDP by augmenting the patient's dependency on a powerful authority figure, proving more hindrance than help in the long run. Although therapeutic confrontation may be valuable in certain circumstances, such confrontation should not be confused with subtly or overtly pushing, manipulating, seducing, coercing, badgering, controlling, exhorting, or indoctrinating the patient. TLDP requires a collaboration between patient and therapist, for which the patient freely takes active responsibility. The focus, in this spirit, should be arrived at jointly in a manner that brings more of the patient's world into relief and interrelation.

TLDP Focus as a Structure for Interpersonal Narratives

The TLDP focus is a working model (Peterfreund 1983) of a central or salient pattern of interpersonal roles in which patients unconsciously cast themselves, the complementary roles in which they cast others, and the maladaptive interaction sequences, self-defeating expectations, and negative self-appraisals that result. The focus helps therapists to make their description and understanding of these problematic patterns more systematic and coherent. The focus provides labels and an organizing structure that makes therapeutically relevant information more accessible and that ideally helps both patient and therapist to reach meaningful discriminations and integrations.

The TLDP focus is grounded in two principles:

1. *For the kinds of psychological problems treated by TLDP, the primary arena for construing life experience is interpersonal.*

2. *The primary psychological mode of construing life experience, for the therapeutic operations central to TLDP, is narration: the telling of a story to oneself and others.* Hence, the TLDP focus is organized in the form of a schematic story outline. The TLDP focus combines the two principles, providing a generic structure for narrating the central interpersonal stories of a patient's life.

Why an Interpersonal Emphasis? Interpersonal transactions are emphasized because they provide a common psychological stage on which problematic life dramas originate and are repeatedly played out. Yalom (1980), for example, illustrates this point with the case of unresolved death anxiety. He points out that such anxiety is associated with (and perhaps maintained by) characteristic patterns of interpersonal transactions. In one common pattern, persons comfort themselves with fantasies of rescue, which lead to desperate dependency on powerful figures. Alternately, death anxiety may elicit defensive belief in one's specialness and secret invulnerability; these beliefs, in turn, are associated with arrogantly narcissistic devaluation of other persons who become, in this view, less special.

The Dynamic Focus

People develop cognitive, affective, and motivational structures, struggle with existential and philosophical issues, and form visions of self and reality in a deeply interpersonal context that itself unfolds one transaction at a time. Each transaction contains something of the larger whole. Correspondingly, issues become evident in therapy primarily through the role they play in patients' transactions with significant others and, more immediately, with the therapist. The TLDP focus attempts to capture the most therapeutically central aspects of these transaction patterns.

What is Narration and Why is it Important? The central model of psychological activity, structure, and organization, for psychotherapeutic purposes, is the story—also referred to by cognitive psychologists in a more restricted sense as the script (Schank and Abelson 1977). In a story, experiences and actions become sequentially organized into more or less predictable patterns of situational feeling, perceiving, wishing, anticipating, construing, and acting. These patterns, when they lead to problems in living, become the subject matter of psychotherapy.

Many aspects of life stories are frequently, even typically, unconscious. Because we are unaware, we live out these organizing life scripts as if they represented absolute truths, rather than being simply versions of reality. Conscious knowledge of these life stories is promoted by TLDP so that patient and therapist may come to see the currently problematic reality as relative, and together may make appropriate revisions. Knowledge of a life story is acquired in the course of attempting to tell it; narration is the name given to this process of coming to know one's organizing life stories through the effort of telling them. Narration is thus a process of discovery, a kind of investigation. Retelling or renarrating refer to the concomitant process of change through creating alternative (therapeutic) understandings of a life story. Although the terms *narration* and *renarration* have a certain cognitive quality, the processes themselves should not be intellectualized and to be therapeutically useful must be sustained by vividly experienced emotions.

In TLDP the patient and therapist are engaged in a joint narration and renarration of the central interpersonal dilemmas of the patient's life (Schafer 1983; Sherwood 1969; Spence 1982). Through this activity patient and therapist collaboratively author a framework for understanding, a new story, within which the patient's awkward, confusing, and self-defeating experiences appear intelligible and purposeful, as occurring for reasons that are understandable within the world as the patient has construed it and within the dramas being enacted in that world. Through the process of reiterative story making the patient and therapist come to appreciate different possibilities for understanding, feeling, and acting with more flexible and perhaps controllable outcomes. This recognition of alternate possibilities signals the beginning of therapeutic change.

Defining Characteristics of a TLDP Focus

The focus takes the form of a prototype or schematic interpersonal narrative. This narrative is built upon an abstract format or conceptual template (to be described) which aids in its construction.

Just as the rules of English grammar do not specify the content of any particular sentence (but do specify that an intelligible sentence should contain a subject, verb, object, and so on), the abstract form of the TLDP focus likewise provides a structural standard, a way of organizing specific and individual meanings into a narrative that makes interpersonal sense. To achieve this goal, a focus must tell something about: (1) the kinds of distinctions the patient makes about himself or herself and others; (2) based on those distinctions, the kinds of actions (including making further distinctions) in which the patient characteristically engages; and (3) the way in which these distinctions and actions are organized by the patient into a rigid and problematic interpersonal drama. More specifically, a focal narrative describes:

1. human actions,
2. embedded in a context of interpersonal transactions,
3. organized in a cyclical psychodynamic pattern, that have been
4. a recurrent source of problems in living and are also currently a source of difficulty.

Each element of this definition will be taken up in turn.

Human Actions. This phrase means that a TLDP focus is constructed of actions and is not simply a collection of traits or other static hypothetical constructs. A life story is a narrative account of a responsible person doing (and experiencing) certain things, in particular situations, for potentially identifiable (albeit often unconscious) reasons. The characters in a life story act: they perceive, think, sense, emote, move, anticipate, and remember. Furthermore, they may do these and other things in various ways, such as reluctantly, enthusiastically, desperately, angrily, sexually, unconsciously, conflictedly, and so on. Conflict may be expressed by attempting to perform incompatible actions, such as submissively ingratiating oneself with an authority while voicing an assertive concern for one's rights, or by striving simultaneously to feel incompatible emotions, such as affection and anger.

As Schafer (1976, 1983) argues in depth, the language of actions is a kind of "native tongue" for constructing narratives about human behavior and experience. In contrast, a focus phrased in abstract jargon or technical language poses significant heuristic and communication problems. It is very difficult, for example, to achieve consensus on the precise referents of constructs like repressed orality, unconscious castration anxiety, or primitive rage. To communicate such constructs intelligibly requires translation from the jargon into terms more resonant with ordinary experience. Castration anxiety, for example, may be redescribed in terms of specific action patterns, such as "feels physically small and incapable of expressing himself in the presence of older males who occupy positions of authority." This translation process can be largely bypassed, however, if therapy proceeds from the beginning with language that is simple, direct, and action oriented. Such language better retains the ability to evoke in both patient and therapist the full experiential complexity that originally gave birth to the focal formulation.

As Schafer (1976) has described, both private actions (thoughts, feelings, images) and public actions (speaking, moving) are best designated by verbs and adverbs, not by nouns and adjectives. For example, it is better to think in terms of feeling angry or acting angrily for some reason than to speak of "my anger making me do it." Correspondingly, the statements which comprise a focal narrative should emphasize verbs and adverbs (actions) rather than nouns and adjectives (entities, traits, reifications). Actions are characteristically concrete; they lend themselves to empathy because their description may evoke in the therapist some experience, remembered or imagined, of acting (feeling, sensing, thinking, choosing, and so on) in a similar manner. For therapists accustomed to thinking in terms of reifications or trait names (dependent, introverted, grandiose, paranoid, narcissistic, obsessive, hysteric, and so on), some mental effort may be required at first to recast these familiar labels in terms of the specific patterns of action to which they inevitably refer. This effort is worthwhile since, as Schafer has persuasively argued, action formulations are "good to think with."

The TLDP focus organizes actions into a structured pattern. This pattern clusters actions into meaningful groups on the basis of their role or function in the narration of interpersonal scenarios. For example, in telling an interpersonal story the actions of the storyteller and the actions of other characters should be grouped separately, lest it becomes unclear who did what. A story which failed to distinguish between acts of the narrator and acts of others may be incomprehensible (although the fact that a patient chose to tell such an incomprehensible story would be of great interest, perhaps suggesting a severe defect in self-boundaries or excessive reliance on projection). In a similar manner, it is useful to identify the role of other groups of actions, such as the narrator's anticipating or reacting to the activities of other persons.

Interpersonal Transactions. Focal action patterns should be embedded in a context of interpersonal transactions, the basic unit of interpersonal scripts. In contrast to simple actions, which may be executed by one person, transactions are executed by two people acting in relation to each other. In telling the story of a transaction, one person's actions are portrayed as explicitly evoking another person's actions. For example: "After you told him the secret, he got angry and slammed the door, and you imagined that you would never see him again." In this case the action of telling a secret is understood as evoking the actions of becoming angry and slamming the door, which in turn evoke the action of imagining a final separation.

Nontransactional narratives may fail to refer to action ("That's a pretty painting"); they may fail to involve interpersonal action ("I mowed the lawn today"); or they may involve interpersonal actions that nevertheless do not describe the actions of one person as evoking the actions of another ("She yelled at me and then she cried and hugged me"). Narration of a transaction, in contrast to narration of an action which occurs merely in the presence of other persons (real or imagined), thus reflects not only one person's contribution to a relationship, but also takes into account the expressed or imagined actions (thoughts, wishes, fears, motives, and so on) of others in response. The concept of transaction will be elaborated further in the discussion of how to actually construct and work with a TLDP focus.

Cyclical Psychodynamic Pattern. The TLDP focus must be organized in a way that makes sense of the self-defeating persistence and inflexibility of a patient's maladaptive and stereotypic interpersonal transactions. The concept of a "cyclical psychodynamic pattern" (Anchin and Kiesler 1982; Wachtel 1982; Wender 1968) best reflects this characteristic rigidity, chronic repetitiveness, and self-perpetuating nature of neurotic problems in living. Traditional explanations invoke linear models of cause and effect to account for this self-defeating persistence and rigidity. These linear accounts view early trauma and unfortunate developmental circumstances as continuing to exert an influence on later behavior, much as a series of billiard balls are set into motion by a first strike with the cue. Unfortunately, such linear models of cause and effect (typified, perhaps, in hydraulic interpretations of Freudian metapsychology) have often led to postulation of highly complicated systems of hypothetical psychic forces and mental structures, and to a misplaced emphasis on distantly past "original" causes.

In a cyclical account the psychodynamic process is not located in the anachronistically preserved past. Instead, this process is understood in terms of presently enacted self-propagating vicious circles. In these vicious circles, self-confirming patterns of repetitive social interchange serve to verify patients' maladaptive views and to validate and reinforce their problematic actions. While some past events set these vicious circles into motion, present continuation of these self-defeating patterns does not depend on the perpetual causal influence of those past events (as a "repressed" psychic force). For this reason, a detailed veridical knowledge of the past (which may be an impossible goal in any case) is not crucial to a cyclical psychodynamic account. The following schematic scenarios exemplify the cyclical psychodynamic concept:

George's mother was abusive and neglectful; his father abandoned the family when George was four years old. As an adult, George now imagines himself to be ugly and unlovable. This perception leads to painful self-rejecting thoughts and to occasional bouts of moderate depression. Rather than endure additional rejection from others, which he is certain is forthcoming because of his ugliness and unlovable nature, George withdraws from others and involves himself in self-destructive overeating, while preoccupying himself with angry ruminations about the "hypocrisy" of other people with regard to standards for physical attractiveness. Although he imagines his behavior to be self-protective, in fact others experience George's withdrawal and anger as unrewarding or even noxious, and they are led to subsequently reject and avoid him. George interprets their behavior not as a reasonable response to his own actions, but rather as proof that he is hopelessly ugly and unlovable. Awareness of this "proof" supports George's self-rejection and also prompts his continued self-defeating withdrawal from and preemptive rejection of others.

Mary was alternately and unpredictably pampered and punished by her father. With him, Mary learned that her own wishes and feelings were inconsequential, and she spent a great deal of time obsessively and anxiously analyzing his behavior, searching for clues that might portend his next change of mood. Mary developed an obsequious and ingratiating style of relating to her father, in the hope that such behavior on her part might induce him to continue pampering her and might minimize the seemingly inevitable episodes of harsh punishment. This ingratiating interpersonal style was also particularly attractive to men whose own role preferences involved the complementary stance of dominance and control. Consequently, Mary had the greatest social success with dominant men who showered her with gifts and who enjoyed their ability to extract unquestioning submission and obedience from her. She married such a man after a brief courtship and discovered only later that he was also inclined to episodes of heavy drinking and physical violence. While Mary recognizes her husband's faults and fears for her safety, she also imagines that if she only tries harder she can "bring out the good" in him. Consequently, she spends a great deal of time obsessively and anxiously analyzing his behavior, looking for clues that might help her know better how to please him. He, in turn, regards her as contemptibly weak and deserving of whatever punishments he elects to inflict. Mary does not interpret these intermittent punishments as evidence of her husband's sadistic nature, but continues to view the problem in terms of her own failure to please him. Consequently she feels guilty and berates herself for imagined inadequacies, and resolves to try harder.

These examples illustrate the self-confirming selection and shaping of experience that is central to a cyclical psychodynamic process. This self-confirming shaping of experience results from both private actions (selective thinking, feeling, perception) and also interpersonal (public) actions that elicit responses from others which validate one's preconceived characterizations of them. Through these largely unconscious patterns of action, patients repeatedly reaffirm the implicit premises with which they construe themselves, others, and situations; accordingly, contradictory evidence and experience are unlikely to be encountered or appreciated. Neurotic problems in living thus acquire a persistent and self-defeating quality, and this persistence becomes an understandable function of the patient's repetitive transactions with others including, eventually, the therapist.

Historic and Current Significance. A TLDP focus should ideally encompass a pattern of interpersonal transaction that is both historically significant and also a source of current difficulty. However, while currently enacted patterns are of primary importance, the specific nature of these patterns may be ambiguous, even when they are enacted within the treatment relationship. Historical knowledge aids therapeutic understanding by providing a disambiguating context in which confusing meanings of present events may be more easily interpreted. Because the primary value of historical material in a cyclical psychodynamic account is limited to clarifying current actions, the search for historical antecedents should always be subordinate to a reconnaissance of the present. This emphasis is diametrically opposite to a linear-causal approach, in which evidence from the present is used to deduce and confirm some supposedly crucial events which presumably occurred in the past.

Therapists must understand that veridical historical knowledge may be impossible to obtain, and that a psychotherapeutic history is always a history as narrated—a story told to a particular clinician under the constraints of a particular conversational situation. Because memory processes are reconstructive, and because these reconstructive processes are influenced by experiences apart from the events being recalled, what transpires between patient and therapist in the here-and-now exerts a significant influence on what is remembered. As Spence (1982:95) succinctly puts it: "Recall of the past is a hostage to the transference." A dynamic focus furthers the TLDP process by participating in this here-and-now reconstructive narration of the past, and more importantly, the present. Most often, as the therapeutic narration progresses, patients develop a greater tolerance for anxiety, an increased trust in the therapist, and a richer sense of their own past. Consequently, while it is not uncommon to begin a therapy with little sense of the patient's past, in a successful case at least a partial life history (that most relevant to the patient's main problems) will have been collaboratively authored by the end of the treatment. The TLDP focus thus facilitates the collaborative making of a meaningful history, in contrast to the traditionally unilateral taking of a history.

Because history is always as narrated, and because the narrative process cannot be separated from the present patient-therapist relationship, TLDP therapists rely on that relationship as the primary arena for psychological exploration and change. In order to use the patient-therapist relationship in this manner, the patient's problematic interpersonal patterns must become manifest in that relationship. Of course, to allow or encourage patients' interpersonal difficulties to become evident in their present relationship with a therapist poses some risk, since it is typically these same difficulties that underlie the problems for which the patient seeks help. However, along with this risk comes an enormous potential benefit. When a patient's interpersonal difficulties become evident in the therapeutic relationship, the subsequent therapeutic work may acquire a persuasive sense of immediacy and affective conviction that cannot be duplicated by even the most penetrating and astute analysis of material about other relationships.

General Format of a TLDP Focus

This format of a TLDP focus was empirically derived from analysis of the categories of information to which expert therapists addressed their comments when constructing focal interventions (Schacht, in press). It specifies four categories of information which constitute minimal requirements for a well-formed narrative about an interpersonal transaction pattern. To make minimal narrative sense of an interpersonal transaction we should know something about (1) what the interpersonal actors do (perceive, think, feel, expect, and so on); (2) what each actor expects his or her behavior will or should lead the other to experience; (3) how each actor believes the other will or should behave in response; and (4) how the aforementioned activities influence the actors' opinions and treatment of themselves.

The TLDP focus contains four structural elements which express, in schematized fashion, these narratively fundamental categories of action. Collectively, these four categories of action, and their interrelations, compose a framework for the narrative description of interpersonal action patterns. The four action categories are as follows:

1. *Acts of self.* These may include all domains of human action, such as affects and motives ("I feel affectionate toward my mother" or "I wish my wife would pay more attention to me"); perceiving situations ("I sensed we were in a competition together"); cognitions ("I can't stop thinking about how ugly and inferior I am when I meet someone attractive."); or overt behaviors ("I can't refrain from avoiding eye contact with my boss when I'm angry with him"). Acts of self include both private and public actions (feeling affectionate as well as displaying affection), and may vary in the degree to which they are accessible to awareness.

2. *Expectations about others' reactions.* These are imagined reactions of others to one's own actions and may be conscious, preconscious, or unconscious. To achieve a transactional understanding, these should be articulated in specific relation to some acts of self. Statements in this category should emphasize imagined anticipation of others' actions rather than overtly voiced demands regarding others' behavior (these latter events are classed under acts of self). Expectations about other's reactions often take a form such as: "If I speak up, I imagine that she will disapprove of me" or "If I ask her out she will just laugh at me."

3. *Acts of others toward self.* These are observed acts of others that are

viewed as occurring in specific relation to the acts of self. That is, these actions of others appear (or are assumed) to be evoked by the patient's own actions. As previously, acts may include all domains of human action, including both public and private actions. Acts of others are typically expressed in a form such as this: "When I asked for the money he ignored me."

4. *Acts of self toward self (introject).* This category of actions refers to how one treats oneself (self-controlling, self-punishing, self-congratulating, self-destroying). These actions should be articulated in specific relation to the acts of self, expectations of others' reactions, and acts of others which compose the remainder of the format. An introject prototypically takes a form such as: "When my husband praises me I feel guilty and remind myself of my shortcomings" or "When I get angry I just try to slow myself down and think things through. I give myself all the time I need."

In a complete TLDP focus, information about the foregoing categories of action is organized into an outline of a prototypic, maladaptive, cyclical interpersonal transaction pattern. If therapists systematically compare the structure of their formulations to this standard, then the format may also aid in recognizing when a tentative focus is incomplete and it may organize the pursuit of missing information. Like many other conceptual tools available to a psychotherapist, the TLDP focus format is primarily a heuristic aid for the clinician and should not be mistaken for what is ordinarily communicated directly to the patient. Everything the therapist understands about a focus is not necessarily transformed into an interpretation.

Example of a TLDP Focal Narrative

This example outlines a problematic interpersonal transaction pattern that was observed first in the patient's current relationship with her therapist, and later was narratively integrated with her childhood history and her current marriage.

Presenting problem. The patient complains of depression and marital difficulties.

Acts of self. Frances assumes a passive interpersonal position in which she refrains from disclosing her inner self, avoids social contact by withdrawal or procrastination, defers and submits to others' wishes, and spends much time in private thinking and wondering rather than in active communication.

Expectation of others' reactions.   Frances expects that other people will ignore or reject her. She validates this expectation with recollections of being ignored or rejected by her mother and by various significant others.

Observed reactions of others.   Others find Frances's passivity unappealing and do not spontaneously recognize her distress and come to her aid. However, Frances does not see this as an understandable reaction to her passivity, but instead interprets this as evidence that others are actively rejecting and ignoring her.

Introject (how patient treats herself).   Frances views herself as helpless in a hopeless situation. Rather than endure the imagined negative reactions of others, she inhibits and controls herself and refrains from asserting her desires or complaints (hoping that this interpersonal passivity will make her mere presence more palatable to others).

How to Construct a TLDP Focus

Formulation of a TLDP focus does not require that therapists adhere to any particular theory of personality. Most personality theories identify certain interpersonal or action patterns as prototypic. For example, in the Freudian psychosexual scheme, interpersonal behaviors are understood in terms of prototypic oral, anal, phallic, and genital patterns. The TLDP focus, in contrast, does not identify any particular interpersonal perspective, theory, or pattern as primary. Rather, the focus mainly addresses how a complete and intelligible interpersonal story may be told, and speaks less to what specific content the story should convey. Accordingly, the content of a TLDP focus may be drawn from any number of broad story metaphors, cultural myths, and psychological theories of personality.

For clinical purposes the ability of a personality theory to sustain a process of intelligible and collaborative therapeutic narration is more important than its so-called objective or scientific validity. In practice this means that a focal formulation must respect the phenomenology of the patient's and therapist's experience. Although there are many possible variants in telling any life story, neither stereotyped theoretical assumptions nor sheer imaginative fiction can substitute for a narrative that is reasonably faithful to the specific details of the patient's life and the particular therapeutic relationship. Sheer charismatic persuasion *cum* coercion may lead some individuals to uncritically adopt a ready-made life story; however, there is no place in TLDP for this kind of Procrustean "one-size-fits-all" formulation.

Malan (1976a:55) points out that ability to formulate a focus is separate from a patient's motivation and ability to work within the focus. In TLDP this distinction between formulating and working with a focus has less meaning since the two processes are joined. That is, formulating a focus in TLDP is understood as a central part of the therapeutic work, rather than being simply a precursor to it. Both the process and the outcome of this activity are useful to the patient. The process of constructing a focus, for example, may require activities which improve patients' ability to introspect; to differentiate feelings, images, and thoughts; to regulate and organize their attention; and to observe themselves and others interacting.

The first step in constructing a TLDP focus is to refrain for a while from doing so, and rather to observe patients telling their stories in their own language, their own time, and with their own structure. This permits assessment of patients' spontaneous capacity for gaining access to their inner lives and for organizing their life stories in a continuous, coherent, and relevant way. By initially allowing the patient free rein, the therapist may observe the ordinary complexity of the patient's narrative themes and the influence of emotion and interpersonal relatedness (especially with the therapist) on the patient's narrative capacity. When certain affectively charged material is discussed or when the therapeutic relationship moves into certain domains, some patients may respond with loosened or disorganized thinking, with seemingly inappropriate affects, with heightened anxious struggles to control impulses, or with defensive maneuvers designed to restore psychic and interpersonal equilibrium. Therapists who too vigorously take the lead may handicap themselves by short-circuiting the patient's expression of these important tendencies.

However, by the second or third session therapists often have sufficient information to begin more systematic work toward and/or with a focus. This systematic work involves two general steps. The first step is to gather information about recurrent patterns of interpersonal transaction from the ongoing flow of the therapeutic dialogue. The second step is to sort, interpret, organize, and assemble these raw data about interpersonal transactions into a coherent outline of a repetitive problematic interpersonal transaction pattern, using the four-element structure of the TLDP focus as a guide.

In actual practice, these two steps occur at virtually the same time. That is, the therapist simultaneously gathers and interpretively organizes information. For convenience and clarity each step will be discussed separately. Also, as presented here these activities are laid out in a very deliberate step-by-step manner. Ordinarily, with sufficient practice therapists can work more fluently and less deliberately than this presentation might suggest. However, the value of having an explicit step-by-step model of the therapist's task becomes evident even for experienced clinicians when something unexpected or disorienting happens in therapy. At such times it may be extremely helpful to have a consciously available guide to fall back on.

Gathering Interpersonal Information

As various microanalytic studies have shown, even brief conversational interchanges contain overwhelming amounts of interpersonal information (Labov and Fanshel, 1977). When extracting information about interpersonal transaction patterns from the ongoing flow of communicative activity in therapy, clinicians must reconcile their desire to be thorough with the numerous limits to information gathering posed by constraints of time, motivation, financial resources, and human intellectual capacity. It is important to recognize that a therapeutic reconnaissance can never approach exhaustive completeness, and that, fortunately, effective psychotherapeutic work does not ordinarily depend on having an encyclopedic familiarity with the patient. Two basic principles aid in the task of gathering interpersonal information. These include: (1) seeking transaction, and (2) evaluating the functional salience of identified transactions.

Seeking Transaction

Because the TLDP focus expresses a prototypic transaction pattern, therapists naturally cannot generate a focus until they have understood the patient's problems in transactional terms. However, while much that transpires in therapy may relate to interpersonal transaction patterns, patients' spontaneous narratives about interpersonal events are often fragmented or superficial. Consequently, their accounts lack information necessary for a fully transactional understanding of what is being discussed. Consider the following verbatim example from an early therapy hour with a college student:

They could, like you could use it when your friends, when it was like something you had had always, or feelings you had acquired, you know, when you were a child or something like that. Something that comes to mind was when, when my mother was, when we were living in (name of town) when I was in the second and third grade, my (pause) we were living with my grandparents too (pause) it was my grandparents and my mother and my sister and my brother and my mother was going to school (pause) and I often got, you know, scolded and things like that for (pause) one thing that sticks in my mind is one night my mother came in late and we were watching TV and she was tired and, uh, or something (pause) or maybe she wasn't even there (pause) she wasn't even there (pause) and it was just with my grandmother and I (pause) somehow an argument started and she started screaming, you know, at me (pause) I was sort of a (pause) I could, I could, I guess I could provoke fights easily when I was young 'cause I got into a lot of them with my mother and grandparents and people, and I can't remember (pause) well anyway, somehow I was told that you don't love your mother, you don't love your mother, this sort of thing (pause) and then I don't know if that happened before (pause) something happened, and then when my mother came home I told her about it, and then something else started. I can't remember, I can remember.

Clearly, this narrative represents a major challenge to even the most insightful interpreter of interpersonal transactions. Although the context for the patient's remarks is clearly interpersonal, his account is vague, loosely organized, self-contradictory, and does not clearly present one person's actions as eliciting or evoking another person's actions. Consequently, the therapist's task of seeking out the transactional implications of whatever the patient is saying and doing becomes very difficult.

In the foregoing example, what appeared at first to be disorganized thinking was, in fact, part of an organized interpersonal scenario being enacted between patient and therapist that did not become apparent until some time later in the session. This patient had heard in a psychology class about the concept of free association and was attempting to say everything that came to mind without consideration of interpretability. He construed his efforts to free associate as a gift to the therapist, whom he consciously wanted very much to please (the patient made similar efforts to please in his relationships with significant others). The fact that the patient at first neglected to tell the therapist about this experiment in free association revealed other meanings of this behavior, including an opposite wish to challenge or test the therapist's authority and competence ("You're so smart, see if you can figure *this* out!") and a fear of being interpersonally inaccessible ("Can you, or anybody, understand me?").

Vagueness, disorganization, and defensive avoidance are not the only factors which may obscure the transactional significance of patients' symptoms and problems. Psychological difficulties often appear in a symbolized, metaphorically transformed, or poorly differentiated manner that disguises their functional roots in maladaptive patterns of interpersonal transaction. The following examples illustrate this point.

EXAMPLE 1

Arnold was a bright high school graduate in his late twenties, who complained of depression and anxiety resulting from "inability to achieve goals." When questioned further, he stated that although he had "always wanted" a higher education, he found himself unable to take any steps to realize this goal, despite ample financial recources and the apparent support of his family and friends. Arnold sought psychological consultation to determine whether his education aspirations were realistic and to help him get unblocked.

In seeking the transactional significance of Arnold's complaints, the therapist first observed that Arnold's behavior in the therapeutic relationship was overly chummy. For example, in the first session Arnold addressed the therapist by his first name and behaved as if he and the therapist were old friends. The therapist suspected that this behavior might be an effort to prevent an opposite (warded-off) kind of relationship. He hypothesized that, by behaving in a gregarious manner, Arnold was attempting to test (and perhaps foreclose) the possibility that the therapist might not like or accept him. While this pattern of seeking acceptance was first noticed in the therapeutic relationship, the therapist soon discovered other interpersonal contexts in which to elaborate this observation and relate it to the presenting complaint.

The therapist discovered that Arnold's desire for a college education appeared to stem from a wish to be loved and accepted and from a belief that he was fundamentally unlovable and unacceptable. Arnold's parents were self-made businesspeople whose emphasis on success inadvertently communicated that no achievement on their children's part could ever be enough. Arnold reacted to this parental message in two ways: first, by developing a chronic sense of inadequacy; and second, by passively resenting his parents for failing to appreciate him and for having unlimited expectations. This passive resentment took the form of a superficial toughness and a striving for independence. In this transactional context, the goal of going to college became understandable as part of a wish to make himself acceptable and lovable. Likewise, his failure to achieve this goal became understandable as a resentful rejection of what he imagined were the conditions for his becoming acceptable, and his sense that any effort was hopeless, since no achievement could ever be good enough.

These concerns appeared centrally in Arnold's current relationships with women. Because he was bright, interpersonally skilled, and handsome, Arnold began relationships easily. However, these relationships repeatedly foundered because he managed to choose high-achieving women who refused to become serious with a man who had only a blue-collar job (regardless of how stable or well paying it might be).

It eventually became clear that the very fact of being in therapy represented the enactment of a version of this transaction pattern. Arnold sought treatment at the suggestion of a current girl friend, in the hope of salvaging their deteriorating relationship. In this case, simply seeking therapy was part of a neurotic transaction pattern in which Arnold sought love by wishing for achievements but asserted his independence by failing to achieve his stated goals. Therapy was, in this instance, another achievement goal that might eventually be added to his list of failures. By remaining alert to this possibility the therapist was able to prevent Arnold from sabotaging his own therapy, and was able to help Arnold understand (renarrate) his inability to achieve goals in a new light.

Dynamic Focus for Example 1

Acts of self. Arnold seeks acceptance from others (and prevents rejection) by (1) behaving in a gregarious manner which conceals his anxiety; (2) attempting to structure relationships so that issues of control and power are avoided and opportunities to give and receive nurturance are maximized; (3) responding in an overly compliant manner to others' expressed wishes so as to avoid conflict; and (4) asking others to help him reach goals of which he thinks they will approve.

Expectations of others. Arnold believes that others want to control and direct his aspirations, choices, feelings, and life direction. He imagines they expect him to act and feel in ways that he is unable to; and he further imagines that in failing to live up to their expectations, he will be summarily rejected.

Observed reactions of others. Arnold recognizes that others offer support and encouragement. However, he construes this encouragement as concealing the veiled threat of rejection and humiliation if he fails to perform what he is being encouraged to do.

Introject. Arnold berates himself for his inadequacy and lack of "achievement," feeling depressed and unlovable. He suppresses brief experiences of anger (at those whom he imagines make demands) and forces himself to acquiesce to what he imagines are their normative expectations.

EXAMPLE 2

Catherine was a twenty-seven-year-old educated professional woman who entered therapy complaining of depression and of feeling that she was a freak because she devoted several hours each evening to meticulously trimming her hair. Her hair was so shortened from this activity that she felt forced to wear a wig when in public. Catherine was extremely embarrassed to even relate her presenting complaint to the therapist, and she was mystified by her complusion to the point of seriously doubting her sanity.

In seeking the transactional significance of Catherine's complaints, the therapist began by noting two features of the therapeutic relationship. First, Catherine displayed dramatic, incongruous, and repetitive changes in her emotional state and nonverbal style during the early treatment sessions. Second, she maintained an assiduously professional distance from the therapist. Even when her tone of voice clearly indicated a strong emotional reaction to the therapist's comments, she steadfastly denied having any personal reactions to him. The therapist identified these features of the patient's transactional style as sources of possible hypotheses about her hair-cutting symptom. In an effort to discern something about the concrete experiential and interpersonal context that evoked Catherine's desire to cut her hair, the therapist repeatedly stopped her when there was a sudden change in affect or communication style, or when she gave nonverbal evidence of having an emotional reaction to the therapist. On these occasions the therapist inquired about Catherine's inclination to cut her hair *at that moment.* In this way the therapist was able to connect the strength of the patient's compulsive wishes to the interpersonal and affective events transpiring in the therapeutic relationship.

Over time, this process revealed a pattern of sexualized associations to the activity of hair cutting. Roots of this pattern began to appear in Catherine's descriptions of her family and childhood. She had grown up in an extremely perfectionistic and prudish family, in which sexuality was not discussed except to be prohibited, and in which she had been deprived of physical affection. Catherine's only memories of physical contact from the grandmother who raised her related to contact that occurred while the grandmother was trimming Catherine's hair. As she related these memories, Catherine's face softened and her ordinarily tense posture visibly relaxed.

As a teenager Catherine had long elegant tresses, of which she was very proud. Her first episode of hair cutting occurred when a boyfriend (who had been making unwelcome sexual advances) announced to Catherine that she was never to cut her hair because, since she was "his girl," her hair belonged to him. Catherine's response was to reject his sexual advances and to defiantly demonstrate her independence by cutting her hair into a shorter style. Regular trimming was necessary to maintain this hairstyle, but the activity was not initially compulsive.

Subsequently, Catherine suffered a tragic loss, in which the first man with whom she had allowed herself a deeply romantic (and sexual) relationship vanished mysteriously. The circumstances of his disappearance were ambiguous, but Catherine blamed herself, believing that she could have taken some preventive action but had neglected to do so. At this time Catherine's regular hair trimming first acquired a compulsive quality. She experienced great anxiety unless she devoted several hours each evening to perfectionistically trimming her hair, making each strand the same length as all the others on her head.

Over time, Catherine and her therapist came to understand that this compulsive hair cutting was in part a kind of restitution, a way of reducing her guilt about her lover's disappearance. By cutting her hair off, Catherine made herself sexually unattractive (in her mind) to men, thereby remaining "faithful" to her lost lover. At the same time she enjoyed a certain autoerotic pleasure from stroking her hair. As therapy progressed, Catherine's hair cutting also came to be understood as a means by which she coped with a wide variety of interpersonal stresses, especially anticipated heterosexual rejection. Her short hair provided a ready-made excuse for rejection. This self-inflicted reason for heterosexual rejection was a lesser evil, as rejections go, because she retained control over the reason for the rejection.

Dynamic Focus for Example 2

Acts of self. Catherine imagines herself to be globally flawed and defective. She spends many hours trimming her hair, and is especially prone to engage in this behavior when she is feeling distressed about herself. The activity of trimming hair reflects multiple interpersonal actions, including: (1) symbolically making restitution for her imagined failure to prevent her lover's disappearance; (2) making herself unattractive to ward off the tempting but forbidden attentions of men and especially the possibility of becoming intimate and having her unworthiness exposed; (3) retaining a sense of control (by perfectionistically cutting each hair to a precise length); and (4) comforting herself through the self-stroking and manipulations of her hair that accompany the trimming activity.

Expectations of others. Catherine imagines that others find her inadequate, especially with respect to her physical appearance. She believes in particular that most men will demonstrate this lack of appreciation by becoming intrusive or attempting to take sexual advantage of her.

Observed reactions of others. Catherine observes that most people have little to do with her. She interprets this as validation of her negative expectations, rather than as a reasonable consequence of her withdrawal.

Introject. Catherine punishes herself with verbal self-recriminations and by refraining from opportunities to engage in potentially pleasurable social activities in order to devote the time to trimming her hair.

EXAMPLE 3

Adam was in his late twenties when he sought hypnotherapy because he was unable to eat anything but an unusual sandwich made of strawberry jam and salami. He had read about hynotherapy as a way of achieving greater self-control, and sought a therapist who could (paradoxically) *make* him control himself. Although Adam desired to eat other foods, he reported becoming nauseated whenever he attempted to consume anything but one of these sandwiches. Adam dreaded the experience of eating, and would typically go hungry until evening, when he would hastily construct three or four such sandwiches and would wolf them down in private, usually in the bathroom.

In seeking the transactional significance of Adam's difficulties, the therapist began with inquiry about how his eating habits might affect his relationships with others. When the issue of relationships was raised (in the first session) Adam rather suddenly revealed that his main reason for seeking treatment was to improve his marital situation. The issue of idiosyncratic eating habits was important, in his view, only because it was the main topic about which he and his wife disagreed.

Over the next three sessions the therapist discovered that Adam came from a family in which his father was helpless and ineffectual, and in which his mother was extremely intrusive, controlling, and domineering. Even as an adult, Adam feared getting a telephone call from his mother. Only one relative in the entire extended family showed any ability to stand up to Adam's mother. It was this relative who introduced Adam to straw-berry jam and salami sandwiches (when Adam was in grammar school), and it was this relative who had helped Adam assert his wish to eat these sandwiches despite his mother's insistence that he join the family in eating food she had prepared. Transactionally, then, Adam learned to eat unusual sandwiches as a way of preserving his identity and self-respect against the influence of a tyrannical and overbearing parent. His eating habits were a kind of last stand, a way of saying to his mother "I control what I put in my body. Your influence stops here!"

Unfortunately, while the therapist was busily unearthing the details of Adam's history, he was neglecting the status of the therapeutic environ-ment and relationship. Recall that Adam had originally requested hyp-notherapy. Based on the emerging formulation of the transactional signifi-cance of his symptoms, the therapist had discouraged hypnotherapy as simply a further manifestation of Adam's preoccupation with issues of control and of his difficulties relating assertively to women (his mother and his wife). However, the therapist communicated this message somewhat categorically (that Adam's difficulties were embedded in ongoing patterns of interpersonal transaction and that hypnotherapy was inappropriate in this case). Adam's response to the therapist's handling of this issue was, in retrospect, a predictable extension of the established pattern: he resisted the therapist's controlling stance and terminated therapy abruptly.

Dynamic Focus for Example 3

Acts of self. Adam asserts himself autonomously against the expectations of others. He avoids situations in which he is dependent on others.

Expectations of others. Adam believes others want to control him and want him to behave in a compliant and dependent manner. He sees others as ready to punish and humiliate him if he fails to acquiesce. These expecta-tions provide a context for his eating behavior, which he keeps secret, imagining that anyone who knew about his food preferences would try to make him change his diet.

Observed reactions of others. Adam sees others as treating him normally (as not making excessive demands), but he believes that this occurs only because he so diligently communicates his unwillingness to be influenced.

Introject. Viewing self-control as a prerequisite to resisting the influence of others, Adam struggles to control himself (by eating only one kind of food, by seeking hypnotherapy).

The foregoing examples illustrate how a diverse array of symptoms and complaints may relate to underlying roots in interpersonal transaction patterns. It is even possible, on occasion, to discern the essence of a transaction pattern in relationships that do not involve real persons, or that do not even involve persons at all. Consider the example of Jennifer, age 28, who sought treatment because she was excruciatingly shy and socially sensitive. As part of enacting this transaction pattern in therapy, Jennifer would not initially discuss details of her interpersonal relationships. When questioned she would become extremely anxious, blush dramatically, and artfully change the topic or become vague. If pressed to respond she would experience a kind of dissociative reaction, in which she could force herself to answer only by transporting herself in her imagination to another setting.

Jennifer was more comfortable, however, in discussing her favorite activity—riding show horses. Her relationship to her horse was psychologically rich and complex. She freely anthropomorphized the animal, attributing to it a variety of thoughts, feelings, wishes, and personality characteristics. Jennifer also experienced intense emotions in relation to her horse (she would become very angry if she felt the horse was "deliberately" failing to perform). In contrast to the reticence which she experienced in discussing human relationships, Jennifer spoke more freely about her relationship with her horse. The therapist used this animal-human relationship as a source of hypotheses about the kinds of transactions in which Jennifer engaged with human beings. He eventually began to wonder aloud about possible similarities between transaction patterns that had been elucidated in the context of the horse relationship and similar patterns that might have existed in her human relationships. Jennifer was able to respond to this indirect approach, which was shortly thereafter abandoned as she became more comfortable and able to relate. As this and the foregoing examples illustrate, the process of adducing transactional roots may be subtle and complex, and ordinarily the therapist's task cannot be reduced to simply asking a few routine questions.

There are two basic and complementary modes for conducting an inquiry into a patient's characteristic transaction patterns. In the first mode, therapists function as participant-observers (Havens 1976), attending to the nuances of the therapeutic relationship and to their private experience of the patient. Diesing (1971:282) elaborates on this point:

> The participant observer and the clinician work their way into the system [patients' experience] they are studying and try to become an active part of it in order to understand it from the inside. They conceptualize their knowledge in terms that the [patients themselves] use or could understand, though they also try to go beyond the understanding that [patients] have achieved. They test the objectivity of their knowledge

in part by seeing whether it is intelligible and acceptable to [patients], and in part by attempting to act on it and seeing whether their actions are understood and accepted . . .

In the second mode of seeking transactional information, therapists supplement their participant observations with direct efforts to talk *about* interpersonal transactions. (If the transactions being discussed refer to what is currently being enacted between the patient and therapist, this is known as metacommunication [Anchin and Kiesler 1982].) Although the capacity to converse in transactional terms is essential to achieving the kind of interpersonal understanding sought by TLDP, patients do not automatically know this. Some patients will persistently report on the actions of only one person ("he did this, then he did that . . . .") or they will fail to make explicit connections between the actions of two individuals ("I did this, she did that, they did something else"). Likewise, a few patients may restrict themselves to impersonal topics that do not involve human actions ("Nice weather today") or that involve actions out of an apparent interpersonal context ("I took a shower, then I made lunch, then I felt depressed").

To participate successfully in TLDP, patients must learn to attend to interpersonal relationships in transactional terms, and they must relate to their own transactional experiences in an immediate, affectively vivid manner. Therapists should gently but persistently strive for a dialogue in transaction statements; that is, statements in which the actions (feelings, beliefs, expectations, and so on) of two people are represented as evoking each other.

Sometimes the therapist's pattern of systematic questioning to elicit transactional content provides a sufficient example for patients to grasp the idea of transaction. At other times, however, the therapist must adopt a more direct approach, collaboratively evaluating nontransactional utterances for possible transactional relevance. For example, a statement that "the weather sure is lousy" says nothing, denotatively, about interpersonal transaction. However, if the statement itself is recontextualized and understood as part of an ongoing transactional enactment with the therapist then it could be revealing to explore why a patient whose life was in disarray and who suffered painful symptoms would choose to spend valuable therapy time discussing the weather. Statements which neglect an interpersonal context ("I mowed the lawn" or "I felt depressed") can be evaluated for possible unstated interpersonal or transactional aspects ("I mowed the lawn to please my mother who was coming to visit, but I imagined she would still criticize the house and then I felt depressed again").

Process and Content. To achieve a useful understanding of interpersonal transaction patterns, therapists must attend equally to the interpersonal process and to the content aspects of the therapeutic dialogue. The content of a dialogue is that portion which is most accessible (although not entirely so) to mechanical recording. The content is what is being talked about; it is the participants' literal understanding of the subject matter of a conversation, perhaps eventually including some of its unconscious aspects.

In contrast, the interpersonal process of a dialogue involves not what is being talked about but how the conversational relationship is proceeding. The process reflects what is being enacted interpersonally between the conversational partners, as distinguished from the putative topic of conversation. The meaning of a particular conversational content may be modified by its accompanying interpersonal process, or vice versa. A thorough understanding of both process and content requires knowledge of the situational and interpersonal context in which a statement is uttered. For example, the content of the statement "I'm sorry for you" ostensibly carries a message of compassion; this content carries very different process connotations, however, depending on whether it is uttered at a wedding or a funeral, or in a tone of voice suggesting contempt rather than empathy.

Interpersonal content often appears in various latent, indirect, disguised, or unconscious forms of expression. Also, although verbal exchange is central to the talking cure, language is only one of the symbolic modes within which people can represent and communicate their experience. Accordingly, information about a person's interpersonal world may be communicated in virtually any representational medium, including kinesics (gesture, posture), paraverbal expression (vocal intonation, timing, phrasing, emphasis), manner of dress and makeup, paintings, drawings, poems, stories, or songs created by or reacted to by the patient, and so on. Early memories and dreams may also offer indirect information about a patient's interpersonal world (Binder and Smokler 1980; Mayman, 1968), as may responses to psychological testing (Blatt and Lerner 1983).

These indirect modes of symbolizing interpersonal information should be examined carefully, with special attention to the kinds of interpersonal and affective discriminations, transactions, and outcomes that occur. While the structure of symbolic productions may be enormously elaborate (Foulkes 1978), these observations may nevertheless provide useful hints about how a patient habitually represents interpersonal relationships. As with most clinical data, the significance of this information should not be evaluated apart from the mediating context of the ongoing clinical relationship in which it was observed.

Interpersonal process, as distinct from content, is often less immediately accessible to awareness. People tend to follow their private rules for conducting and interpreting interpersonal transactions more or less unconsciously. Consequently, clear understanding of interpersonal process is often elusive, and therapists should discipline themselves to wonder systematically about the nature of the scenario the patient is trying to enact. As a rule of thumb, it is useful to evaluate everything the patient says as being in some way a possible commentary about the ongoing process, a potentially disguised allusion to the therapeutic relationship (Gill 1982). This recommendation respects the fact that interpersonal neutrality does not exist, and that all communications, however mundane, include messages about the state of the relationship between the communicators. Of course, every patient utterance is not inevitably also a disguised reference to the therapeutic relationship. However, such disguised indices of interpersonal process are common and may not be noticed unless the therapist makes a deliberate effort to do so.

When evaluating interpersonal process, useful starting points (see also chapter 3) include repeatedly asking oneself: What context or situation does the patient seem to imagine that we are in? What is the patient trying to do to me, for me, with me, in spite of me, without me? What is the patient trying to get me to do with, for, or to him or her? What is the patient trying to prevent me from doing with, for, or to him or her? What is the patient trying to prevent himself or herself from doing with, for, or to me? When evaluating possible answers to these questions, it is important to avoid false either/or dichotomies. Therapists must remember that neurotic conflict may not follow ordinary rules of logic or consistency, and that often these questions may have multiple and even contradictory answers. The therapist's personal reactions may be a useful source of possible answers to these questions.

Therapists should notice their reactions to patients (that is, their feelings, associations, wishes, fears, behaviors toward the patient), and should wonder how a patient may have contributed to evoking those responses. This kind of therapist introspection may provide the earliest awareness of the kinds of transactions the patient is unconsciously attempting to enact. Of course, therapists should evaluate such countertransference clues cautiously and tentatively, as hypotheses rather than as conclusive evidence. (A more detailed discussion of the therapist's use of personal reactions appears in chapters 3 and 7).

Discrepancies or incongruities between the apparent process and content of a patient's statements are commonplace (for example, when terrible news is delivered with a smile, or when a compliment is delivered in such a way that it becomes, in its impact, a subtle insult). Common wisdom leads therapists to attend to such discrepancies as likely markers of psychological conflict. Since content is carried largely through verbal means, and since expressions of interpersonal process often appear in nonverbal channels of communication, therapists routinely attend to both verbal and nonverbal expressions, inferring existence of conflict when there is a lack of congruence between the two modes. However, it should not be assumed automatically that one mode of communication is more true than another. For example, if a patient smiles repeatedly while relating a tale of woe, it should not be assumed that the smile reflects a real message that the patient's complaints are not genuine and in fact represent a secret source of pleasure. This is certainly a plausible hypothesis, but it is not the only possibility. The patient's smile might be an effort to obtain a reciprocal reassurance from the therapist that the reported problems are not, in his or her professional opinion, of a catastrophic or highly pathological nature; or, the patient's incongruous smile might be an effort to present himself or herself as a "good" person, in the hope that the therapist will therefore refrain from criticizing or blaming.

When faced with a discrepancy between verbal and nonverbal modes of communication, therapists do well to consider contexts in which both messages may be interpreted as true. For example, if a therapist perceives that a patient's hostile verbalizations are accompanied by an erotic nonverbal invitation, it is a dangerous oversimplification to assume that the erotic message is the real one, and that the patient is simply concealing this message with a superficial display of hostility. It could be more instructive in this case to remember that neurotic conflict routinely involves attempts to carry out simultaneous contradictory actions, and to explore ways in which the patient imagines both seducing and attacking the therapist, as well as engaging in various strategies to refrain from these actions.

Additional indirect information about patients' transaction patterns may be gleaned from examination of expectation and imitation. An expectation is the mental completion of an incompletely expressed story. In the same way that responses to projective tests may reveal unconscious psychodynamics, the manner in which a patient repeatedly expects himself or herself and others to act is also an important source of information. Also, as with projective tests, we may gain information by examining both the thematic interpersonal content of expectations (affiliative, aggressive, controlling, and so on) and also by evaluating the structure of the expectations. (Are the patient's expectations expressed in the form of transactions in which differentiated persons engage in actions that evoke and are evoked by others?) Many expectations can be elicited from the patient simply by asking for them. Often, however, expectations are unconscious, and it is helpful to examine the therapeutic relationship, dreams, and other less direct sources of information. By encouraging patients to report not only their observations and perceptions, but also their imaginings, inferences, dreams, fantasies, and expectations, the therapist (as well as the patient) may gain valuable insights into the lines along which the patient habitually constructs interpersonal meanings.

Therapists should also pay careful attention to the patient's efforts to imitate others, whether this appears to be a conscious effort (modeling) or an unconscious one (identification). The patient's choice of whom and what to imitate, and the quality of the imitation, may reveal important information about the lines along which interpersonal scenarios are constructed. Therapists should notice who is idolized by the patient and also who is reviled (or idolized in the guise of being reviled). Analysis of these relationships may provide clues to warded-off interpersonal patterns which the patient tries to deny, conceal, or be the "opposite" of, and also to wished-for patterns which the patient idealizes but has been unable to achieve.

Because transaction patterns may play themselves out over an extended time, therapists' moment-to-moment observations should be complemented by sequence analysis. Much useful information may be gained from considering therapeutic events as part of an organized transactional sequence, rather than viewing them simply as separate units of behavior. Therapists should note the sequence of themes, of affects, and of interpersonal maneuvers that occur both in the therapy hour and in the patient's reports of extratherapy relationships. Transactional sequences can be relatively easy to observe when they occur within a single therapy hour; however, such sequences may be enacted across sessions as well, and therapists should always consider how patients' actions may be related not only to what is immediately preceding, but also to what occurred last week or last month, or what is expected to occur in the future (see especially chapter 9, "Termination"). Analysis of transactional sequences provides information about what stimulates, elicits, or suppresses what in the patient's relationships. Sequence analysis can be crucial to understanding cyclical patterns.

For example, a patient may arrive for a session appearing tentative and apprehensive (evoking support from the therapist). The patient becomes warm and friendly (in response to the support), but then displays competitive behavior (distancing the therapist because too much closeness is frightening). Finally, the patient experiences difficulty in leaving at the end of the hour (fearful that his or her competitive behavior may have damaged the therapeutic relationship). The patient in the foregoing example could be very different from another individual who engaged in the same behaviors, but in a different sequence. A patient might arrive feeling apprehensive (evoking support), but then become competitive (reacting to support as if it were a type of control), and subsequently express concern about possible separation from the therapist (fearful that the therapist will dislike a patient who is too autonomous), and finally leave in a warm and friendly manner (after seeing that the therapist does not respond with dislike or with complementary countercompetitiveness).

Identifying Functional Salience

All interpersonal transactions are not equally important for psychotherapy. A useful focus separates salient transactional events of central interest from those which are more epiphenomenal. Identifying functional salience involves the task of relating an interpersonal transaction pattern to the psychological problem(s) which the therapy seeks to ameliorate. A salient transaction pattern not only embodies the presenting problem; it eventually becomes the problem that is being treated within the therapeutic relationship. The following vignette illustrates the importance of a focus that is salient in this manner:

A young woman sought therapy to understand why she remained engaged to a man who usually treated her coldly, who had previously been unfaithful, and who openly doubted that the couple would remain together for long. The patient stated that the only satisfaction she obtained in the relationship was connected with her fiancé's ability to remain emotionally composed and supportive when she was upset.

The patient's female therapist tried to help the patient understand why she remained so attached to her fiancé by focusing on her relationships with other men, especially her father. In this connection, the patient recalled characteristic incidents when, as a young girl, she had witnessed her father verbally abusing her mother and other members of the family. When she repeatedly pleaded with her mother either to force her father to get professional help or to leave him, the mother calmly denied that there were any serious problems. The patient also contrasted the therapist's steady supportiveness with her father's frightening emotional lability.

Despite persistent effort the therapist soon felt that she was having little impact on the patient (even though the patient remained appreciative of the therapist's interest). Two months after treatment began, the patient married her fiancé, following which the marital relationship immediately deteriorated.

With the help of her supervisor, the therapist began to question why she felt so powerless with this patient. In seeking to identify what the patient did that elicited this feeling of powerlessness, the therapist eventually perceived that she was being treated by the patient as if she were a kindly but completely ineffectual helper. This attitude recapitulated the patient's view of her mother, who had been unable to assert herself against her father's tyranny. Thus, the interpersonal predisposition initially enacted in therapy reflected an important aspect of the patient's relationship with her mother which, in turn, was an important accompaniment of her conflictual relationship with her father and, currently, with her husband. However, by limiting the focus initially to the obvious relationship difficulties with men, the therapist missed the significance of what was being enacted in the therapeutic relationship. Since the patient unconsciously identified the therapist with her mother, and thereby expected the therapist to be similarly ineffectual, the therapist's failure to address this enactment undermined her therapeutic effectiveness.

The task of assessing salience is synonymous with the task of generating coherent cyclical psychodynamic accounts that relate patients' experienced symptoms and problems to their characteristic patterns of interpersonal transaction. Salience, in this context, refers to functional or causal primacy, rather than to standing out (as in the perceptual sense of figure standing out from ground). Whatever belongs in the cyclical psychodynamic account is salient; whatever is not yet part of the account is not yet salient. Therapists thus face the task of identifying which information about a patient is most likely to prove useful when constructing a cyclical psychodynamic formulation. While there are no infallible rules for selecting this information, several guidelines can aid the therapist's endeavor.

First, extremely high or low frequency and/or intensity of an action or experience often reflect rigidity or preoccupation with particular topics, and thereby mark salience. Repeated traumas, serious losses, or major illnesses should be investigated. Repetition may also be metaphoric or symbolic rather than literal; this becomes evident in patients' recurrent characteristic responses to seemingly diverse events.

Second, salience may be indicated both by what is omitted from a patient's behavior and experience and by what is invariably included. It is often significant that a patient never mentions certain types of affects or certain kinds of interpersonal activity (sexual, aggressive); or that, if these topics are mentioned, they are discussed only in a circumscribed way (the patient complains of "competitive problems with men" and never mentions anything about relationships with women). Therapists should suspect that important areas of difficulty are not being discussed if average expectable responses are omitted from the patient's repertoire (the patient fails to experience resentment following a blatant injustice or fails to grieve following the death of a loved one). The transactional significance of such omissions typically resides in the ways in which patients have taken pains to arrange their relationships so as to prevent certain threatening experiences or activities from occurring. In evaluating average expectable responses therapists should be certain to consider the possible effects of normal ethnic, subcultural, or even familial variations.

Third, there are certain contextual indicators of salience. Major life changes (job, education, family, health, and so on) should not go unnoticed. Transaction patterns that occur redundantly within or across contexts (relationships, times, situations) are often more narratively significant than transactions that occur in a more contextually flexible and modulated manner. Ideally a therapist can identify similar problematic transactions in reports of the past and family relationships, in reports of contemporary relationships with significant others, in expectations for future relationships, and in the roles which the patient attempts to enact in the therapeutic relationship. Of these contextual possibilities, the most salient transaction patterns will likely be those that can be observed in the therapeutic relationship and in contemporary relationships with significant others.

The search for highly salient interpersonal information should not be construed to mean that only one most salient feature should be described. Transactional systems have multiple elements, and it is a fundamental error to select a single element to represent the entire transaction pattern. This point is well illustrated by the following example taken from Mortimer and Smith (1983). A hypothetical patient is speaking:

He was really putting me down with his superior looking helpfulness. The more he hovered over me the dumber I got. It was like my mother used to treat me, like I was retarded or something and needed her to do everything. Then, when he turned his back on me, it was just too much. If I had stayed around, I'd have hit him for sure, so I ran out of there. I needed to pass his course to graduate, but there was no sense in going back there anymore after what I did.

Mortimer and Smith identify a wide range of possible themes in this passage, including vulnerability to feeling degraded; a transference pattern of experiencing others who offer help as hovering and depreciating; feeling threatened by dependency wishes and degraded by a wish to be helped; a style of defending against anger by taking flight, and so on. The authors then suggest that any one of these themes could potentially be selected as the central issue for a therapy.

A TLDP therapist, in contrast, would not attempt to select only one of these repetitive actions or experiences for the focus; nor would a TLDP practitioner select several of the issues and keep them separate. Rather, a TLDP focus would integrate as many of the identified issues as possible into a coherent account of a repetitive cyclical psychodynamic transaction pattern. The TLDP therapist's task would not be to select from among unitary focal alternatives, but rather to pursue a formulation that made sense of as many of the observational data as possible. Although the sketchiness of Mortimer and Smith's example makes it difficult to develop a point-by-point illustration, the following TLDP focus demonstrates how the themes they identified could be incorporated into a single focal narrative.

Acts of self. The patient assumes an avoidant interpersonal position, in which confrontations are evaded by fleeing from situations in which persons in authority expect the patient to attempt difficult tasks. As part of this avoidant pattern, the patient displays various signs of emotional distress, including visible trembling and stuttering.

Expectations of others. The patient expects others to view him critically as incompetent and stupid, and to hover over him because they believe he cannot be trusted to function successfully on his own.

Observed reactions of others. The patient observes that other persons often pay close attention to his performance. However he does not see this as an understandably helpful reaction to his distress messages, but instead interprets other people's proximity and attention as a readiness to criticize, attack, and control him.

Introject. Rather than expressing his anger toward others, who are seen as condescending and critical, the patient instead berates himself for failing to perform better and for not coping more effectively with criticism. These failures confirm in his mind the imagined message that authorities have been delivering; namely, that he is inadequate and incompetent. Convinced of his own unworthiness, the patient avoids situations in which others might have an opportunity to evaluate his performance. Even if this avoidance ultimately proves self-defeating by preventing the patient from accepting needed help, it is better than enduring the castigation and humiliation which the patient believes inevitably accompanies such help.

Using Interpersonal Information to Formulate a TLDP Focus

It is quite unlikely that any two clinicians will gather information in precisely the same way. This variation occurs because each therapist possesses idiosyncratic perceptual and narrative-constructing capabilities, and because each therapist-patient dyad will find unique portions of the possible common experiential range on which to base their communication. In the course of their initial assessments, therapists will accumulate a variety of clinical observations, empathic intuitions, preconscious impressions, personal fantasies, emotional reactions, and so forth. Although these intuitive processes underlying much clinical information gathering will lead to differences among therapists, the inescapable role of intuition should not be used to rationalize a casual abandonment of disciplined and critical thinking. Indeed, effortful reflective thought is an important means of training one's clinical intuition (what is at first effortful later becomes fluent and intuitive with practice).

Sometimes collected observations and impressions may not seem to hang together in a coherent manner, and therapists may ignore, discard, or devalue certain observations simply because they can't understand their significance. This temptation to close one's eyes to confusing information must be resisted. It is necessary to persevere in the faith that one may ultimately make sense of what seems, at first, like an impossibly ambiguous and complex aggregation of information. To persist in this way demands that therapists be willing and able to sustain the tension which results from confronting such ambiguity and that they be diligent enough to accept responsibility for the hard work of doing so.

The TLDP focus format provides a heuristic structural standard for the evaluation, organization, interpretation, and analysis of *both* systematic observations and intuitively derived impressions. The format helps the therapist to organize his or her impressions into a prototypical schematic narrative which: (1) includes central problematic aspects of a patient's habitual modes of relating to others, and (2) organizes these interpersonal transactions into a self-defeating cyclical psychodynamic pattern. Using the four-element TLDP focus model as a template for structuring inquiry, a therapist begins to assemble a focus by considering pertinent questions such as: Which actions and transactions appear redundantly? What cyclical-causal relationships appear among the observed actions and transactions? Which expectations of others appear related to which of the patient's actions; and which of these actions, in turn, lead others to behave in ways that confirm the patient's initial expectations? How have behaviors of others toward the patient (past or present) led him or her to introject? How does a particular way of treating himself or herself affect the patient's expectations of others and transactions with them?

The result of this systematic reflection is a set of statements, organized into the four categories of the TLDP focus format, that express a patient's central interpersonal difficulties in a schematic narrative. While this preliminary focus may be well developed, and the therapist may feel convinced of its validity, a useful rule of thumb is to regard the focus as always partial and preliminary (and therefore subject to continued scrutiny and revision as necessary). Maintaining a tentative attitude toward a focus is a reminder that people's lives are complex and multifaceted, and that therapists cannot hope to achieve an exhaustive or final understanding of a patient, no matter how long or intensely therapy continues.

Difficulty in Formulating a Focus

It is possible that a therapist may be unable to construct a complete focus, either because information relative to one or more of the four action categories is deficient, or because the available information cannot be organized into a coherent cyclical-psychodynamic account. The first hypothesis should generally be that the therapist lacks sufficient information to formulate a focus. However, persistent difficulty in formulating a focus may point to other handicapping factors, including problems with the information-gathering process or even becoming overwhelmed by too much information. More specifically, these difficulties may include the following issues:

1. The patient's character organization may be too rigidly armored, preventing the therapist (and the patient) from obtaining necessary information. Such patients often have very constricted and poorly differentiated inner lives. Alternately, the information may be available but presented in such disguised, transformed, chaotic, or unusual (psychotic) forms that it goes unrecognized or is uninterpretable even by experienced and sensitive observers.

2. Maladaptive modes of relating may be so pervasively woven into the patient's character structure (ego-syntonic) that the boundaries between problematic and reality-oriented interpersonal patterns may be virtually nonexistent. Patients whose characterological difficulties are this rigidly entrenched often maintain that any problems in their lives are due to the unreasonableness of other people, and it may be impossible to establish an effective therapeutic collaboration.

3. The patient's capacity for experiencing and relating to other persons may be severely constricted. Rather than experiencing others as whole objects with thoughts, wishes, fears, and inner lives of their own, these patients may experience others predominantly in terms of fragmented attributes (what they wear, own, or do for a living) or in terms of functions which gratify basic needs. Such patients are unable fully to perceive themselves in transaction with another person, and hence cannot easily provide the information necessary for a complete TLDP focus.

4. The patient may have a problem that is not maintained in a cyclical psychodynamic fashion. Typical examples of such problems include various adaptive failures caused by ego defects which result from central nervous system or metabolic disorders (attention deficits, impulsivity, problems with affect modulation), or stress reactions due to extreme but discrete trauma. Ordinarily such patients will not meet the basic criteria for selecting TLDP as an appropriate treatment (see chapter 4). However, because the selection criteria cannot be perfect, therapists may (erroneously) attempt TLDP with some patients whose problems don't fundamentally arise in a transactional matrix (although they may have interpersonal sequelae). Persistent difficulty in formulating a complete focus may be a clue to this possibility.

5. Therapists' own experiences may interfere with their perceptions, producing a confusingly fragmented and overly selective picture of their patients, or yielding a premature and misplaced sense of conviction. Negative enactments by the therapist may alter the openness and content of the patient's self-disclosure. Patients who persistently keep the therapist in the dark often believe something like this: "If I let you really know me, then you will humiliate me." Although this behavior and its underlying reasons may properly become part of the work toward a focus, therapists should not fail to consider the possibility that their own behavior contributes to this enactment.

6. The therapist may be attempting to integrate too much information. As discussed previously under "Seeking Transaction," people may enact interpersonal transaction patterns in numerous forms and contexts. The

picture may be further complicated by various ways in which a manifest or currently operative interpersonal pattern may serve as a functional component in a concealed or warded-off pattern (the patient uses one mode of maladaptive relating as a means of avoiding a more feared alternative). If the therapist fails to recognize that a variety of superficially different behaviors and experiences all express a common underlying transaction pattern, then it can be very difficult to formulate a focus because the apparent amount of relevant information becomes overwhelming. When struggling to understand a patient whose transaction patterns seem overwhelmingly numerous, a useful rule of thumb is to cluster actions or transactions that all make the patient feel the same way about himself or herself (transactions that converge on a common introject). This common introject—usually experienced as a redundant affective theme—may provide the clearest clues to what the patient is reenacting.

In TLDP, difficulty in formulating a focus does not necessarily portend therapeutic failure. Since the explicit focal format represents both a description of a recurrent problem and also a plan for inquiry and action, it offers a basis for identifying what remains to be accomplished if a focus is to be generated. Suppose, for example, that a patient recounts a pattern of problematic transactions with his wife but in his telling fails to include any mention of her expectations or of how he felt about himself while with her. The therapist should then inquire about the missing information, using the structure of the TLDP focus as a general guide to formulating questions. What does the patient imagine his wife might have expected? How would he have acted had he been aware of that expectation? How did the way he felt about himself influence his choice of what to do and his construal of his wife's beliefs and motives or how she felt about herself?

Using the TLDP focus format as an observational guide makes it very difficult for patients to be uninteresting and makes failure to generate a focus almost as informative to the therapist as a successful fabrication of a focus. The TLDP therapist who has been unable to chart a focal direction for treatment may always refer to the structure of the focus for clues about where to go next. Each time difficulty is encountered in formulating a focus, the problem may be related to the basic definition of a focus and to the fundamental tasks of: (1) gathering interpersonal information relevant to the four elements of the focal narrative; and (2) organizing that information into a narratively coherent cyclical psychodynamic account. The four elements of the TLDP focus model, as a standard for structural comparison, allow therapists to judge when and how completely a focus has been formulated. Or, if a focus has not been formulated, the model points to what is absent and the therapist may then set about obtaining the missing information.

When assessed against the focus format, partial data tell the therapist which aspects of the therapeutic reconnaissance should be emphasized if a complete or well-formed focus is to be generated. For example, it may be that the patient has failed to provide information that is interpersonally or transactionally interpretable. This can occur when patients talk about objects or abstractions rather than human activities. In this instance, the therapist knows that he or she should work toward understanding the action implications of what the patient is reporting, because a focus requires understanding in action terms. In other cases, patients may have discussed only the activities of others, or only those of themselves, or may have avoided discussion of their expectations or of how they treat themselves. Here, the therapist's task in generating a focus is to pursue information pertinent to the unarticulated categories. With the guidance of the explicit four-element focal model, this work toward a focus may be just as systematic (and therapeutically important) as subsequent work with a focus. A brief clinical example will illustrate:

The patient was a professional man in his mid-thirties who complained of depression and inability to accomplish goals. Predictably this problem with accomplishing goals was also enacted in therapy, which quickly became a rather stagnant and boring affair. When the content of the therapeutic dialogue was reviewed with reference to the interpersonal information required to formulate a focus, it became apparent that neither the patient nor the therapist had discussed anything which fell into the category of expectations of others. Accordingly, the patient's self-report had the quality of a travelogue, in which he simply recounted a series of "I went there . . . I did this . . . then she did that." Other people, including intimates such as two former wives, were presented as uncomplicated characters without inner lives or expectations of their own. This patient's inattention to or denial of others' expectations was further acted out in the therapy when he neglected to pay his bill, thereby communicating that, among other things, the therapist's expectations were also insignificant. When the therapist became aware of this pattern and brought her own expectations into the therapeutic relationship by confronting the patient over the unpaid bill, this marked a turning point in the heretofore becalmed treatment process. Subsequent therapeutic work productively continued to give attention to the neglected subject of other people's expectations and inner states.

Working With a Completed Focus

The TLDP focus is not a substitute for an overall clinical assessment, and it should be considered in its overall clinical context. Just as treating a cut finger becomes a very different therapeutic task depending on whether or not the patient is a hemophiliac, so dealing with a particular maladaptive transaction pattern must proceed according to each patient's characteristic strengths and weaknesses for participating effectively in the therapeutic work. Collaboration in generating a focus does not mean that patients can effectively participate in the extended psychotherapeutic tasks. They must also meet other criteria of suitability for TLDP (chapter 4 deals in depth with these matters).

Ideally there is no single event that is isolated and labeled as the "presentation" of a focus to the patient. Rather than speaking of presenting a focus to the patient, it is better to understand the process as one of collaboratively arriving at a shared view of what is important to work on in therapy. This work involves more than simply creating intellectual generalizations about experience. Thus, while the focal work should be broad enough to serve as a prototype for dealing with other important situations in the patient's life, it must also involve specifically detailed and vivid reliving of pertinent emotional and transactional experiences. Throughout this process the therapist should maintain an atmosphere of collaboratively finding out rather than one of authoritatively having the answer.

A focus should be articulated as a specific problematic interpersonal scenario that the patient consistently anticipates as his or her fate. This perceived interpersonal destiny ideally unites the technical and experiential components of the therapeutic process by capturing a pattern of interpersonal transaction that is significant both outside of therapy and also in the patient's relationship with the therapist. In an ideal (and therefore impossible) therapy, material emerges during each session that is clearly related to the focus (expresses some part of the focal pattern or defends against such expression). This material typically updates and elaborates the core understanding captured in the focus. "Deep" interpretations should not be required for these relationships to be evident.

Focal comments should rarely (if ever) address the entire cyclical psychodynamic pattern, as this would ordinarily be too much for a patient to digest at once and would probably lead to overly intellectualized understanding. Rather, therapists should work toward clarifying, elaborating, and interpreting the individual manifestations of the focus before attempting to interpret patterns or links between the elements. Like storytellers, therapists should organize their comments and questions so that the proper affective and associative background is in place for focal narratives to make convincing sense. However, the therapist cannot force this background into being and validation of this process must come from the patient. Often it is necessary to work slowly, bit by bit, or even simply to wait for the patient to take an expectable next step. This is an essential feature of that aspect of psychological interventions traditionally called "timing."

Focal comments should also strive for specificity (in action terms) and should avoid overly broad generalizations such as "conflicts over anger," "competitiveness with older men," or "attacks of feeling inadequate." Because it is important for patients to feel affectively as well as intellectually understood, and because excess verbiage may interfere with access to mental imagery and affective experiences (Appelbaum 1981; Spence 1982), therapists should value brevity and should phrase their remarks in concrete and emotionally evocative language. Highly abstract words and long compound sentences rarely belong in psychotherapy. Indeed, it is often a sign of important relationship difficulties (a patient who makes the therapist feel insecure) when it seems necessary to speak in a pompous or jargon-laden manner.

While a focus may be extremely useful as a structure for listening and for interpreting and organizing ongoing observations and impressions, therapists should beware of overextending a focal narrative. It is dangerously easy to force therapeutic events to fit a focal formulation and, subsequently, to find "corroborating" evidence. The fact that something can be plausibly related to the focus doesn't mean that the connection is affectively convincing or, most important, that it is consonant with the patient's experience at the time. The risk is that once sensitized to the presence of a particular characteristic in a patient, and especially once that characteristic has been named and incorporated into an organized formulation, a therapist becomes more likely to perceive that same characteristic again, and becomes less likely to perceive opposite, contradictory, or alternate characteristics. For example, a comment by the patient about the therapist's clothing or appearance will be understood one way if the prior interpersonal process was perceived as expressing aggressive competitiveness, whereas the same comment will be heard quite differently if the process was perceived to be one of nurturance or seduction. Likewise, if a patient casts himself in the role of a bad boy, the therapist may become especially alert to evidence that the patient is seeking signs of displeasure or forgiveness in the therapeutic relationship. Correspondingly, the therapist may become less sensitive to alternate possibilities which do not fit the bad boy formulation. Therapists do well to be skeptical of themselves and to alert themselves to the possibility that their observations are contaminated by the effects of self-fulfilling prophecy and selective perception.

Having created a plausible focus, therapists may subsequently feel a certain narrative pressure to apply their hard-won understanding. This pressure is increased by the therapists' need for mastery, order, and understanding (which a focus appears to fulfill) and by patients' demands for a quick fix. If therapists yield to this narrative pressure indiscriminately, the result may be a rigid or even frenzied interpretive pursuit of focal connections. Therapists may succumb to an unwarranted sense of conviction in the correctness of their formulations (hardening of the categories) and become blind and deaf to evidence from the patient and the therapeutic relationship. It is crucial to repeatedly reconfirm the validity of the focus by establishing an elaborated experiential and associational context for what the patient brings to each session. In this process patients must be working partners who experience what is being verbalized and who are able to support, revise, or disconfirm the therapists' comments as well as make contributions of their own. *A focus does not explain everything: it is a map, not the territory itself.* There will inevitably be significant residual ambiguity in any narrative formulation. Therapists should not forget the essentially tentative and incomplete nature of any focus.

Patients, too, may embrace a focus with excessive zeal, learning what their therapist "wants" to hear and shaping their comments and reactions accordingly. To some extent this is unavoidable and can even be positive: a patient may develop an enhanced capacity for empathy. However, patients who persistently say what the therapist wants to hear may seem to confirm the focal formulation, when in fact the focal work is being distorted by the interpersonal enactment between patient and therapist.

In this circumstance, the patient-therapist collaboration may itself reenact the focal problem, with the content of the focus being unconsciously shaped by both participants' needs for certain things to be true in order to maintain their relationship. For example, patients' needs to please may impel them to make things hang together for therapists who, for their part, feel duty bound to make sense of their patients' problems. Such patients may be willing to accept plausible constructions uncritically, but such acceptance may in fact represent an enactment of an excessively deferent and dependent interpersonal pattern. In this case, a therapeutic misalliance risks yielding only a maladaptive illusion of understanding. Therapists should beware of being seduced by the seeming coherence of a patient's narrative (what Spence 1982, refers to as "fool's gold"). What patients say, no matter how plausible or coherent, should not be interpreted outside the context of when, how, and why they say it. In particular, a patient's responses to focal work should always be evaluated with the status of the treatment relationship in mind.

Efforts to articulate a focus should simultaneously foster patients' beliefs that their difficulties and suffering are being understood and that their situation is not hopeless. However, helping patients to feel understood (or even understandable) is a delicate task that cannot be accomplished merely by saying "I understand" or by nodding empathically at regular intervals. To this end it is important to respect patients' affective distress and to recognize how their symptoms and maladaptive actions also represent healthy motives and genuine (if failed) efforts to deal with their problems. Therapists also will inevitably make some inappropriate assessments and interpretations. Indeed, sometimes it is only through such errors that the therapist gets to observe, in the patient's reactions, details that elaborate further understanding. To participate effectively in TLDP, patients must occasionally tolerate such failures of empathy and then be able to return to collaborative work. Therapists, for their part, must openly allow themselves to be corrected by feedback from the patient.

Another problem occurs when patients' implicit requests for understanding are also woven into the maladaptive interpersonal patterns that are the subject of therapy. Patients frequently entertain curative fantasies as corollaries to their focal patterns. In such fantasies, patients imagine that if they are to feel or act "better," they must have a certain kind of person who will interact with them in a particular way. Thus, as part of their maladaptive transaction patterns, patients may need to cast the therapist in a certain role in order to feel that he or she is capable of listening, understanding, or accepting. For example, a patient who relates to others deferently and dependently may feel most comfortable with a therapist who enacts a complementary authoritative and directive role. However, by assuming such a role, which the patient implicitly demands as a precondition for being understood, the therapist may also foreclose important opportunities for the patient to develop a more autonomous mode of relating. Of course, to meet their own needs, patients may perceive a therapist as authoritative and directive even when objective observers would make a different assessment. The therapist's task is to understand the patient's experience without necessarily validating any distorted perceptions or maladaptive interpersonal preconditions for being understood.

Patients' responses to development of a focal narrative are often a mixture of both positive and negative reactions. On the positive side a patient may respond with appreciative recognition, acknowledging that despite previous awareness of this area of discomfort, it was never so clearly articulated as a problem. Or, patients may realize for the first time that various disturbing elements in their experience are not disconnected, but can be organized and understood as part of a pattern of conflictual interpersonal relationships. This recognition sets the stage for investigations into how patients play an active role in creating and maintaining their difficulties. Alternately, since the focal subject matter is painful, patients may become anxious and back away from the therapist, or they may back away from themselves by responding with habitual defensive techniques that ward off awareness of experiences associated with the focus.

All reactions to the focus, whether positive or negative, may provide further material for the elaboration of the focus. Both avoidance or zealous embracing of the focal content in the therapeutic dialogue may paradoxically be accompanied by an enactment of the focal pattern in the therapeutic relationship. To examine these enactments without thereby suppressing them, therapists must give the patient adequate latitude to respond. Specifically, therapists should maintain a collaborative approach and should ordinarily abstain from forcing the direction of the dialogue.

While refraining from overtly managing or directing their patients, TLDP therapists must also deal effectively with diversionary resistances, such as persistent vagueness or avoidant changing of topics. Throughout, however, emphasis should be placed on understanding when, how, and why defensiveness occurs, rather than on confrontively getting patients to admit to their defensive actions. Avoiding a controlling or adversarial stance also does not imply that therapists do not exert persuasive influence. It is impossible for a therapist to be truly nondirective, and it is undesirable to pretend or even aspire to the myth of neutrality. It is most important that therapists exert influence in a manner that fosters autonomy, allowing patients to discover and own their personal capacity for change. While exerting influence to increase patients' autonomy may seem self-contradictory, properly accomplished the task is no more paradoxical than the influence a mother uses to ease a young child into opportunities for independent activity.

Staying With a Focus. If a patient's communications repeatedly seem irrelevant to the focus, then the therapist should attempt to bring the patient back to pertinent material. This work should follow two guidelines: (1) the principle of "selective attention and selective neglect" (Balint, Ornstein, and Balint 1972), and (2) the principle of "least possible confrontation."

Selective attention and selective neglect are not the same as arbitrarily ignoring whatever appears unrelated to a focus. Ignoring anything that a patient says or does is an unfriendly and generally counterproductive action in TLDP, since everything that a patient says or does communicates something, however disguised, and thus cannot be safely disregarded. Selective attention and selective neglect properly involve a subtle process of influencing what is figure and what is ground in the therapeutic discourse. The therapist's patterning of questions, the timing and shaping of the context for questions, the choices of what to name and what to leave nameless, should all create an associative atmosphere in which focally relevant material predominates because it seems most narratively natural.

The principle of least possible confrontation instructs therapists to use the gentlest means available to promote awareness. It is almost never useful to sacrifice a collaborative therapeutic relationship in order to confront a patient. To paraphrase Peterfreund (1983:198), the adversary is not the patient but the patient's problem. While some patients may forgive a therapist's abruptness and tactlessness, this forgiveness may well be part of their difficulties; in any case, the fact of a forgiving patient does not justify a coercive approach to the therapeutic relationship. It can be necessary at times to provoke anxiety, especially with obsessional patients (Sifneos 1972; Davanloo 1980), and this may even be desirable, so long as patients do not become so anxious that they lose the capacity to observe themselves and to collaborate effectively. However, even anxiety-provoking confrontation can be gentle, and ideally, therapists should prefer to help patients learn how to confront themselves. The inevitable impediments to speaking freely should arise from within the patient, and not from reactions to a confrontive relationship offered by the therapist. The principle of least possible confrontation recognizes that a TLDP focus is a means, not an end. It should never be understood as some sort of critical interpretation which produces change all by itself and therefore must be gotten across to the patient at almost any expense.

Although the principles of selective attention/neglect and least possible confrontation may sound simple, a therapist's task in this regard can be quite delicate and difficult. The therapist must function somewhat as a narrative artist, creating a background of associations and interpretive elements that makes focally relevant themes easy to see. If carried out in a crude, mechanical, or unempathic manner the patient may reject the therapist's efforts as tedious carping and the therapy may reach an impasse. An empathic collaborative relationship is an essential prerequisite for selective attention/neglect and for therapeutic confrontation, and maintaining this relationship generally takes precedence over other therapeutic work.

If therapists persistently fail in their efforts to engage the patient in focally relevant dialogue, they should: (1) review the patient's overall clinical status (see "Guidelines for Assessment," chapter 4) to ensure that the patient possesses the basic resources for effective participation in TLDP, and/or (2) consider the possibility that the content of the chosen focus is currently unworkable. A focus is, after all, just a hypothesis. If correct it may not be uniquely so, or it may be excessively inaccurate or incomplete. In some cases, exploration of the focal topics evokes unmanageable anxiety. This is especially likely if the therapist fails to take an affirmative approach and places excess emphasis on the defective, pathological, and maladaptive aspects of the patient's life. In such cases patients may self-protectively divert themselves from the focal material by becoming preoccupied with unconnected events, current or historical. Although such events may be relatable to the focus, the connections may be too obscure to be plausibly interpreted. Furthermore, in such a case the therapist's primary task would be to establish (or restore) the patient's sense of safety in the therapeutic relationship.

If excessive anxiety and defensiveness persist, a therapist may have to abandon or revise a focus in order to restore an effective collaborative process. In general, however, a focus should not be abandoned unless there is reasonable evidence suggesting the potentially greater viability of another focal pattern. It is important to persevere, and to tolerate the ambiguity, uncertainty, and tension which inevitably accompany efforts to make sense of the heretofore incomprehensible. Such perseverance, if not carried to fruitless extremes, is frequently rewarded by new understandings based on generation of unexpected connections between seemingly unrelated events. If through their therapist's example patients also elect to persist in trying to understand, rather than choosing to run away from themselves and others, the result may be increased hope, a strengthened sense of mastery, and a heightened awareness of themselves as active agents in their lives.

Chapter 6

Clinical Illustration of the Assessment Process and the Development of a Focus

IN CHAPTERS 4 and 5 we have presented the TLDP approach to the diagnostic assessment process and to the development of a focus. We have also outlined technical strategies for achieving the dual aim of obtaining a general diagnostic picture as well as a focus for subsequent therapeutic work. The present chapter seeks to illustrate these tasks more concretely. We do this by following the course of an initial TLDP assessment interview, accompanied by commentary.

The patient is a woman in her mid-thirties who has been married for several years. The couple had agreed not to have children. She is employed as a librarian and is reasonably satisfied with her position. She sought psychotherapy because of chronic, periodic depression and an inability to form satisfying interpersonal relationships. The interview to be presented is her first full-length contact with the clinician (not the therapist). Prior to this interview she had been seen briefly by another interviewer to rule out psychotic features and other factors that might contraindicate TLDP.

The Interview

I: Why don't we start with you telling me about yourself and what brought you in.

P: Well, there's a twofold reason why I came in. Uh—one is that I guess the area of depression brought me really, more than anything else because I've suffered from depression off and on all my life and my father also has severe periods of depression and they've gotten more severe as he's gotten older. And it's really an unpleasant situation to be around. I'm very uncomfortable around him and I really don't like the idea to think that I may progress and get to this point at some time in my life. He gets to the point where he's nonfunctional.

I: How do you mean nonfunctional?

P: He sleeps 24 hours a day, seven days a week.

I: Uh. Is he being treated for it?

P: He has in the past, but he does not really care for therapy and he hasn't continued it.

I: He doesn't care for what?

P: He didn't care for the therapy and he has not continued it.

I: So he's not on any medication or anything.

P: No.

I: How old is he?

P: Uh—sixty.

I: Is he retired?

P: Yes, he took early retirement.

I: Now, why don't you tell me something about your depression. What's it like and how do you experience it?

The patient's presenting complaint is chronic, periodic depression, along with the fear that, like her father, she will get progressively worse. The interviewer does not assume that at this early juncture he and the patient share a common understanding of the subjective experience characterizing her "depression." Therefore, he asks the patient if she can articulate her

experience. In this way, he attempts to gather information about the interpersonal referents of her depression. At the same time, he begins to assess
her capacity for recognizing and communicating her emotional experiences
—a basic task in any dynamic psychotherapy.

P: Generally it comes on suddenly. Sometimes I can figure a triggering
event and most of the time I can't. But I have an overwhelming desire
to eat. I eat everything and anything. I have no feelings of hunger
but then again I have no feelings of satisfaction either. I get to the
point where I do the bare minimum of anything. I go to work and
that's about all. I do minimum housework and—

I: But you are able to work?

P: I'm able to work, right.

I: When you eat, is it anything or certain things, or what do you eat?

P: Anything. It doesn't matter.

I: Do you gain and lose a lot of weight?

P: I gain weight. I've been on a weight-loss program which has helped.
But if I binge I will gain weight.

I: Approximately how much weight do you gain when you binge?

P: Five to ten pounds.

I: Then you usually take it off?

P: Eventually.

I: How long does it last?

P: It varies, sometimes six weeks–two months and there has been a
period when it was about eighteen months or two years.

I: When was that?

P: That was—well, there have been two periods of that length. One was
my last two years in college, and then about two years ago.

I: How old are you now?

P: I'll be thirty-two in December.

I: Do you identify anything that set those long periods off or any of
the shorter ones? You mentioned sometimes you do.

P: I really can't put my finger on it.

I: Now you've described what you do, you get lethargic and you eat.
Can you say any more about what it feels like? How you experience
yourself—other people?

The interviewer has learned that the patient finds it easier to describe
her depression in the language of symptoms, suggesting that she may
find it difficult to discuss affective and interpersonal issues. However, he
uses the opportunity to gather information about the severity of the de-

pression. Is it more a neurotic depression (dysthymic disorder according to the *Diagnostic and Statistical Manual of Mental Disorders* [DSM-III]) or are there indications of a more severe affective disorder? The patient reveals that even when depressed she is able to work; weight loss or gain is not extraordinary, and, at least so far, she does not spontaneously offer any indications of serious psychopathology or suicidal ideation. Consequently, the interviewer's initial diagnostic hunch is that the patient is not suffering from a major affective disturbance, and once again he attempts to assess her capacity to describe her affective experience in interpersonal terms.

P: I don't like myself.

I: How do you mean?

P: I'm not happy with myself physically. Uh—just basically not happy with myself. I know—I guess I feel guilty for not doing anything. I know I have all these things to do but I don't do them. I just sit.

I: Now what does the guilt feel like? How do you experience that?

P: Well, I feel like I ought to be doing all these things. Like my housework and shopping and cleaning and all this.

I: Uh-huh.

P: And I feel bad because I don't do it. But it's not bad enough that I'll get up and do it either.

I: Are there any other feelings that go along with the depression?

P: I feel weighted down. Just physically weighted down.

I: Is there a painfulness or an emptiness? What's the primary experience?

P: I feel very alone.

I: Alone? How about your experience of other people?

P: Well, I don't get along very well with other people. I just—

I: Generally, or when you're feeling depressed?

P: Generally, but when I'm depressed it's even worse. I don't want to be bothered with anybody.

With further gentle encouragement, the patient is able to communicate more specific feelings (guilt and loneliness) that are associated with her depression. Since a central diagnostic aim is to identify a conflictual relationship pattern associated with the patient's painful affects, the interviewer pursues the patient's subjective experience in relationships with others. She reveals a sense of failed responsibilities and a tendency to withdraw from others when depressed. Thus, the interviewer already has begun to assemble a potential salient relationship pattern as well as to determine that the patient is capable of discussing her experiences in relationships.

I: What do you do? How does that get expressed?
P: I just have minimal contact.
I: How often do you get depressed?
P: I would say two or three times a year.
I: Any particular times of the year?
P: No.
I: And they usually last from six weeks to two months except for those two longer periods?
P: Yeah.

At this stage of the initial assessment interview, the interviewer is attempting to counterbalance the search for a circumscribed maladaptive relationship pattern with the necessity of obtaining a broader diagnostic picture. At this point he could have chosen to pursue the patient's interpersonal behavior when depressed. Instead, as we will see, he steps back and inquires about other problems that may have led the patient to seek help. This is the sort of clinical judgment with which the TLDP therapist is continually faced. It is essential that no matter what topic the interviewer pursues, he always remain alert to evidence relevant to a potential focal theme. The patient reveals a general difficulty in forming satisfying relationships, thus suggesting that her presenting complaint of depression refers to a more basic disturbance in interpersonal relationships—on the face of it, a suitable problem for TLDP.

I: Are there other particular things that brought you in?
P: Well, my inability to relate to other people.
I: Can you elaborate on that?
P: Well, I've never been able to form friendships.
I: You don't have any close friends?
P: No.
I: Do you have any kind of social contacts or friendships?
P: We have one couple in town that we see fairly often.
I: You don't feel close to either one of those people?
P: Not really.
I: Can you describe what it's like for you when you're with people that makes it difficult for you to get to know them, form friendships, get close. What happens?
P: I just withdraw, I don't have anything to say. I may or may not participate in the conversation. Generally not.

I: How do you feel about yourself at those times?

P: I feel like I don't have anything to offer.

I: That you have nothing to offer. What do you imagine people are thinking about you then? What's their attitude toward you when you're with them and you feel like you have nothing to say?

P: Really, that I'm present and that's about all.

I: That you are present. They're not attracted to you or they have negative feelings toward you. They just don't feel about you one way or the other?

P: Right.

I: Like you're invisible.

P: Just like I'm not there. It doesn't really matter whether I'm there or not.

Here, the assessment of the patient's ability to discuss interpersonal "transactions" begins in earnest. As discussed in chapter 5, the crucial elements include: (1) the individual's view of herself in relation to others; (2) her (affectively influenced) expectations of others' attitudes and intentions toward her; (3) her perceptions of the actions of others toward her; and (4) her acts toward herself. This inquiry is advanced with any form of intervention (from open-ended or specific questions to clarification and interpretation) that promises to deepen understanding of the patient's experience. In this sense, a trial therapy to assess the patient's motivation and capacity to engage in the therapeutic task required of TLDP begins as early as possible. Already the initial presenting complaint of depression has begun to assume an interpersonal context. Specifically, a prototypic interpersonal transaction has begun to take shape: the patient feels that she has nothing of value to offer to others, who in turn are seen as treating her as if she were inconsequential, and she reacts by withdrawal (and perhaps with feelings of loneliness and depression).

I: Do you feel that more with men and women or is it—you can't distinguish any difference?

P: I'm probably more uncomfortable with women than I am with men.

I: More uncomfortable with women. What's the difference that you see?

P: I don't know. I'm able to relax more around men than around women. I don't really know why.

I: But then you still don't feel like you could form any kind of close relationship. You still have that same feeling like you're just present. But you feel more relaxed about it?

P: Yeah.

I: With women, what's there that's not there with men that makes you less relaxed? Do you have any sense of the nature or quality of the discomfort?

P: Hum—Uh, I would say it's just generally, I don't know. I never thought about it. I guess it just has to do with the different type of conversations and situations that go on between two groups. When you're with a group of women you're talking about family and home and children and things of this nature which are not of primary interest in my life.

The preceding brief passage is another illustration of the blending of assessment and treatment in the TLDP approach. The careful exploration, through questions and clarifications, of the patient's discomfort in relationships encourages her to attend to her subjective experience in new ways; it fosters therapeutic introspection. She begins to wonder about the nature of her greater discomfort with women. In this way the interviewer obtains diagnostic information, while at the same time the patient derives immediate benefit from the therapeutic exchange.

I: What is (of interest)?

P: I guess I'm more involved in my work and outside interests.

I: What are they?

P: Well I like to read and I do some needlework and go to quite a few movies.

I: Those are things you don't think women are interested in?

P: Most of the women I know don't read and don't go to movies. Their whole interest is their house and their children. And most of them don't have a job.

I: What women are these? Where do you know them?

P: Well, like I said there's a couple we know that we see quite frequently and most of the rest of the people either, well, through church. That's where we have most of our social contact.

I: Now this couple that you see regularly, you don't feel comfortable with them but who initiates all these contacts then?

P: My husband. He bowls with them.

I: I see, so they're friends—but you're not really friends with the wife.

P: I just go along.

I: Do you sense any tension in that?

P: Well, the husband and I do not get along, but—

I: Why not?

P: Well, everything has to be his way and he jumps around a lot. It's the type of thing where one night we went out to dinner and we wound up going to three different restaurants before we found the one that suited him.

I: Uhm—How does your husband feel about that?

P: Well, he doesn't really care for it but he likes him, so he puts up with it.

I: How does that leave you feeling toward your husband? When he puts up with that?

P: I get a little annoyed.

I: A little annoyed? What do you do with it?

P: Nothing.

I: You don't say anything to him about it?

P: No.

I: How come?

P: Well, because really it would not do very much good.

I: How do you mean?

P: We will continue to see the couple.

I: You sound like you don't feel that your opinion would count much with your husband in that situation. Is that a general feeling you have?

P: It depends on the situation. Sometimes he pays attention and then again he doesn't.

I: Do you see that as much of a problem? A big problem in your relationship?

P: I think I've learned to live with it.

I: That doesn't mean it's not a problem.

P: Well that's true, it bothers me on occasion but then again, like I say, it doesn't bother me.

I: Because you've resigned yourself to it.

P: Right.

I: What effect has that had on your relationship?

P: I guess we both have a tendency pretty much to go our own way.

I: Really? So you don't feel you have a close relationship with your husband?

P: Not particularly.

I: Why don't you tell me some more about it.

The preliminary therapy focus that has quickly begun to crystallize, through the interviewer's attempts to seek a salient, conflictual relationship pattern, is examined in one of the patient's most important relationships—that with her husband. Its presence in the marital relationship provides supporting evidence of the importance of this pattern. As the diagnostic reconnaissance continues, the therapeutic component deepens with the interviewer's confrontation of the patient's first clear-cut resistance, associated with active examination of her sense of being ignored by her husband: "I think I've learned to live with it." The resignation reflected in this statement adds another element (the patient's reaction to her expectation of others) to the preliminary therapy focus being assembled, and by this process the therapeutic work of this first interview is advanced.

P: Well, we've been married a little over ten years and we have no children by choice.

I: Both of your choice?

P: Huh.

I: Both of your choice or—

P: Yeah.

I: So you don't plan to have children?

P: No. He has a teenage son.

I: Does he live with you?

P: No. We have him on weekends. But—I'd say we pretty much go our own ways. He's a salesman and he's now in town. He came off the road when we got married and he's working in the city. So his hours are very flexible. He changes hours three or four times a year.

I: He works in the city?

P: Yes.

I: Oh, okay.

P: And I've yet to be consulted about what hours he's going to work. He just comes in and tells me that tomorrow he's going to work at 7:00 in the morning. And this may go on for six weeks and then he'll come in and tell me he's going to work at 1:00 in the afternoon. So after a while you get where you just learn to live with this. I worked quite some time to get my hours changed so we could work the same schedules. So two weeks before I finally got my hours changed so that we would be on the same schedule, he changed back to his other schedule. Which is exactly opposite of what I'm working.

I: So you don't get together much.

P: That's true.

I: How do you feel, now that you're talking about it?

P: It doesn't bother me.

I: Are you trying to convince both of us?

P: No, it just really—

I: Why not?

P: Well, I feel like he's entitled to work the times that he wishes to work. It's his job and he's going to have to be happy with it. And I try to make accommodations and I could have gotten my hours changed back but I happen to like working my current schedule. I guess I finally decided that he might as well adjust to my hours as well as I have to adjust to his.

I: Did it used to bother you?

P: It did.

I: What happened? How did it stop bothering you?

P: I just decided I was going to have to accept it and live with it if I was going to live with him.

I: What do you feel is good about the relationship now?

P: We enjoy each other. The times we have together are good. In a lot of ways I guess we're both very similar. We don't—he likes people and he likes to be around people on occasion but then again he likes to be by himself too. Or the two of us together. And as I say we enjoy being together the times we have together.

I: So there are good things about the relationship, but you feel that he really—at least in terms of his scheduling for work and planning for your being together he doesn't—your opinion doesn't count and you've learned to live with it.

P: That's true.

I: What do you do with the resentment that you feel?

P: I work it out on my own.

I: How do you do that?

P: I carry on a lot of conversations with myself. And by the time I talk it out with myself then it's gone.

I: What do you say to yourself to make it go away?

P: Well, if I'm upset about something I try to figure out why I'm upset about it and what I'm going to do about it and then by the time I work out a solution then the anger or resentment is taken care of.

As the interviewer takes a more direct reading of the patient's motivation to work on uncomfortable topics such as her marital relationship ("How do you feel, now that you're talking about it?"), he again confronts her defensive denial. This time he explicitly pursues her resistance as manifested in her reluctance to acknowledge negative feelings to the therapist. Thus another important assessment issue for TLDP is introduced, namely the patient's willingness to discuss her reactions to the therapeutic interchange. The interviewer deepens the therapeutic work by interpreting the resentment that accompanies the patient's resignation to being discounted. The patient's acceptance of this trial interpretation informs the interviewer that her resistance to exploration of feelings is not particularly rigid. This is a positive prognostic sign for TLDP. Although the appearance of more rigid defenses would not rule out TLDP, they would alert the interviewer to specific difficulties that would have to be addressed during the course of treatment. So far, a general dynamic hypothesis has been generated in which depression is associated with resentment and anger that is not allowed expression and often is turned back on the patient in the form of "guilt" and a sense of unworthiness.

Of greater relevance to the TLDP therapist is progressive articulation of how these conflictual feelings are managed within a specific interpersonal transaction: The patient harbors hidden anger and resentment over feeling discounted or ignored and expects any complaint on her part to be met with further neglect. Thus, she "talks (herself) out of it," ending up by turning the negative feelings back on herself in the form of self-depreciation. Finally, she withdraws into resignation. Furthermore, her passivity and withdrawal may very well encourage others to ignore her enough to confirm her expectations. A corollary hypothesis is that the patient's depression is associated with anger turned on herself and with despair accompanying her resignation to being seen as inconsequential. Another hypothesis is that this interpersonal pattern will characterize the salient transference-countertransference scenarios enacted within the therapeutic relationship, perhaps even within the interaction in this interview. The preliminary dynamic focus that has been articulated so far offers sufficiently detailed interpersonal referents to provide the therapist with a clear-cut blueprint for organizing subsequent therapy material and for identifying potential expressions of the focal theme in the form of transference-countertransference enactments.

I: Do you ever get angry at anybody?

P: Very rarely.

I: What would make you angry?

P: I don't know, it takes a lot to make me really angry.

I: You can't think of anything? Going back to your relationship with your husband, how have these things affected your sexual life—if it has?

P: Well, it's definitely decreased it. We don't see each other but for about 4 hours a day. Two in the middle of the afternoon and 2 when I get home from work when he's usually asleep. Other than that I don't guess it has.

I: When you say decreased it—to how often?

P: Once or twice a week.

I: From what?

P: Well, three or four times a week.

I: Is that recently or has that been going on for—

P: It's been coming for a long time. Part of it has to do too with a physical problem that he has. He has extremely high blood pressure and his medication has affected—

I: He can't get erections?

P: Yeah.

I: Is that a serious problem?

P: No, it's not really. I think it bothers him more than it does me. But, it definitely—when he went on the medication, it definitely created a strain there for a while.

I: Does it make it more difficult for him to get erections or he just can't?

P: It makes it more difficult.

I: But he's still able to?

P: Yeah.

I: When you have sex, is it satisfying for you or do you feel that lack of closeness, some of the tensions in the relationship? Does it get expressed in less satisfaction sexually?

P: There was a stage where there was less satisfaction. In the last month I would say that it has definitely become more satisfying.

I: Can you identify that with anything changing?

P: I think I've just become more relaxed.

I: Any reason you can think of?

P: No.

I: How do you feel talking about this subject? Your sexual life is pretty personal.

P: I'm a little uncomfortable. It's something I don't normally talk about.

I: But you answered pretty readily. Just going along again? Just resigned yourself to answering the questions?

P: I think it's something that I've wanted to talk about. I just haven't.

I: Is there more that you wanted to say about it?

P: I don't think so.

Here the interviewer attempts a trial transference interpretation in order to assess the patient's ability to examine within the therapy relationship what is now part of the preliminary focal theme: her resentment and resignation. He asks her if she is "just going along again" in discussing a very personal topic. The patient has already demonstrated her willingness to communicate affective reactions about the therapeutic dialogue and about the therapist although she denies that they amount to much. Here she confirms her motivation for the therapeutic work. It is likely that the interviewer's interpretation fell somewhat flat at this point because it was made without sufficient data (it was premature), rather than reflecting entrenched resistance on the patient's part. Nevertheless, it was put tentatively—allowing the patient to accept or reject it easily—and at least offer the model (examining the patient-therapist relationship) for subsequent therapeutic work in TLDP.

I: Why don't you tell me some more about you in general. I've asked some specific questions and I want to get back with some more I want to ask you too, but tell me more about you.

P: I don't know what to tell. It's just not—

I: Whatever you feel is important.

P: There's just not a whole lot to tell.

I: You mean you're just present?

P: Yeah.

I: Well, tell me what you did and—well, let me ask you about that. What do you mean there's not a whole lot to tell, you're thirty-two years old, lived for thirty-two years! Nothing to tell about all that?

P: Nothing I consider interesting or—

I: Nothing that you consider interesting?

P: I can't see that anybody else would consider it interesting either.

I: Why not?

P: It's just a very average life.

I: You know what's happening now sounds very similar to what you described what happens when you're out with people. That you feel you have nothing to say. There's nothing that you can say that you think about that's happened with you that would be of any interest to anybody else.

P: It's true.

I: I wonder why you feel that so strongly?

P: I don't know. I've always been—I've not found myself an interesting subject of conversation.

I: Do you wonder about that? Why do you feel that way?

P: I have.

I: What have you concluded?

P: I don't know. I say I wonder about it on occasion but it's not something I've reached a conclusion about.

I: Have you come up with anything?

P: No, not really.

I: Do you think it's realistic?

P: No. But yet my experience with others, it does seem to be.

I: So it seems like something worth looking at. As you've been talking with me today what's your—how do you imagine I'm reacting to you? My attitude toward you, things that you're saying about yourself?

P: I really can't imagine that you're the least bit interested.

I: I'm bored to death?

P: Basically.

I: How does that leave you feeling? If that's the way you see me—my attitude toward you? (Pause)

P: Just that I'm here and answering questions. That's about all.

I: That we know. It doesn't bother you at all?

P: No.

I: Why do you think that's the case?

P: I think that it's something that I've built up over the years. And I don't care whether—

I: You've sort of steeled yourself to it?

P: Right.

When the interviewer shifted to asking the patient, in open-ended fashion, to describe more about herself, she essentially stated that there was nothing of interest to tell. The interviewer reacted reflexively with a specific question and then caught himself, realizing that her implicit self-depreciation might signify enactment of the salient interpersonal pattern they had been examining. Consequently, he encouraged the patient to look at this self-deprecatory attitude. In fact, she acknowledged the expectation that he would be bored with her. By directly examining the patient's reluctance to talk spontaneously about herself, rather than circumventing it with specific factual questions or assurance of his interest, the salient relationship pattern was identified "alive" at the moment in their relationship. This occurrence further confirmed the relevance of the preliminary focus, and it gave the interviewer an opportunity to assess further the patient's willingness and ability to examine the focal issue as it was being enacted between them.

At this point the patient still considers it her fate to be of no consequence to others. However, she evidences a willingness to consider this attitude further, and the interviewer takes the opportunity to suggest that this particular topic might be worthwhile to examine. Thus, elements of the preliminary focus are presented during the interview as an outgrowth of their collaborative inquiry into her presenting problems. The interviewer then makes another judgment to temporarily suspend direct examination of the focal theme in order to obtain further general diagnostic information. However, by asking about the patient's background, he also is looking for specific data concerning the origin and early occurrence of the focal interpersonal pattern.

I: Can you, in looking back—do you have any sense of when you started feeling that way?—that you're not of any interest to anybody?

P: As far back as I can remember.

I: Why don't you tell me something about your background. Your growing up, your parents, relationships with them, and family members.

P: Well, I have a mother and a father and two sisters. One older and one younger. I guess on the whole, a very typical struggling middle-class income, trying to make it on one salary. I guess on the whole it was a good childhood. I don't really know. I guess I put most of it out of my mind. Very few things that I remember about growing up.

I: If it was basically a good childhood, why do you think you've put it out of your mind so much?

P: I don't know, I don't remember things like that. Things in the past are just gone. I'm sure they're there somewhere, I just don't recall them.

I: Do you remember if you felt in your family this way? Feeling that nobody finds you interesting—that you don't matter to anybody?

P: Yeah. I felt myself, I was just there. And I fit into everybody else's schedule and worked my way around it.

I: In your family as a child?

P: Yeah.

I: What gave you that feeling? Do you recall any experiences, the way things were?

P: It just seemed that everybody else was more important.

P: Who's everybody else?

P: Well, in particular, my two sisters.

I: What were the age differences?

P: My older sister is three and a half years older than me and my younger sister is less than a year younger.

I: Less than a year?

P: Yes.

I: So she came pretty fast. Do you remember when she was born?

P: No.

I: I guess not, that's pretty young.

P: (laugh) Entirely too young to remember it.

I: In what ways did they seem more important to your parents?

P: Well, they always had places to go and things to do and activities they were involved in and mine seemed to be left over and if they fit in somewhere and didn't interfere with somebody else that was fine but if they didn't, well, then they could be rearranged.

I: You mean your experience was that your parents always sort of made arrangements to do things for your sisters, take them wherever, and you always were the third. You were caught sort of in there between them, lost?

P: Yes.

I: As you think back on that now, how does it make you feel?

P: I resented it at the time. But then I just resigned myself to the fact that this was the way things were going to be and I would learn to live with it.

I: You've resigned yourself to an awful lot over the years. [The statement communicates empathy and support; it also raises the question of whether this pattern is in the patient's best interest. Thus it subtly hints at the possibility of change.]

P: That's quite true.

I: I imagine it hasn't left you feeling very happy. [Ditto]

P: On occasion it upsets me. But, it's all in the past; it's not worth worrying about now. [A clear case of denial. The patient seems to say: "Let's not rock the boat."]

I: It seems like it still upsets you a little now.

P: I resented it.

I: I wonder if an important reason that you don't want to think about these things, you don't want to get upset about them is because you don't feel that you can do anything about it. Nothing is going to change, so why be upset. [The interviewer highlights the patient's self-assigned victim role.]

P: That's true. It's not going to do any good. [The patient stands her ground. She is not going to be budged!]

I: What happened in your family, the way you experienced it, like you say the past is in the past, you can't change that. But this feeling you have that you don't count, that you don't matter, that there's nothing about you that's interesting to anybody—you think that could change? [The interviewer pursues the focus, applying gentle pressure in the direction of self-exploration.]

P: I would like to change it. But I don't know how. [A hopeful sign indicating that the patient really wants help.]

I: Maybe that's something you can find out in therapy. Because that is inside you, that's not anyone else. [A good way of defining an agenda of therapeutic work, underscoring the interviewer's belief that (1) change is possible and (2) the patient is ultimately the architect of her fate rather than a passive bystander.]

When the patient is asked to describe her family background, resistance is immediately evident. This resistance takes the form of an inconsistency: the patient states that "I guess on the whole it was a good childhood," yet she also states that she "put most of it out of my mind." The therapist confronts her with the obvious question of why she would want to put good memories out of her mind. When the patient has difficulty going further, the interviewer, mindful of the focal theme, offers a tentative reconstructive interpretation; namely, that even as a child the patient felt neglected by her parents. The patient confirms the validity of this interpretation and proceeds to reveal more specifics about the origin of the focal interpersonal pattern: as a child she resented feeling neglected and then "just resigned myself to the fact that this was the way things were going to be and I would learn to live with it." The focal pattern is firmly established and acknowledged by the interviewer: "You've resigned yourself to an awful lot over the years." With that ostensibly simple statement, and the patient's straightforward response—"That's quite true"—a level of rapport has been obtained that can form the basis of collaborative therapeutic work.

They go on to fortify the therapeutic contract with explicit agreement that the patient's fixed, pervasive expectation of neglect, and her accompanying resignation, is a valid focus for therapy. The preceding passage is another illustration of how the focus in TLDP is presented not as a formulation given by the therapist but as a mutual understanding that crystallizes through the therapist's search for a salient interpersonal pattern structured in the format of the TLDP focus (see chapter 5).

I: Do you think this experience that's been with you all your life has anything to do with your depressions?

P: I think so. I think when I get to the point where it builds up where

I really feel like I'm not worth anything, that will start off a cycle. And then I will eventually work through it.

I: So you can muster a good bit of strength when you get right at the bottom and pull yourself out.

P: Whenever I can't go any further.

The interviewer makes another tentative interpretation, to test whether the patient's two presenting problems, depression and an inability to form satisfying relationships, are of the same cloth; he suggests that the patient's depression refers to unpleasant affects associated with the pattern of resignation to feeling neglected. The patient confirms this in describing her depression as a by-product of feeling neglected and worthless over a period of time. She also offers evidence of sufficient personality resources to keep her depressive reaction from becoming overwhelming. Thus, in this brief passage, data are obtained regarding further specifics of the focal pattern and the broader diagnostic question of the severity of her depressive disorder. With regard to the latter question, evidence continues to mount of a differential diagnosis of self-limiting depression (dysthymic disorder) rather than a major affective disorder. Furthermore, the patient's depression is the affective component of a chronic characterological disturbance.

The interviewer encourages further description of the patient's background. He is particularly interested in continuing to assess the patient's subjective experience of people (assumed to reflect the developmental maturity of the patient's repertoire of object relationships) and her capacity to communicate descriptions of transactions with them. As discussed in chapter 4, both of these capacities are dimensions of ego functioning relevant to the therapeutic tasks required of TLDP.

I: Can you describe your parents? Are they both alive?

P: Yes.

I: Can you describe them as people a little more? What they're like as people.

P: Ah, well, I like my mother. My mother and I are very much alike. In fact the older I get the more I like her. She's a very quiet person. Very unemotional person. We've never been particularly close up until, I'd say, the last four or five years.

I: What made the difference?

P: I think I just grew up and accepted her. And realized that she and I are very much alike.

I: Do you recall much physical show of affection as a child?

P: No, she's not physical. In fact I can't ever remember her initiating a show of affection. In fact, I never remember her ever saying that she loved me.

I: Uh.

P: But I don't think she ever told the other two she did either. I'd say she shows very little emotion.

I: It sounds like the only way you would have gotten any signs that she did care about you would be things that she would do. And as you recall it, she always did more for the other kids. So it left you feeling, what, that she loved them more? (pause) In retrospect, looking back now, do you still feel that way?

P: I don't think so, looking back now.

I: What do you make of your recollections then that they did more, that she did more for the other kids. Why do you think that was the case?

P: I think she did more because they demanded more. They expected these things. And I didn't.

I: So for some reason you feel that you backed off real early?

P: Uh-huh.

I: Like you do now?

P: Right.

I: How about your father? What's he like as a person? What's your relationship with him?

P: Well, he's entirely different now than what he was when I was growing up. When I was growing up he was a very demanding person. Everything was black or white, there was no gray. He was not really strict, but stern. He always seemed to be a very strong person. Able to handle all the situations and everything.

I: What did he do for a living?

P: He worked as a factory supervisor. He's a physical person. He likes to touch and hug and kiss.

I: Did he do much of that with you?

P: Yeah.

I: Did you feel closer to him?

P: Not really. Because I did not like a lot of physical contact.

I: You didn't?

P: No.

I: What do you make of that?

P: I think it goes along with everything else of being a very close reserved person.

I: Is there anything you recall from your childhood that was particularly traumatic or extraordinary? Anything that happened in the family or to you?

P: There was a—the only thing that stands out, there was a fight between my father and my mother's parents. I don't know what it was about to this day. But I can remember there was a period of, like two years, where he did not set foot inside their door. He had nothing to do with them. I can remember it as being a strained period. But I don't know—that's about all I remember about it.

I: What effect did it have on you?

P: Well, it kind of put us in the middle because my mother was—we still went to see her parents, but it was kind of like—he knew about it, he wouldn't stop us. But it was something he did not want to happen.

I: Uh. What was it like when you were in school? Elementary school, high school? What were your relationships like?

P: I just went to school every day and studied and made fairly good grades. School was probably about the only thing I enjoyed.

I: So you liked school. Did you have friends in school?

P: No.

I: What did you do with your time?

P: I read a lot. We lived in a very old neighborhood, like only five kids in the whole four-block area and so there wasn't a whole lot of intermingling. My sister and the little girl across the street were very close and—

I: What about in high school, did you date?

P: No.

I: Never dated?

P: No.

I: Was your husband the first person you dated?

P: No.

I: Tell me something about your—what dating history you have had.

P: I dated some in college, not a whole lot. Nobody steadily.

I: How did you meet your husband?

I: Through a mutual friend that I went to school with.

I: So he was the first person that you really were involved with.

P: No, not really. [The pattern "there is nothing interesting about me" reasserts itself.]

I: Want to tell me about it?

P: (pause) Well, I, you know, what's there to tell?

I: I know that it's not going to be interesting (with a smile) or is there another reason that you don't feel much like talking about it?

P: Well, like I said we met through a mutual friend. When I met him I was living in B———, working at J——— and I'd come to K——— — to visit the girl I went to school with and she was dating him at the time and over the process of a long weekend I spent with her she kept throwing us together. So by the end of the weekend she had left entirely. She got mad about halfway through the weekend and stayed somewhere else.

I: Were you about twenty-four when you married?

P: Twenty-three.

I: What attracted you to your husband?

P: He was fun to be with. He's a very pleasant person. He's the type of person who always talks to strangers.

I: He's real outgoing?

P: Yes. The first afternoon we spent together we absolutely hated each other. I wouldn't talk to him all afternoon. Then we went out again that night, and the next afternoon. By then I'd begun to enjoy myself. [The patient shows a certain flexibility, a good prognostic sign.]

I: How soon did you get married after the first date?

P: We met in January and got married in May.

I: That's pretty quick. Now how many other men had you been involved with before your husband?

P: Two.

I: What happened with those relationships?

P: Well, really the problem was distance. Both of them were in R——— — and I was in C——— at the time. And they just wore out over going back and forth, trying to keep up the relationship. It just didn't work out very well.

I: Was this after college, during?

P: With these two people—I had dated in college and then continued dating afterwards.

I: Did you have sexual relationships with them?

P: Yes.

I: Where they satisfying or were there any problems?

P: The only problem was that with one of them he really couldn't get satisfied unless we had a fight beforehand. This just got a little old and on my nerves.

I: What do you do for a living?

130

P: I'm a librarian.

I: Do you like your work? Do you want to do something else?

P: I'd rather do something else. I don't know what, but something.

I: Did you graduate from college?

P: Yes.

I: What college?

P: I have a B.A. degree from T—— and then an M.A. from G——.

I: How do you feel you do at work?

P: I'm good at what I do.

I: So you're happy with your work. That's one area that you have some good feelings about yourself. How do you get along with your colleagues?

I: Some of them are okay and some of them—just marginal politeness.

I: No particular close relationships or bad relationships?

P: No.

I: Do you feel at work that they have the same attitudes toward you that you feel in other places that you could be there or not be there and it wouldn't matter? What about in terms of your skills? Do you think they value, or appreciate—

P: No, not really. I can be replaced.

P: What's the earliest memory that comes to mind for you? A scene you can visualize in your mind's eye.

P: I guess I can remember looking out the front door and seeing my grandfather and grandmother coming up the front steps. I must have been four or five at the time.

I: Anything stand out in this scene?

P: I guess why I remember it is because they never did that before and never did it since.

I: Your mother or father's parents.

P: My mother's parents. It's the only time I ever remember them coming to the house, I guess.

I: Do you remember how you felt at the time?

P: I guess surprised, and wondering why they were there.

I: Why didn't they visit more than that?

P: Well, they did not like my father. Simple as that. And neither one of them drove and they lived across town and they did not visit.

I: What's the next earliest memory? Again as a scene that you can visualize in your mind's eye.

P: I remember being at church one Sunday and being very upset because they had to call off something. I guess maybe a picnic or something. Because it was pouring down rain. I remember that upset me greatly. Because I remember crying.

I: Why?

P: I don't know. I can't imagine why that would upset me so much.

I: What comes to mind?

P: I remember being in the building, I get the feeling of a large room and I remember crying and somebody picking me up and rocking me.

I: Then how did you feel when you're being rocked?

P: I just felt very upset and very alone, really.

I: You sound almost inconsolable.

P: I don't know. See I don't know why this stands out. I just— (laugh)

I: Do you remember how old you were?

P: I couldn't have been over five or six.

I: Do you recall any recurring dreams or a particular vivid dream that stands out in your mind that you recall?

P: I have one that keeps occurring about I'm in school and it comes to the end of the semester and I suddenly realize that I have not been to these two classes at all the whole semester. Here it is time to take finals and finish up and I don't even know where the classes are much less what they were. Or what they were about.

I: How does it leave you feeling?

P: Desperate.

I: You missed these classes?

P: I missed them altogether.

I: How often do you have the dream?

P: I haven't had it in a while and then there have been times when I've had it every night for, like two or three weeks.

I: Uhm. The memory you mentioned, the second one—you're going to miss out on this picnic—and from your reaction it seems like you're really upset about missing this picnic and then in this recurrent dream you've missed out on these classes. Something of a missing out on something. Does that bring to mind anything?

P: No, not really.

I: You do feel that you've missed out on a lot over the years. Certainly as a child. [The therapist identifies what may be an important theme in the patient's life.]

P: I guess I do. I guess I feel like I've missed all the interesting things there are to do.

I: Do you take any kind of drugs or medications or—

P: No.

I: How about—how much do you drink?

P: Very, very little.

I: Going back to the beginning when you talked about the depression. The inability to relate has been there a long time. How about the depressions, how long since they first started.

P: I was probably in high school. That's about the earliest I can remember.

I: In high school. When did your father start getting his depressions?

P: About—the worst of it started about six or seven years ago. Now looking back, you know now, I can see spots before which he had a very bad spell. But the worst of it—

I: His middle fifties? Has he been hospitalized at all for it?

P: No.

I: He's been on medication?

P: He's been on medication but he's not been hospitalized.

I: His medications help?

P: Yes.

I: But he doesn't want to take them?

P: No.

I: What made you finally decide to—have you ever had therapy before? What made you decide now and how did you decide to make the call here? [It is always important to inquire in an initial interview why the patient has decided to seek professional help *at this particular time.* See also chapter 5.]

P: I've thought about it off and on but have never done anything about it and I guess this program just came up at a good time—it caught my attention because I was just coming out of a period of depression. And I thought now is as good a time as any to do something about this. [Public announcements have the effect of attracting prospective patients who may be "sitting on the fence." Thus it is easier for the person to rationalize his or her decision by saying: "I came in response to an announcement."]

I: Now you talked about depression. Do you feel anxious and nervous, tense?

P: Sometimes, like if I'm going into a new situation.

I: Socially, at work or—?

P: Either one.

I: How bad does it get?

P: Not really terribly bad. I have a nervous stomach.

I: What do you do about it when you feel this way?

P: Just keep going and figure I will get through the situation and eventually it works out and smoothes over.

I: We talked a bit about some of the things you might want to look at in treatment. How do you feel about getting into therapy? How much do you think it might help?

P: I think it really might help. I think it will help me to look at things that I have—that I don't want to look at. That I haven't looked at and help bring new ideas, possibilities that I have not thought about for dealing with situations.

I: What kind of situations?

P: Well, reacting with other people and with my depression to help me understand why I go through these cycles. And what I can do to work through them. [Patient shows reasonable motivation and has given evidence of good ego resources. All of this augurs well for TLDP.]

I: Okay. Is there anything more that you wanted to add?

P: No.

I: How have you felt about the interview so far? What's your reaction to the interview so far?

P: I'm beginning to feel a little more relaxed.

I: You were kind of tense at the beginning?

P: Yes.

The initial assessment interview draws to a close with a further survey of the patient's interpersonal history, as well as other diagnostically relevant matters including vivid early memories and dreams. The existence of a conflictual pattern can be glimpsed from these data and serves to establish a focus for therapeutic work. The interview ends with an explicit agreement that the patient will enter psychotherapy with specific issues to be examined. From this interview the interviewer has obtained a general diagnostic picture of the patient, as well as a focus to guide subsequent therapeutic work. Equally important, the patient has had the experience of being faced with thought-provoking questions and observations by another person who appears to understand her distress. She has surely benefited from this brief encounter and indicates that she is more at ease with continuing the therapeutic work.

Chapter 7

Technique

Process: Blueprint for Technique

The problem of technique fundamentally relates to the question of how the therapist can best serve the person who seeks professional help. There are many ways in which one human being can help another: by providing material assistance, or by providing information, advice, and so forth. The primary purpose of the dynamic psychotherapist, in our view, is to provide a constructive experience in living. By this we mean that the patient-therapist relationship inevitably takes a form that, in part, reflects the patient's current difficulties in achieving a sense of autonomy while at the same time relating comfortably to other human beings. Thus, to the extent that difficulties in relating to the therapist as a co-equal adult can be identified and rectified, the patient will be in a better overall position—to paraphrase Freud—to achieve greater productivity and greater enjoyment. This may appear to be a large assumption. However, it is common wisdom that in many areas of life the most effective learning (or relearning) takes place when the task to be mastered is vividly brought into focus. The effectiveness of therapeutic learning during the immediate experiencing of a conflict situation was recognized by Freud (1917, *S.E.*, 16) and has been reiterated by contemporary clinicians (Gill 1979).

Thus, by assuming a particular stance in the patient-therapist relationship, the dynamic psychotherapist sets in motion a therapeutic process.

We suggest that this goal is achieved more readily and with fewer detours if therapists have a clear understanding of the process they seek to initiate. Such an understanding presupposes a firm grasp of the "rules" governing therapeutic learning and the ability to implement them.

In dynamic psychotherapy it is difficult, if not impossible, to make specific technical recommendations. This is true, in part, because the meaning and function of any given technical intervention are determined by the context of the therapeutic interaction. However, a clear conception of the therapeutic process and an understanding of the transactions in the patient-therapist relationship can provide valuable guidelines to the therapist. For these reasons, we will begin our discussion of technique by elucidating our conception of the therapeutic process.

We adopt as a basic working assumption that patients suffer from the ill-effects of previous interpersonal experiences, notably those with significant figures in their childhood. As part of these earlier experiences they have acquired certain attitudes, cognitions, and beliefs which are associated with unpleasant feelings that serve them poorly in their current lives. These maladaptations prominently include the symptoms of which the patient currently complains. The latter, in turn, are part of other problems that make the patient's life unnecessarily difficult.

As therapists we assume that if one human relationship has made the patient "ill," another human relationship can, within limits, make him or her "well." The extent to which it may be possible to remedy the ill-effects of previous experiences depends on a number of factors, including the degree of previous damage, the quality of the new experience, the patient's ability and willingness to work on the problem, and external circumstances. To achieve desired goals, the therapist proceeds on two major fronts by (1) providing a new human experience, and (2) in the context of that experience, seeking to effect changes in the faulty learning which the patient has carried forward from the past.

There are, obviously, numerous ways in which one can modify previous learning. For example, one can instruct or persuade a person to behave differently, one can forcibly prevent the occurrence of certain behaviors, and so on. The dynamic psychotherapist places greatest emphasis on helping patients to understand the symbolic meanings of their behavior. Without being recognized by the patients, these meanings have exerted and continue to exert a powerful effect on their interpersonal behavior. The TLDP therapist anticipates that (1) troublesome patterns of interpersonal behavior will presently be activated in the patient-therapist relationship; and, (2) when an appropriate affective context exists, their hitherto unrecognized meaning can be identified and recast (interpreted). What is therapeutic, then, is a new interpersonal experience with a significant other. That experience, in itself, is helpful; beyond that, however, it serves to correct more systematically the maladaptive products of previous interpersonal experiences. Ideally, all aspects of the therapist's behavior should satisfy one fundamental criterion: It should provide the patient with a constructive experience in living. The therapist sets an example of caring, reasonableness, predictability, maturity—in short, presenting the best model of adult behavior of which he or she is capable. This is done as consistently as possible throughout the course of therapy.

At the same time, the TLDP therapist adopts the working assumption that the patient's response to the therapist represents an amalgam of preexisting and long-established negative expectations of others. The patient makes "plausible" interpretations of the therapist's behavior and attitudes which, in turn, serve to confirm the patient's negative expectations. Nevertheless, the patient usually gains an appreciation of the therapist's attempts to be caring, reasonable, and helpful (Hoffman 1983). In general, the TLDP therapist assumes that by becoming part of the patient's affective world, he or she will inevitably be influenced by the patient's habitual patterns of managing and responding to interpersonal events.

With respect to the second task—probably the more difficult of the two —the therapist helps patients discover, identify, and understand the meanings of the beliefs, feelings, and action patterns that interfere with their current living. These produce untoward effects because they are built on erroneous and obsolescent assumptions (for example, that the patient is a small child and his wife is his mother). Without ever having been closely examined, these assumptions have been carried forward automatically from earlier phases of the patient's life. The assumptions, and the accompanying attitudes and behavior, persist because patients unwittingly and self-defeatingly orchestrate significant relationships so as to evoke reactions from others that confirm their fears and anticipations. Thus, interpersonal relationships serve as a vehicle for self-perpetuating vicious cycles.

The affect accompanying patients' action patterns, it must be stressed, is painfully real. Partly for this reason, a pattern can usually be abolished only if patients are able to recognize it adequately in the context of the patient-therapist relationship and provided the therapist is able to identify (recast, interpret) the anachronistic character of the current experience in a manner that allows patients to modify it. Thus, the therapist seeks to engage patients in the cognitive task of identifying and understanding the preexisting sets which influence the manner in which they construe interpersonal relationships, as well as the ways and means by which they unconsciously seek to induce the therapist to conform to the interpersonal scenarios dictated by those expectations. By taking this interpretive stance, the therapist disconfirms the patients' expectations, thus providing them with a new and more constructive experience. The combination of achieving insights into the nature of these maladaptive action patterns in collaboration with a person who acts differently represents a process that is mutative because of its affective immediacy (Gill 1979; Hoffman 1983; Schafer 1983).

What is the place of technique in this conceptual framework? In principle, the answer is simple: The therapist's actions either provide patients with a new and direct experience in adult relatedness or they are a step in the direction of helping patients understand symbolic meanings that are hypothesized to govern their maladaptive patterns of behavior. In a strict sense, the two functions coalesce. Thus, we may say that both are aspects of a new interpersonal experience that is therapeutic.

It is important to add another point: While the therapist may at times make a direct suggestion, imply that a particular course of action may be in the patient's best interest, or discourage a feeling or action, he or she feels most comfortable when functioning in the role of an adult model or a decoder of hidden meanings. This stance is designed to create optimal conditions for the patient's maturation since it interferes least with the goal of encouraging the patient to make discoveries and arrive at solutions. In short, the therapist views this as the most constructive help he or she can give. Indeed, there is no other human relationship which is so uncompromisingly dedicated to this proposition.

With respect to the objective that psychotherapy should provide a new and constructive interpersonal experience, it is clear that much depends on the therapist's basic attitude toward the patient and the quality of the emerging relationship. Caring, empathy, interest, and respect are obviously essential characteristics the therapist must bring to bear on the relationship; they cannot be prescribed or legislated; either they are present in reasonable amounts or they are not. There is no doubt that therapists will encounter patients with whom they do not wish to work; conversely, there are also certain therapists who evoke strongly negative reactions in many patients. When these issues are honestly faced, as we recommend they should be, less harm is likely to result than when there is dissimulation. Many patients, almost by definition, are keenly sensitive to rejection or similar experiences, and—what is most detrimental from the standpoint of therapy—they may not consciously recognize that they are adapting in neurotic ways to negative attitudes on the part of the therapist. In other words, they may repeat with the therapist the same scenarios they have experienced with a hostile or rejecting parent, with predictably disastrous results (Strupp, Hadley, and Gomes-Schwartz 1977).

The point to be made is this: A basic ingredient of psychotherapy is the healing quality of a good human relationship (Frank 1979; Strupp 1973). While we disagree with Rogers (1957) that these qualities are the necessary and sufficient ones in psychotherapy, they are certainly *sine qua non*. By that we mean that they cannot be replaced or compensated for by cleverness, astuteness, or technical expertise.

While the therapist's caring may occasionally be communicated directly, the most common as well as effective communication of this basic attitude occurs *nonverbally*. In human relations, actions—it should not be necessary to belabor the point—always speak more loudly than words, and for therapy to be truly effective the two should be minimally disjunctive. Most patients, in one way or another, have been victimized by parents who have specialized in the double bind. We believe that therapists who are reasonably mature are capable of implementing, even with very difficult patients, the kind of therapeutic relationship in which the patient can feel accepted and engage in productive therapeutic work.

At the same time, we take it for granted that, while the therapist's maturity contributes to the foundation of a good human relationship, the quality of the patient-therapist relationship is persistently challenged and potentially undermined by the patient's conflictual behavior patterns and the therapist's unavoidable, but ideally, limited recruitment into them. The overarching goal of technique in TLDP is progressively to improve the quality of the therapeutic relationship. More specifically, this is accomplished by systematic and thorough examination of the patient's maladaptive action patterns and their effects on the interaction of the two participants. In common psychoanalytic terminology, the TLDP therapist's technical approach emphasizes the analysis of transference and countertransference in the here-and-now.

As Fromm-Reichmann observed, the patient needs an experience, not an explanation. What is crucial, therefore, is the patient's experience with another human being who is dedicated to the proposition of helping the patient achieve greater maturity. What matters is not what the therapist says but what the patient carries away from the interaction with the therapist.

At the same time, a significant part of what the patient internalizes is a function of the therapist's verbal messages—usually not the effect of a single one but their cumulative value.* But we must ask ourselves about

---

*Rarely does a single communication by the therapist make or break the therapy. From a scientific viewpoint, we are as yet grossly ignorant of how single messages combine to form

each and every intervention: Does it help or is it likely to hinder? There are times when we cannot be certain, and we recognize that in all human interactions there is a certain amount of filler material, which simply serves the function of reassuring the participants that they are in touch with one another.

The process of psychotherapy necessarily places limits on the therapist's spontaneity. The therapist endeavors to make the patient a collaborator without losing sight of the fact that the relationship is a professional one —as someone noted, a highly personal relationship within a highly impersonal framework. For therapy to progress, there needs to be a therapeutic alliance, and one hopes that, as the work proceeds and the patient's self-awareness grows, that alliance will be strengthened. As already noted, it will be reinforced as both participants arrive at a better understanding of the patient's recurrent need to reenact with the therapist those interpersonal patterns that, in one way or another, are related to the core of the disturbance. Thus, a major task is to limit the extent to which the therapist becomes enmeshed in these scenarios, a goal that is facilitated by a certain reserve and neutrality. The therapist's self-imposed restraint creates the field in which the patient's "illness" can manifest itself. This field is the context in which the technical operations to which we shall now turn must be understood.

Technical Goals of TLDP

Focus on the Therapeutic Relationship

Our conception of the therapeutic process represents a line of thought that cuts across the traditional psychoanalytic schools. Although terms like *transference* and *countertransference* clearly refer to interpersonal transactions between patient and therapist, Freud remained faithful to a model that conceived of the therapist as a relatively static figure. Later writers (Macalpine 1950) continued to characterize the patient's behavior in therapy as unidirectional—from analysand to analyst. A therapist whose behavior deviated from the model was said to manifest countertransference. Indeed,

---

the therapeutic influence and how we might maximize their effect. Therapists seem to have a clearer awareness of those operations that impede or obstruct therapeutic progress. In the absence of more precise knowledge, we must assume that to a greater or lesser degree, each communication does count, and as therapists we should tailor our behavior accordingly.

early recommendations that the therapist undergo a personal analysis were designed to calibrate the therapist as a scientific instrument which only records but is unaffected by the phenomena at which it is aimed. Such an ideal, it was recognized later, was unachievable even in a hard science like physics (Heisenberg's principle of indeterminacy), and most improbable in a discipline involving human relations. With respect to psychoanalysis and psychotherapy, a truly interactive model—based on the realization that patient and therapist are continuously engaged in dynamic transactions that have a significant bearing on the conduct of therapy—was slow in evolving. It may be said that at this point in time we are entering an era in which the implications of this new conception will be more fully explored.

Historically, Alexander and French (1946) seem to have kindled an interest in the therapeutic importance of patient-therapist transactions when they advocated that the therapist actively promote a "corrective emotional experience" by deliberately relating to the patient in a manner that dramatically refutes the latter's transference expectations. Authors following the teachings of Harry Stack Sullivan have consistently stressed the importance of therapists remaining attuned to their participation in the patient's maladaptive modes of relating (Epstein and Feiner, 1979; Levenson 1972; Marguilies and Havens 1981). Therapists with a Kleinian orientation have applied object relations theory to the study of countertransference reactions evoked by patients' transference enactments (Kernberg 1980; Racker 1968). The recent writings of prominent Freudian therapists have likewise viewed the key to therapeutic change in the here-and-now analysis of patient-therapist transactions (Gill 1979; Hoffman 1983; Schafer 1983).

We emphasize, as we have done throughout this volume, that the therapeutic relationship consists of two persons who are engaged in a structured interaction. Each participant experiences the relationship from several interdependent perspectives. In turn, the attitudes and behaviors that reflect these perspectives reciprocally influence both participants.

The patient may be seen as being influenced by three general perspectives:

1. He or she is capable of perceiving and reacting to the therapist in a flexible (that is, adult) manner, which allows the patient to achieve an adaptive, reasonable attitude toward their joint work. This capacity has been termed the *observing ego* and its influence on the patient-therapist relationship has been viewed as a crucial component of the therapeutic alliance.

2. At the same time, the patient is prone to interpret rigidly the thera-

pist's attitudes and behavior in terms of preexisting sets which represent expectations of others that promote insecurity, fear, and mistrust. This perspective we have termed *anachronistic relationship predispositions* or, in traditional parlance, transference.

3. The patient unwittingly behaves in ways that tend to provoke others (including the therapist) to respond reciprocally. This has the effect of confirming the patient's expectations of how the kind of person he or she is evokes certain responses in others. In other words, the patient's behavior becomes a self-fulfilling prophecy. This unconscious and self-defeating conduct is the *action* component of transference, and is rarely mentioned in standard discussions of this topic (Hoffman 1983).

Each of these perspectives profoundly affects the patient's experience of and conduct in the therapeutic relationship. They represent an amalgam of feelings, fantasies, attitudes, and behavior whose relative influences are continually shifting.

The therapist, on the other hand, is influenced by four perspectives:

1. The therapist attempts to maintain a caring, reasonable, and dispassionate attitude, as well as a professional (interpretive) stance.

2. At the same time, the therapist's professional manner is influenced by personal style, which has a complex impact on the patient (often experienced as "positive" or "negative").

3. The therapist is also continually pulled into reactions that conform to the roles designated by the patient's maladaptive interpersonal scenarios (these reactions may be termed countertransference evoked by the patient's transference patterns).

4. At times the therapist's manner of experiencing and relating will be determined by strictly personal meanings which have their origins in his or her own unresolved neurotic conflicts (the traditional meaning of countertransference).

Each of these perspectives colors the therapist's experience of the therapeutic relationship, and in ways that often reciprocate the patient's conduct, their relative influence is continually shifting. However, by virtue of the therapist's professional reserve and understanding of the therapeutic process, he or she is in a position to be more sensitive (than an untrained person) to these influences and to turn their impact to therapeutic advantage. The therapist does this by examining them both overtly with the patient and, covertly (silently), in preparation for interpretive interventions.

It follows that the principal technical strategy of TLDP is the careful, systematic elaboration of the interpersonal transactions between patient and therapist. As these transactions are explored, the patient's conflictual modes of relatedness—of which his or her transactions with the therapist are empirical manifestations—increasingly come into focus. A patient rarely enters therapy expecting to make the relationship with the therapist an area of examination. This is true regardless of the nature and intensity of the feelings and fantasies initially experienced in the presence of the therapist. Nevertheless, when the therapist is continually sensitive to the character of the unfolding relationship, the patient eventually comes to appreciate its importance. Once attention is focused in this direction, the patient comes to realize that the therapeutic work does not take place in an interpersonal vacuum and that patient and therapist are active participants in a process that needs to be studied and understood as part of the therapeutic effort. Equally important, patients gradually discover that the therapeutic relationship encounters the same difficulties that led them to seek therapy in the first place.

Guidelines for Understanding the Patient's Conflicts

1. The Role of Transference

As we have noted, a good therapeutic relationship provides an ideal medium for experiencing one's maladaptive interpersonal predispositions, while at the same time facilitating their correction. However, in order to foster a therapeutic process, technical interventions must be organized around working conceptions of the manner in which the patient's conflicts influence the patient-therapist relationship. The most basic and widely used of these conceptions is the transference, which refers to the patient's proclivity for enacting emotional conflicts through the relationship to the therapist. This conception was introduced by Freud (1917 *S.E., 16*) when he postulated that therapeutic progress occurs solely and uniquely through the patient's relationship to the therapist.

While all psychoanalytic approaches consider transference to be the primary vehicle for understanding and ameliorating emotional conflict, there are great divergences concerning the nature of transference and its technical management. The most conservative view holds that transference behavior develops slowly and can only be dealt with after a transference neurosis develops. However, questions have been raised about the existence of such an entity, as opposed to "a panoramic process of transference pictures merging into each other or momentarily separating out with special clarity, in a way that is frequently less constant than the symptoms and other manifestations of the neurosis" (Greenacre 1980:420). More in line with the conception of transference as a variety of continuously shifting affective themes is the view that transference behavior may be productively dealt with from the inception of treatment.

Some contemporary authors (Blum 1983; Coltrera 1980; Rangell 1980) contend that excessive attention has been lavished on transference issues; other writers (Gill 1979, 1980; Schafer 1983) have argued that while analysis of the transference is stressed in theoretical writings, these recommendations are often not being adequately implemented in clinical practice. In our own clinical work we have come to adopt the position that analysis of the current transactions between patient and therapist (traditionally called analysis of the transference and of the countertransference) constitutes the most effective means for dealing with chronic patterns of interpersonal conflict. As stressed throughout this volume, these maladaptive patterns find pervasive expression in the therapeutic relationship where, if circumstances are propitious, they may eventually be modified. In studying the therapeutic work of younger colleagues and in supervising them in TLDP, we have become convinced that transference analysis is frequently not well understood and is greatly underutilized in general practice.

The major short-term dynamic therapies to some extent share this view, and as we have described previously, they advocate transference interpretations from the inception of therapy. However, these approaches also share the assumption that current evidence of transference is primarily a beacon guiding the therapist toward interpretive reconstruction of childhood patterns of conflict (the core conflict or nuclear conflict). This technical assumption is based on the conception of transference as *repeating* childhood conflicts by projecting them onto a neutral therapist, like an internal movie projector projecting an image upon a screen—hence the notion of the therapist as a blank screen (see chapter 1). Thus, we believe that the major versions of short-term dynamic therapy tend to exclude many patients because there is an insufficient appreciation of, or an unwillingness to deal with, the dynamics of the patient-therapist relationship.

In contrast, TLDP makes greater use of the therapeutic relationship for rectifying interpersonal conflicts. The interactive conception of transference proposed here is consonant with viewing the therapeutic relationship as a dyadic system. Thus, regardless of its childhood sources, conflict persists in the form of transference experience and behavior because circular interpersonal patterns (similar to Horney's "vicious cycles") confirm the patient's mistrustful expectations of others. Accordingly, the patterns perpetuate the patient's anxieties and defensive maneuvers (see chapter 5).

Our definition of transference is in keeping with that proposed by Hoffman (1983:394):

> The distinguishing features of the neurotic transference have to do with the fact that the patient is selectively attentive to a certain facet of the therapist's behavior and personality; that he is compelled to choose one set of interpretations rather than others; that his emotional life and adaptation are unconsciously governed by and governing of the particular viewpoint he has adopted; and, perhaps most importantly, that he has behaved in such a way as to actually elicit overt and covert responses that are consistent with his viewpoint and expectations. The transference represents a way not only of construing but also of constructing or shaping interpersonal relations in general and the relationship with the analyst in particular.

Accordingly, the patient's transference experience and behavior are not simply representations of the past superimposed upon the therapist as "distorted" images. Rather, the patient has certain preexisting sets or fixed expectations with which he or she interprets the meanings of interpersonal occurrences. The therapist proceeds on the working assumption that these plausible (from the patient's point of view) interpretations are always in response to something actually occurring (conscious or unconscious attitudes and behaviors of the therapist; aspects of the therapeutic arrangements, such as office fixtures, fees, appointment times, and so forth). In other words, the patient's transference experience does not distort some consensual reality, but rather is based on rigid proclivities to interpret events in a certain way without the flexibility to consider alternatives. The latter would be at odds with the affective themes that unconsciously govern the patient's life (Gill 1979; Hoffman 1983). This view of transference has important implications for technique which will be discussed shortly.

Furthermore, it is important to remind ourselves that the therapist rapidly becomes a highly significant person in the patient's life. As Freud (1917, *S.E.*, 16) perceptively observed, this attachment becomes the motive force for therapeutic change. Having turned to the therapist for help and unconsciously prepared to relate to him or her as a love object, the patient becomes exquisitely sensitive to all that transpires in the evolving relationship. It follows that any clinical data, whether generated in the form of references to people and events outside the therapeutic relationship, the patient's mood, dreams, or the emotional climate of the interviews, must be viewed as "disguised allusions" to the transference (Gill 1979). In other words, whatever else they may represent, such data should always be scrutinized for what they might reveal about the patient's experience of the therapeutic relationship. Direct references to the therapist, however fleeting, are, of course, always taken as important communications about the patient's reaction to the therapist.

A final point concerns the relationship of transference to the TLDP focus. In chapter 5 we defined this focus with reference to patterns of interpersonal experience and conduct that continue to prove troublesome to the patient. It can be seen that our conception of the focus represents a decision to attend selectively to a "transference picture" (Greenacre 1980) that appears salient at the inception of the therapeutic relationship. The TLDP focus is a method for conceptually specifying that aspect of the therapeutic relationship termed the *transference,* which reflects the patient's current version of chronic maladaptive patterns of relating to others. It directs a spotlight on that form of the transference which has the greatest impact on the therapeutic relationship.

While the initial formulation of the focus often remains the primary emphasis throughout treatment, not infrequently the focal theme will shift or will come to include several themes. Maintaining a focus in time-limited therapy should not entail attempts to fit the patient or the therapy to a Procrustean bed. As pointed out in chapter 5, it is the structured, interactive format of the focus which provides continuity to the therapeutic work, even as the content changes. At the same time, there is a redundancy in emotional conflict, and the act of focusing—as well as the method for doing so—encourages the therapist to attend in a disciplined manner to the unfolding of conflictual themes, without being sidetracked by less important issues and diversions inspired by defensive operations.

2. The Role of Countertransference

The traditional psychoanalytic position postulates that countertransference is the therapist's version of transference; accordingly, the patient comes to represent an object of the therapist's past onto whom feelings and wishes derived from unresolved conflicts are projected. However, questions concerning the definition and technical significance of countertransference continue to be actively debated (Arlow 1980). A major reason for the continuing controversy may relate to the topic's direct bearing on the character and degree of the therapist's personal involvement in psychotherapy and psychoanalysis. Of particular importance here are the views that have emerged from within object relations theory in recent years. This position can be summarized as follows: Through conscious and unconscious modes of relating, the patient evokes in the therapist internal affective reactions that symbolically represent facets of the patient's internal world. The therapist's reactions to this stimulation may directly reflect the patient's conscious and unconscious wishes or other aspects of his or her self-experience, or they may reflect disavowed aspects of the patient's self-representations and object representations (Kernberg 1980).

Regardless of their specific emphasis, the various contemporary views of countertransference testify to a greater appreciation of the significant emotional impact that patient and therapist have on each other. The older view of countertransference assumed an internal driving force, a repetition compulsion in the therapist that generated countertransference reactions in the same manner that transference was assumed to be generated within the patient. In contrast, the conceptions of countertransference derived from object relations theory evidence a greater appreciation of the interactive nature of the therapeutic relationship. Consequently, they assume that a therapist can learn much about the patient's conflicts by attending to reactions that are evoked by the patient (Racker 1968).

Nonetheless, much of the contemporary psychoanalytic literature, and the clinical teaching based on it, still depicts the therapist's role as that of a more or less dispassionate observer who analyzes and presents interpretations to the patient at the correct time and in the correct form. Thus, even if the patient evokes an emotional reaction in the therapist, these reactions should be limited to internal experiences that remain fully under the therapist's control. In other words, as the patient enacts his or her transference scenarios, the therapist may have inner reactions, but should not "join the game" (Greenacre 1980).

The literature on time-limited dynamic psychotherapy deals with countertransference either in accordance with the classical view or what we choose to call the conservative interactive view. For some authors, a therapist who is affected by or participates (even to a limited extent) in the patient's neurotic scenarios is engaged in a pathological reaction which, almost by definition, hinders therapeutic progress. Accordingly, it is held that countertransference occurs only intermittently, that competent therapists should be largely immune from it, and that in any case it represents an undesirable interference. When countertransference does occur, traditional views demand that it be expunged as rapidly as possible through self-analysis or consultation (Mann 1973; Sifneos 1979).

Those time-limited therapists who often deal with more difficult patients do acknowledge that countertransference may occasionally be a reaction evoked by the patient's conflictual struggles enacted within the therapeutic relationship. Consequently, they acknowledge that counter-transference reactions are not necessarily pathological. Indeed, they advocate that the therapist attend to countertransference reactions for clues to the nature of the patient's conflicts. At the same time, consonant with their view of the therapist's role as a relatively dispassionate observer of reactivated infantile conflicts, these authors maintain that it is detrimental to the progress of therapy if the therapist is induced to participate in these conflicts even to a limited extent (Davanloo 1978, 1980; Malan 1976a).

As we have already seen, the therapist's role and function in TLDP is radically different from that advocated by other short-term approaches. By attempting to treat patients who are often very persistent in their attempts to draw others into their rigidly fixed modes of relating, the therapist cannot help but join the game. We suggest that a therapist who relates to the patient in an empathic manner will inevitably become a participant in his or her unconscious scenarios whose purpose (in part) it is to seek confirmation of unconsciously preconceived expectations of significant others. We further believe that the therapist's inevitable involvement in and response to the patient's maladaptive modes of relating has been a neglected topic in the literature of time-limited dynamic psychotherapy. Because of its crucial importance in TLDP, we shall proceed to examine the issue in greater detail.

In our view, the patient and the therapist are always co-participants who are reciprocally influenced by the affective restrictions placed on the relationship by the patient's conflictual modes of relatedness (see also Epstein and Feiner 1979; Racker 1968; Sandler 1976). Transference, as previously described, is seen as the enactment of certain internal structured role relationships around which the patient's emotional life is organized and which in turn color experiences of the self and the world: "[T]he patient's transference would thus represent an attempt by him to *impose an interaction and interrelationship* between himself and the [therapist]" (Feiner 1979; emphasis added). In this conception, the therapist's countertransference is an empathic "role responsiveness" (Sandler 1976) to the specific relationship which is the only way in which the patient can relate to the therapist at the moment. Thus, emphasis rests on the quality and meanings of the specific transactions which activate the patient's self- and object images as well as associated feelings and fantasies.

Countertransference in these terms is still conceived of as a form of empathy, a "trial identification" (Greenson 1967) with portions of the patient's inner world. However, the common view of countertransference restricts it to internal reactions of the therapist evoked by the patient. In contrast, we hold that the conception of countertransference should be broadened to encompass those therapist actions and reactions (including attitudes and behavior as well as thoughts, feelings, and fantasies) that are evoked by the patient's transference enactments. From this perspective, transference and countertransference are ineluctably intertwined. They constitute an interactive unit which characterizes, in part, the nature of both participants' involvement in a transaction or set of transactions.

Countertransference, in TLDP terms may be described as a form of interpersonal empathy, in which the therapist, for a time and to a limited degree, is recruited into enacting roles assigned to him or her by the patient's preconceived neurotic scenarios. The therapist's empathy, however, encompasses more than the patient's inner world—it can expand to include the firsthand experience of participating in that world as it is translated into interpersonal behavior. Thus, the therapist does, indeed, join the game to a limited extent.

The empathic process goes awry when the therapist is unable to pull back and reflect upon his or her reactions to the patient. In that event, the therapist ceases to be empathic and instead identifies with the patient in a manner that reinforces the patient's neurotic expectations in interpersonal relationships. If countertransference goes undetected it may impede therapeutic progress; and if it is conceived of in traditional terms, it may be lost as a primary tool for guiding the therapist's work from moment to moment. It follows that at the center of the therapeutic process in TLDP is the therapist's ability to become immersed in the patient's modes of relatedness and to "work his way out" (Gill and Muslin 1976; Levenson 1982). If the therapist succeeds in this task, he or she is in a position to turn a vivid emotional experience to therapeutic advantage by fostering the patient's examination of what they both have been living through.

There are times when it is extraordinarily difficult for the therapist to avoid enmeshment in the patient's scenarios. As we have stressed, patients are often impelled to force the occurrence of self-fulfilling prophecies by making the therapist a co-participant in their struggles. These pressures may be exceedingly subtle but they may also take the form of placing the therapist in a vise. Patients continually test the therapist (Weiss, Sampson, and Mount Zion Psychotherapy Group, in press), and their skills in this regard are often uncanny. The fact that the entrapments and their underlying purpose are unconscious does not make it easier for the therapist to deal with them. It is helpful, however, for the therapist to keep in mind that the enactments proceed from the patient's pervasive sense of weakness, neediness, and vulnerability and that, at bottom, the patient is always suffering.

In these scenarios, the patient is driven—again, unconsciously—to ferret out and exploit the therapist's own weaknesses. For example, the patient may sense that the therapist needs adulation and praise from patients, is prone to guilt induction (to some extent, everyone is), "needs" the patient for a variety of other purposes (income, prestige, and so on), must succeed with every patient because failure is intolerable, and the like. Seductive behavior by patients, while common, has received perhaps more attention than it deserves. For many therapists a more difficult problem is the management of anger. The following example, taken from the Vanderbilt I study (Strupp 1980*b*) illustrates the therapist's response to provocation by a hostile and negativistic patient:

The patient, a nineteen-year-old male sophomore, was profoundly depressed. Slouched in his chair, avoiding eye contact with the therapist, and appearing withdrawn and glum, he portrayed the classic picture of a severely depressed patient. In seeking therapy, the patient was apparently under a great deal of internal pressure. There was a sense of desperation, but it was not the kind of motivation that generally bodes well for TLDP. Our purpose in presenting the following exchanges is to exemplify the patient's provocative behavior toward the therapist, his hostility, anger, and above all his unconscious need to defeat the therapist by arousing reciprocal negative emotions. Unfortunately, the therapist became enmeshed in the patient's game without being able to work his way out. The therapy essentially ended in failure.

The stage for failure was partly set by the therapist's rational and cognitive approach. He attempted, from the beginning, to make the patient a collaborator in examining the irrational beliefs that appeared to guide his behavior. However, a sense of irritation was already apparent from the therapist's comment at the end of the first hour: "Your view of yourself is very limited. You say a lot of people view you with contempt and you view yourself with contempt. You teach people to treat you with contempt. Others then see you the way you see yourself. One big help therapy can provide is to look at yourself, your beliefs, and the messages you are sending others."

As therapy proceeded, the patient exhibited other facets of his sense of inferiority, inadequacy, and self-hate. He dwelled on his physical appearance, describing himself as looking funny, ugly, weird, skinny, awkward, underweight, walking with sloped shoulders—in sum, a "jerk." (In fact, the patient's appearance was average and unremarkable.) Adding to the vividness of his negative self-image, he related an incident in which a girl he had asked for a date laughed at him. The therapist chose to deal with the issue by actively confronting the patient: "What do you do to catch people's attention? You must be doing something . . . usually people don't notice. You sit there and look mad." The patient responded with the challenge: "There is nothing to feel cheery about." Pursuing the attack, Dr. Y observed: "People don't like you. I haven't heard anything that might get them to act differently."

P (defiant):   I can't do anything different.

T (apparently being drawn into an argument):   Of course you can . . . you make yourself very poor company . . . Let's find out why it happens and what you can do to change. . . . Make a start by looking at what you can do to change. . . . Make a start by looking at what you do to get people to pass over you.

P: I have a sour attitude toward life.

T: It can be changed.

P: How can I have any other attitude?

T: Change your behavior—that might change your attitude.

P: So what do you want me to do, put on an act?

T: At the moment, just look at yourself . . .

P (insistent):   This is the normal me.

T: I don't know what the "real you" is.

In the ensuing interchange, the therapist asked for examples of how the patient presented himself to others, again focusing on "messages" he might be sending to others. One of these, in relation to peers, seemed to be "Go ahead, put me down, fellows." The patient admitted that this might be a mistake. Dr. Y proceeded: "You are moderately intelligent and decent looking, but there is something . . . a general statement to the world: 'I am no good, not too bright, put me down' . . . Try to put some distance between your eyes and yourself . . . see how you get others to treat you."

Elsewhere, Dr. Y attempted to stimulate the patient's curiosity about himself, and to enlist his cooperation in the therapeutic task. He conveyed a sense of hopefulness by indicating that there were things the patient could do if he seriously tried. He gave him a homework assignment of watching for specific instances in which he put himself down, tried to get attention, and made others feel sorry for him. He allowed that "this won't solve the underlying problem, but it will give us a start."

The preceding patterns of interaction continued with relatively little change. It emerged that an important source of the patient's current conflict was the relationship with his mother. As he put it: "She tries to goad me into doing things. I've never had any long-term grudges against her because usually what she said made sense over the long run." Significantly, she was highly critical of the patient, but when he succeeded she bestowed scant praise. Yet, when the patient openly complained and indicated that he felt bad, his mother would be more loving and supportive. She was also reported as having "embarrassed me a lot." The patient's current girl friend, too, was noted by the patient as being very possessive and demanding.

The therapist tended to offer the patient life-directing principles such as these:

"If you do well, it's your doing, and if you do poorly, it is also your doing.

"You have allowed your feelings to control your actions and your behavior. You don't have to do this. You are not at the mercy of your feelings. You can stop a spiral like that.

"What is unusual about you is not your looks but your concern about your looks. Frankly I don't understand where that arises. I do know that you have a brother who you say is very good-looking.

"I am sure it is true that often you don't realize that you view yourself in a negative light. But there are lots of times when you could say: 'Whoa, let me think about this.' Write the points down maybe and see whether your first view isn't askew.

"Much of your depression and much of your unhappiness are almost self-induced. . . . I think you are capable of learning some new things about yourself and learning new ways of dealing with the world and people.

"If anyone says you look funny, they're not talking about your physical appearance but about the way you act, which is under your voluntary control. It's just like succeeding in English because of the work you do instead of making your teacher feel sorry for you.

"You don't have to look rotten because you feel rotten . . . you find many excuses not to try anything new . . . it's time you stop crying in your beer about your looks."

Reviews of recordings and transcripts of the therapy hours revealed a good deal of tension. On the one hand, the patient was detailing his complaints against his parents, early childhood, peers, as well as himself; on the other hand, Dr. Y exhorted the patient to change his behavior by deliberate attempts. The following example typifies the exchanges:

T: We can certainly accept that you've been taught at home to be concerned about your physical appearance, but does it serve you in any way to hang onto this concern the way you do?

P: I can't see where it is a disservice or less than helpful. It is a fact of life.

T: No, it is not a fact of life at all. The fact of life is that you're a fairly average size and appearing individual. But you go around all the time complaining about your looks and worrying about them. Now what service does that provide you? How is it useful to you?

P: It wouldn't bother me if people didn't come to me and say things to me.

T: What service does it give you?

(Pause)

P: I guess you could call it an excuse for failure.

T: Absolutely! Over and over again it's an excuse! . . . and it won't work. Looks are an excuse for failure in only one situation and that's a beauty contest.

P: I've missed getting jobs and everything else.

T: No, I reject that. It's just an excuse . . . Your manner may make you lose a job but not the way you look. Your behavior will make you lose a job but not your appearance.

The patient continued to challenge:

P: I have developed a sullen expression.

T: Sullen, that's the right word, exactly the right word! But sullen has nothing to do with physical appearance. That's how you choose to look. It has nothing to do with your weight or your build or your hair or anything else.

(Long pause)

P: How do I change being sullen? I don't know whether I want to or not.

Another theme concerned the patient's relationship with his girl friend. She frequently called him, and after these lengthy telephone conversations he would feel depressed. Like the patient's mother, she appeared to be possessive, and he felt as if she was pulling "a good sized net" around him. The dilemma seemed to be that on the one hand he was eager to win her affection and on the other he was terrified by her engulfing attitude. In particular, the prospect of marriage filled him with fear. However, little progress was made in dealing with the issue in therapy.

Dr. Y's emphasis throughout was on the patient's performance rather than his anxieties. The primary goal of therapy, he noted, is the achievement of self-awareness and insight. The patient's wish, on the other hand, appeared to be for nurturance and consolation. In one of the last sessions (the therapy lasted 11 hours) he accused the therapist: "You sound like my mother. You don't understand."

We may take it for granted that no therapist is able to fulfill all of the patient's wishes for love, support, approval, the gratification of dependency needs, and so on. Hence it is inevitable that sooner or later the patient will feel frustrated. Frustration is closely related to anxiety which is readily transformed into anger. That anger eventually becomes directed at the therapist. Let us also recall that virtually no one will be in therapy unless he or she is struggling with a host of unfulfilled needs. These are activated as therapy proceeds, as the therapist becomes a significant other, and as he or she plays the self-assigned role of benign but relatively neutral and uninvolved listener. The patient's frustrations are a part of his or her "illness," and they will come into play as the patient comes to feel sufficiently secure in the relationship with the therapist. We believe that the anger surrounding the emergence of unfulfilled needs into consciousness poses one of the most difficult problems for many therapists. If the patient succeeds in evoking anger from the therapist, he or she may feel that they are "closer," which, in turn, reduces anxiety.

One patient became recurrently incensed at the therapist because of his alleged failure to respond to requests for "direction" (control). This patient who was in the throes of a grief reaction (due to a death in her family), wanted the therapist to advise her on how to handle various behavior problems involving her children, about whose welfare she had become deeply concerned. On one of these occasions, responding to the patient's insistent plea, the therapist recommended a child psychologist, whom the patient subsequently consulted. Predictably, this acquiescence in the patient's (partly) legitimate request proved insufficient, and the patient was soon disappointed and angry again at the therapist. She accused him of being insufficiently understanding and caring, unresponsive to the patient's needs, and generally inadequate. As on previous occasions, she threatened to discontinue therapy although, almost in the same breath, she volunteered that the therapist had been helpful to her. This patient had a great need to control significant others, including the therapist.

In situations of this kind, the therapist faces a dilemma: In striving to gratify the patient's wishes, he or she abdicates the therapeutic role and becomes a pawn in the patient's neurotic struggle for control; by declining participation, the therapist becomes the target for the patient's unfulfilled dependency needs. The only therapeutic solution is to enlist the patient's observing ego; that is, to have recourse to the therapeutic alliance. If the latter is viable, the patient is able to take a step back and observe, with the therapist, what is going on, what he or she is trying to do in the relationship, and to understand the neurotic character of the wishes that are rising to awareness. In such cases, the patient may turn out to be a rather unreliable ally. In other words, the internal pressure to have powerful needs gratified in the therapeutic relationship may be more compelling than to tolerate the pain of nonfulfillment which is the price that must be paid for gaining insight into a neurotic constellation.

If the alliance is ambivalent, as it typically is, the patient may leave therapy, rationalizing this decision in terms of the therapist's alleged incompetence, coldness, lack of understanding, and the like. At such times, the therapist's appeal to the patient's intellect may prove fruitless, as Freud (1917, *S.E., 16*) clearly recognized. The patient may then win a Pyrrhic victory over the therapist; that is, the therapeutic relationship has been sacrificed as the patient's neurotic structures remain intact. Through skillful handling of the therapeutic relationship the therapist may succeed in forestalling such an eventuality; however, the patient's need to defeat the therapist—and ultimately himself or herself—may prove more powerful. If in the process the therapist has been provoked to express anger or rejection, the patient will be convinced by this "evidence" that the action taken was the only reasonable one under the circumstances. Despite the therapist's best efforts, such unfortunate outcomes are sometimes unavoidable. They illustrate the enormous obstacles that are commonly encountered with "difficult" patients as well as the limitations imposed on the therapist by the patient's pathology.

3. The Interpersonal Theme of the Session

A typical therapeutic hour will be found to center around one or two themes which in one way or another are related to the TLDP focus which has been previously identified (see chapter 5). Salient emotional conflicts and interpersonal action patterns in which they become manifest are redundant across relationships. They are also continuous over time. In other words, the version of the patient's life story or narrative theme (Schafer 1983) which constitutes the major source of his or her current unhappiness will be retold to the therapist in many forms and reenacted continually within the therapeutic relationship. In order for the therapist to attend to the focal theme (or themes), he or she must view each session as directly connected to and following from the previous one, as though no time had elapsed between sessions. Each interview generates hypotheses in the therapist's mind about conflicts and their interpersonal manifestations. Similarly, each interview ends with questions in the therapist's mind concerning the emotional meanings of what the patient has talked about, as well as how he or she has behaved during that session.

These hypotheses and questions should be kept clearly in mind in the subsequent interview, and they should serve as guidelines to the therapist in attempts to make sense of what the patient is currently communicating.

It is well to remember that specific hypotheses and questions may serve as guidelines over many sessions. For example, a transaction between patient and therapist in a given interview may carry an important meaning for the patient which the therapist does not understand at the moment. By keeping such a question in mind, the therapist may come to understand it at a later time (see examples given in chapter 8). Although therapists may feel that they do not adequately understand a transaction, they may recognize it as "loaded." This is usually sufficient reason to avoid interpretations or other interventions (giving direct advice). If the therapist keeps the field open, and if the issue is important in the patient's life, there is a good chance that the theme will be replayed later in therapy, at which time its unconscious meanings may come more clearly into focus. Premature interventions, on the other hand, may prevent further elaboration of the topic and, more important, make the therapist an unwitting participant in a neurotic pattern. Furthermore, as the therapist attempts to decode the patient's communications and activities, it should not be forgotten that decoding is aimed at translations into the theme of the TLDP focus as it unfolds across sessions. Therapy thus comes to assume continuity and coherence over its entire course.

It should also be recalled that the patient's developing relationship with the therapist acts like a magnet which attracts to it attitudes and feelings, both positive and negative, pertaining to earlier love objects in the patient's life. In TLDP, the most important facet of a theme in any interview is its interpersonal manifestation in the therapeutic relationship. In order for the therapist to identify the general form of the patient's relationship predisposition (that is, the interpersonal expression of the focal theme currently being enacted), he or she must maintain constant alertness and curiosity about the state of the therapeutic relationship. At the same time, while attempting to understand the current interpersonal transactions, the therapist does not ignore whatever else the patient is talking about. Any area of his or her life the patient chooses to discuss (unless the therapist identifies it as a diversionary tactic) should be jointly examined, although the issues may be so complex and intertwined with defensive operations that elucidation is temporarily precluded.

The therapist must always begin a session by entering the patient's affective world where admittance is given. Needless to say, much can be gained by clarifying and interpreting conflicts that are manifested in relationships outside of therapy. Simultaneously, however, the therapist maintains a mental set aimed at applying what is learned about conflicts in other relationships to understanding the immediate state of the patient-therapist relationship.

The translation back to the latter is attempted when the therapist identifies a similarity between patterns of conflictual experience and behavior in other contexts and what transpires in the therapeutic relationship. Interpretations of these connections are made with a degree of conviction that is commensurate with the clarity of the evidence and the patient's "openness" (i.e., lack of defensiveness) to accept them. At other times, the therapist may not readily see a connection between the transactions in other relationships and those in the patient-therapist relationship. This does not mean that no connection exists, for "disguised allusions to the transference" (Gill 1979) are often exceedingly subtle. We take it for granted that such connections always exist, even if they cannot be readily discerned. Consequently, when an emotionally charged situation or pattern can be identified and clarified in another context, the therapist may ask the patient if he or she is aware of the same experience with the therapist. Even if the patient denies such a connection, the question itself alerts the patient's attention to such a possibility. It may also communicate the therapist's tolerance for the patient's disagreement.*

At other times, the therapist may directly invite the patient's attention to an examination of the state of the therapeutic relationship. This is particularly germane when the therapist senses tension or other disturbances (absence of affect, boredom) in the climate of the relationship. The activation of old scenarios within the therapeutic relationship may become manifest in the patient's verbal communications as well as in the manner in which he or she relates to the therapist. The evidence may be embedded in seemingly trivial details—"casual" comments, gestures, dreams, fantasies, and so on. Consequently, the therapist must maintain a disciplined naiveté in seeking to understand the meaning of a patient's actions or descriptions of interpersonal events or inner states. Concomitantly the therapist should not hesitate to investigate the patient's experience in detail until it makes sense. This is particularly true of communications which the therapist experiences as charged with affect (which sometimes may appear incongruous).

Affects are usually a complex amalgam of experiences, feelings, fantasies, recollections, and so forth; they rarely refer to specific experiences nor

---

*Merton Gill (personal communication) refers to "one of the most common perversions of the technique by those who first learn about it and become enthusiastic about it, namely its mechanical application." He goes on to illustrate: "The patient says he's angry with his wife, so the therapist mechanically says: 'Aha, you must be angry with me,' (Incidentally, among other possibilities, it's at least as likely that he feels the therapist is angry with him, so-called 'identification in the transference'). So the therapist has to have a plausible basis for drawing a parallel." We would add that the therapist should also be mindful of any activity that may be resisted by the patient as a gimmick or a routine. Sooner or later all patients will be searching for targets at which to vent their anger and frustrations.

do they have invariant meanings. The therapist, therefore, must carefully explore the context in which they occur. For instance, a verbal report of depression cannot be taken at face value; it may embody features unique to the patient-therapist relationship at a given moment, but yet may differ markedly from depression the patient may have experienced in a different interpersonal context. Affects typically occur at varying levels of awareness, and they may refer to highly idiosyncratic experiences associated with the core of the patient's identify.

In each session the therapist seeks to identify the nature of the current conflict by focusing on those elements of the patient's communications which carry the strongest affect, always keeping in mind that valuable clues may come from his or her own affective reactions to the patient's communications (irritation, boredom). Sometimes descriptions of an event may impress the therapist as being strangely devoid of affect; the omission then, may be more significant than the verbal description.

By closely attending to all facets of the patient's communications, as well as his or her own associations and fantasies, the therapist will often gain a reasonably clear picture of the issue with which the patient is currently struggling. As a participant in the patient's interpersonal drama, the therapist's first glimpses of understanding may come from "tugs" that are part of the reciprocal role the patient unconsciously assigns to him or her. To ignore these tugs as well as the emotional reactions to which they give rise would be tantamount to dismissing the most relevant material. Similarly, a therapist who responds to a provocation by verbalizing counter-anger is clearly abdicating the role of therapeutic listener. (Such reactions, as we have observed in a research context, are not nearly as rare as is commonly believed.)

It is not unusual, however, for the therapist to remain puzzled as a session is proceeding. Even if he or she has a reasonably clear conception of the TLDP focus, the material for the current session may fail to provide further elucidation. As noted previously, at such times it may be particularly appropriate to scrutinize the transactions between patient and therapist for evidence of the momentarily elusive theme. If this fails, one may openly acknowledge one's puzzlement and directly seek to enlist the patient's aid.

This approach may have several salutary effects: It underscores the fact that therapy is a collaborative enterprise; that the therapist is neither omniscient nor infallible (indeed, at the end of a long day he or she may be fatigued or not sharp for other reasons); not every interpersonal process is readily understandable; and the current difficulty may be a function of the patient's unconsciously determined defensive operations. These may be important lessons in tolerance, patience, and forbearance that are also applicable to other areas of the patient's life. It should never be forgotten that one of the therapist's most important functions is providing a role model the patient can identify with and emulate. Contrary to some extant misperceptions, the therapist is neither an interpreting nor a reinforcing machine!

Once an understanding of the patient's experiences and behavior has been gained, the therapist intervenes to clarify and interpret their meaning. We have separated our discussion of the processes of gaining and conveying understanding in order to promote a clearer elucidation of each task. In actual practice, of course, the two are woven together, reciprocally reinforcing each other.

Guidelines for Therapist Interventions

1. Examination of the Therapeutic Relationship

It is apparent that the unfolding therapeutic relationship provides the therapist (and the patient) with the most vivid and affectively powerful material potentially available to the treatment. For therapy to proceed, the patient must experience an affect and must see himself or herself in action before an intervention (other than simple facilitations, and so on) can become meaningful. Just as a tennis coach cannot correct a student's errors until both can observe them in the course of a game, patient and therapist must become engaged in an interaction before mutative change can occur. First, the patient must act; then, with the help of the therapist, he or she must step back and observe the action; finally the meaning and purpose of the action must be explored.

A therapist who is sensitive to the patient's enactments will recognize their emergence and, at appropriate times, freeze the action in order to engage the patient in a rational and dispassionate discussion of what has transpired. This process entails recasting (interpreting) the patient's emotional experience in terms of the therapist's emerging understanding of its meaning. The interpretation represents an attempt to reorganize what is partly implicit and partly explicit in the therapeutic interaction.

The example set by the therapist's activity just described may have another long-range benefit as it comes to serve the patient as a model for dealing with emotional reactions and conflicts. It may allow the patient gradually to take some distance from automatic reactions and to examine their meaning from a more rational perspective. Thus, therapy expands the patient's repertoire of inner resources for coping with conflicts. It is also critically important to note that the patient comes to identify with the therapist's attitude of tolerance, equanimity, and acceptance of the patient's inner turmoil.

2. Four Organizing Questions

We have previously described (see particularly chapters 2 and 5) the format used to conceptualize interpersonal transactions. In order to clarify the components of the patient's experiences in the therapeutic relationship, four basic questions may serve as a guide to interventions:

1. How does the patient experience me, and what is the nature of his or her feelings toward me?

2. What might be the patient's experience of my intentions, attitudes, or feelings toward him or her?

3. What might be the patient's emotional reactions to fantasies about me?

4. How does the patient construe the relationship with me, and how might his or her current reactions be a consequence of our previous interactions?

Thus, the therapist endeavors to make optimal use of all opportunities for exploring and explicating the patient's experience in the therapeutic relationship. This goal is systematically pursued over the course of therapy. The decision to inquire at any given time about the state of the therapeutic relationship is a clinical judgment involving intuition, empathy, and personal style. It also embodies a conception of the therapeutic process, for example, the kind set forth in this book.

3. The Use of Material from Outside the Therapeutic Relationship

As a general rule, direct examination of patient-therapist interactions is advisable during periods when the therapist senses tension or there appear to be other forms of emotional pressure. For example, the patient may be lethargic or seemingly devoid of affect; the therapist may experience boredom or drowsiness, and so on. At other times, attention is directed to the state of the therapeutic relationship when the therapist identifies a correspondence between the current state of the therapeutic relationship and patterns of interpersonal conflict that are evident in the patient's descriptions of outside relationships.

The modern approaches to short-term dynamic therapy originated in attempts to treat psychiatric combat casualties in World War II. Clinical reports of that period are characterized by an emphasis on extratransference interpretations; that is, treatment was aimed at the reduction of symptoms through examination of acute stresses in the patient's life, without recourse to an analysis of the therapeutic relationship (Small 1979). Subsequent attempts to deal with more chronic neurotic symptomatology and character malformations utilized the more traditional psychoanalytic treatment strategy of genetic transference interpretation. As we have noted (see chapter 2), this emphasis is also apparent in the writings of Malan (1976a), Davanloo (1978, 1980), and Sifneos (1979).

In earlier sections of this chapter, we have shown that the TLDP therapist more thoroughly examines immediate expressions of transference. The patient's communications about all areas of his or her current and past life are examined for what they may reveal about the current state of the patient–therapist relationship. Admittedly, while many aspects of the patient's behavior have such implications, they are frequently not in focus. Thus, no therapist can be oblivious to the patient's difficulties in relationships outside of therapy; indeed major portions of the therapeutic sessions will typically be devoted to them. Yet, by being alert to parallels, information is acquired that may further the participants' joint understanding. It will also become clear that exploration of an external issue may often be less threatening to the patient. Thus, information relevant to the therapeutic relationship is often obtained more readily when attention is focused on topics that appear to lie outside.

It is therefore good practice to examine whatever areas of his or her life the patient chooses to discuss and to elucidate the nature of the patient's actual or fantasied transactions with others. This effort has a twofold aim: (1) to help the patient understand the nature of interpersonal difficulties in "real" relationships, and (2) to further clarify, by analogy, the patient's current experience in the therapeutic relationship.

The narrative content of dreams (and associations evoked by dreams) may also yield valuable data about the patient's construal of the therapeutic relationship. Furthermore, dream actions and objects both animate and inanimate, may symbolize aspects of the patient's interpersonal experiences that are otherwise inaccessible. It is often worthwhile to examine the manifest content of dreams and related associations in terms of the patient's view of himself or herself and others, the nature of the interactions between characters, and particularly the feelings associated with these interactions. It is also well to remember that a recalled dream is often an affective communication that contains poignant comments about the current state of the patient-therapist interaction. The participants may then seek to understand recent interactions that may have given rise to the dream.

At the risk of tedious repetition, we want to state emphatically that any aspect of the patient's narrative concerning outside experiences, no matter how ostensibly trivial, may be a symbolic commentary on the relationship with the therapist. Our supervision of other therapists and our own clinical work has repeatedly confirmed that "disguised allusions to the transference" (Gill 1979, 1980) are easily missed unless the therapist maintains a consistent attitude of disciplined alertness. To illustrate: Once an issue pertaining to the therapeutic relationship is identified, the therapist can typically find symbolic evidence for it in the patient's communications about seemingly unrelated material brought up earlier in the session. With sufficiently disciplined attention, the therapist can learn to identify such issues when they first appear in disguised form. He may thus increase the efficiency of his work—an important consideration in time-limited therapy. It is also true that important transference issues are often bypassed *unless* the therapist is able to identify them when they appear in disguised form.

When parallels are identified, linking them may be an intermediate step in expanding the patient's self-awareness. However, the line of inquiry always returns to a study of the therapeutic relationship. With systematic attempts to explore the dynamics of the therapeutic relationship, there is clearly the danger of applying this technical strategy in mechanical fashion (Blum 1983; Gill personal communication). As is true of any dynamic technique, the proper timing of here-and-now transference interpretations is ultimately a matter of clinical judgment, which can be improved through supervised experience. Still, there are certain helpful guidelines: If the patient makes an explicit reference to the therapist or the therapy, however fleeting, it is well to explore the implications. If any of the patient's communications appear relevant to some previous event or transaction in the therapeutic relationship, it is worth pursuing the possibility of a disguised reaction. If there is an abrupt or incongruous change in the patient's mood or manner of relating to the therapist, it is likewise advisable to inquire further. Finally, if the patient is describing an affectively charged situation, it may be helpful simply to ask if the patient has ever experienced—or is currently experiencing—similar feelings in relation to the therapist. Recall that feelings, attitudes, and behaviors are typically being transferred from one significant person to another!

Technique

4. When to Make Interpretive Links to Outside Relationships

In psychoanalysis and psychoanalytic therapy it is customarily assumed that therapeutic change is a function of insight. The latter is thought to refer to an affective experience of conflictual behavior in the transference, combined with cognitive understanding of the connections between current conflicts and their inferred childhood origins. Accordingly, the primary technical strategy consists in preparing the way for genetic transference interpretations, and these transference-parent links (T/P links) are considered to be singularly conducive to therapeutic change. We have previously voiced our disagreement with the notion of a unique class of therapeutically mutative techniques as well as with assumptions regarding the therapeutic use of historical reconstructions (see chapter 5).

In our view, insight refers to learning the value of interpretive thinking; that is, learning to appreciate the capacity for differentiating and integrating contradictory experiences (the therapist as a helpful professional and as a punitive authority). It involves a growing capacity for making connections of various kinds and integrating diverse facets of emotional and interpersonal experience (Neubauer 1980). Of great importance in this effort is helping patients to understand how they actively contribute to their unhappiness and interpersonal conflicts through their actions, rigid construing of experience in accordance with a limited set of interpersonal themes, and accompanying expectations of others. Thus, T/P links are considered but one form of technical interventions that may at times further the broader therapeutic endeavor.

As is true of all technical interventions, the interpretive linking of experiences between patient and therapist with outside experiences calls for good clinical judgment. Some therapists offer specific rules for implementing this type of intervention, including timing. Most writers on short-term dynamic therapy advocate the use of T/P interpretations as often as possible (Davanloo 1978, 1980; Malan 1976a; Sifneos 1979). In contrast, Gill (1979, 1980) recommends the use of genetic transference interpretations only when the patient has first spontaneously introduced relevant historical material; in short, no blanket rules exist.

The TLDP approach to interpretation resembles most closely the procedures proposed by Gill (1982). In accordance with our emphasis on therapeutic learning based on systematic examination of the transactions between patient and therapist, interpretive links to outside relationships are used relatively sparingly. Forging such links serves two primary functions: (1) it strengthens the patient's capacity to achieve emotional distance from stereotyped predispositions, and (2) it reinforces the patient's awareness of

163

their profound effect on the current relationship with the therapist. Thus, as a general guideline, interpretive connections to outside relationships can be helpful in placing a particular transference enactment in broader perspective *after* the enactment has been carefully explored in the here-and-now and the patient has gained an appreciation of its impact on his or her experience and behavior.

There are times when connecting interpretations may be essential for overcoming serious obstacles to therapeutic progress. For instance, a critical point may be reached when the reality of a transference enactment becomes so affectively compelling to the patient that it threatens the stability of the working alliance. At such junctures, the therapist may encourage the patient to examine whether the immediate experience is representative of the overall state of the treatment relationship. As part of this evaluation, the therapist directs the patient's attention to patterns of similarities between the therapy experience and other current or past relationships. By highlighting such similarities the therapist promotes the patient's insight into his or her history of disappointments, frustrations, and traumas that have exerted a lasting influence.

It should be noted that the interpretive linking we have been discussing does not necessarily presuppose exhaustive history taking. If, through careful examination of the patient-therapist transactions, a particular maladaptive relationship pattern has been articulated, it can be hypothesized with reasonable confidence that the pattern also occurs elsewhere. Concomitantly, the patient may be the one to observe the congruence and arrive at an interpretation. Such self-discoveries appear to be particularly effective because the patient has engaged in active learning.

5. Interpretation in TLDP

In dynamic psychotherapy, classes of interventions are commonly viewed as lying along a continuum with regard to their relative therapeutic potential. Primary points on this continuum refer to questions, confrontations, clarifications, and interpretations. Since interpretations are considered the most important technical tool in dynamic therapy, it will be helpful to scrutinize their function more closely.

The art of interpretation in psychoanalysis originally referred to understanding the unconscious meanings of the patient's conflicts. More recently, it has been redefined as the technical skill of formulating timely interventions that are emotionally meaningful to the patient (Sandler, Dane, and Holder 1970). Thus, major emphasis is placed on what the therapist elects to interpret, when the interpretation is made, and the form in which it is done. Thus, in the various forms of analytic therapy, interpretation is still considered the ultimate technical objective and the primary means for imparting "correct" knowledge to the patient at the most propitious moment.

In TLDP we view interpretations as the product of a collaborative inquiry in which patient and therapist learn together about the patient's conflicts. Accordingly, interpretation per se is not the linchpin of treatment. Rather, it is one important activity in a process of understanding the transactions between patient and therapist, and the manner in which their relationship reflects episodes in a fixed scenario.

Therefore, interpretation in TLDP is defined as an intervention that enlarges the patient's awareness of his or her current psychological state by a communication that facilitates understanding of a current interpersonal experience and the factors complicating it. Interpretation promotes insight in the manner previously described. Furthermore, its purpose is to restructure or reorganize the meanings of the current experience to the end of making it more congruent with present-day reality. While this process involves a reliving of painful experiences, the growing understanding provides relief of the patient's suffering, thus constituting one of the healing functions of psychotherapy. In this process, the collaborative exploration of the transactions between patient and therapist plays a central role.

By the same token, the distinctions between the classic types of intervention appear less important than their aim. Questions, clarifications, suggestions, interpretations—in short, any verbal or nonverbal action by the therapist—can further the progress of therapy as long as they are made in an empathic manner and as long as they capture some important aspect of the patient's current struggle.

When a therapist offers an interpretation he or she sends a message with a particular intent. However, since the patient's understanding of the actions and intentions of others are to varying degrees governed by prepotent interpersonal themes, the therapist's interpretive communication may be received in terms of a preexisting set rather than in terms of the therapist's intention. For example, the therapist may comment on the patient's diffident behavior toward a spouse. Although the therapist attempted to identify a pattern of inhibited aggression, the patient may hear the observation as disapproval, similar to the experience of harsh criticism from the spouse. The result may be compliant agreement with the therapist's observation, mirroring the patient's diffident compliance with the spouse. To cite another example: A woman patient who engaged in a considerable amount of volunteer work obliquely expressed her resentment of working without recompense. Concomitantly, she appeared to be angry at her husband who did not wish his wife to work for pay. When the therapist reflected the patient's feelings that she would like to get paid for services she had rendered, she felt criticized by the therapist who had done no more than paraphrase her feelings (which, however, she needed to disavow).

In sum, a therapist contemplating making an interpretation must carefully seek to anticipate and gauge the patient's response. If, in the therapist's judgment, the patient will be unable to grasp an interpretation (for example, when the evidence, available to both participants, appears thin or is built on a great many assumptions) it is obviously unwise to make it. Similarly, if the therapist anticipates that the patient will oppose or reject an interpretation, there is no point in risking a confrontation. Problems, however, arise when the therapist is unable to foresee the patient's reaction. As we have illustrated, it is virtually impossible always to prevent such misapprehensions and misconstruals. The best one can hope is that subsequent amplification by the therapist may elucidate the difference between what the therapist meant and what the patient heard. An important feature of therapy is the opportunity it provides for such corrections.

Of course one hopes that interpretations will, more typically, lead to increased self-understanding. There appears to be no foolproof way of ascertaining whether an interpretation has been correct or wide of the mark. The patient's immediate agreement does not necessarily confirm that the therapist had succeeded in effecting a cognitive reorientation that carries with it therapeutic benefits. By the same token, lack of agreement or disagreement does not prove the opposite. As is increasingly being recognized (Peterfreund 1983; Spence 1982), there are no historical truths to be discovered in psychoanalysis or analytic therapy; there are only new —and, one hopes, more constructive—meanings which the patient can assimilate. To further this enterprise, it is quintessential that the therapist take special precautions not to hurt the patient's self-esteem by the kind of interpretation advanced and the manner in which it is presented. If this caveat were stringently followed, there would be fewer negative effects in psychotherapy than there appear to be (Strupp, Hadley, and Gomes-Schwartz 1977).

This stance follows from another important distinction between TLDP and classical analysis. In studying the analytic literature one often gets the impression that a problem is being analyzed for the sake of analyzing it, that is, for establishing a "truth" about a person's unconscious motivations. In such attempts the therapeutic value of discovering symbolic meanings may be quite remote or even totally lost. This appears to be a consequence of the old dichotomy between psychoanalysis as an investigative method and a therapeutic one (see chapter 1). The TLDP therapist's attitude, by contrast, is always therapeutic. This is the case because the therapist never loses sight of the interpersonal problems with which the patient is currently struggling. Though keenly interested in how the patient got that way, the therapist is far more interested in why an old trauma, loss, or deprivation continues to exert a powerful influence on the patient's life in the present. The latter influence accounts for the patient's being in therapy—not to be analyzed but to be helped! In pursuing a line of inquiry or in weighing a possible interpretation, the TLDP therapist is consistently aware of the question: Is this intervention likely to help the patient in coming to terms with the past and in leading a more constructive and satisfying life? Since the patient's difficulties in the present are often usefully explained by reference to the past, the therapist seeks to identify continuities between beliefs and assumptions guiding past interpersonal relationships and present ones, including prominently the one with the therapist. This realization also conduces to greater parsimony in the therapeutic endeavor: The TLDP therapist does not pursue byways or "interesting" excursions into the patient's psychic life but remains focused on those topics that are likely to make a difference.

Every therapy session entails the formulation and rejection of numerous hypotheses that suggest themselves as the therapist listens to the patient. Each therapist clearly has pet ideas and it is clearly easier to find support for them than to entertain alternative hypotheses. Sullivan once remarked on the great difficulty many therapists have with respect to the latter. Peterfreund (1983) has recently criticized the tendency of many therapists to conduct analyses or psychotherapy in stereotyped fashion. We recommend that the therapist carefully weigh evidence that comes from within a given hour. Such evidence gains greater credence when it is checked against what the therapist knows about the patient from previous interactions. We also recommend that in making interpretations the therapist favor *parsimony* by positing the fewest possible assumptions. Analytic jargon and broad generalizations (penis envy, masochistic attitude) are always useless; but beyond that, any interpretation needs to be based on observations and data that both patient and therapist have jointly developed. For example, if the therapist comments on a woman patient's attempt to ingratiate herself with the male therapist and with other men, he must base himself on data the patient has supplied and which are almost as clear to the patient as they are to the therapist. Furthermore, there must be appropriate affect, and the patient must be ready for the interpretation. An interpretation usually says something new to the patient since it presents a problem in a different context. However, in our experience it is wise to restrict oneself to interpretations that are readily understandable to the patient and are consonant both with analytic principles and the patient's growing self-understanding.

6. The Use of Free Association

Therapists conducting psychoanalytic forms of therapy are taught that a patient should be encouraged to free associate. While most dynamic therapists probably have only a general notion about the behavior to which this concept refers, in practice encouraging free association is routinely interpreted as taking up only those subjects that the patient spontaneously introduces. The psychoanalytic rationale for this stance by the therapist is twofold: (1) any interruption in the patient's stream of thought will obscure the development of unconscious, conflict-laden themes; and (2) the introduction of topics by the therapist constitutes a form of "suggestion" which is another means of obscuring the true picture of the patient's conflicts.

We agree, as already discussed, that the therapist's main task is to listen empathically to the patient's story. However, we also believe that empathic listening can take place during an active dialogue between patient and therapist. In any conversation between two people, the extent to which either party truly listens to the other reflects the quality of his or her attention more than the amount of verbal participation. It is also well to remember that the main affective themes influencing a patient's life are robust, otherwise how could they have such lasting and pervasive influence? It follows then, that they are replayed in many different ways and are redundant in the patient's communications. In other words, they are not easily sidetracked by the therapist's interventions. In any event, genuine understanding of a patient's conflicts may be obscured by stereotypes imposed by the therapist's clinical theories, regardless of how much latitude is allowed to the patient's free associations (Peterfreund 1983).

The psychoanalytic principle of encouraging free association is based on the classical view that the patient's unconscious conflicts are projected onto the person of the therapist, as a personification of the past. A corollary principle states that this process will occur only if the therapist acts as a blank screen; in other words, the therapist remains passive and quiet, intervening only when the patient's associations become constricted or blocked. We have already discussed our disagreement with this concept of the therapeutic process (see chapter 1 and earlier parts of this chapter). Put simply, if the therapeutic process is conceived of as a dyadic system requiring the active collaboration of both participants, then a therapist who remains passive will not foster this process.

A therapist who rigidly adheres to the principle of *only* responding to content that the patient has currently introduced will be unable systematically to focus the therapeutic material. While organizing and focusing the therapeutic content may eventually be accomplished, doing it in this manner tends to extend the length of treatment. This is true for psychoanalysis conducted four or five times a week; the problem is greater in dynamic psychotherapy which is conducted once or twice a week, and it becomes acute when therapy is time limited.

Let us use an example to illustrate our point. Say the patient introduces a topic highly relevant to the therapeutic focus. A productive discussion ensues but the topic is by no means exhausted. In the next session a week later, the therapist is alert for further material relevant to the topic from the previous week. However, the patient talks about unrelated matters (perhaps a defensive flight from the emotionally charged topic of the previous session). Furthermore, the therapist sees no way to tie the new material to the therapeutic focus. If the therapist adheres to the principle of not introducing topics which the patient is not currently discussing, important material from the previous week may be lost for an indefinite period of time. On the other hand, if the therapist—practicing in the spirit of TLDP—calls the patient's attention to his or her "forgetting" of the previous session's discussion, the therapeutic focus will be restored.

This action by the therapist is not leading the patient in terms of imposing the therapist's view of what constitutes conflict-laden experiences. Rather, it implements a primary technical objective of TLDP, that of consistently attempting to keep the therapeutic focus in sight. Of course, the therapist must strive to maintain a balance between empathic listening and intervening, which is similar to (and often intertwined with) the course navigated between participation in transference-countertransference scenarios and dispassionate observation of his or her involvement. This balance is achieved through training, experience, and the disciplined self-observation to which we have referred throughout this volume.

7. The Importance of Therapist Flexibility in TLDP

The patients for whom TLDP is particularly suitable have marked difficulties with closeness and intimacy. The conscious and unconscious maneuvers they employ to ward off such experiences often make it difficult for the therapist to understand their emotional states and to intervene effectively. These patients tend to evoke negative reactions from the therapist who may feel "excluded" from the patient's emotional experience or drawn into it in a way that undermines the therapist's sense of integrity.

To deal with these problems, the therapist must be flexible, and in particular, adaptable in the communications, and in the kind of relationship offered. Flexibility can be expressed in a variety of ways that are not restricted to the technical or stylistic aspects of the therapist's activities. The therapist does not have to do something to promote the patient's enactments or to prove something about himself or herself. Indeed, to a considerable extent the therapist must be free enough to let things happen. This does not mean abandonment of the task orientation but it does mean an ability to participate in the patient's experience, to follow the patient's associations and fantasies, to engage in what Polanyi (1966) calls "indwelling." In this task, a measure of warmth, humor, and an appreciation of social graces can be extremely helpful. It is expected that good therapists possess these interpersonal skills.

Flexibility can be conceived of as an *attitude* that is incorporated into therapists' personal styles and implemented through their techniques. Among other things, it involves respect for the restrictions in the patient's interpersonal behavior. The therapist should not expect the patient to be someone he or she cannot be or to act in ways unnatural to the person. At the same time, the therapist does not subscribe to the view that the patient's current modes of relating are the only options.

The therapist accepts patients as they are, but also expresses a keen interest in their interpersonal relationships and their experience in these relationships. The therapist maintains an attitude of curiosity about patients, how they came to be who they are, why they cannot change, and the price they pay in terms of self-defeating behaviors, conflict, and pain. Without "pushing" patients (for example, by demanding that they reveal facets of themselves that are currently too painful to expose) the therapist seeks to help them understand why seemingly simple problems in interpersonal relations present such formidable difficulties.

The Therapist at Work (1). In the following account of a single therapeutic hour we shall exemplify a number of important principles and procedures followed by the TLDP therapist. In particular, the sequence illustrates in action terms the therapeutic alliance, the unfolding of a focal theme, and the therapist's interventions.

The patient, a professional woman in her mid-twenties, began the hour by reporting comments made by her husband about her moodiness. She soon turned to a discussion of "worries" relating to her job. Lately she had been waking up early, ruminating about her relationships with bosses and co-workers, and seeking advice and support from her husband. In her interaction with the therapist she expresses frustration mixed with anger. She is obviously distraught and seems to be on the verge of confronting the therapist with the message: "No one is helping me; you are of no help, either. I am angry at you and everyone else. Can't you see that I am helpless?" It may be seen that this woman is enacting a particular scenario with significant people in her life, including prominently the therapist, with whom she has a good working relationship and whom she tends to idealize. (The counterpart of placing men on a pedestal is her anger at them when they fail to "deliver," either because they are unable or unwilling to do so. Then she disparages them and in other respects gloats over their lack of omnipotence [the common shorthand term *castrating* might be applied to this pattern].) We may expect that her present-day behavior has roots in her childhood. Such is indeed the case, as we shall see, and reference to this background may help to make the pattern more vivid although it is probably not essential in order to bring about therapeutic change.

To understand the patient's current frustration, we must take a closer look at the work situation. During the preceding year, when the patient was new on the job (in which she demonstrated considerable skill, ingenuity, and leadership), she had the support of a male supervisor with whom, for the most part, she got along quite well. We shall call him Joe. In keeping with her general tendency, she idealized him. In the more recent past Joe had increasingly withdrawn from the supervisor role, putting the patient more on her own. She resented this (watch for parallel behavior with the therapist!) although, as the therapist pointed out later, Joe's behavior might also be interpreted as a vote of confidence since he seemed to consider her fully capable of managing the job more independently. (The therapist should also be forewarned to watch for the patient's dependency needs and not to gratify them.)

The preceding interpretation, in which the patient's experience of anger and helplessness at the boss's withdrawal is contrasted with an affirmation of her apparent strength, is often a useful therapeutic technique. It may be seen as an example of cognitive restructuring along lines also recommended by cognitive therapists.* Needless to say, such activities on the therapist's part are frequently resisted or dismissed by patients who may

---

*It may be opportune to comment here on the fact that the psychoanalytic approach and the recently popular cognitive orientation (the latter is often linked to behavior therapy) have important features in common. The same is undoubtedly true when techniques in other forms of psychotherapy are being closely examined. This fact underscores the virtual impossibility of isolating single techniques from any therapeutic approach to prove their effectiveness. We must recognize that all therapeutic approaches are broad gauged and extremely difficult to dissect.

turn their anger at the therapist. However, if a good therapeutic relationship exists and if the patient finds it difficult to dismiss or oppose the interpretation, it is more likely to play a constructive part in effecting change.

To complicate matters, the patient experienced marked anger at a co-worker, a woman of approximately equal rank in the organization, with whom she had various disagreements relating to the utilization of office space. One of the co-worker's tactics had been to cast aspersions on the patient's competence, which the latter deeply resented. However, she felt unable to defend herself or to fight back. Instead, she turned to male figures (Joe, her husband, and the therapist) for support. (Incidentally, the patient sought, from the beginning, to induce the therapist to give advice, a plea the latter had steadfastly declined because he identified it as loaded; that is, as a transference maneuver fraught with considerable although obscure meaning).* A previous therapist had complied with these requests. In the early phases of her work with the present therapist she sometimes compared him unfavorably with the previous one pointing to the latter's greater willingness to comply with her wishes. The present therapist had identified the situation as one in which one is damned if one does (by perpetuating the patient's dependency wishes) and damned if one declines (by frustrating these wishes).

The therapist gradually managed to make the patient see that (1) she was quite capable of making her own decisions; (2) it was clearly in her best interest to take charge of her life and to take action that was more in keeping with *her* own desires which she was in a better position to assess than anyone else; (3) she fundamentally resented advice proffered by others, even when she explicitly requested it; and (4) it was more important for both participants to understand her intense need to induce others to take charge of her life. (The latter, admittedly, is often not a very effective ploy because it may be seen as too intellectual and tantamount to reasoning with a child who urgently desires a piece of candy. Nonetheless, if there exists a measure of basic trust in the therapeutic relationship,

---

*Such occurrences are not uncommon; that is, a therapist may feel put upon, manipulated, or otherwise pressured to engage in a particular action, the reasons for which neither the therapist nor the patient may adequately understand at the time. Although there is no universal agreement on the subject, a therapist may succumb (while silently noting the event) to minor manipulations, such as questions about the therapist's health, the destination of a trip, and so on, rather than making an issue. However, where major dynamics are concerned, most therapists will draw a line, decline to participate in a scenario, and invite conjoint examination of the problem. It may take some time before the issue can be clarified. However, in keeping with the reenactment paradigm, we can expect the problem to be replayed in therapy at a later time provided it is an important issue and provided the therapist has done nothing to interfere with the reenactment.

the patient as an adult may be more amenable to tolerating the frustration and delay than would a three-year-old.)

The patient was the oldest child in a large family. Her mother, with whom she continued to have a markedly ambivalent relationship, was a rather controlling woman. In particular, she stifled her daughter's desire for independence in a variety of ways. On the other hand, she provided little genuine affection and seemed to harbor deep resentments of the feminine role (as did the patient). As might be expected, the father was experienced by the patient as a rather weak and ineffectual man who rarely enforced discipline and in other respects was also remote. Nonetheless, the patient had deep and affectionate feelings toward her father (and other men) whom she wished to please and by whom, in turn, she wished to be admired and loved. Not surprisingly, she saw her mother as a dangerous rival for her father's affection. Resenting and rejecting her mother's aggressiveness (which she detected within herself) it was difficult for the patient to assert herself, both on the job and in relation to her husband (as well as the therapist). Thus a familiar dilemma was created: If she asserted herself, she would "become" her mother, a prospect she abhorred; if she submitted, she might retain her father's approval and love but fail to realize her (rather considerable) talents. Either alternative would leave her angry and unfulfilled.

The parallel between the parent-daughter constellation and the conflict at work is striking. In therapy, too, the patient was avidly seeking the therapist's love and approval, alternately idealizing him and placing him in a position of power. Then, if the therapist fell short of the patient's expectations (by declining to give advice), there was the continual tendency for love to turn into anger and rage. The latter affects, however, had to be inhibited because of the pervasive fear relating to loss of love.

The therapist's stance throughout therapy was clear: He consistently communicated a respectful, accepting, and empathic attitude. (This was easy to do because the patient had many fine qualities including feminine appeal, and the therapist became genuinely fond of her.) Furthermore, the patient being a highly intelligent woman who possessed considerable ego resources approximated the "ideal patient." Accordingly, a productive collaborative relationship came into being and was sustained despite periodic punctuations by the patient's anger, impatience, demandingness, and frustration. The therapeutic task largely consisted of helping the patient understand the vicissitudes and turmoil in relationships with significant others (mother, husband, boss, co-workers, therapist). The latter was accomplished by listening to and partially participating in the scenarios that were enacted in therapy. At appropriate times, the therapist would present a succinct statement of the current conflict as he understood it. In so doing he consistently took the position of an ally who helped the patient realize her potential without interfering in the process. This took the form of identifying the nature of her conflict as it manifested itself again and again in seemingly diverse forms in her current life. It meant, in part, pointing out the manner in which she stood in her own way (for example, by pursuing mutually contradictory objectives, such as the wish to be assertive and independent while at the same time wanting to be "Daddy's little girl"; or her pronounced aversion to being a woman, which she identified with becoming like mother).

The dynamic focus in this case history may be seen in terms of several facets centering around her feminine identity. Of greater immediate consequence for therapy than such a broad overarching theme were the *action patterns,* a few of which have been mentioned in the foregoing discussion. Let us also emphasize the necessity of identifying and dealing with these patterns in detail and depth over a period of time. Certainly, no single interpretation is sufficient; indeed, it is far more common to recognize the necessity of many repetitions. The latter, in our experience, is a more typical course than for single, one-shot interventions to produce lasting change. It is in keeping with our belief that engrained cognitive, affective, and behavioral patterns are far more difficult to modify in most instances than is suggested by the writings of cognitive therapists.

In relating her complaints the patient expressed a fair amount of anger which was mixed with tears. Also, her feelings were, at least in part, directed at the therapist. The therapist's comments are paraphrased:

"Now let's take a look at the situation together. You experience quite a bit of anger at Joe whose support you feel you no longer have. Instead of letting you down, as you see it, we might say that he believes you are eminently capable of managing the problems yourself. In other words, he seems to have a good deal of confidence in your ability.

"But let us also take a look at something else. The struggle you have with your co-worker and the context of the job situation reminds me quite a bit of what you experienced at home when you were growing up. There seemed to be chaos in the sense that your father did not enforce discipline or 'lay down the law.' Anything went. You hoped he would assert himself, especially take your side against your mother (analogous to your co-worker) and in general support you. He failed to do so, and you were quite angry at him (as you are now angry at Joe). You also see yourself (as you saw yourself then) as weak and helpless. Thus, as you see it, it takes a man to take charge, run interference, straighten things out. What this ignores is your very marked ability to stand up for yourself and fight whatever battles need to be fought. We have seen a good bit of evidence that you can do it. In other words, you are not at all helpless.

"And there is still something else: As we have said before, if you assert yourself and, as you say, become 'bitchy,' you become your mother, something you definitely want to avoid. To be sure, whatever you do, you are not your mother. (This seemed important to underscore: similarity is not identity!) The way you resolve this conflict is by assuming a passive, compliant role. That denies your aggressive impulses and at the same time assures you of your father's continued love and affection. At least you then look to a powerful man to come to the rescue and bail you out. If he fails to do so (which, as you experience it, is Joe's situation as well as mine), you become angry and depreciate the man (there was some tangible evidence of this during the hour). Thus you wind up feeling angry and frustrated. If you assert yourself, you may not get exactly what you want but there is always that possibility."

The foregoing themes were being elaborated further during the hour which the therapist (and presumably the patient) experienced as quite productive. There appeared to be an appropriate context for making the particular comments and interpretations, and the timing seemed right. What made it right? Among the important ingredients, the following appear important: There was a solid and generally positive working relationship; there was ample empirical evidence to substantiate the comments advanced by the therapist, and the groundwork had been laid in previous therapy hours (the therapist said, in effect: "Here is another instance of what we have been talking about for some time"); sufficient affect had been mobilized so that the interpretations were far from being an intellectual exercise, which usually falls on deaf ears; a number of facets of the patient's current and past life appeared to fit together—they made sense to the therapist, and, the latter judged, also to the patient; the patient was willing to listen to the therapist (in other words, resistance was not too strong); and the therapist's comments, made in a spirit of collaboration and support, predictably strengthened the therapeutic alliance.

It is always possible to raise questions about the "correctness" of clarifications, constructions, and interpretations. We are in full agreement with other writers (Spence 1982) that veridicality cannot be established or proven. What matters is that the story which patient and therapist jointly create represents a constructive rewriting of the patient's history in terms that help the patient to view himself or herself in a new and more adaptive light. It must lead to development of a more constructive and valid self-image; and it must lead to more adaptive actions vis-à-vis significant others in the patient's current life. Psychotherapy of the kind we are describing involves the examination of specific experiences and events in the patient's current life, from which it is possible to abstract common themes, scenarios, scripts, and so on that unnecessarily complicate the person's interpersonal functioning.

The Therapist at Work (2). The following is another vignette of therapeutic work within the TLDP framework. In many respects, this patient presented greater challenges to the therapist than the preceding one.

The patient was a professional man in his late twenties. Highly intelligent and quite successful, there had been several detours in his professional development. Only lately had he shown a desire to build a career and settle down, which included marriage. A persistent problem had been perfectionism, rebelliousness, and considerable anger. The latter was directed at significant others in his life, notably male authority figures, including of course the therapist. The course of therapy vividly expressed the patient's interpersonal difficulties. For example, he frequently canceled scheduled hours requesting a different time than the one that had been mutually agreed upon, arrived late, and chose a chair farther away than the one designated by the therapist. While appropriately respectful toward the therapist, he portrayed an imperious and arrogant attitude, challenging the therapist to provide quick and easy solutions. At the same time, his attitude appeared to be a thin veneer hiding the keen desire for a powerful (male) helper upon whom he could lean and who might mitigate his corrosive self-critical attitudes.

The latter set of attitudes may be seen as manifestations of an excessively severe and punitive superego. Indeed, the patient's difficulties, and the dynamic focus, might be characterized as hypertrophied superego. In common diagnostic parlance, the patient is readily seen as suffering from a relatively severe obsessive-compulsive personality disorder. In daily life, the problem manifested itself in terms of marked intolerance of shortcomings, both in himself and others, perennial anger when someone made a mistake or otherwise demonstrated imperfection which underscored the patient's failure to be in full control of his life or insufficiently conscientious in discharging his duties and obligations. While attempting to achieve a state of perfect control in himself and others—a task in which he obviously failed—he would become enraged and engage in verbal fights with his fiancée and other significant people in his life. Thus, confronted with failure of his missionary zeal, he would become angry and, secondarily, depressed. (One might also note that this pattern produced greater interpersonal distance.) A major presenting complaint was his waning sexual interest in his fiancée and recurrent sexual preoccupations with women whom he passed on the street. In short, his life, while superficially okay, was a "living hell" from which he sought escape.

The major therapeutic task, in the therapist's judgment, was to mitigate the patient's overly severe superego (a task, as seasoned therapists will recognize, of sizable proportions). Let us consider the array of forces: On the positive side, we have a patient who is highly intelligent and reasonably well motivated for therapy. Although a relatively unreliable collaborator in therapeutic work, he is sufficiently troubled by his problems to enlist therapeutic help and he may be expected to collaborate with the therapist at least up to a point. While his attitudes toward the latter were markedly ambivalent, he respected the therapist as a person and as a professional. He also had certain skills of introspection, was not greatly impelled to engage in significant antisocial acting out, had a sense of humor, and was experienced by the therapist as quite likable. On the negative side of the ledger were the patient's pronounced anger and hostility, his rebelliousness vis-à-vis male authority figures, his need to challenge and defeat them, his perfectionism, rigidity, and corrosive self-derogation.

The therapist's objective was to build a good therapeutic alliance and to establish himself as a more accepting, benign, and nonpunitive authority figure, with whom the patient could identify and who might thus aid in the task of ameliorating a tightly organized superego. While proceeding on this major front it would also be important to invite careful scrutiny of the manner in which the patient's tightly knit belief system was linked or gave rise to a series of maladaptive and self-defeating behaviors. The latter were the problems of which the patient complained, over which he claimed to have no control, and which interfered seriously with his present-day adjustment. As with other symptoms, the patient must come to realize that instead of being the victim of powerful forces he plays a crucial role in abetting them. (This is the operational counterpart of Freud's epigram: Where id was, there shall ego be.)

This is an ambitious objective, the likelihood of whose realization, as experts have recognized (Salzman 1968), is rather slight in the short run. This would be true particularly if therapy were restricted to 25 hours. (It would be more realistic to think in terms of several hundred hours!) Yet an initial block of 25 hours might serve to induct the patient into the patient role, demonstrate that therapy can help, and perhaps raise his motivation to engage in more intensive and prolonged therapeutic work.

In working with this patient, the therapist recognized the following major hazards: On the one hand, he ostensibly came to enlist help; on the other, he was unwittingly but firmly committed to sabotaging the therapeutic effort. As previously noted, this would take the form of tampering with the external arrangements. Failing to provoke the therapist, a likely alternative was to depreciate him. This, of course, would maintain the homeostasis of a system in which the patient aggresses, is then being aggressed against, revolts, submits, and ultimately is defeated.

In the hour under discussion (the 12th) the therapist sought to implement the task previously described. While pursuing his role as a benign but firm and incorruptible authority, he endeavored to help the patient recognize the manner in which his rigid patterns which seemed to reel off automatically were in fact maneuvers which were both created by him and in whose enactment he played a very active role. The hour was one of those instances in which the therapist was keenly aware of the reciprocal role the patient intended him to play but in which there was no explicit discussion of the patient-therapist relationship. In our experience there are many such hours, and we see their occurrence as no contradiction to major TLDP principles. Rather we believe that there must be sufficient flexibility in the conduct of therapy to permit the pursuit of major therapeutic objectives without slavish adherence to a formula. In other words, while we would insist that the therapist should always be cognizant of his or her intended reciprocal role as well as the transactions between patient and therapist, there should not be a monolithic rule that the topic must be discussed with the patient during every hour. If such a formula is invoked, patients tend to defeat it, saying, for example: "I knew you would get around to asking how I feel toward you. What I discussed has nothing to do with you and I have no feelings about you."

With this patient, the therapist introduced the concept of the superego, describing its controlling, disciplining, and punitive function as well as its inexorableness and peremptory demands. This occurred after the patient had given numerous examples of his perfectionistic trends, his intolerance of human failing in himself and significant others, and his general discomfort in the face of these events. He was also emotionally aroused, that is, distraught, by what appeared to be happening to him. The therapist outlined some of the important consequences of the patient's conflict: "You alternately criticize and punish yourself for any imperfection you might detect in your own or someone else's behavior. Your superego insists on perfection. If there is the slightest flaw in someone's behavior, you are in for criticism and punishment. If you rebel against your superego or try to flout it, you evoke its displeasure which then necessitates your being punished. If you obey its dictates, you feel controlled and subjugated; you then feel the urge to rebel. When you rebel, you feel guilty for being disobedient, and you must then be punished. So you can't win ... The only solution I can see (this was said *very* calmly) is to work out some kind of compromise that allows the warring parties to have greater tolerance for each other." (The therapist might have expanded the discussion to include the father-son relationship in childhood but pursuit of that topic seemed premature or inopportune.) The interpretation, if one wishes to call it that,* appealed to the rational and reasonable part of the patient's ego; it averted a potential attack upon the therapist while instead strengthening the therapist's position as an ally; it opened up avenues for further discussion as opposed to foreclosing the issue; it stringently avoided disapproval or criticism of the patient (which might be the single most counter-therapeutic move in this case!); and it began to build a wedge between the patient's automatic behavior and potentially greater autonomy.

Obstacles to Therapeutic Progress

In attempting to implement the TLDP approach, the therapist often faces serious obstacles produced by the emotional conflicts typical of TLDP patients. Their chronic and severe difficulties in interpersonal relationships inevitably become manifest in psychotherapy as resistances to therapeutic work, and these impediments are clearly of great importance in TLDP.

1. The Concept of Resistance in Psychoanalytic Therapy

According to the traditional psychoanalytic view, resistances serve three major psychodynamic functions: (1) they impede the uncovering of an unconscious conflict; (2) once a conflict is reactivated in therapy, they interfere with the renunciation of unconscious wishes and fantasies associated with the conflict; and (3) they reflect the patient's general reluctance to experiment with new and more adaptive behavior (Dewald 1982).

*We have increasingly come to feel that *interpretations* may be a poor and potentially misleading term. *Restructuring* may be preferable because it describes more precisely the process of infusing the patient's self-experience and view of the world with new meaning. Interpretation, on the other hand is reminiscent of crystal-ball gazing or Joseph's interpretations of Pharaoh's dreams. The latter carries with it the implication that there is a specific underlying meaning that must be discovered by the therapist and communicated to the patient. In our view, the process involves identification of a belief, fantasy, and so on, that is rarely specific or capable of being translated in the manner suggested by the term interpretation. More typically, we are dealing with attempts to impose a different and more adaptive structure on the patient's mental processes. These are approximations to truths which are plausible and internally consistent but at least in part idiosyncratic of the patient-therapist relationship. There are no immutable truths in this realm!

Freud (1909, *S.E., 10*) originally viewed resistance as an obstacle to uncovering and resolving the patient's repressed conflicts. Accordingly, the goal of therapy was to overcome the patient's resistances. As Freud's (1923, *S.E., 19;* 1926, *S.E., 20*) thinking evolved, resistance assumed an expanded role in the ego's defensive functions which came to be seen as permeating the patient's character structure and modes of interpersonal functioning (Reich 1933). Building on these changing conceptions, A. Freud (1936) further developed the view of resistance as a reflection of the defensive organization of the ego. Thus, analysis of resistances came to be seen as crucial for understanding and modifying the patient's maladaptive patterns of behavior. By the same token, sensitivity to even subtle signs of resistance became an increasingly important part of the therapist's skill.

Today, the prevailing view of resistance remains based on the ego psychological model. Thus, resistances are activated in therapy to prevent the therapist—and of course the patient—from grasping the nature of the neurotic conflict. Resistances, however, are no longer viewed as obstacles to be eliminated as a prelude to change; instead, they are to be examined and understood as psychic operations that interfere with the therapeutic process, of which they are an integral part.

This view still assumes that resistances are forces within the patient that function as impediments to therapeutic progress. With more recent developments in ego psychology, therapists have come to appreciate how massive the barriers may be. Thus, the emphasis of long-term dynamic therapy has gradually shifted from uncovering unconscious conflict to the more difficult and time-consuming task of working through the patient's character resistances. A related assumption is that as a psychic mechanism resistances operate impersonally, as though they were programmed automatically to oppose exploratory and interpretive efforts. In particular, resistances obstruct the full expression of transference and the articulation of genetic connections (Schafer 1983).

The major short-term dynamic therapies are to varying degrees influenced by these assumptions about the identification and management of resistances. Without the luxury of unlimited time in which cautiously to analyze resistant behavior, some short-term therapists believe that resistances must be confronted and attacked with a relentless spirit, in order to pave the way for genetic transference interpretations (Davanloo 1978, 1980). The adversarial tenor of this approach, however, may cause many therapists to shrink from a systematic analysis of resistances. The result is a situation akin to the traditional status of transference analysis: more attention is given to it in theory than in practice (Schafer 1983). Another untoward consequence of the confrontative approach is that the patient may affectively run for cover and engage in more subtle forms of resistance. In other words, if the therapist views resistances as a form of oppositional behavior, he or she may lose touch with the manner in which patients are prone to construe the therapist's interpretive efforts in terms of conflictual interpersonal themes. For example, the patient may experience the therapist's confrontation of intellectualized communications as a reprimand and respond with masochistic submission, seeming compliance with a person in authority, or secret defiance. Other forms of subtle resistance may be digressions to issues outside of therapy or preoccupations with childhood history—all in order to escape from what patients may experience as potentially dangerous antagonism between them and the therapist.

Despite its many ramifications, the concept of resistance remains central to all forms of psychodynamic psychotherapy. The concept embodies theoretical assumptions concerning the meaning of neurotic conflicts and their behavioral expression. In practice, the meaning and function of resistance is anchored in the therapist's theoretical conceptions of the therapeutic process and its goals. As Schlesinger (1982) pointed out, *resistance* is not a term that describes behavior but one that seeks to explain it. While resistances may take many forms, all dynamic therapists agree that they serve to protect the patient from experiencing painful affects which are related to conflicts. Resistances, like all behavior, have no invariant meanings and their clinical significance depends on the therapeutic context.

2. The Definition of Resistance in TLDP

In keeping with the interpersonal perspective developed in this book, resistance is viewed as a process phenomenon—an integral part of the transactions between patient and therapist. Resistances, specifically, refer to the nature of the relationship in which patient and therapist participate. We view resistances not as the mere expression of oppositional psychic functions but rather, from the patient's viewpoint, as unconsciously derived personal actions aimed at maintaining a sense of security and avoiding some form of danger, and directed by unconsciously held convictions about oneself and others. We conceptualize resistance as patterns of construing experiences and as modes of behavior based on those subjective views (Schafer 1983; Schlesinger 1982).

In this context resistances represent impediments to a collaborative experience. The feelings and fantasies underlying the patient's defensive operations may be obscure, but they are more or less subtly woven into the nuances of the patient-therapist relationship. They may be transformed into the metaphoric content of the patient's associations, the actions and reactions of either participant, the inner experiences of the therapist, or other aspects of the therapeutic relationship. Consequently, in dealing with the patient's resistances, the therapist effects changes in the therapeutic relationship and therefore in the patient's personality structure. It is important to remember that we are referring to personal actions, no matter how the therapist may experience their consequences. The following vignette illustrates our meaning:

The patient was a young woman in her early twenties who had been unable to follow through on educational or career goals. Furthermore, she had been unable to sustain a satisfying romantic relationship and repeatedly engaged in angry exchanges with her parents regarding her future. She suffered from periodic bouts of depression associated with her inability to find a direction for her life. In the treatment a transference enactment emerged which paralleled the pattern of conflictual relations with her parents. She acted like an ineffectual, helpless waif who needed others to guide her. By engaging in various sorts of self-defeating behaviors, she provoked others (her parents, her therapist) to assume an authoritarian role. However, the patient experienced the attempts by others to advise her as judgmental and condescending, and she reacted with anger and stubbornness. During one session, the patient related how she had missed several days of work, thus endangering her new job. When she told her parents, they had accused her of being irresponsible. Her female therapist had attempted to engage the patient in an examination of the consequences of her recent actions but at the same time had realized that she was irritated with the patient. The therapist also had sensed the patient's anger. However, when she attempted to explore the patient's feelings, the latter quickly stated that she did not know what she felt.

In supervision the therapist had stated that she repeatedly ran up against a blank wall and that the patient was very resistant. However, as the supervisor examined this metaphor with the therapist, it became clear that it reflected the therapist's exasperation with her patient as well as her feeling of being at a loss over what to do. Together they were able to see that the therapist's association of a blank wall captured her reaction to a specific pattern of personal action by the patient, namely, her stubborn refusal to cooperate with an adult who was experienced as judgmental and condescending. In other words, this resistant patient was unconsciously taking a reasonable course of action in terms of how she experienced the therapeutic relationship; she was protecting herself against the ridicule and criticism she expected from her irritated therapist. Once the therapist was able to view the patient's behavior in this light, she was able to intervene in a more helpful manner. At the next opportunity, when the patient stated that she did not know what she felt, the therapist inquired about the rapidity with which the patient responded, which did not even afford her the opportunity to think about the therapist's question. This opened a discussion of why the patient took this stance, which led to a more profitable examination of the transference enactment in which they both had been immersed.

3. The Identification of Resistances

Clearly, the most important clues to the existence of current resistances are found in the patient-therapist relationship, and more specifically in the patient's manner of relating to the therapist from the first interview on. The following vignette illustrates the operation of resistant behavior in the third interview. By examining this resistance, the therapist was able to further the joint understanding of the therapeutic focus:

The patient was a recently divorced professional woman in her late thirties. Married for fifteen years, she had obtained a divorce within the past year because of chronic unhappiness in her marriage to a man whom she described as emotionally insensitive and critical. While intellectually evaluating the relationship as unsalvageable, the patient still found herself longing for a reconciliation. She suffered from symptoms of depression and anxiety, and could not bring herself to date. Furthermore, she was preoccupied with the fantasy that her husband was a changed man with his new girl friend; he was considerate, empathic, loving—in short demonstrating all of the qualities lacking in the marriage. Part of this fantasy was the nagging belief that the new girl friend could bring out these qualities, whereas the patient had not been able to do so.

The initial focus was directed at attempting to understand why the patient could not emotionally let go of longings to reunite with her ex-husband. At the start of the third session the patient asked the therapist for guidance concerning topics to discuss, ostensibly because she was concerned whether she could adequately handle her part of the undertaking. Rather than remaining silent or again asking the patient to free associate, the therapist questioned the implications of the patient's lack of confidence in participating. Together they identified the patient's vulnerability to feeling criticized for disappointing someone in authority, whether it was her employer, ex-husband, and so on. The therapist was able to point out that even in their first session the patient had feared that the therapist would disapprove of an affair that had occurred several years previously. They also were able to articulate a particularly painful concern that the patient had failed her ex-husband and, consequently, had lost a special and irreplaceable relationship. The patient was struck by this realization because she knew that her marriage had not had these qualities. As a result of this work, the patient evidenced increased involvement in the therapeutic relationship.

It can be seen that resistance is part and parcel of the patient's characteristic mode of relating and can, therefore, manifest itself in *any* form of behavior, no matter how seemingly innocuous, trivial, or characteristic. Because therapists can be lulled into ignoring such characteristic behavior, let us further illustrate this point:

A married man in his early thirties entered treatment because of a chronic sense of occupational failure, unhappiness in his marriage which included almost no sexual activity, and a profound sense of worthlessness. He was the oldest of two children whose parents had divorced when the patient was four years old. The mother was a cold, strict woman who appeared more interested in her work than in child rearing. Since childhood the patient had felt that his mother and sister were allies and shared a contempt for men, including the patient. In therapy with a male therapist, the patient presented himself as a cosmic flaw who did not deserve to take up any of the "godlike" therapist's time. This self-effacing presentation, and the patient's corresponding intense dysphoria, continued until the therapist finally realized a dramatic inconsistency in the patient's behavior. For some time the therapist had been impressed with the eloquence of the patient's style of talking; he demonstrated an impressive vocabulary, used metaphors with astonishing creativity, and his grammar was flawless. What finally struck the therapist was the contradiction inherent in the patient's relentless self-denunciations of being flawed and worthless and the impressively eloquent style in which these denunciations were delivered. When the therapist confronted the patient with the contradiction inherent in his captivating manner of depicting himself as worthless, it ushered in important work on the patient's competitiveness with men, his secret feeling of power over them, in certain circumstances, and his sense of magnanimous grandiosity. The inception of work on these issues marked a turning point in the treatment.

It can be seen that a therapist will be most likely to identify resistance if he or she attends to immediately observable behavior. The therapist is aided by the fact that a current theme will usually be replayed by the patient with many variations that eventually make sense to the sensitive listener.

Clinical discussions of resistance are often inconsistent. In dynamic terms, as we have noted, it is often characterized as an oppositional force; at other times, it is described in more static terms as a wall which must be chipped away. It can be assumed that such diverse metaphors represent therapists' subjective reactions to the particular quality of patients' resistant behavior. By remaining attentive to specific reactions to the patient, including the metaphors that occur to the therapist, the latter can often further understanding of the current resistance. Let us illustrate this point with a clinical vignette:

The patient was a chronically depressed young, single woman. She evidenced a pattern of behavior in heterosexual relationships in which, by portraying herself as helpless and childlike, she seduced aggressive, macho men. Once the patient entered into a sexual relationship with these men, she would entice them to open up emotionally and then she would drop them. Concurrent with these brief relationships, the patient maintained a long-standing relationship with an emotionally subdued, passive man, whom she considered a wimp. While this sexual relationship was unsatisfying to her and while she found him intellectually uninteresting, she considered marriage to him. Although the patient was quite successful in her career, she felt directionless. Her family background was tumultuous. She had a brother who was an alcoholic and two sisters with whom she felt intensely competitive. Her mother, who had died some years before, had paraded around the house inappropriately dressed in scanty clothing. The patient's father, who had died a few years after his wife, had been a compulsive gambler and had carried on affairs for many years.

Early in the therapy, the patient had openly attempted to seduce the therapist. When this had proven unsuccessful, she had begun to examine her profound ambivalence toward men. After a few months, however, the patient began to express increasing frustration with her male therapist for not opening up and revealing more of himself. The patient described herself as stuck and expressed a growing disinterest in working in the treatment. While in supervision the therapist described feeling up against something and that the therapy had reached an impasse. In the course of discussing these metaphors referring to the state of the therapeutic relationship, the therapist was able to see that, unable (in her typical manner) to seduce the therapist, the patient had been forced to struggle with her fearful mistrust of men. Similarly unable to freely experience emotions with her therapist, she felt stuck. On his part, the therapist experienced the patient's profound mistrust and consequent affective constriction as a barrier which he was up against. During this discussion, it occurred to the therapist that his patient was not able to open up sexually unless she felt in complete control of the sexual activity in which she participated. He realized that his patient was terrified by the prospect of losing control of her feelings, of losing herself in sexual passion, and of unleashing murderous rage toward men. He returned to the therapeutic work less confused and frustrated.

While in TLDP the therapist continually evaluates the state of the therapeutic relationship for evidence of resistant behavior, patients tend to avoid recognizing that they experience and react to the therapeutic relationship in any way other than an uncomplicated professional fashion. The fact that the therapeutic relationship, like any human encounter, is influenced by hopes, fears, and the gamut of other emotions, tends to be ignored. In addition, the specific constellation of affects, attitudes, and behavior characterizing a particular transference enactment tends to be experienced as the only reality of the moment, and therefore it is not questioned. These "resistances to the awareness of transference" represent the most pervasive form of resistance in psychotherapy, yet therapists too often fail to examine them systematically (Gill 1979; Gill and Hoffman 1982). By endeavoring to make this form of resistance the primary target of therapeutic work, TLDP attempts to rectify a major technical deficiency in the routine practice of dynamic psychotherapy, whether it be time limited or open ended.

4. The Management of Resistances

In inviting the patient to examine a resistance, the therapist is implicitly challenging a rigid mode of relatedness. Since patients (unconsciously) dare not relinquish habitual patterns that serve to maintain some form of interpersonal security, it is expected that they will often intensify defensive efforts (dig in) or substitute others that serve the same purpose. Patients are impelled to cling tenaciously to their view of the world and to structure current experience with significant others, particularly the therapist, in accordance with these expectations.

Thus, the patient's immediate responses to the therapist's interventions may reflect increased attempts to guard against revealing the details of discomforts in interpersonal relationships. At such times, the wisest course of action is not necessarily to retreat until greater rapport develops or the patient becomes less apprehensive. Similarly, if the therapist's interventions produce increments in anxiety, it does not necessarily follow that the therapist is pushing the patient too hard. It must be remembered that resistance, transference, and the patient's characteristic ways of relating to the therapist are all different facets of the same attitudes and behavior. Consequently, as noted earlier, by not immediately and systematically attending to resistances, the therapist may become oblivious to patients' character styles and accept them as the "way they are." The result can be that the therapist begins to question characterological expressions of resistance much later than is desirable, which at the least, may unnecessarily prolong the treatment.

In general, it is to be expected that when the therapist approaches affectively charged issues, the patient will become anxious and seek protection by habitual techniques (anger, withdrawal). The therapist's response may then consist of pointing out the specific ways in which the patient seeks to keep himself or herself (and the therapist) in the dark about the affective experiences. The following case material is an example of this point:

A divorced woman in her late thirties sought treatment, complaining of depression and loneliness. She had a few superficial relationships with women and no current contacts with men, even though she was very attractive. She viewed as the source of her problems several childhood episodes in which she had been sexually fondled by her father. The patient felt that these experiences had left a mark, and she wanted her male therapist to discuss the consequences. While this woman appeared to be of at least average intelligence, she acted scatterbrained and flaky. Furthermore, she repeatedly called herself a dodo and contrasted her alleged stupidity with the therapist's assumed great learning and intelligence.

From the first couple of interviews, the therapist focused on examining how the patient sought so relentlessly to present herself as flighty and dumb. When the therapist questioned why the patient appeared to cling so tenaciously to this self-image, she would often ask what he thought or request constructive guidance. At such times, the therapist would point out that the patient was again acting as though she had no resources that would aid in their collaborative work. After numerous interchanges on this topic over several sessions, the patient was able to begin talking about her disappointment and bitterness toward men, starting with her father and reinforced over several unhappy romantic relationships. They were also able to articulate her fear that were she to begin expressing her bitter feelings, she would be consumed by them and appear ugly to other people. It became apparent to the patient that her dumb act served to avoid the danger of becoming an ugly embittered recluse; accordingly, it was preferable to be thought of as a good-hearted dodo.

Conscious affects may disguise as well as disclose the patient's focal conflict. Some patients may manifest intense and recurrent affect; others may not recognize or express relevant affects and they may be seen as intellectualizing. The therapist who advances interpretations in that context may likewise intellectualize. As therapists generally recognize, interpretations made in the absence of affect tend to have limited impact although at times they may clarify an issue in a preliminary way. Yet both ways of dealing with affects may be expressions of resistance which may blind the patient to the possibility of alternative ways of relating to the therapist. In all instances, the therapist must attempt to understand which aspects of the therapeutic relationship give rise to the observed patient state.

If the patient becomes so caught up in a currently enacted scenario that the working alliance is impeded, the therapist may wonder aloud whether the patient's way of construing their relationship is the only valid or possible one. If the patient can experience the therapist's questions as supportive (as opposed to being antagonistic, critical, or demeaning), the stage is set for a resumption of collaborative examination.

5. The Therapist's Resistances

Since resistance arises in the patient-therapist relationship, it can therefore be expressed by either participant. The patient relates in the only way he or she can. If the therapist fails to empathize with the resisting patient or plays a reciprocal role (by becoming impatient, attacking, and so on), he or she becomes an opponent in the battle the patient needs to wage for self-protective reasons. In that event, the therapeutic relationship becomes a replica of the past, without the possibility of a new ending. On the other hand, by participating in the patient's struggle as a limited coactor, the therapist can mediate therapeutic change. Resistance, as we have noted, is inextricably interwoven with transference and countertransference; indeed, all are facets of the same process.

We previously described the young woman who felt "stuck" in her treatment, and it was determined that she was profoundly mistrustful of men and frightened of losing control of her sexual and aggressive feelings.

It will be recalled that her mother had walked around the house in inappropriately scanty clothes and had died. The patient's father had been an alcoholic and had carried on affairs for many years. When drunk the father would accuse the patient of being a slut. As the treatment progressed and the patient became emotionally freer with her therapist, a new theme emerged in her communications: the expectation that people of importance to her would be insensitive to her emotional turmoil, would not help her control her behavior, and in fact would leave her. It was during this time that the therapist took a short vacation and "forgot" to inform the patient until the last session before he left. When the therapist returned, the patient appeared more depressed and talked of moving to another city where she might be happier. She shared with her therapist old letters written to her father before his death, which revealed her longings for a close, affectionate and protective relationship with a man. While discussing these letters, the patient entered into a long monologue about her interest in writing, and the therapist found himself being bored.

This therapist was usually empathic, conscientious, and was specifically fond of this patient. He wondered why he had neglected to inform the patient earlier about his short absence, and he further wondered why he had felt so bored with her recently. In discussing his recent actions and feelings with his supervisor, the therapist realized that as his patient felt that their relationship was assuming greater importance to her, she had self-defeatingly (and unconsciously) acted so as to evoke his boredom, thereby confirming her expectation that someone of importance would be insensitive to her feelings and needs. In this instance, at the same time that the patient talked of longing for a closer relationship, the intellectualized monologue about her writing interests served to deaden the therapist's sensitivity to her longings.

Therapist resistance may also arise from the manner in which TLDP is conducted. The therapist must appreciate the forces working against remaining consistently attentive to the contemporary transactions in therapy. By asking patients to explore feelings about the therapeutic relationship, therapists face the discomfort of evoking emotional pain as well as allowing themselves to become the target of feelings, fantasies, and perceptions that may threaten their own self-image and self-esteem. The therapist's consequent counterresistances may lead to a variety of rationalizations that may take the following forms: (1) the patient needs more time to develop trust in the therapist before painful issues can be broached; (2) if an interpretation of resistance is made and the patient does not give up the resistance, it is best to wait for a more propitious moment; (3) if the patient does not respond positively to an interpretation of resistance, the therapist may conclude that he or she is off the mark. These considerations can sound convincing because they may contain a kernel of truth, but in the final analysis, it is often preferable to confront resistances directly, particularly if they threaten the working alliance.

6. Consequences of not Examining the Therapeutic Relationship

The TLDP therapist can face the tension generated by examining the therapeutic relationship only by means of consistent self-discipline. In falling short of these requirements, the therapist avoids the emotionally arduous work of understanding his or her own role in the patient's maladaptive modes of relating. Under these circumstances, therapeutic progress may still occur; however, it may turn out to be illusory because it rests on an unwitting collusion with the patient's self-protective but maladaptive modes of coping.

For instance, it is almost axiomatic that if the therapist takes a relaxed, friendly, and supportive stance from the beginning, the patient tends to form a significant although sometimes disguised attachment to the therapist. The patient may then feel more secure and comfortable than in any other relationship. However, if this positively toned relationship has been engendered by a therapist who primarily attends to the patient's difficulties outside of therapy, there are certain regularly occurring consequences: The patient may feel supported in struggles with day-to-day problems but sense that underlying basic issues are being bypassed. From time to time the patient may have fleeting thoughts about the therapeutic relationship. However, if the therapist deals superficially with these concerns or ignores them, the patient will tend to dismiss them as trivial, which in turns reinforces the avoidance of unsettling feelings about the therapeutic relationship.

Although a positive relationship with the therapist can result in therapeutic improvements, failure to identify and resolve conflictual relationship predispositions results in their continued influence on relationships outside of therapy as well as within therapy. In a similar vein, Langs (1976) refers to "misalliance cures," and Malan (1976a) speaks of "false solutions." In time-limited dynamic psychotherapy such developments may lead to an undesirable prolongation of therapy because at the planned termination the patient may feel that the work has just started or, if the therapist adheres to a specified termination date, the patient may feel abandoned.

A Note on Inertia. One of the notorious failings of young therapists is their lack of patience. Having identified a neurotic conflict and made an interpretation they at once expect miraculous changes in the patient's feelings and behavior. Conversely, they become discouraged when they observe that change is often painfully slow and that patients persist in their habitual patterns of behavior regardless of their adverse and painful consequences. Freud dubbed this phenomenon "repetition compulsion," and behavior therapists have written at length about the patient's "reinforcement history." The term *functional autonomy* (Allport 1937) is yet another way of speaking about the persistence of human behavior. Whatever the terminology, every therapist has made the observation that behavior change tends to be slow, sometimes excruciatingly so. There is a strong conservative element in human behavior, for the good reason that what one has always done lends security and predictability to one's behavior and that of others. Many patterns of behavior have been acquired automatically, that is, their rationale has never been examined in the cold light of day. Often they have been learned in childhood when the individual was weak and helpless and unable to assess the long-range utility of a particular way of acting or reacting. Examples are ubiquitous: One feels neglected and has one's feelings hurt. One experiences a setback and blames oneself for one's alleged shortcomings. One asserts oneself in relation to a spouse or subordinates and finds that the other person has withdrawn his or her unconditional love, which proves devastating. One's child appears to be unhappy, a state of affairs which "obviously" must be the parent's fault.

In terms of systems theory, one continually programs and is in turn programmed by significant others to behave in particular ways. We have chosen partners who, for reasons of their own, engage in patterns of behavior reciprocal to ours. For example, we may have a need to hold someone responsible for our feelings of discouragement or depression. But we have also selected someone who stands ready to assume guilt: we aggress against them, and they aggress against us; we punish them, and they punish us; they collaborate in our self-defeating behavior, and we often reciprocate in kind. Unless a relationship fulfills complementary needs, it does not endure. Consequently, if one partner, perhaps as a result of a therapist's interventions changes his or her behavior, this disturbs the equilibrium of the system, and the other partner, now confused because the expected pattern of behavior is no longer forthcoming, may become disturbed and fight for its reinstatement. In this way, therapy sometimes leads to divorce. The thrust of the attack may become directed against the therapist who, intent upon inducing change, becomes a disturber of the peace, someone who evokes anxiety, and who, therefore, is being opposed. As always in therapy, the trick is to steer a course which on the one hand maintains sufficient tension, thereby keeping the patient motivated, and on the other, prevents the experience of too much anxiety.

Therapists who push for change may be particularly vulnerable to being defeated but those who avoid the issue may defeat themselves. Freud already recognized that a phobic patient must eventually confront the anxiety-provoking situation and learn to tolerate the unpleasant affect. In other words, analyzing the determinants of a conflict may not be sufficient to resolve it. In modern times, behavior therapists have similarly noted the salutary effects of *in vivo* exposure to anxiety-provoking situations. Even when we are not dealing with a full-blown phobia, the reluctance to abandon well-worn patterns of behavior may be considerable. The kinds of behavior (patterns of thinking, feeling, and acting) we are seeking to change in psychotherapy are often deeply entrenched—they have been practiced (overlearned) for many years and the patient's world has been built around them. There are no magical solutions, and the best a therapist can do, after a conflict has been exposed and dealt with in some measure, is to define the problem for the patient and to leave its management in his or her hands.

7. Therapist Errors in TLDP

Errors in psychoanalytic psychotherapy are usually viewed as a mixture of two types: (1) technical errors (misapplications of technique, such as premature interpretations), or (2) failures of empathy (being insufficiently attuned to the patient's subjective experience, misunderstanding the nature of the patient's current conflict). It is generally expected that the therapist will become aware of errors and thus be able to take appropriate steps to correct them. Self-awareness, consultation with colleagues, supervision, and personal therapy are the traditional means by which technical skills are perfected and honed.

By its very nature, TLDP may create special hazards. For example: (1) the patient may subtly pressure the therapist into abdicating a neutral stance; (2) the role as participant observer may make the therapist more vulnerable to acquiescing in the patient's wishes and demands; (3) the activity demanded of the therapist may, by itself, increase the opportunity for errors; (4) the therapist's continual awareness of time limits may induce a sense of inadequacy, of not doing enough, or seeking to accelerate the therapeutic process in a variety of ways.

It is almost axiomatic that the TLDP therapist cannot be effective without risking entrapment in the patient's scenario. He or she may become victimized by a seemingly innocuous question, a sly provocation, an innuendo, and a wide range of other snares. Patients are often singularly adept at ferreting out the therapist's weak spots and vulnerabilities. Thus, the therapist is bound to commit involuntary errors. While often irksome and sometimes infuriating, they are an integral part of the fabric of therapy. Judiciously used and understood for what they are—namely, inevitable responses to the patient's self-protective maneuvers in the face of misperceived interpersonal dangers—the therapist's errors may further rather than hinder the progress of therapy. They may also provide a valuable antidote to the therapist's sense of omnipotence, perhaps the single most serious occupational hazard in all forms of psychotherapy.

Chapter 8

Case History Illustrating the TLDP Approach

Introduction

In order to illustrate the TLDP concepts that have been discussed in the preceding chapters, we will present an annotated version of an actual therapy. While reviewing this case, we realized that there were many places where, in retrospect, we could have handled things in a different manner. Of course, this reaction reflects the inevitable (and healthy) Monday morning quarterbacking that is associated with reflecting upon one's own clinical work or that of one's colleagues. In addition, however, it reflects continued changes and, we hope, improvements in our conceptual understanding of the therapeutic process and corollary modifications in technique. Some of our most recent thinking has been incorporated into the commentary that accompanies the case transcript. However, a case presentation can only illustrate an approach as it is understood and practiced at one point in time. It cannot capture the continuing evolution of the approach as new ideas are incorporated into a working model.

As we struggled with this communication problem, it occurred to us that many of the time-limited therapy models are presented as though they were final products of their creators. There is, of course, no area of human endeavor, whether it is in science or art (and psychotherapy surely has elements of both), in which complete understanding or final truths, have been achieved. Certainly in the area of psychotherapy—where there exist so many competing theories, where technique is so intimately intertwined with the therapist's style, and where research technology is still so new—it is axiomatic that there must be continual improvement in theory and technique.

The point to be made is that TLDP represents an attempt to integrate experiences accruing from our clinical practices, selected contemporary theoretical developments, and the most recent products of our research efforts. Each of these components is continually changing as a result of new clinical observations, reworking of concepts, new research evidence, and of course, the interaction of all three. The case history is presented in that spirit of tentativeness which, we believe, should characterize all writings on psychotherapy.

Background

The patient was a career woman in her late thirties, who had been married for ten years and had two children. She sought psychotherapy for feelings of anxiety and depression which had lasted for several years. She described herself as having little joy in her life, feeling overwhelmed by work (even though she performs well), and having no sexual interest in her husband. The patient expressed resentment of her husband for not helping enough with child rearing but was unable to confront him. Furthermore, she felt guilty over whether she was pursuing her career at the expense of her children. Even prior to having children, the patient felt a growing emotional distance from her husband. After her children were born, the patient suffered a serious physical illness and felt that her husband was unsupportive. She remained bitterly resentful of this but had been unable to discuss it with her husband. Currently they were not close and had sexual relations only infrequently.

The patient was raised in a religiously conservative family, the youngest of three children. She had an older sister and brother, but felt close to neither. She described her father as an emotionally aloof man who was uninvolved in the child rearing. However, she respected his stability and reliability. The father died when the patient was in college, and she apparently mourned. She had no recollections of ever feeling angry at her father, although she vividly recalled incidents where, hoping for closer contacts, she instead felt hurt by his criticisms and rebukes. The patient described her mother as controlling and dominating. While she never fought with her father, she recalled, as a teenager, having had frequent arguments with her mother.

After dating casually in high school, the patient became engaged in college but severed the relationship after a short time. In her middle twenties she became involved with a man twenty years her senior but refused to marry him because of life-style and age differences. After the end of this relationship, she entered psychotherapy and was seen by a male therapist individually and in a group. She grew dissatisfied with not having more individual time with the therapist but could not bring herself to tell him, and finally left therapy after several months. The patient has had no further therapy contacts until now.

The patient entered therapy as part of the Vanderbilt research project on TLDP. She was initially interviewed for approximately 1½ hours. The interview followed a standard protocol for selecting potentially suitable patients for the program. Content covered in the interview included information about her current life circumstances and functioning, her background and family relationships, and the problems that precipitated her seeking psychotherapy. The interview was videotaped and the patient filled out various clinical and research assessment forms before and afterwards. Judged to be a suitable candidate, she was seen by one of the TLDP training therapists, who happened to have been the initial interviewer. What follows is a description of the treatment beginning with the first session after the initial standardized interview and after the patient had been informed who her therapist would be. Interviews were conducted twice a week for fifty minutes. The therapy lasted for 27 sessions.

Session 1

P: I don't know exactly where to start. I've been having some real uneasy feelings about this whole thing and some questions came up after we last talked that I felt I didn't get answered, or else if they were answered I don't remember the answers to them. But if you

would, would you repeat to me again so I'll have a clearer understanding about this project and how it differs from what I would
encounter if I were to go to see somebody else, in the community,
in private practice as far as getting help with my anxiety and depression. What is the difference, other than this is shorter? Is that the
only difference that it's compacted into a shorter period of time or
is there any other difference?

T: I'll try to answer that as best I can in a while, but it might be helpful
first to get a little bit of understanding of what your concerns are,
what motivates the questions.

A patient's questions frequently have multiple meanings, some of which
may be clear to the therapist whereas others embody a hidden agenda; that
is, they have transference implications which need to be explored. In this
interview, the patient's request for information is quite reasonable—she
wants to know about the somewhat unusual therapy arrangements and
how they might differ from ordinary ones. However, she is also asking
implicitly: "What kind of therapist are you? Can I trust you? Will you use
me, as I have felt used in the past (see later sections)? Am I being coerced
by you?" In all such instances it is good practice to explore underlying
feelings and fantasies rather than to foreclose the inquiry by giving factual
answers and thereby ignoring the patient's real concerns that she may not
be able to articulate herself. At the same time, to withhold answers to
reasonable questions reinforces the patient's fear that the therapist is
someone not to be trusted. Questions can always be answered after exploring their meanings for the therapy relationship, at which time they are not
as loaded. Toward the end of this interview the therapist does attempt to
answer some of the patient's questions. As indicated in the following
segment, this served to strengthen the therapeutic alliance.

P: Well, I don't know why I'm so uneasy about it, except the money
is one thing. I haven't even talked to my husband about it, which
for some reason I'm having a really hard time saying to him that I've
looked into this and this is what I'm doing. I don't know. I've just
had some sleepless nights about it. I don't really know what it is.

T: Can you say more about what this uneasy feeling is? What goes
through your mind and how you experience it?

P: It's hard to describe. I get kind of tied-up feelings inside. A queasy
stomach and I've lost some sleep over it. I'll wake up in the night at
2 o'clock and start thinking about it. I guess I'm worrying if I really
want to do it and I'm having some second thoughts.

T: What are those second thoughts? When you wake up in the middle of the night what comes to your mind?

P: (Silence) I guess part of it is I realize, maybe, I feel there is some risk to what I'm doing and I'm wondering if I'm ready to risk it and opening up some areas maybe that I've kept squelched for a long time.

T: What risks?

P: In that it might make me face something I don't want to face. I don't know if it's the unknown and I don't know exactly what that is except that it probably has a lot to do with what's going on between me and my husband. [This opens the possibility of exploring the interpersonal significance of the patient's problems.]

T: What comes to mind that you would fear?

P: I guess maybe the question whether it's going to help strengthen our relationship, which is what I hope it will do in giving me a better insight into myself and maybe more coping skills or whatever. Or is it going to make me, is the situation not going to improve with us and is it going to lead to a separation or divorce, which is something I really don't want to look at right now.

T: You think that's one important contributor to your queasy feelings and butterflies in your stomach? Fear that you might find yourself feeling so dissatisfied with the marriage, that something might happen that would destroy it?

P: Yeah, sure deep down that's probably something.

From the opening moments of the first TLDP interview, the therapist attempts to focus in on the patient's current problem, especially as it is manifested in her apprehensions and expectations toward the therapist. Attempting to clarify the meanings of affectively loaded words and phrases is particularly helpful in this effort. Here the therapist also helps the patient translate her physical symptoms into the language of fantasy and feeling within an interpersonal relationship: "queasy stomach" is related to fear of the therapy causing harm to the patient's marriage.

The therapist seeks to explore further the patient's fears about how therapy might harm her marriage. She responds with the intellectual rationale that therapy could be a "growing process," but her therapist points out that her fears are emotional. They continue to explore why she finds it so hard to tell her husband that she has sought therapy. The patient recalls that when they were dating, she made arrangements to be away for several weeks for advanced career training. She was reluctant to tell him, fearing that he would be displeased and their relationship would be damaged. The therapist suggests that the patient felt her future husband would leave her. She agrees and adds that he also might have been angry, which she would have found intolerable. However, her future husband accepted the news well, and the therapist raises the question of why she had been so convinced that he would be angry or rejecting.

> T: So then it meant something to you that you wanted to do this, get this training. It had some meaning for you, some emotional meaning for your [life] that you felt would be, your husband would take very badly.
>
> P: Yeah, that's what I thought at the time.
>
> T: And it sounds like a similar thing, coming here. Even though intellectually you feel it's to strengthen the marriage, to bring you closer together. Somehow emotionally there's something about it that you fear is, what? An attack on him? What comes to mind?

Early clarifications and interpretations further collaborative inquiry and serve the trial function of assessing how well and in what manner the patient responds to interpretive work. At this stage of therapy, the therapist is attempting to identify a focal theme, and he looks to the beginning therapeutic relationship as the primary source for clues. The patient begins to express a theme to which she will return later: "I must be a good girl, not experience anger toward significant men (husband, father, therapist), and do their bidding. Unless I do so, they may leave me, withdraw their love, abandon me. I can prevent separation—and the disturbing feeling of loss—by acting right. By implication, too, whatever may go wrong in a relationship, it is my fault and it is my responsibility to prevent such occurrences." The therapist, in keeping with the TLDP model, relates these feelings to the patient-therapist relationship.

> P: I guess I don't really want to—want him to think that—I guess I'm afraid he'll interpret it as this is the beginning of the parting process or something. And I don't really want him to feel that way. But for some reason. . . .
>
> T: It's as though you're turning away from him.
>
> P: Yeah.

The patient recalls that during previous discussions her husband had expressed approval of her seeking therapy. The therapist points out that during her recuperation from her physical illness the patient had felt that her husband had turned away from her to devote himself to further professional education. Now she appeared to feel that her seeking therapy was a rejection of him, to which he would respond with the same hurt and anger that she had felt toward him. Indeed, throughout their relationship the patient had felt that anything that she did for herself would be taken badly by her husband. The patient acknowledged that she had a hard time being direct with her husband out of fear of hurting his feelings or anticipating his angry reactions. Yet, she realizes that she hurts him indirectly with mean looks or a cold attitude. The therapist wonders if she sees therapy as an angry, retaliatory act against her husband. She quickly denies this but agrees that it does not make sense that she cannot tell him about it. She then begins to wonder if therapy, in fact, symbolizes an angry gesture toward her husband and comments that she has "so much" anger and resentment stored up.

The therapist, by staying close to the patient's affects as she experiences them in the present, attempts to clarify a particular scenario that is played out with her husband. He helps the patient become aware of this pattern with interventions that are simple, short, gentle, but searching. In addition, he asks questions that point to incongruities and overreactions behind apparently self-evident feelings and behavior: "Which raises the question, why would you imagine he would feel that way?" These questions cannot be answered quickly but they stimulate the patient's curiosity, foster a collaborative effort, and provide thematic direction, all by saying implicitly: "You can see that there is more here than meets the eye; it is a problem that we can explore together." The patient is talking about her husband but the therapist can safely assume that she feels similarly toward him and that this problem will sooner or later make its appearance in therapy. Important feelings are always tied to "objects" (significant persons) and these feelings can be transferred from one to another object: At one moment, the patient may be expressing feelings toward her husband but they may readily be transformed and apply to the therapist.

The patient feels that her children often are the innocent targets of her anger, that she is too impatient and critical with them. The patient goes on to describe her angry behavior with her children, and the therapist picks up on her characterizing this behavior as instinctive.

T: What comes to mind about why you would respond automatically that way as opposed to some other way?
P: Because I think that's the way I was treated.
T: By whom?
P: Primarily by my mother.
T: Your mother would yell at you and criticize you?

P: She is a very criticizing person, very critical, and I am aware of that and I'm aware of how critical I am a lot of times in the relationship to my husband and my children and everybody, and that bothers me and I've tried to work on it. I've made some progress slowly and I don't want my children to grow up being criticized all the time. I have to work very hard to praise them for things they do that are worthy of praise.

T: You feel you didn't get much praise from your mother?

P: Yeah.

T: How was your father different?

P: He wasn't a very critical person and he didn't have a lot to do with disciplining us on a day-to-day basis. He would get involved periodically. I can remember being spanked by him one time and that was because I told a lie. He asked me if I had washed my hands and I hadn't and I told him I had. And he would say things like "don't talk back to your mother," if I said something wrong, snippy. He would always support her and not allow us to act that way toward her. But mother is the one who would pick the switch off the bush and switch us if we did something that annoyed her. I don't remember getting a lot of spankings. It was a lot more verbal: "Why did you do that? You shouldn't have done that."

T: So on a day-to-day basis you felt that you were constantly under the gun of mother's criticism and didn't get much support, much praise, and it sounds like you might have liked father to be on your side and balance it but he wouldn't. He was kind of in the background or he took mother's side.

The therapist presents a succinct summary which clarifies what the patient has said and which also serves the important purpose of communicating his empathic understanding. The focus rests on the patient's view of things and the affect she is currently experiencing.

P: Supporting her, yeah.

T: You felt kind of ganged up on.

P: The way I think of him is he set the standards for what—I think this is right, this is my perception but I may be wrong—for how things were. But mother was the enforcer.

T: But what happened if you tried to stand up to mother? Talk back?

P: Well, I was told I couldn't talk like that or mother would hang up the phone on me, wouldn't allow me to continue, or the conversation would be cut off. She would leave the room.

T: What about father?

P: I never got into any confrontations with dad that I can remember.

T: Why not?

P: I don't know why not. It seems like it always came from mother. The decisions were made and partly because probably he wasn't there some of the time and he never seemed to be that much involved in the arguments, about what was going on, and I don't know why.

T: So your experience was that if you tried to stand up for yourself, talk back when you were getting criticized, or there was an argument, that if you did you'd be—mother would turn away from you, and you'd just be left there.

P: Or she'd just say, "I don't want to hear anymore. That's the end of it. I don't want to talk about it any more. I said no." Period.

In looking for a reason why she is often impatient with her children, the patient associates to the way she was treated by her mother. This provides the therapist with an entrée into forming an initial picture of primary childhood relationships. In TLDP this historical information serves the background role of helping to elaborate and explain the origins of current predispositions being clarified with her husband and therapist. In clarifying and summarizing the patient's recalled experiences with her parents, the therapist is laying the groundwork for returning to the primary area of examination in TLDP, the therapeutic relationship. As an intermediate step, the therapist offers a link between the patient's experience with her parents and the way she construes her relationship with her husband.

T: Do you think that influences your fear of speaking out to your husband? That he'd do the same thing except maybe even worse?

P: Well, I think it probably is my preconditioned pattern of response and there've been times when we have gotten into confrontations and he really overpowers me and I back off. I get really upset with that kind of force.

The discussion continues with the patient's experiences in the infrequent arguments with her husband. On the rare occasions when she overtly expresses angry feelings she characterizes herself as "obnoxious." She usually reacts to her husband's anger by crying and having her thoughts scatter, then "I just shrink away and clam up." However, recently the patient experiences herself as becoming emotionally numb in these situations, which her therapist clarifies as turning away emotionally and sexually from her husband. This new behavior frightens her and contributed to her seeking therapy. The therapist turns attention back to her initial uneasiness about therapy and the patient responds with renewed questions about the situation. Once again the therapist postpones answering her questions, and with the recent information obtained, suggests that she is afraid that he will somehow hurt her. The patient agrees and expresses her concern that he will become angry with her. In response to the therapist's request for her associations about this issue, the patient expresses the fear that the therapist will push her to seek a divorce and if she resists become angry with her.

Bringing the patient's attention back to the therapeutic relationship stirs up renewed concerns and questions. At this point, however, the therapist is able to interpret more specifically some of the motivation behind the patient's questions. He continues his effort to articulate the focal theme as it emerges in the therapeutic relationship. This strategy differs from other dynamic time-limited approaches that view the focal theme in the immediacy of the therapy relationship as secondary to its "reconstruction" in primary childhood relationships.

T: I would say, "you ought to get out of that relationship," and you would say, "I'm not so sure," and I would get angry and what do you imagine would happen? How would that hurt you?

P: I don't know how it would hurt me except the anger. I guess I just have this thing about anger. Just from our last meeting when I said, "When did you want to get started," and you said "Right away," I felt really pushed. I wanted to say, "No I've got to wait a couple of weeks," but I didn't say that. But you said, "I'd like to get started right away." And that made me nervous for some reason. I don't know why. Maybe because I was still feeling a little unsure about the whole thing. Part of it too is because I know my schedule is like unreal this week and next week. But I felt when you said, "I want to get started right away," I felt pressured. And I think I probably thought, "Okay what other kinds of pressures are you going to lay out on me that I'm not going to be able to say, Stop, wait a minute I can't deal with that or that's not for me. "

The therapist's offer to accept the patient for therapy without delay was prompted by his desire to be helpful. Instead, the patient had felt pressured. This contradiction provides an illustration of misunderstandings and distortions that regularly arise in psychotherapy. At times, the therapist has no inkling of how seemingly innocuous or neutral communications are heard by the patient. This ubiquitous tendency to distort underscores the importance of the therapist's remaining attentive to the manner in which his or her comments and actions are being experienced by the patient. The latter is prone to construe the meanings of interpersonal transactions in terms of his or her salient relationship predisposition.

> T: Well it sounds like, looking back over and kind of pulling together what you've talked about today, our earlier interchange about getting started right away stirred up in you a feeling that once again you were going to be caught in a situation that is very familiar for you, where you were feeling like either the wife being dragged along with things that she didn't want to do but had to for fear of something even worse happening, or like a child—"this is the way it's going to be and I don't want to hear anything from you." Like you experienced when you were a kid. And once again this would happen again here with me. And the only way you would have, the most comfortable way at this point that you would have in dealing with that, is to try to kind of pull back, not speak up about it, but protect yourself and draw back.
>
> P: That's my pattern.

The therapist introduces the first approximation of a focal theme, defined as a particular relationship predisposition, with associated self- and object images, feelings, fantasies, and expected consequences. By articulating the tentative focus in these terms, the therapist succeeds in capturing the patient's tendency to feel like a child in relation to a powerful but uncaring parent ("dragged along"). He outlines the patient's pattern of self-protection through withdrawal. The patient recognizes and resonates to the description by saying simply, "That's my pattern."

> T: Which maybe is what's behind your concerns about can you afford it, can you fit it in your schedule. All of these things that are very reasonable, and behind that is really, "Are you going to hurt me, are you going to get angry at me if I don't want to do what you want me to do?"
>
> P: Well, I think I have a fear of being boxed in.
>
> T: That really seems like an important area to explore, why it is that —I think we looked today at some of the things that make you feel boxed in. You're being pressured or that you feel like you're being told this is the way it's going to be by someone who's important to you, whether it's your husband, your parents when you were a kid, and you feel pressured. But it doesn't explain why you feel so over-

whelmed by it. That you're boxed in, you can't do anything about it, you can't stand up for yourself. That might be an important area to explore. When we talked before about one of the characteristics of this kind of therapy is to try to find a circumscribed area of primary importance emotionally and look at that carefully and this certainly seems like that kind of an area. It's what brought you in, or an important part of what brought you in, and we also saw it emerge immediately in our relationship.

The therapist continues to identify a focal theme, staying close to the patient's immediate feeling state. At this point, additional nuances are added, namely, the patient's anger and resentment at feeling boxed in, her sense of helplessness in dealing with these feelings of being coerced by powerful adults to whom she must submit if the danger of desertion is to be averted. Simultaneously, the therapist outlines a tentative goal (exploring the foregoing configuration) and invites the patient's collaboration in the joint task of therapy.

P: Yeah, I thought about—well I couldn't really talk when you called me at home the other night because everything was just in a mess, but I thought about calling you at home and I thought, no I don't want to do that because he might not like it. (laugh)
T: Yell at you?
P: Well, I don't know what I thought. I don't think I thought you'd yell at me. I don't have that perception yet of you. (laugh) I just—and then I'd wake up at night and stew around.
T: Call me to tell me what?
P: To tell you I was feeling really uneasy about this whole thing. I had some questions that I didn't feel like I'd settled and couldn't we wait. Put if off a couple of weeks. (laughs)
T: How do you feel now?
P: Well, I feel a little better except I still don't have some of my questions answered.

There follows a discussion of the specific questions she has raised, and then the arrangements are made for payment and scheduling of appointments.

The salient predisposition has been identified primarily by attending to the nature of the relationship which spontaneously unfolds between patient and therapist. Current relationships outside of therapy and childhood recollections provide additional information and confirmation, but the primary source is the patient-therapist interaction. The patient's apprehension about the therapeutic relationship caused her to be guarded and reticent. The therapist responded to this problem with some frustration and with the urge to question her actively. He also felt put on the spot in terms of how well he would treat the patient in reaction to her vigilant, stony stare. At the same time, she responded cooperatively, with introspection and feelings, to his efforts at examining her affective experience in the therapeutic relationship. We believe it would have been a mistake to respond immediately to her many questions about the therapist and arrangements of therapy. On the other hand, if the therapist had only treated these communications interpretatively, he would have colluded in her scenario, thus confirming her belief that powerful adults do not respect her feelings. By trying to answer her questions at the end of the session, the therapist provided a corrective experience.

Session 2

As the session begins, the therapist describes the patient's task, that is, trying to verbalize whatever comes to mind.

P: I have the feeling that it's been a mishmash of things coming out.

T: Is that the way you felt at the end of last time?

P: Not really. I felt much better by the end than I did when I got here. I felt good about that. I didn't feel quite as bad, as nervous about coming this time as I did the first time.

T: What did we talk about, do you think, that made you feel better?

P: I think talking about the fact that I haven't been able to tell my husband what I'm doing yet helped and I think your response—I don't know what I expected but it—I felt like it was okay. I must have been expecting or had the fear that you were going to think: "You crazy thing, you haven't told your husband you're doing this." (laugh) That's really stupid and childish. I was thinking you were going to react to me that way and I know better than that, but that's what I think I was feeling.

A salient focal theme or relationship predisposition emerged in the first interview. This may be described as an expectation that the therapist would respond critically to the patient's reluctance to tell her husband about her desire to seek therapy. By discussing this issue with her therapist, the patient is quickly being provided with an opportunity to see the contrast between her transference expectation and what actually occurred. This kind of experiential (*in vivo*) learning is central to TLDP.

T: "Stupid and childish." Why do you think that was the reaction you expected?

P: Because I'm supposedly an adult and should be mature and it seems like that would be nothing so drastic to tell your husband about what you're doing.

T: Do those names ring any bells for you? [Here the therapist probes for evidence of the same reaction in current and past relationships outside the treatment context. Better TLDP technique would be to explore what the patient might be reacting to in the therapeutic relationship that led her to suspect such ridicule. Chances are she would have little basis for this reaction and thus would be faced with its irrationality.]

P: Not really. Except maybe my own insecurities I feel sometimes about not being able to tell him up front. Not feel so inhibited about telling him. I feel guilty about it and I think I feel guilty about some of my behavior toward him. I know when I do things that I think are not very nice or very appropriate for a mature person. I feel guilty about that.

T: When you say you feel guilty, how do you experience the guilt?

The therapist seeks to elaborate on the patient's feelings in relation to the therapist. He focuses on what appears to be a loaded phrase—"stupid and childish"—that may compress a wide range of experiences, fantasies, feelings, and important aspects of the patient's image of herself and others. Emphasis on such loaded terms may open up larger vistas. Similarly, it is good procedure to attempt to clarify the meanings of such apparently self-evident terms as *guilt.* Terms of this kind often have specific idiosyncratic meanings that need to be explored.

The patient attempts to specify the feelings she calls guilt by saying that she does not feel mature and sometimes treats people badly. However, she apparently cannot expand further and states that she has a hard time putting feelings into words. She goes on to express relief that in the previous session the therapist had eventually answered her questions about therapy. She then begins to describe her initial negative expectations about the therapist but shifts to criticizing herself for thinking too much about what is happening during a session. Essentially she reports how anxious and on the spot she felt during the first interview. She then articulates her fear of running out of things to say and that the therapist would not help out.

T: And you felt I was just going to leave you there tongue-tied with thoughts whirling in your head. (Silence) The image that you had of me coming in sounds pretty bad—that I was going to be rigid, opinionated, easily angered, unsupportive—doesn't sound very pleasant. Not much to look forward to.

P: It's interesting that you say that because when my husband and I were talking about some things last summer, he made a comment to me: "Am I really that bad?" Something I said—I was trying to tell him that it's hard for me to talk to him and at one time he responded with, "Am I really that bad?" I did a similar sort of thing.

In further exploring the manner in which the patient was initially predisposed to view the therapeutic relationship, the therapist calls attention to an important image which the patient had of him. This image is part of the focal theme which the therapist has been formulating. By spontaneously linking this current experience with similar experiences with her husband, the patient provides supporting evidence for the evolving focus.

T: What comes to mind about that?

P: (Silence) The only thing that comes to mind is that I wonder if it has something to do with men.

T: You recall feeling that—having that kind of experience and apprehension toward other men besides me and your husband?

P: I can't think of any one specific other person.

T: How about women? Do you recall feeling similarly?

P: (Silence) Nobody in particular. There are some women that I'm associated with at work who can easily put me down and it's the same kind of thing. I back off. If I begin to feel uncomfortable because they're disagreeing and I'm feeling that my opinion is being wiped out—if a woman is like that then I feel intimidated.

T: Do you experience them as actively and directly putting you down, or even if they disagree with you it feels to you as if your opinions don't count for much?

P: I'm not sure that it's me individually, I think—I'm really thinking about one individual in particular—I think she is just like that with a lot of people. But I find it hard to retaliate once she has stated her position; I get the feeling there's no room for any further discussion.

T: And you back off, feel intimidated, and don't talk. So if somebody is forceful in stating their opinion they don't have to necessarily put you down.

P: Not necessarily, it can be a general sort of thing.

T: And you just feel intimidated. Do you feel anything else?

P: (Silence) Sometimes I think of myself—okay, I really think I know what I'm talking about—just forget it. That sort of a response. Sometimes I have decided, or in response to that I will just decide or make a decision to do what I want to do in that situation.

T: So there's a silent, a secret resistance, defiance, you try to do what you want anyway. Just quietly.

The therapist is always on the lookout for both the conscious and unconscious components of a relationship predisposition, keeping in mind that a major purpose of such themes is to ward off anxiety. Here evidence is unearthed of a predisposition embodying hostility—a "silent, secret resistance"—beneath the patient's overt feelings of intimidation. The therapist attempts to stay close to the patient's affect.

The patient seeks to avoid the topic of hostility by shifting to an intellectual discussion of strategies for implementing her ideas at work. She denies wanting to get back at anyone. The therapist confronts her attempt to rationalize her indirect expressions of hostility.

T: Now, in a work situation you're working sometimes quietly as you described and can be effective and it's very useful. Works out fine. But you have also described that you do similar kinds of things with your husband and there it doesn't work out so well.

P: I think I feel more like I'm doing it to get back at him—to hurt him.

T: The mean looks, the coolness, lack of sexual interest.

P: Smart remarks.

T: There it hurts you as much, maybe, if not more.

The patient describes feeling guilty over such "childish" responses and proceeds to describe a recent incident in which she felt her husband had ignored a request for attention by their daughter. The patient responded with anger and anxiety.

P: Angry and my heart racing and just feeling sad for her, I think—I got emotional.

T: Sounds like you felt pretty intensely, that you felt angry—sounds like you felt furious, not just angry.

P: Yeah, probably.

T: And at the same time that made you very anxious. Your heart was racing and then you felt sad. Why do you imagine you would have such a strong reaction? I can see you interpreting it that way [empathizing with her] but why such a strong reaction?

In TLDP there is a consistent focus on the collaborative exploration of the patient's feelings and reactions. Accordingly, questions that engage the patient's curiosity about feelings and reactions are used with some frequency. Here the question concerns the intensity of the patient's reactions to her husband's behavior with their child.

The patient expresses dissatisfaction with her husband's alleged inattentiveness to their children's feelings. The therapist suggests that the intensity of her reaction may point to her taking the husband's behavior "personally"; that is, her husband neglects their children in the same way that he neglects her. The patient recalls an incident some years ago when she had felt hurt and rejected by her husband's insensitivity to her feelings. She begins to look teary.

T: How do you feel now as you're talking?

P: I'm beginning to feel like I'm going to cry.

T: What's the feeling that goes with this?

P: (Crying) Like I'm not important enough to him that it makes any difference. I don't mean enough to him that he can listen to what bothers me. He cares as long as everything is going along real smoothly and nothing upsets the applecart, but if I have a need to talk about what's bothering me he's not interested in listening. That's the same sort of feeling I have when I have wanted to talk about things that were important to me, like issues of being a parent and how we're going to work that out, what's important to us in our life and what are our goals and how we're going to reach those kinds of things. Whenever they're brought up I get what I interpret as a curt response and that's the end of it—"let's don't talk about it any more."

T: And what do you do then?

P: I clam up and withdraw and get stomachaches and headaches and I get, I think more than that, I get busy.

T: At those times when you get a curt response from your husband, do you experience him as, and you as—that you don't count for much, you're not important enough for him to be bothered with these things?

P: I've either thought that it's that or he is threatened by my bringing things up that require some kind of a discussion or dialogue.

T: That's an intellectual analysis of him. That's not what makes you clam up though, is it?

P: No. It's the feeling that I'm not worth listening to, I guess.

T: And it sounds like you attempt to try and struggle with those feelings by using your knowledge and your intellect to try and understand why he would do this. But it really doesn't help much.

P: Yeah, I do a lot of that.

T: The more immediate question is why you feel so strongly at times like that. Not only irritated or hurt but very intensely that you don't count for anything. You're not important. Where does that come from?

The therapist always attempts to organize the items of information as they emerge from the patient's narrative. He also assesses the patient's response as tentative formulations of the focal theme are presented. Here a new emotionally charged element is added: the patient feels that she doesn't count for much with her husband, that she is "not important enough for him." In addition, more is learned about the patient's characteristic (defensive) reaction to these feelings: she clams up. Her withdrawal now appears to be associated with her inability to express anger and to ask her husband for more care and attention.

A focal theme is usually replayed many times and numerous facets are illuminated in the process. Since there is a good deal of redundancy in human communication, the therapist will eventually be able to identify a theme, even if he does not succeed in doing so immediately. The patient may be counted upon to show him the way if he does nothing to interfere with the process.

The patient describes herself as feeling insecure, which she attributes to problems in the relationship with her parents. This feeling has become more noticeable as she has felt unsupported by her husband in the parental role. While the patient feels "indecisive" and agonizes over possible mistakes, her husband appears to make decisions quickly and easily. Her husband's confidence in the parental role contrasts with her own sense of inadequacy as a parent. However, she also feels "cut off" when she attempts to discuss problems with her husband, as though her feelings don't matter to him. She begins to cry. When her therapist asks what she is feeling, she says "pushed away." The patient continues to express her frustration over not being able to interest her husband in a discussion of their respective views on parenting.

T: Now even in recalling it now it's very much alive here, perhaps because it's still very much an alive issue.

P: Yes.

T: As well as affecting you very strongly.

P: I think the thing that bothers me, he cuts me off in that way but then —but physically he wants me and that just doesn't—I can't respond physically when he cuts me off emotionally.

T: How do you feel when he makes sexual overtures?

P: Sometimes I could scream.

T: Scream?

P: Just SCREAM!

T: Scream what?

P: "Leave me alone!"

T: In hurt and resentment?

P: The other night he started trying to help get the children ready for bed and he never does that—well very seldom unless I ask him. And I thought, this is unusual. And then we got in bed and I realized he wanted me to get them to bed earlier so that we could have intercourse and it just made me furious. Because I thought, Why don't you help me otherwise!

T: How did you feel then?

P: Angry. (Teary)

T: But you went ahead and had intercourse? How does that work for you?

P: (Sigh) It's just an ordeal most of the time.

T: But you submit to it, right?

P: Because I know, based on last summer at least—I really don't want to go through another thing like that but . . .

T: You're afraid he'll threaten to leave you?

P: I think he would. I think he—I just dread the yelling at me and screaming, worse than the threat to leave.

T: Sounds like you almost feel like a child who has to do a chore because if you don't, no matter how much you dislike it you'll get yelled at and it's just overwhelming.

The patient agrees that she feels intimidated. The therapist suggests that she feels hurt when her husband refuses to discuss their roles as parents. She then experiences him as inattentive and uncaring. The patient readily agrees with this interpretation and recalls the first time in their marriage when she experienced him as cold, which left her feeling crushed. She recalls further incidents where she felt "unimportant" to him but wonders if she may have been too quick in interpreting his behavior as rejecting. The therapist poses the question of why she would so readily feel rejected. He also recalls to himself that in the first session the patient was reluctant to examine her feelings about the marriage but has been doing so throughout this interview. Consequently, he calls this fact to her attention and invites her to look at her feelings more closely.

T: Going back over all we've talked about today the thing that stands out most strongly, that you felt most strongly, is your husband pushing you away, acting like you don't count for much with him. How hurt and resentful and furious you can get. And how distant you feel from him. Last time your really big fear was that our talking together, that you were afraid that I was going to be pushing you to face things in your marriage that might be real harmful to the marriage, and that was very frightening to you. Given that was a fear of yours last time, how do you feel about what we've talked about today?

P: Well, I just feel like crying. (Cries) The thing that frightens me the most is that my own feelings of coldness toward him frighten me because it hasn't always been that way and I don't want it to be that way. But I can't seem to get a handle on what has happened and it scares me to think that my feelings may never change back the other way.

T: The feeling of coldness I would suspect is really very much tied up with your feeling so intimidated when you feel pushed away and not counting for much. You feel hurt, angry, furious. At the same time you get very intimidated and feel overwhelmed that you can't do anything else, so you clam up and back off. And then you let it out in all kinds of ways. Coldness perhaps. To go back to what seems a very primary question, why do you feel so intimidated in reaction to those feelings? At precisely those points when you feel pushed away and you feel like you're not counting for much and you want to talk about what is going on, it's then that you're least able to. That seems like a real important path to explore.

The therapeutic focus is presented again, this time in more specific and elaborated form. The therapist always stays at the level of the patient's emotional experience, avoiding complex constructions or interpretations. He uses simple language and remains attuned to the clinical data.

The patient describes her difficulty in talking with her husband about things that bother her. She wants to be more forceful with him but she can't and ends up "stewing." As the interview draws to a close, the therapist explains the procedure for videotaping the next appointment as part of the research protocol. The patient expresses concerns about confidentiality and possible harmful effects, but she defers, stating that all she can do is "trust" the therapist. Again, attentive to the expression of themes finding expression in any facet of the therapeutic relationship, the therapist points out that the patient is vulnerable to feeling coerced and intimidated. In turn, this leads to a tendency to submit. He wonders if this is occurring around his request for videotaping. The patient says that is exactly how she feels. The therapist states that he would like to videotape but if she feels that it would interfere with their work, he will desist. They proceed to discuss the videotaping arrangements, including the uses of the videotapes and procedures for ensuring confidentiality. The patient agrees to allow videotaping of the next interview but the therapist reiterates his position that if she feels it would interfere with their work, he would respect her wishes.

The therapist recognizes the continuity of behavior, particularly the fact that all aspects of the therapeutic relationship can be influenced by a dominant focal theme. Thus, he relates the patient's feelings about the videotaping to the central theme elaborated earlier. She responds by saying: "Yeah, that's exactly it; I fell right into it. Because I guess I feel like you are in control. . . ." The therapist's behavior also proves that actions speak more loudly than words: He does not support her independence on the one hand and then, when it suits his purposes, infringe on it in the way she feels others have done.

In the next three sessions variations of the focal theme are enacted in the therapeutic relationship, where they are examined and repeatedly linked to similar experiences with the patient's husband and, earlier in life, with her mother and father. In the 3d interview, the patient has second thoughts about videotaping as part of the research protocol. However, since she fears the therapist's "harsh" and "rejecting" response, she feels impelled to clam up. When the therapist interprets her feeling that she is worthless and therefore must strive to please others in order to gain acceptance, the patient feels overwhelmed. The therapist suggests that she experiences his remarks as criticisms. The patient begins the fourth session feeling better but wonders whether the therapist had put her down in the previous meeting. The experience of being put down recurs several times during the session, and each time it is examined and linked to similar experiences with her husband and parents. In addition, the therapist begins to explore her inability to tolerate expressions of hostility: She can feel discouraged, hurt, and tongue-tied, but she cannot feel indignant or offended. The patient begins to realize how often she masks certain feelings. Early in the 5th session, therapist and patient clarify the latter's discomfort with not receiving more positive feedback from the therapist. She is prone to feel helpless and admonished. They articulate her self-image of wanting to be of help to people, to please them, or alternatively, feeling victimized. The therapist interprets her aloof and reticent attitude in the session as reflecting her belief that she must guard against being emotionally abused by him.

Session 6

T: You look like you're ready for me to begin.

P: I sort of feel that way this morning for some reason. Usually I come in and have something on my mind, and I'm sort of blank this morning. I don't know if it is the hour of day.

T: You mean there's nothing at all. . . .

P: Well. . . . It's just that I don't know if I have anything to say right this minute, and usually when I come in there is something that I've been thinking about. Sitting around, using my mind a little or thinking about this morning.

T: What comes to mind about why you might not have anything to say? Anything from the last session come to mind that is contributing to this?

P: I don't know if there is anything specific. It's just that I have noticed that I haven't spent as much time thinking about the last session as I have previously. I talked with my husband a little bit about it. Some of the things that have occurred, but . . . and I just haven't had it on my mind like I usually do . . . the previous sessions.

T: What do you make of that?

The therapist's opening remark is in response to the patient's characteristic stance of aloofness, which he experiences as a stony stare. Presumably, it reflects her vigilance in interpersonal relations and her ingrained fear of incurring someone's displeasure. When she has nothing to say, the therapist assumes that the primary reason has to do with feelings she has about their recent transactions. The patient supports this assumption here by mentioning that she hasn't been thinking about the past session as she usually does. The therapist recalls to himself that in previous sessions the patient tried to take a passive position and, not surprisingly, she has felt that he had been insufficiently directive. Notice the paradox: On the one hand, the patient complains about a significant person's intrusiveness and authoritarianism, feeling pushed around, and so on. On the other hand, if the therapist leaves the initiative with her, encouraging her to take charge, he is experienced as unhelpful. A directive therapist is someone with whom the patient can potentially fight and whom she can resist; if the therapist is adhering to the role of an empathic listener, the patient is then thrown off-balance—it is a role she is not accustomed to.

The patient tries to tell the therapist why she finds it difficult to express herself. In an unemotional and polite fashion, she begins to press him for answers to what bothers her. When he declines to answer her questions, the patient accepts this. The therapist begins to inquire how she handles his response.

> P: Well, if you gave me an answer for every question, I would probably fall right into the trap of saying "Okay, you're the authority. You know what's right. So, you must be right." You have more knowledge than I do. If I try to figure it out for myself, it may help with the problem I have of forming my own opinion again, having something to base it on.

The therapist begins to work on an important character resistance—her polite, unemotional, and undemanding manner of relating. He assumes this to be part of a scenario he hopes to elaborate. The patient presumably experiences the therapist as "holding out" but she can't press him for what she wants, nor can she display anger if she feels unfairly treated. As always, the therapist attempts to stay close to the patient's feelings.

> T: Okay, well, that sounds like a reasonable rationale. You get upset that I know and that I'm not telling you. But how do you *feel* about the idea that I know and I'm not telling you?
> P: Well, it would be a lot easier for me if you would tell me.
> T: That's a thought.
> P: That's a thought. How do I feel? I feel like I'm going to get flustered and confused just trying to answer your question.
> T: What's flustering or confusing?
> P: I can't express my feelings!
> T: Can you tell me what you're experiencing?

216

The patient is becoming upset. The therapist's hunch is that she is misconstruing his questions in terms of her predisposition to feel bullied by a harsh and critical authority. The task is to bring these issues into the open where they can be examined. Thus, he asks her to scrutinize her immediate feelings, and then, in order to reinforce their working alliance, invites her to step back and assess whether her current experience reflects a pattern recognizable to her.

P: I'm trying to keep from crying.

T: There is a box of tissues.

P: Is that your private stock? (Laughs) Well, I don't know. I just have a terrible time trying to describe what I'm feeling. It makes me feel about something about responding to you and your behavior directly.

T: Well, is what you are experiencing now, does that ring any bells for you? Do you feel that way at other times, if so when? This confusion, kind of discombobulated, crying. [Here is another example of how easy it is, even for a TLDP therapist, to lapse into the more traditional approach of seeking material with which to make linking interpretations. The correct TLDP approach would be to encourage a more detailed examination of what about the therapist's behavior is disturbing the patient.]

P: The thing that pops into my mind first is that same thing that we talked about before. In wanting to talk to him [husband], get into some dialogue with him about something that's important to me, and he squelches the discussion and that's when I start getting all confused.

T: He doesn't tell you what his feelings are . . . what he's thinking. You feel that you are angry at those times?

P: I don't think of it as anger, I think of it as more as rejection or, "I don't want to . . . listen to you . . . I don't want to talk about it. Don't bother me, go away."

T: You feel it's like a put-down, discounted? You feel all confused, tongue-tied?

The patient describes her inability to cope with her husband's alleged insensitivity, but the therapist assumes that this is also a commentary on the patient-therapist interaction. At this point early in therapy, however, he is apparently uncomfortable with the patient's unhappiness that is obliquely directed at him. Thus, he diverts the discussion to another subject—the patient's impatience with her children. The therapist's action can also be viewed as his becoming too embroiled in a role complementary to the patient's role in her current neurotic scenario: the therapist will not tolerate the patient's complaints (as she experienced her parents' impatience with her as a child). After a short time, the therapist realizes what has happened and attempts to articulate it.

> T: Let me point out something, where we should begin. You see how you look and feel—very calm, working together, it's very helpful, productive. I won't tell you what I'm thinking. I won't help you out. Because I have good reason for it, and you accept it as good reason, and yet when you look at it, it's all camouflage. I mean that you pretty well may find a kind of truth to it, which makes it even better camouflage in that you say it's helpful for you to figure things out for yourself. That's reasonable. But it makes an even more effective camouflage for another part of this. Once again, someone you want to count on won't support you, pushes you away, won't help you out. And you are really very effective at camouflaging that other reaction from yourself. Then that leads to the question, why this particular reaction? Why feel all discombobulated and confused?

The therapist attempts to describe the patient's immediate affective state covered by her "reasonable" exterior. Striving to further collaborative inquiry, the therapist raises questions to stimulate the patient's curiosity about herself and about their relationship.

> P: (Silence.) I don't know. I mean I could say, okay, you won't tell me, so what? That's your prerogative. Without even, I don't know, sometimes I may, sometimes I don't think I know really when I am angry. Maybe that's a part of the confusion. I get so involved with it that I label it something else.
> T: That may be. You see the first reaction is for you to see yourself as very reasonable and me as wanting to help you, and also being reasonable. Two mature adults without any feelings, working together. You ask and if I won't tell you there is a good reason, you can see the reason and that's fine. But when we get behind that, then, it was what you said before, one way of looking at how you feel, at how you present yourself is: "Why do you hurt me so, why do you do this to me, look what you're doing to me. How can you be so cruel, insensitive, not helpful?"
> P: You see, I don't even put it into those kinds of words in my mind.

The therapist persistently confronts the patient with her manner of relating politely and reasonably, which serves to hide from both her feelings of mistreatment and associated resentment—a state of affairs characteristic of her close relationships. In other words, the therapist contrasts the patient's reasonable attitudes in the working alliance with her irrational attitudes toward the therapist. In this instance, however, the patient's reasonableness also serves a defensive role. The patient comments on how foreign it is for her to attend to these feelings, even though they continually interfere with her comfort in relationships.

As the patient's feelings are discussed, she recalls similar experiences in childhood with her parents. These recollections point to the origin of the patient's current interpersonal difficulties, as well as indirectly serving to elaborate the nature of her current problems.

T: Does anything come to mind about the person you are telling me about?

P: You mean the confused thoughts?

T: Yes. In the context of feeling unsupported or pushed away.

P: I don't remember a specific age. And I don't remember specific incidents. It's just my mother coming across to me as: "Don't bother me with that question." "I said no, there is to be no more discussion." "You're asking too many questions, go find something to do, get out of my way." That kind of thing. There is one specific time I remember she hung up the telephone, that's when I was more like a teenager, that incident stands out in my mind and always has. I called her to ask if I could do something with the kids and she said "no," and I said "why?" She hung up the phone. She didn't even answer the question. I can remember just the general feeling that there were times when I was reprimanded that I can remember just walking away and going outside and talking to my dog, telling him what an awful person she was and how I hated her and all this kind of stuff.

T: You could get furious at her when she wasn't around?

P: But to show that in her presence would have been horrible. If I had even expressed feelings or said something back, it was this: "That's enough, you're not to talk that way, there is no point in further discussion." And if my father was around, he supported it. He said, "You don't talk that way to your mother, period." So, I'd go tell my dog how terrible I felt, how they treated me. And I don't even remember a specific incident when I said that to her specifically. I think that later these feelings of being rejected began to come out with my husband, the feeling of nonsupport.

T: I wonder if you don't feel that especially at those times when you feel that I know something that would be helpful to you and I'm not telling you, that you fear that if you got pissed at me, "So why don't you tell me, look what you are doing to me. Why do you make me feel worse, instead of better." That I would not take that, I would just make you get out and not come back.

P: I don't think you would tell me to get out, literally, from the room. I think you might choose to not tell me. Again, I may go back to this for a good reason.

T: You go back to excusing these . . . feelings, getting worked up and angry.

P: Well, I feel that part of my expectation with some of this was that you would tell me some things where it will help. There may be times when you won't. And granted I would like to not have to struggle all the time. I think there is some obligation on your part to help me. But I also think that maybe part of it is allowing some time for me to process things and try to figure things out too.

T: That sounds very reasonable . . . but if you think about it, isn't that really awfully reasonable for somebody who has felt so unsupported from so many people and is so sensitive to that, and looking for someone who will share the load and help out, that you could then come here and be so awfully reasonable and tolerant?

P: I think I have a right to be reasonable sometimes (said with irritation). In some situations to have a reasonable, or to take a reasonable attitude about it.

T: Sure, but you are all the time, aren't you? At least on the surface. What we are talking about is the opposite of that. That part of you feels that you don't have a right to be unreasonable anytime . . . (long silence). You know, when I said that, I had the feeling that your reaction was sort of to stiffen up. "I've got to watch you, I don't want to get unreasonable."

P: Well, what I'm thinking was deep down I probably feel that there are times when I am unreasonable and probably feel guilty about it.

Again, the therapist looks for opportunities to examine the patient's relationship predispositions in the immediacy of their interactions. Childhood recollections are employed to make sense of her present experiences and modes of relating. With her characteristic reasonableness, the patient attempts to disavow any feelings of hurt or anger but the therapist challenges this attitude. He points out an incongruity between her reasonable demeanor in the face of feeling ignored and her acknowledged sensitivity to such situations. She becomes irritated with the therapist's (somewhat overeager?) persistence, which he eventually points out along with her defensive "stiffening up" and becoming more guarded. These interchanges, as well as the previous segments from the sixth interview, illustrate the TLDP therapist's efforts to engage the patient in a collaborative examination of chronic interpersonal conflicts.

The patient's expectation that her feelings and opinions will not be tolerated by those important to her—including the therapist—continues to be the therapeutic focus in the next several interviews. In the 7th interview the patient felt anxious and reluctant to talk. She had given in to her husband's request for sex, although she had felt cold throughout. Afterwards she felt guilty and sad over her reaction. When the therapist attempted to examine the absence of any resentment toward her husband, the patient complained that he was putting her through an ordeal and accusing her of being "angry all the time." She then related a dream of a friend's husband dying but the patient felt guilty. The patient withdrew into a painful isolation and recalled how she felt similarly as a child after fighting with her mother and feeling unsupported. In the 8th interview, the patient was apologetic about her behavior in the previous session, but in response to her feeling more warmly toward the therapist she experienced him as "tuning her out." The therapist interpreted her fear that overtures for closeness with him would be rebuffed. He also wondered if she was not experiencing his impending one-week vacation as a rejection of her. The next session (9th) continued an examination of her expectation that the therapist would not tolerate her attempts to be more open with him. The patient also revealed that she had been more assertive with her husband, rather than withdrawing when feeling unsupported, and he had responded positively to this. In the 10th interview, the patient had resolved to tell the therapist that he always "bursts her bubble"; that is, when she comes in feeling good he tries to convince her how she really has other more upsetting feelings. The patient expressed apprehension about telling the therapist, because she expected him to be offended and to reject her.

P: It's really amazing. I came in here feeling just incredible. I came here feeling really good, confident, and I felt like I was going to tell you what I felt like saying, and I said it, and I just fell apart. And that's the feeling that I have right now. It just feels like I came in and it just went "phfft," and I was feeling good about having thought about that and having been able to, feeling that I could say it. It seems that once I said it I just disintegrated.

T: Well, there are a couple of things about what you experienced that are pretty striking. One is you felt that you had a legitimate complaint, and once you voiced this, your experience with me is somebody who is very intolerant, that however legitimate you feel your complaint is, I don't want to hear it, I don't think it counts for anything. It's as though you have offended me, that you have no right to say anything about how I treat you. And that my response would be to dismiss it and to dismiss you, angrily. And if I do that, you seem to fall apart. My attitude toward you is very important to your well-being. And it's very precarious.

P: Which is not news to me.

T: How do you mean?

P: That has come out before. Not having enough confidence in my own opinion, thinking I deserve a right to feel that way. And, that what other people think of me determines to a large degree what I do. It seems like too, that I try to figure out ahead of time what the person is going to do and how he can react, and probably as a protectiveness, to try to prevent it, being rejected, feeling like I'm being rejected.

It now becomes clear that the patient's self-punitive attitudes are being directed at and enacted with the therapist. The patient fears punishment and rejection, but at the same time subtly provokes the therapist. She confirms that the therapist is on the right track by acknowledging his observations as a familiar experience. This allows her to experience the contrast between negative expectations of important figures and the more realistic view provided by her therapist. These activities are central to the therapeutic process in TLDP.

T: This feeling that I was kind of sternly intolerant, easily offended, easily rejecting person, where I do seem angry at you, dismiss you, you say you are kind of left floundering. Isn't that sort of like a little girl struggling with a difficult parent? More specifically, isn't that what you experienced in your relationship to your mother?

P: Yes, I think so. And, it looks like I relate to most people that way. But it seems to be more people who are either in an authority position or who somehow seem to be, or I perceive as being above me or having a power over me or something.

The therapist links the current experience with the past, thereby also highlighting its anachronistic character. The patient can recognize the distortion ("I relate to most people that way"), which reflects useful learning.

However, it should be kept in mind that there may be compliance with the therapist as someone who has power over the patient and whom therefore she must please at all cost. In part, she may tell the therapist what (she thinks) he wants to hear. This may be another enactment. If so, it is fostered by the therapist's impatience to make a genetic interpretation. It would have been preferable for him to explore in greater detail the patient's experience in their relationship which contributes to her view of the therapist. This effort would more directly highlight her preexisting, maladaptive "sets."

T: Well, that makes sense, doesn't it?

P: Yes, because my mother was a very authoritarian sort of person. Very controlling and dominating. And also, she was the source of emotional support. It sort of seems to get back to something that has come up before. Why have I not been able to grow out of that?

T: Well, what are your thoughts about that?

P: I think it's something that I haven't really dealt with. I guess it has taken this long for my life to just about fall apart at the seams, to find some ways of dealing with my feelings. Maybe I, it's been easier for me to behave that way. It's obviously the way I learned to behave growing up. Behavior is very hard to change anyway. To some degree. It probably is something, I think, a lot easier to be dependent and blame other people for my problems and lack of this and that and the other.

T: Why would that be easier?

P: Well, it's that I avoid confrontation which is a very difficult thing for me to deal with. I think one of my biggest problems is like I said, dealing with my feelings of not being a worthwhile person and having the right to speak up for what I think I must do. (Long silence)

Mother, like the therapist, was a source of emotional support. However, she was also controlling and dominating. As shown earlier, the patient unconsciously wishes for the therapist to be that way as well. According to her experience, that's what a love object needs to be. Therapy should help the patient to make better and more realistic differentiations. The therapist fosters these differentiations by linking the present experience to similar ones with her mother. This kind of genetic transference interpretation (T/P Link) is viewed in TLDP as an intermediate, but not essential step along a line of inquiry that returns to a focus on the therapeutic relationship. However, as we have pointed out, by introducing these links as frequently as he has, the therapist may have short-circuited valuable examination of the patient's reactions to what transpires in the therapeutic relationship. Such linking interpretations should be used sparingly.

T: Have you noticed that with just about anything you say, you are very sensitive to what my reaction will be? That is, I keep coming back to that comment that you alluded to today that you made before, when you saw that I was looking somewhere else in the room and your sense of that was that I wasn't listening to you, dismissed you. I wonder if that isn't a constant presence for you, what do I think about everything you say.

P: I do want to know what you are thinking. I say a lot of things to you that I don't say to anybody else. And which I probably guard saying to other people just because I don't want to risk what their reaction will be.

T: Does it seem to you that the feeling is that unless there is proof otherwise you assume that someone is not interested in what you have to say?

P: You're saying . . . (Silence)

T: No matter how, like with us, no matter how, even when you feel that I am interested and am concerned about what is going on with you, even then there is still a nagging doubt, that's the best case, that you are always looking for some indication that you expect to be there that, in fact, I'm not. That any indication of interest in you and respect for your opinion is really a very thin veneer, that's not really how I feel. I would not say that's how you feel all the time, in other words, if there isn't always a part of you that wonders, a nagging doubt? You're looking stony faced again. (Chuckle)

The patient abruptly turns the tables on the therapist and aggressively questions him about his feelings. She evidently tries to put the therapist on the defensive. He responds by sharing his impression that the patient looks very vigilant and he wonders about that.

P: I've done most of the talking about the way that I feel. You ask me a lot of times, "What are you thinking about, what are you feeling?" It leaves me wondering what you feel. I don't know what you feel. (Laughs) But I also feel like I don't . . . this is another problem that I have. I think a lot of times I behave or I say to myself: "I'm not supposed to behave that way in this situation," and that goes back to my childhood. The thing that brought it home to me the most was listening to my mother talk to my children and say "You don't want to do such and such" and "You don't feel like that" and "You don't want to do that" and that kind of response. It suddenly hit me one day that if she talked to me like that when I was a child, she was constantly telling me something contrary to what I wanted to do or what I was thinking at the time. And so out of that, I got a lot of "You're supposed to do this" and "You're supposed to do that" and "You're supposed to feel this way" and "You're supposed to behave this way." And one of the things I have been feeling here is, and I was thinking about our relationship, and I think I've been thinking I'm supposed to behave and act in a certain way and things are supposed to be a certain way during the time that I am here, and that is, you're the therapist and I'm the client, and I talk about my feelings and you don't talk about yours (laughs nervously), you know, that sort of thing. And that has been bothering me lately because I think it hinders me from really knowing you as a person, as opposed to a therapist. Is that clear?

T: Yes. There are a few things that you are saying there. One it seems very pertinent to what we have been talking about is this recollection of the repeated experience of your mother telling you what you are really feeling. It sounds like that may be one of the things that really irritates you about what I say. That you come in feeling one thing, in fact you said that right at the beginning, you're feeling one thing and I tell you that you are experiencing something, I tell you, you shouldn't feel that way or you don't feel that way, this is what you *really* feel. That I treat you like your mother did. That your feelings don't count or they are wrong.

The therapist remains alert to how the patient experiences his actions and communications in terms of the focal theme. This includes how she misconstrues his attempts at helpful interventions. In listening to her description of childhood fights with her mother, the therapist comprehends an implicit complaint about the therapeutic relationship, particularly about what has just transpired between them. The therapist picks up on her latent message and shares it with her: he doesn't care about her feelings, because he knows how she "really" feels. As indicated in the following passages, this intervention hits home, and the patient begins to talk more freely about her irritation with the therapist and her difficulty in revealing it to him. It should also be noted that the therapist made a T/P linking interpretation subsequent to the patient spontaneously introducing material about her mother. While linking interpretations do not always require this condition, it is a useful guideline for the appropriate timing of such an intervention.

P: (Quietly) I hadn't thought about that. I think what I was trying to do with that, see, I was saying to myself, okay, you're the therapist, you have the skills to understand behavior and interpret it, and so forth and so . . . I was thinking that therefore, you must be right.

T: I'm your mother.

P: Yes, (Laugh) right. Rather, until today, well yesterday, when you did it again, I think I got more irritated. I was able to say to myself, "I am irritated, because he did it again." Whereas before, in the other incidents, I cried, when I said, "Yes, he's right."

T: You cried again today.

P: Yes, but I think that was more related to the fact that I said to you that I was irritated. In fact I was thinking about saying it, and when I got here, even saying the phrase "You irritate me," I was trying to think, I was trying to almost describe it in terms of the situation and avoiding saying "you," pinpoint you directly.

T: Well, before when you would cry when I would point something out, in the context of what you are remembering now about your experience with your mother, I wonder if that wasn't more of a feeling of being admonished and chastised by me, like a little girl being chastised by your mother. You cry because you felt hurt and disapproved of, rejected, and today I wonder if it wasn't more crying and feeling of falling apart because of the feeling of like criticizing your mother. Then you feel like your mother would be offended, like I would be offended. Like your mother would. That I would say that you're a bad little girl. I don't love you.

P: Which I was told as a child: never to talk back to my mother.

T: It seems that a lot of feeling would be involved in. . . . The feeling that you hurt me, that I would dismiss you, kick you out. Fear, loneliness.

P: Which rationally, I don't believe that. But, as you pointed out before, emotionally, that's the way I understand it. Automatic.

T: That's a good word for it: *automatic.*

P: I'm not even aware of it. When it happens and I respond that way.

T: Which is part of the question that we asked before: why is it continuously present? It's automatic.

P: I can't recognize ahead of time. I can't recognize how I am going to respond ahead of time. It just happens.

The patient produces further evidence of therapeutic learning. She has realized that she tends to relate to important figures in an automatic manner in terms of fixed expectations, rooted in relationships with significant figures from the past.

In the 11th session the focus appeared to shift from issues around the patient's inhibition of anger and assertiveness to behavioral inhibitions as well as guilt and shame associated with affectionate and sexual feelings. During a visit by the patient's mother, the patient was able for the first time to tell her how badly she feels when her mother is critical. The patient then grew silent and uncomfortable in the session. She recalled a dream during the therapist's one-week vacation. For the first time in years she dreamt of her husband; they were in bed and she felt warm and cozy. When the patient described this dream to her husband, he responded with a sexual overture from which the patient recoiled with irritation. The therapist suggested that, in part, the dream represented the patient's desire for a closer, more affectionate relationship with the therapist, but she feared the sexual implications. The patient agreed and stated that she "forced" such thoughts out of her mind. This interchange ushered in a discussion of sexual feelings about the therapist.

In the 12th interview, the patient continued to experience warm and sexual feelings toward the therapist and "guilty" feelings as well. The therapist continued to explore her reactions. She recalled an earlier memory in which she felt neglected by her husband while she was away obtaining further professional training. The patient was attracted to another man who paid attention to her but she felt guilty and refrained from getting involved. Now she realized that subsequently she had never allowed herself to feel even affection for another man and rarely feels it for her husband. In the following passage, the therapist attempted to interpret the patient's recent positive feelings for him.

T: That recollection does have similarity to what you are experiencing now, because there you felt that this man was there, he was interested in you. You were feeling lonely. You were away from home. And, you first had tried to contact your husband and he wasn't there. He wasn't available. You were disappointed, angry. It was in the context of being angry at him and hurt and disappointed that you feel this closeness and sexual arousal with this guy that is there. It's the same situation that you are feeling with me. In contrast to your husband, who is there physically but you feel is not there emotionally. I wonder how much of it is the sexual feelings themselves.

Or could they somehow be a way of expressing that you are disappointed or angry at your husband?

P: And feeling guilty about being angry.

T: Yes. I was wondering about that. It's almost as though the way you describe the contrast now between the way you feel about him and me and this recollection you have. One way of looking at it is that you're feeling warmly and sexually about me, and sexually interested in me, while on the one hand, it's a response to what you feel in our relationship, it is also a way of putting your husband down. He's not with you.

P: Because of the anger.

T: Well, anger is part of it, but he has disappointed you.

P: Now that makes me wonder what you feel. It sounds like my feelings toward you could be more a result of wanting to get revenge on my husband rather than a genuine feeling toward you. I think the feelings are there and they are genuine, but the source of those feelings may be more a way of getting revenge.

The therapist is surprised by the sudden upsurge of warm, sexual feelings in this characteristically emotionally controlled woman. He is also puzzled by his own lack of reciprocally warm feelings, because he is genuinely fond of her. However, the therapist ignores his puzzlement and pursues the idea that the patient's professed fondness for him represents revenge against her husband, whom she experiences as insensitive and neglectful. The patient attempts to accept the therapist's assertions but she appears to feel indignant and hurt over what she hears as the therapist's criticism. In fact, the therapist does feel that he has inadvertently devalued the patient's positive feelings. Furthermore, he realizes that he has lost empathic touch, having failed to understand how difficult it was for the patient to share her positive feelings with him. The therapist assumes that he has become caught in a countertransference reaction. He begins to ask himself what complementary role he has unwittingly enacted and the meaning of the patient's scenario. The answers are not immediately clear to him.

In the 13th interview the patient appeared distraught and stated that she felt bad after the previous interview. Furthermore, there was a resurgence of self-critical feelings, of being ugly and inept. The interview was confusing for the therapist, although he assumed this tone was in reaction to his previous unempathic response to the patient's positive overtures; that is, he assumed that the patient was having a negative reaction to his countertransference.

Case History Illustrating the TLDP Approach

The 14th interview occurred a day later than scheduled because the patient had canceled, complaining of a persistent headache. She begins this session by relating how harassed and out of sorts she had felt the past few days. The therapist immediately attempts to link her recent upset to events from their previous meetings.

T: In addition to all that and whatever busy stuff that was going on during the week, is there anything that you can recall from our session Tuesday morning that might have added to your pain in the head?

P: (Laugh) I was feeling really low from the previous session and I didn't feel too good Tuesday either, mentally, emotionally. And, I don't right now recall anything specific we talked about, I just was in one of those states where I felt generally bad about myself and everything, and the headache came on sometime after our session Tuesday in the afternoon or later in the day. I remember having sensed that it was coming. I came in here feeling rotten and I didn't leave feeling a whole lot better, except that I didn't feel quite as bad as I did when I came in. But I wasn't feeling very good about myself.

T: How do you mean?

P: I think I can describe the feelings I had as inadequate and ugly and generally ineffective and not happy with anything. I vaguely remember and we talked a little bit about your response to my feeling foolish and ridiculous, about the feelings I had toward you. I felt better about what went on here Tuesday than I had the previous time, but I wasn't really clear. Sometimes I'll come in here and things will be very clear and we talk and I understand what you are saying and there are other times that you'll say things that I'm not quite sure of, understand what you're saying and I have a sense of confusion, no clear feeling for what went on. I sort of had that feeling when I left Tuesday.

Often a confusing session—for the therapist as well as the patient— reflects the emergence of an important affective state that has not yet been adequately identified and acknowledged by the therapist. This certainly happened in the previous two interviews, in which the therapist realized that he had been unempathic but was not clear how this occurred.

T: This was this past Tuesday. Well, what was confusing?

P: Right now I can't think of anything specific. It's not coming back to me very readily as to what we talked about.

T: I've given it some thought and the more I've thought about it the more striking it seems what happened and it is not surprising. It seems that you would feel foolish about it as well as rotten because you had expressed some feelings which in retrospect are really—and I should have realized it at the time—are really difficult for you to express, personal feelings, both your feeling warmly toward me as well as sexually interested and my reaction was to—maybe this is exaggerated maybe not too much but it is certainly how you heard it—was to say, "Well, those feelings aren't real, you're just mad at your husband and trying to take it out on him." And given that's what you heard as my reaction, it's not surprising you feel foolish and you feel rotten about yourself. What's missing though and seems equally reasonable that you would feel pissed off at me, for responding that way.

P: For discounting the feelings. Did you intentionally do that (Laugh) . . . respond that way?

T: I'm not sure why I picked up on that and whether there is a kernel of truth in it or not, which in a way is not as important as the fact that I did, and could be seen as discounting you. So for me it raises two questions. One is you felt foolish and you felt rotten, but where is the anger? The other question is why it happened as it did?

P: Why it happened as it did?

T: Yes. Whatever part I contributed to that is something that I need to look at. But for our purposes, for you, we need to look at what is going on between us.

P: But the time where you responded that it may be the anger toward my husband.

T: Well, more generally, you reached out to me, expressing feelings that are very personal, very important, and intimate. And felt discounted. In terms of what is going on there, I wonder if that is simply an experience that you had with me.

P: Where I have reached out and gotten that kind of response?

T: Yes.

P: Are you asking if I can remember anything specific, a similar kind of thing?

Between sessions the therapist has been trying to clarify in his own mind the nature of his countertransference reaction in the 12th session and how it might shed further light on the scenario currently being enacted in the therapeutic relationship. In the preceding passage, he describes how the patient must have felt, thus reestablishing empathic contact with her, and he acknowledges his role in what has happened between them. Having admitted his error, he begins to inquire about the patient's reactions. The goal is not to blame the patient (her transference) or himself (his counter-transference), but to work collaboratively to understand the transactions. Furthermore, the therapist endeavors to incorporate the material into the focal theme—the patient's inability to constructively assert herself and express anger.

The patient had felt that the therapist had been detached and stern in response to her expression of positive feelings toward him. However, he seemed less so now and she didn't feel he was usually that way. The patient recalled her mother's disapproving attitude. She then talked about a phone call she had made to the therapist to reschedule the current session. She felt that he had been perturbed. The therapist commented on her use of his first name during this phone call.

P: Well, I've thought about that a lot . . . about what to call you. And I've always had the tendency to call you Dr. L. I don't know, for some reason I felt like calling you M. So I did it. But I had a funny feeling about it and then you weren't very friendly over the phone, and I thought, well, you didn't like for me to do that. But, I did it.

T: What do you make of having experienced me in reaction to your making overtures, your expressing a closeness to me? That I seemed stern and detached?

P: What do I make of that?

T: Yes, did I disapprove of you, like your mother? (Pause) What possibility is it of having the misfortune of ending up with a therapist just like your mother, or something else?

P: No, I don't think you are like my mother. I discount that, immediately (laughs).

T: Let's see what else we could come up with (smile).

P: The only thing that comes to mind is that it is part of that conflict I feel about what is appropriate behavior and what isn't. Even though I think you are open to hearing anything I have to say, and even though I have those feelings, there shouldn't be anything wrong with it. But you are a part of it and I don't know. It gets all mixed up in my mind in terms of I am here to work out any problems and that it's not appropriate to start having these feelings about you personally. In that way. I don't know why I see you as disapproving unless it's part of my problem of dealing with my own self-concept.

That I don't think highly enough of myself to think that would be flattering to you or be a compliment to you or whatever.

T: See, making a distinction between working out your problems and the feelings you are having toward me, is there any difference? Aren't those precisely what you've been feeling toward me both before and then most recently, precisely the things that have been causing you a problem? The way you experienced me in the first few sessions was as very bristly and disapproving and critical and you had to be very careful. And you described that as like your mother. Always ready to discount what you have to say. To disapprove, to be critical. And then you began to feel more warmly toward me. You felt that I wasn't that way. That I listened to you in a way that your mother didn't, that your husband didn't. And you began to have feelings toward me, maybe a lot of them were because you wanted to have a closeness with me, maybe in a way you wanted to with your mother. And that ended up again with you feeling rebuffed and chastised.

The therapist again articulates the patient's focal theme (in its current variation) as the reenactment of an earlier predisposition. The patient is struggling with the realization—now experienced as well as intellectually understood—that her central relationship problems have also shaped the therapeutic relationship. But their appearance in this relationship provides the opportunity for examining and correcting them. The therapist helps her in comprehending this opportunity. He has succeeded in turning his "mistake" in session 12 into constructive therapeutic learning.

P: I went back to sort out my expectation of coming here and I, it looks like, I don't know how to say this, it looks like I expected to come here and talk about what is bothering me and try to figure out what the problems are which started all of it without getting involved with you as a person. It . . . I was thinking about that because I don't think I ever thought about that too much. Does that make sense?

T: Why would you ask me?

P: I am having trouble and I don't think I sound very clear. I didn't anticipate or expect that I would relate to you as a person or something. You are a therapist and you are going to be off out here somewhere, listening to my problems and everything and relating to you as a person and getting involved with what is going on and how to feel in relating toward you, I didn't even think about that initially. Which is kind of ridiculous.

232

T: Why is it ridiculous?

P: Because you can't relate to people that way. There is always going to be some type of interaction, some kind of response.

T: You are the same person here that you are outside.

P: Regardless of who I am interacting with. It's just exactly what you were saying. It would seem likely that the same kinds of things would happen here as would happen in my relationships with other people.

T: What we have seen is your expectation that around feeling that in response to your overtures for closeness, I'd be very detached or again, disapproving, discounting, that somehow it happens again.

P: The interesting thing is that, intellectually, I can say that it's probably not true, it probably would not happen. But, that's, emotionally that's the way I respond. It seems like I'm always setting people up to be that way.

The 15th interview witnesses a further shift in the patient's predisposition to perceive the therapist as stern and disapproving like her mother. While she continues to experience her husband in this fashion, she increasingly tries to protect her image of the therapist as a "good object." They discuss the possibility that this behavior recapitulates her childhood avoidance of confrontations with her father, in order to protect her wish for a special and close relationship with him. The patient had been on a trip with her husband between the 14th and 15th interviews and felt closer and more sexually responsive with him than she had in years. On their return, however, her old coolness and resentment returned. The 16th session began with the patient describing how she woke up that morning feeling angry at everyone and everything. This was a new experience for her, perhaps reflecting improvement in her ability to recognize and experience feelings that previously had been disavowed because she considered them unacceptable.

P: I got up this morning feeling horrible, furious at everybody in the world. And, I don't know what's gone wrong, who I'm mad at, who I was mad at, who has made me angry or what. I feel a headache coming on. The same kind of physical symptoms I felt when I have been angry before. I am really puzzled about how to figure out what is the source of the anger and how to identify what is bringing it on. I can't, nothing comes to mind about what we talked about in our session that made me feel that way.

The patient is able to acknowledge that she feels "furious." Furthermore, she begins spontaneously to examine previous events in the therapeutic relationship for the source of this feeling. In so doing, she has accepted an important facet of TLDP's modus operandi. Her behavior is also indicative of the existence of a solid working alliance.

T: How would you put it into words?
P: How would I put it into words? You mean "I am furious"?
T: Yes, whatever that feeling is, just blurt it out.
P: I feel as if I am irritated. I am frustrated.
T: About what?
P: That's what I can't figure out.
T: Whatever comes to mind.
P: Well, the only thing that really comes to mind in terms of looking back at what has happened in the last few days. This is just terribly hard for me to say . . . when I talked to you on the phone the other night, you said it was Dr. L, and it has bothered me ever since, and you are smiling as if you expected that. (Laughs)
T: I am smiling because I was going to ask you how you felt about me doing that.
P: Why were you going to ask?
T: Well, it struck me again that you did call me by my first name. And I called myself by my last name. It happened a couple of times over the last few weeks. So, it sounds like you're furious at me.
P: It sounds like it, but I keep saying that's ridiculous and the same old thing. I keep saying to myself that if that is what you prefer to call yourself to me, then why should I get so furious, be so upset about it, be so sensitive about it, try to rationalize the way I feel.
T: Rather than try to rationalize it, let's try to look at it some more.

Patient and therapist are on the same wavelength; both have a hunch that her anger is directed toward the therapist and that it has something to do with another phone conversation about appointment times. A seemingly unimportant matter, such as the use of the first or last names, can become the carrier of important feelings (in this case relating to emotional closeness). The therapist should not unreflectively go along with the patient's preferences about this (or other facets of the therapeutic arrangements) nor should he rigidly adhere to a routine mode of working without remaining alert to the patient's reactions.

The patient felt "slapped in the face" but wished to avoid confronting the therapist. Although she views her reaction as "ridiculous" she proceeds to describe her dislike of using last names with subordinates at work, by implication accusing the therapist of being rigid about how he addresses her. The patient can't confront the therapist directly and becomes teary. He assumes, in the following passages, that the patient's tears hide her anger.

T: Are you feeling furious with me now?

P: I'm feeling teary when I talk about it (crying). It's the same old thing. I bring up something that is very uncomfortable, then I start crying, and I guess it's all trying to express something that upsets me, the anger or whatever, directly to you and I don't really expect any particular kind of wrath to come from you as a result of it or any kind of violent reaction, but I cannot understand why I get so upset about it (crying harder). And, I knew that if I didn't say something about it, I would have the worst headache there ever was by the time I got out of here.

T: You said it would be difficult, but it was a lot easier for you to tell me you were angry at me, than it has been before. But in crying, do you have a sense of what the feelings are that are there? Is it that anger or is it something else?

P: It doesn't seem like anger, it seems like hurt. That's the only way that I can describe it.

T: So, we know that you feel hurt and really furious at me, but what you can experience with me is just the hurt.

Here again, the therapist carefully explores the patient's affective state. He attempts to examine the nuances of her feelings, how she handles them (defensively and adaptively), and what they reveal about the manner in which she construes the immediate transactions in therapy.

The therapist reiterates how the patient was primarily "furious" at him for, as she saw it, rebuffing her overtures for closeness by refusing to go along in using first names. Furthermore, he points out that she acts as though her anger doesn't count for much, thus demonstrating how she has internalized her perception of the attitudes of others toward her feelings. They briefly explore the origin of this part of her self-concept in terms of the patient's experience of parental disapproval when she expressed her feelings. The therapist then brings the discussion back to what has been happening between them.

T: Getting back to why, what came to mind for you was the scenario about your employees and your becoming more flexible about it and you figuring that when you felt that, when you wanted employees to call you by your last name, that's a way of keeping distance, pushing away. I wonder if that is how you experience things here.

P: I think that that is the only thing that I really had to compare it to. I didn't think about that until this morning, when I was walking across the street. Probably that would be the initial reaction, based on my behavior.

T: And what we have been talking about in the last few sessions is your desire to have a close relationship with me, share with me affectionate feelings toward me, your sexual feelings toward me, and before felt that I had pushed you away. I wonder if again that's the same experience. It's not a question of names, it's a question of that you felt, a part of you felt, that this was the overture again, for us to have a closer relationship. A more affectionate relationship. A different kind of relationship than a doctor-patient [relationship]. And that you felt that my calling myself by my last name, I was pushing you away, and that is why you were so furious.

P: I think that's probably what I felt but I think the thing that bothers me the most is, why should I get so furious about it? If that . . . I just don't understand why I should be so sensitive to that.

T: To be pushed away by someone you want to get close to?

P: Yes.

The therapist weaves events of the last few sessions, and the meanings which the patient has attributed to them, into the focal theme. He does this at each opportunity, attempting to help the patient to recognize, understand and work through the many variations of the predisposition which is enacted in the therapeutic relationship.

The patient begins the 17th interview by relating how a headache she had during the previous session disappeared immediately afterwards. She attributes this to her ability to reveal her anger to the therapist. During this interview the therapist makes a comment about the patient's "overture" to reveal more about himself. She feels that the therapist is tuning her out and then she feels self-conscious. The therapist suggests that her experience is a reaction to interpreting his comment as accusing her of making a sexual overture. The patient recalls a dream from the previous night in which two men are lying on a hard surface and she is joking around with them. Her mother and sister are present and disapprove of her playfulness. In the dream she is thinking: "If only they knew that I enjoy it." The patient disavows any sexual attraction to the therapist or her husband but finds herself between sessions engaging in sexual fantasies about men who are attractive to her. The patient experiences shame over her sexual and playful feelings of which she imagines the therapist disapproves.

Evidently, as a result of working systematically on the patient's expectation of disapproval of her angry and playful feelings, she has become more accepting of them. She is more in touch with her sexual feelings and fantasies but remains ashamed of them. This shift in the salient content of the therapy illustrates the process by which previously disavowed feelings and fantasies become more accessible to examination, resulting in an expansion of the focal theme. Here the patient has begun to deal with her sexual inhibitions and associated feelings of shame. Her predisposition to experience the therapist as a maternal figure who disapproves of assertiveness and anger (and sexual feelings) has begun to give way to experiencing him as a paternal figure who evokes playful and sexual feelings but who may also disapprove of them.

In the 18th session the patient states that she felt more affectionate and sexual toward her husband. She recalled a dream after the previous interview in which she capitulates to the therapist's wish to be called by his last name and she pleads with him not to desert her. She sees a connection between the dream experience and the relationship with her father, with whom she could be playful to a certain extent. The patient feels that she can be somewhat playful with and curious about the therapist, but if she goes too far he becomes disapproving.

While the patient's apprehension about the impending termination date has been implicit in her dream, she directly raises concerns toward the end of the interview. In the 19th session the patient states that she felt closer to the therapist after the last interview. She related a dream occurring between these sessions, in which she was at home with her husband naked and feeling "playful and free." In another part of the dream the therapist was present and inadvertently let slip that he liked pizza. The patient acknowledged that she felt more warmly and sexually aroused by her husband than she had in years. She wore a "mysterious" nightgown to bed one night and they made love in a new and exciting way. The therapist noticed that the patient was giving more information about her sexual feelings and behavior—in her dreams and awake—but was concealing details. He commented that both the manner in which she was relating her experiences and the general atmosphere in the interview had a coy and playful quality. The patient responded that she had been eager to come to the session but just prior to it had the panicky thought: "What is happening to me?" The therapist wondered if that wasn't a reaction to the playful, warm, and sexual feelings she had experienced recently; she enjoyed them but she also feared that they would result in harm to her.

It should be noted that the affective quality of the transactions between patient and therapist is often of greatest significance. In this case the content of the patient's communications should be listened to, but the content may, for the moment play a secondary role in helping the therapist understand the latent meaning of the patient's immediate behavior. In session 19, the therapist notices that he is not getting a clear picture of the patient's sexual experiences and feelings and he is impelled to quiz her about details.

In session 20 the patient raises the impending termination date as her primary concern.

P: Before we get started today, could we talk about the end of this, or the continuation or whatever, in terms of the timing in relation to the project?

T: Well, what are your feelings about it?

P: I'm feeling like I don't want to quit at the end of the time period. I just need to talk about it, and I really respect your input.

T: I think that is something that is certainly timely to talk about. What are your thoughts about it?

P: Well, right now I feel like so much is happening and I feel the sessions are not long enough. I always leave here recently feeling there is so much more I want to talk about and it seems like I am getting sort of a frenzied feeling, I don't know if it is because I know time is catching up with us. I just feel that I am just beginning to put things together and get a sense of what is going on, but yet I'm not really there yet. And I just feel like it is a mistake to stop.

T: I didn't catch the word you said . . . what kind of feeling?

P: Frenzied.

T: Frenzied.

P: I come here and there is so much I want to say and so much is going on and I know that I'm not going to have time to get it all in in this one session, and I can hardly wait to get to the next session. That is kind of the way I am feeling right now. I don't know if that is related to stuff I haven't thought of or whether it is because of a lot of what is going on. But, I need to know what is going to happen at the end of the three months, in terms of this. If I can continue. Is that an option?

T: Sure, it's an option. But before, we should think it over. Let us look a moment at what that experience is like for you. This frenzied feeling that you [have], the session is not long enough, that there is too much to talk about, you can't wait from one session to another. Also, you mentioned the last time that sometimes you get cold feet so you have mixed feelings about it. Can you say some more about what it is like for you? What it is that you feel that you need to get out of the session and why it is not long enough?

The patient immediately raises her concerns about the impending termination date. Her sense of urgency evoked by the time limits is evident: "time is catching up with us." A patient's reaction to termination in this form of therapy inevitably blends common reactions to the loss of a valued relationship with idiosyncratic experiences from the past. This patient presses the therapist for reassurance that they will not have to stop at the agreed upon time. While acknowledging that the termination date is something for both to assess, the therapist maintains the same attitude that he has adopted throughout: He is curious about the patient's experience and its affective meanings in terms of their relationship.

P: Well, just like last time. I wanted to tell you what happened over the weekend. I wanted to tell you about the dream that I had and that it just seems like there are a lot of things going on that I'm coming here to tell you about and try to figure out what it means, if it means anything, and how it fits into whatever and everything else that has been going on. I also feel like I still have a lot of tension about our relationship and what goes on here. I go away sometimes feeling, I just have this sense of, and I'm not sure about what is going on here with us, and I see things getting better with my husband and this is nice, but now I'm concerned that maybe I'm doing some of the same kind of things with you here that I want to try and get straightened out. I hate to see it just stop before that time. I'm uncomfortable with that, I'm concerned about it. I'm not ready to give it up. I think when I get this feeling that you are not listening and you're not concerned or whatever, I haven't really, at the time I'm getting the feeling that a lot of times I don't really stop and say, "What is going on with you right now?" I'm getting this kind of message from you. And I need to check out whether my perception is right, because I know I have a tendency to draw conclusions and just go on and then stew about it, I think that's what I've been doing. I get so wrapped up in what I want to say and what I want to tell you about what's happening that it's hard to think about the other.

The patient is not ready to give up her relationship with the therapist. The therapist's attitude is to examine her wishes toward him and the feared consequences of leaving the therapeutic relationship. These questions are examined in the context of the focal theme. Furthermore, the manner in which the patient copes with the threat of termination is a variation of the characteristic ways in which she has struggled with salient interpersonal conflicts. In the preceding passage the patient states that there are still many things she wants to talk over: her dreams, her sexual behavior with her husband, her reactions to the therapist. While her wish to share this potentially rich therapeutic material reflects a realistic appraisal of work that could be pursued, it can also be viewed as her characteristic attempts to be a "good girl" who capitulates (recall her recent dream about capitulating to avoid desertion) to the therapist's expectations.

They continue to discuss the patient's concerns about terminating at the stipulated time. These concerns increasingly center on her relationship with the therapist.

P: Another part of it is that in coming here I didn't, it just never even occurred to me that that sort of thing could happen . . .

T: What sort of thing?

P: That anything could happen between us. It was like, I'm so puzzled by that, I guess. I have the expectation that, well I didn't have the expectation that I would have feelings about you, and I think that's kind of ridiculous when I think about it. Intellectually, it's kind of ridiculous because how can two people interact and not have some feelings transmitted but I expected, I guess, that not to happen here.

T: What did you expect?

P: What had I expected? That we would never talk about what was going on between us. I didn't have that expectation. I just thought it would always be external factors, and I didn't expect to get caught up in feelings that I had about you and what was going on between us.

T: What are your thoughts about why that's real important to you now?

P: I don't know. As I said, it may not be, maybe I'm not sure at this point that it needs to be brought up, but I feel like I haven't had enough time to get assurance.

T: What do you feel is uncertain? What needs to get done before you feel comfortable inside?

P: I think one thing that needs to happen, I need to be able to react to my feelings when they occur here. And, not just let it go by and stew about it later. Sometimes, I have a sense that I would like to know if what I am sensing from you is what is happening. Because I think I have a tendency to misinterpret you a lot of times.

T: You feel you are able to do that better now in your relationship with your husband?

P: I haven't really done it a lot. That is a whole area that still needs a lot of thought. Last week was the beginning, the first step in terms of my being able to tell my husband about my feelings very easily, and not get all foggy in the head.

Understandably, the patient is apprehensive about terminating and feels that there is much unfinished business. The therapist, for his part, does not attempt to reassure her that "everything will be all right" or that they have accomplished enough. Instead, he treats the patient's feelings and reactions in the same customary manner—as expressions of the patient's central relationship issues. In response to his inquiry, the patient states that she is much more aware of her automatic predispositions but feels that she needs more time in therapy to master them more adequately. The therapist acknowledges the patient's realistic appraisal of progress but continues to search for the meaning termination has for her.

T: It sounds like what has changed most is that it's not as automatic a thing and you're very aware of it now.

P: Uhm Humm.

T: In addition to your feelings about that there are certain things that have started, that you have done some work on. You feel it would be useful for us to do some more in many ways. The things that you feel are important changes that you are making. You have just begun.

P: Uhm, Hmm.

T: In addition to that, in terms of your experience in our relationship, the feelings that you have been talking about, about me. What thoughts do you have about how that takes a role in your not wanting to stop?

P: Initially, when we talked about my sexual feelings toward you and I was terribly frightened by that, it's a question I had and I was thinking about it, I couldn't remember how it was that you happened to ask that, and I was wondering if the whole thing about my behavior kind of lets people, and I know I'm having a lot of trouble with the sexual part versus the whatever. For some reason I seem to want

to separate the two out, and that whole thing is unsettled for me.
And I feel like all my inhibitions that have been squashed since I
came here are ready to explode. (Laughs nervously) And I don't
know what.

T: Well, what comes to mind?

P: Well, I don't know. I feel like I want to learn to play the guitar, I want
to sing, I want to fly away somewhere or something. (Laughs) I have
these real light, kind of airy feelings, to run around the house naked
and carry on. (Laughs)

T: Sounds like fun.

P: (Laughs) Yes.

The patient appears particularly concerned about not completing sufficient work on the issue that has been the primary focus recently: the shame
she feels in reaction to her playful and sexual feelings, which have been
inhibited but which are now less so. She appears to believe that she will
not be able to free her positive feelings without the therapist's support.

P: Well, I think I keep going back to the sexual feelings I had, that being
so unexpected, I just, I get real hung up in relating to men on a sexual
basis versus . . . lately I relate to every man I see in the street, sizing
them up in terms of how good they are in bed or something, and that
is real bothersome to me. I think that's a way I am relating to men.

T: Well, it's one thing to be sizing them up on the street versus inviting
them to proposition you, and the way you respond or your attitude
about it, it's as though they were the same.

P: Yes. It looks exactly that way, as brought out about the feelings I had
toward you. [This would have been a good opportunity for the
therapist to inquire about what the patient currently perceived were
the therapist's attitudes about her sexual feelings for him. Such an
inquiry would have assessed whether the patient's concerns about
termination were contributed to by the fantasy that the therapist still
disapproved of her sexual feelings.]

T: How would you experience men before you started feeling this way?

P: Sort of avoidance. I didn't . . . difficulty relating to them. I have
always had trouble just talking, just conversation.

T: Is that different now?

P: It's a little different now. In fact, I've noticed it. I can even encounter
somebody, a man, who I don't even know and maybe I know a little
bit, not well, and I can joke and cut up, and sort of banter back and
forth, which has always been a real problem for me.

T: Well, now before, when you saw a man as attractive, that would now be attractive to you, inside you're saying he looks pretty good, how would you handle it before?

P: Before?

T: Before you started experiencing these feelings?

P: When I'd talk, I'd really need to control myself and be careful about it, the way I looked and acted, and what I'd say. Afraid I'd be transmitting a "come on" sort of a message.

T: So before you were also aware of being sexually curious but you immediately had to squelch it, so that's not different?

P: That's not really, no not entirely. That's part of the problem. I think because I now just feel less need to control it. I feel like more like I could be playful, but I, it doesn't threaten me. It doesn't mean that anything is going to happen.

T: It sounds like you have started to feel more comfortable with men. You enjoy contact with men. What's bothersome then? What I hear you saying is a little different from what I thought you said before. What I hear you saying is that you have always been sexually curious about men, now you just feel more comfortable with it.

P: Well, I guess it's the whole thing of sexual interest, I guess. And thinking about that before I even know the person, it's like, that part of me that was always taught that sex and intimacy and physicalness, was reserved for someone you were very bound to, and were going to spend the rest of your life with. That sort of thing.

T: That sounds like you still believe that. We are talking about your curiosity.

P: Well, when I'm in a situation where I'm with a man, with the person I'm supposed to spend my life with, and I should not be having all these sexual feelings about other men.

T: Well, do you think that is pretty common?

P: Well, this friend I have, she feels the same way and she and I have had a lot of discussions about that.

T: Then, there are two of you walking around.

P: There are two of us. (Laughs)

T: Well, how would you feel if you never had any sexual curiosity about any other men?

P: Other than my husband? Well, recently I feel like it would cut out a lot of time (Laughs). Maybe that's why I feel all of a sudden, it's a big thing with me. It's becoming more fun. I'm not threatened by thinking something is going to happen if I feel that way.

T: So if you were, felt like you experienced your parents teaching you.

You never had any sexual curiosity or sexual interest in any other man, would that, in terms of what you do, would that make life just a lot less fun?

P: Another thing that just popped into my head was I said that with my husband the other night, I felt like I'd enjoy being somebody's mistress and just being put up in a plush place and not having to do any of the nitty gritty grimy stuff related to everyday life. His response was, "Yes, I think I'd enjoy being somebody's gigolo, too" (laugh) and he said, "Is that one of your fantasies?" and I said, "Well, yes, it's fun to fantasize about it" and he said, "As long as nothing comes of it." I mean, just that flat out answer, and I thought, I wonder if he thinks I'm going to do something! My experience from him was that it was okay to think about it as long as I don't do it!

T: Because he does it, too.

P: Because what? He does it too.

T: It looks like we have two women and one man who walk around here having these fantasies.

P: (Laughs)

T: The population is growing.

P: You are very cynical.

T: (Laugh) Going back to if we look at what we talked about today, in terms of your initial question, you're very concerned about stopping. Try to understand a little more about your concerns in terms of what you said today. It seems like aside from the very real issue that you feel you've worked out some important things, and they're not done, and you don't feel you have done as much as you like. By the way, parenthetically, the question is very realistic that how do you know how much you've done. That's a very realistic concern, but what went into that? It sounds like it is also a feeling that our relationship has gotten to be comfortable. Maybe you don't want to give it up for that reason. I also wonder if there isn't a nagging feeling on your part, even though it sounds like you feel very good and confident, more confident, more optimistic about making changes you feel are very good for you, and that you feel the ball is rolling. I wonder if there is the nagging feeling that somehow it is tied to my sanctioning it and that if we stopped, it will all just collapse, maybe that is not the best word, maybe it is like the barn door will slam shut again.

P: Well, I think that I hadn't thought about it specifically, your sanctioning it, but I had thought about what would happen if we terminated this right now and not at a point where its internalized: "It's my feelings and it's okay with me." I'm not sure.

More evidence accumulates that the patient fantasizes that her new ability to feel closer and more comfortable with people is based on the therapist's approval. This fantasy reflects a continuation of the patient's tendency to view the therapist, in part, as a personification of parental figures; she is a "good little girl" who will not do anything without parental approval. The patient acknowledges the influence of this anachronistic predisposition and in an intellectualized manner speaks of the need to internalize further what she experiences as the therapist's approving attitude. We may note here her defensive use of the therapeutic relationship as a means to stave off termination.

In session 21 termination continues to be the main topic of discussion. The therapist helps the patient further explore her complex feelings about the possibility of stopping soon. The patient feels sad, which the therapist acknowledges as expected when an important relationship ends. In addition, they examine the absence of angry feelings at this point and wonder if the patient's feeling of detachment might not mask her lost anger at her therapist. The patient feels as though the therapist is threatening to reject her, and the recent profusion of complex dreams and other material is examined in terms of her complaint that there is too much going on to stop therapy. In session 22 the patient feels that she has regressed, and all of her old self-doubts and inhibitions have returned. Her mother is visiting, and the patient feels a great deal of tension in their relationship.

T: It sounds again like you feel that this is not at all a good time to think about ending.

P: That I'm sure of it.

T: So you give yourself some pretty convincing evidence that, as we talked about last time, that maybe all of the progress you felt you made was real tenuous, collapsing.

P: That's exactly what I feel like is happening today. I feel like I can handle my husband a little better. I'm beginning to feel better about that, but this whole thing that came up with her [mother] again. . . .

T: We also see that there is, especially the last time, there are a number of reasons why you wouldn't want to stop, end our relationship. Which I think raises the question of how much you are trying to convince us, even at your own expense, that this is a bad time to stop?

P: Why do you ask, well, what's wrong with trying to convince us? I feel that I'm just relating what has happened and that the doubt and questions I have about it which I have a right to convince you.

T: You sound kind of irritated with what I said? [Therapist focuses on the patient's affect—a topic which should always be given priority.]

P: It sounds like what you are saying is that I am deliberately trying to make my case and maybe I interpret that in a wrong way, I don't know. I think right now, today, I feel kind of desperate. And I guess I don't understand, that when we talked about this and I was kind of frantic up until we finally had the session where we finally talked about it, and after that I felt better. Of course, it still hasn't been decided. It hasn't been clear.

T: Part of that decision, an important part of it, is looking at how you react and how you feel about how you react to the possibility of our stopping. When you said, for instance, that you recall that when you were a kid and you and your mother were at odds with each other, that what you could do was vow that you would not speak to her, which must have upset and hurt you as much as her. Is it possible that part of you is doing the same thing now? In other words, that you are feeling that everything is collapsing, that you are having the same problems that you had before, the same inhibitions. That is a way of not speaking, an expression of your disappointment and anger at me. We've been thinking about stopping our relationship, but your reaction is at your expense, because it hurts you.

P: Well, I hadn't really thought about that. What I keep hearing you say is that I'm burying a lot of stuff in relationship to us.

T: That you are what?

P: Burying. That there is a possibility that what I'm saying, I am reacting to something I don't want to hear. I am describing it as totally based on what is going on outside of here.

T: Well, if you think of it that's kind of surprising and striking because all along we have been doing that and it has made sense and all of a sudden it doesn't.

P: That's why I'm saying if I just blocked it out, so it never even occurs to me.

T: That's very likely. It's especially surprising since what we are looking at now is a reaction to something that is very difficult for anybody —ending an important relationship. So it's doubly surprising that you felt it didn't have anything to do with us.

The patient's desperation about terminating is increasing, reflected in the reemergence of her original symptoms in relationships outside of therapy and in emotional withdrawal from the therapist. While the patient may panic at the prospect of termination, the therapist, clearly, should not.

The pressure of time is a reality for both participants and the therapist may struggle with his own doubts about whether enough has been accomplished. However, he should maintain a consistent attitude of examining the meanings of termination for the patient. While he can always take stock of the appropriateness of terminating—even in the last planned interview—we strongly recommend that the therapist adhere to the established termination date. The patient's anger and disappointment with the therapist are increasingly evident though unexpressed. The therapist attempts to examine how she is handling these feelings, in terms of the characteristic ways she has dealt with interpersonal conflicts throughout her life. He interprets her increasing difficulties outside of therapy as a plea for continued contact with the therapist. The patient makes the surprising comment that she never connected her outside experiences with her current feelings about the therapist. The therapist points out this remarkable lapse in the patient's characteristic perceptiveness about the influence of the therapeutic relationship. This lapse further evidences her intense struggle with the idea of terminating.

The patient began session 23 complaining that the therapist has "put me through hell." She was emotionally withdrawn and had trouble listening to the therapist. When he commented on this, the patient became tearful and said that she felt sad. While she consciously felt helpless, the therapist wondered if her emotional detachment reflected an obstinate refusal to vent her anger toward the therapist. Session 24 begins with the patient reflecting on her recent behavior.

P: Well, I've come out of my misery. I feel better today. My husband and I had a talk the other night and he said something to me about the spring of the year and that he had noticed that at this time of the year, just about every year, I get a real low and he asked me if I had thought about it and he said when did I remember one of the first times feeling that way, and I thought back to my illness and that year he went off in the summer and so forth. He said, "No, that's not the earliest time." I said, "When was it?" He said it was the first year we were married, that it was the spring of the year. I wanted to quit graduate school and I was feeling really depressed and low and it was funny because I thought all that happened in the fall. But, then I got to looking farther back and trying to pinpoint separation from somebody I had a very close relationship with. And . . .

T: Go back over that again.

P: Well, I was trying to think farther back, because he was telling me that he was very disappointed that I had regressed and things were not going well and he had really been happy the time I had been in a good mood and it looked like we were working some things out, and I was trying to think back farther and the next thing that I can think of [was] a significant relationship I have had with men I had been closely involved in, it seems like at this time of the year is when I terminated my relationship with the man I talked about and had the dreams about. It's also the time I broke off the engagement with the person before that. It's also the time, I was thinking, my father died in January and just after that was the time I was going through breaking up the relationship with the older man. I was trying to go back farther than that to see if I can think of anything else and the next thing that popped into my mind that I hadn't thought about was the time when I was a real small child and something was wrong with my mother, she was ill, and I was sent to an aunt's house and I knew, it was a terrible experience, I remember being terribly unhappy the whole time I was there, but I remember riding the bus home by myself, and I always wondered if that was in fact what happened. And I couldn't have been over four or five years old. I know my dad met me at the bus station.

T: You rode the bus by yourself?

P: Yes, I rode the bus by myself back home and my dad met me at the bus station. My mother, I don't know where she was, whether she was still in the hospital or whether she was home or what, but, so I asked her this morning. I was just curious at what time of the year that happened and she said it was in the fall. I was asking her what happened that made me have to go off to this aunt's house and she said that she probably had a nervous breakdown, because she was very depressed and she was crying all the time and apparently my older brother had broken his leg playing football and she was experiencing a situation in which she couldn't cope. And so, I was sent off, and I don't remember where my sister was, I guess she was still at home. I just remember the experience being very bad at this aunt's house because she was very authoritarian, worse than my parents. She was just mean. Mother was not real clear on the length of time I stayed up there. She said she thought it was a short time. What had happened was this aunt who was her sister came down to sort of take care of things at home and help mother, and mother said she couldn't stand her. She felt that there was a conflict between them and so she just told her to go back home and take me with her. So we rode back on the bus together and I came back by myself. Mother said she thought I was probably four years old. The thought of putting my child on a bus by herself to send her somewhere just appalls me, it is just horrible to me.

The patient has been through a difficult time struggling with her reactions to the impending termination. At the same time, she has remained committed to the work of therapy. In seeking between sessions to understand why facing termination has been so traumatic, she attempted to recall earlier separation experiences. It turns out that at this time of the year she has endured several major losses, including her father's death when she was in her twenties. Furthermore, she recalled a particularly traumatic separation from her family when she was four or five years old. She had not thought about this for years. In discussing this memory, her strong reaction to how horrible it was for her mother to allow her to be sent away partly reflects her attitude about the therapist holding to the termination date. While the therapeutic alliance remains strong and supports their continued work, at another level the patient still resents the therapist for treating her cruelly. If these feelings are not thoroughly examined, the patient is in danger of experiencing the termination as a recapitulation of what she construed as earlier instances of neglect and abandonment by her parents, over which she had no control.

P: And now I'm thinking about the things we're talking about here, terminating, and here it is, this time of the year again, another relationship that has been meaningful and suddenly it's going to end and I know, like when my daddy died, the thing that I remember thinking, being the saddest about, was that I felt that I never really knew him. And was close to him. Never had developed that emotional closeness that I would have liked to have had.

T: Which is exactly how you feel about me.

P: Uh-huh.

T: When did he die?

P: He died in January.

T: Of which year?

P: Sixty-seven. My husband seems to think that I go through this cycle every year. We talk about it and he thinks he has seen it since we have been married, not necessarily every year, but he particularly related it to the first year we were married and when I was in graduate school.

T: You know, your earliest memory was of being left.

P: Yes, and I don't know what time of year that was. I would suspect that it was spring or summer. Because the weather was warming up and I know the weather was warm because they were going fishing when I left.

T: In a way, it doesn't even matter what time of the year it was. That memory seems to include all of the losses, emotionally. It sounds as if it is a very important experience for you.

P: You know the other day when you said, you made some statement about it's hard when you terminate a relationship that has been meaningful to you, I can't remember exactly what you said, I almost burst into tears. And I thought you were saying to me, I really thought you were saying, this was the end. That's the way I felt. Even though that decision hadn't been made specifically. That's how I felt. My husband and I had a really good talk the other night. But, I brought up the fact that did he expect me to make a lot of changes, and he said no. He said it may take you three years or something like that. I said, "Are you saying that it's a hopeless situation?" He said, "No, I think that the next few months will be critical in terms of what you do and how you handle yourself. But I am willing to stick by you through it all." He was really very supportive. I just thought, unlike him. If he'd talk to me like that once a month, our problems would be okay.

T: What are your thoughts about these memories that are coming up about various losses? How do you feel? What do you make of them in terms of what you're struggling with about ending our relationship?

The patient feels as though the therapist has told her that she must leave at the appointed time. She feels, in part, like a helpless child who is being put out by a callously insensitive parent, regardless of the upset that it causes her. They are clarifying this experience as a recapitulation of earlier traumas, now structuralized into an anachronistic relationship predisposition. The therapist encourages the patient to examine her memories of past separations and losses, in order to shed further light on the meanings of the impending termination. The threat of rejection or abandonment has been one of the patient's greatest fears associated with her conflicts over aggressive and sexual feelings. Thus, the patient's central issues continue to be the focus of therapy. They color her experience of therapy and the way she deals with terminations; while the termination phase generates its own unique features, it also continues the primary work of the therapy.

The patient's spontaneous account of her husband's supportive stance is a demonstration of impressive improvements in the marital relationship, brought about undoubtedly by the patient's therapeutic experience. It is apparent that the patient has become more comfortable with intimacy and that this, in turn, evokes a much more affectionate response from her husband.

P: Well, it's just the fact that that decision is going to be made and my reaction to it has been that I don't want it to end, but I guess, I don't know, it just made me start thinking about why I was reacting the way I was and what the alternatives would be if we terminated, and what I saw would be the consequences. And I guess what my husband said about seeing this in me periodically at times of the year, I just sort of started to think back and he made some comment about that it could go back further—way, way back in my early childhood.

T: What alternatives are possible?

P: Well, termination and see what happens. See if I can cope with the problems I have any better. Looking at whether I need to continue and if so, with you or with somebody else or a different therapy or something like that. I could demand my money back since I feel like I didn't make any progress. That thought ran through my mind when I was feeling so bad. (Laughs nervously) I really didn't feel like I could do it.

T: I know a part of you does.

While still uncomfortable with acknowledging her feelings, the patient's resentment and disappointment do get expressed. In her sarcastic comment is embodied the common fantasy that, unless all of her expectations of unlimited caring and love are met, nothing good has occurred. She knows intellectually that this is not true and emotionally she has experienced significant improvement, but the experience of having suffered through repeated losses with no recourse but to feel despairing and resentful is still influential. While the patient attempts to play the problem down, the therapist acknowledges its continued presence.

P: (Laughs) I am getting back at you if you say we need to quit. (Laughs)

T: You say that with a laugh and smile.

P: I can't help it, that's just the way I do it!

T: That's a little more out in the open than before, that angry feeling. You say it with a smile, at least it's said.

P: Another thing is that I decided that I wasn't going to wallow in my self-pity. I've only got one session left, I don't feel that way today. Other alternatives, well, I'd like to know what you think. I don't know if I'll get that or not. But, in terms of how you feel where I am, the problems that I have mentioned.

T: Well, before I give my opinion, let's hear about yours.

The therapist's stance remains consistent throughout therapy. At the inception the patient had raised many questions about therapy, and the therapist, while acknowledging their legitimacy, offered the patient the opportunity to explore their meanings. Facing termination, the patient again raises many questions about the therapist's role. Again, he acknowledges the legitimacy of her questions but suggests that the work can be furthered by first examining what these questions can reveal about the patient's feelings concerning the impending termination.

P: About my opinion?

T: Yes. Why do you think mine is more important?

P: Not necessarily. I think it has a part. I'd like to know what your perspective is. That might help me look at the situation a little better. I guess part of the nagging and wanting to continue is not opening myself up as much as I'd like to and that sort of thing. Seeing that as just a possibility. I think I've sort of tried to prepare myself for the termination. Maybe I've gone through the grief over what I felt the last two or three times. I feel like I've gone through that, being sad about it and now sort of coming out of it, and look at the future and, well, if it does happen and what's it going to be. I've geared myself up for that possibility. At least that, maybe that's trying too hard to control how I feel, but still I have to do that at this point.

The patient alludes to a grieving process, which is a common reaction to termination among patients who have had earlier physical or emotional losses. As with any grieving process, if not worked through it can continue to exert an inhibitory influence on the patient's relationships. To reemphasize, the therapist views this phase of therapy as a potential mourning period but one shaped by the central issues which have been the focus of treatment throughout.

P: I only have a couple of sessions. I just don't want to do that. I can't function feeling like I did the last couple of times. I had such a terrible stomachache, and had all the physical ailments. It got about to the point where I was going to have an ulcer. But now today it's not too bad.

T: But as you say, grieving is not a pleasant experience. It was like that when your father died. Even anticipatory grieving. (Silence) When you said that one of the things you feel you haven't done up to this point is getting to know me, opening up to me.

P: I think I feel maybe it's that same kind of feeling like I had with my daddy in that I guess I tend to think, look back and think, well, why didn't I reach out? Maybe if I had made the effort and not been so protective of myself, he might have responded to that. I couldn't for some reason, obviously we talked about some of the reasons why, I did reach out one time and got rejected. And, so it saddens me to think, here, I've done it again. I've been in contact with a person and I'm still protecting myself through that, and now that it's about to end, I'm sorry that we are not closer and, granted, you may not allow that to happen, but I'm feeling more sad about my not having reached out or wondering if I did reach out. I think the problem is basically that I didn't.

Later in session 24:

T: Certain things that you would like to do that you are not sure you can do on your own, continue progress or being more open and being more comfortable with your feelings, so that the automatic reactions that you have cause you difficulties, which you are much more aware of can still happen. Also, parenthetically, is it possible that it is pretty difficult to change and not really as important as whether you can catch those things or not? Stop yourself when they get started. What we're also seeing is a lot of feelings you have that have to do with holding onto, making things different than they were before. Today we talked about the experiences you had with your mother and father. So, it's not really an easy decision to sort out what is the right decision. My feeling is that one of the things that was, I think, very strong in your experience of our terminating in 25 sessions, if we did, was that it was permanent. You never said that, but the quality of what you said.

P: Yeah, something just popped into my head. I hadn't mentioned . . . we could terminate and explore the possibility of the future, if I got to the point where I was feeling I needed help again.

T: That is something that clearly is very possible. Sure! Why not?

P: I was acting like it was the end of the world and there was no other possibility to pick up pieces if I got to the point where I was disintegrating.

T: Right. That's another facet which I think you were picking up on today in terms of recalling your father's death and when you were sent away which . . . being sent away at that age, you must have felt like you would never come back. An important part of your experience of this relationship is it is like I was dying. Like you were being sent away never to return. That's one of the things that makes it so frightening and infuriating. When, in fact, sure, if we stop now, and you saw how things went, there is nothing to stop you from coming back.

P: What's interesting is the fact that I reacted that way. That it was going to be final, no options.

T: Related to that is the possibility that it doesn't matter how long it is, three months, or three years, or three centuries, given all the things that get stirred up around ending a relationship, ending our relationship, how would you ever know if you could do it? The only way to know is to try.

P: I need to try.

The therapist points out certain realistic limitations about this form of therapy (or any psychotherapy); that is, the hope for miraculous change cannot be realized. All of the patient's emotional conflicts have not been resolved; however, she has achieved sufficient understanding of and practice in recognizing and coping with her maladaptive relationship predispositions, and one may hope that she will continue her efforts to diminish their influence on her life. The therapist briefly surveys what they have accomplished as well as work that remains to be done. At the same time, the therapist maintains his interpretive stance. He pulls together the patient's recent experiences and interprets an important meaning that termination has for her: it is affectively equated with the "death" of the relationship, leaving no opportunity for reunion. This fantasy grows out of the patient's personal history but its general form is commonly experienced in the termination phase of time-limited therapy (as well as other forms). The patient is impressed by the power of her fantasy and the manner in which it shapes her experience. Again, she is given the opportunity to experience the powerful influence of her maladaptive relationship predispositions. However, we see that her attitude has become more optimistic.

In the 25th interview—the planned termination session—the patient proposed meeting for two more interviews, which would carry her through a particularly stressful period at work. While the therapist had doubts about this rationale, he felt that, given her history of losses, it might be a useful experience for the patient to have some control over the actual ending of the therapy and to be somewhat flexible. The patient expressed her expectation that the therapist would view her as clutching on to the relationship and push her out. They examined this expectation in terms of her previous experiences of parental loss and of feeling rejected by her husband. The patient expressed a sense of well-being and was more comfortable about terminating. She felt that much had been accomplished in psychotherapy. She was "self-satisfied" but sad. It was agreed to meet for two more interviews.

The first part of session 26 was taken up with assessing what had been accomplished in therapy. The patient stated that she was more aware of the difference between responding intellectually and emotionally to things that bothered her. She felt that she was not as sensitive to criticism and did not feel panicky about terminating. She was still concerned about her ability to express angry feelings; however, she realized that she was not as irritable as she used to be and no longer felt like a time bomb. She worried about her marital relationship but was confident that she could return for further therapy if she so desired.

In the last session, the 27th, she brought the therapist a small present. She felt ready to terminate. She was more comfortable in interpersonal situations and felt better about herself. Problems remained in her marriage but she believed that she and her husband were working on them. She also felt confident that she would not "regress." She would like to be more spontaneously "giving" of herself and to express anger more openly. She expressed gratitude to the therapist and became sad and tearful as the interview drew to a close. The patient left with a warm goodbye.

Follow-up

Approximately ten months after terminating, the patient called for an appointment. She appeared slightly nervous but warm and friendly. For the past several months she had been thinking of contacting the therapist to provide an update on her progress but had desisted because of feeling like a little girl who had to make a report. However, a recent and surprising dream had precipitated the call. The patient had continued to notice progress reflected in greater self-confidence, feeling better about herself, and more accepting of her behavior toward others. She had not progressed as fast as she would have liked but realized that her expectations might have been unrealistic. Her report of behavioral changes were as follows:

1. She and her husband were talking more openly about problems as

well as about general matters. They also shared domestic responsibilities more equally. The patient finds that she is not nearly as sensitive to being criticized by her husband. Furthermore, she is much more openly affectionate, touching him more, and generally feeling closer. She is more drawn to him sexually, and while the frequency of their sexual relations has not increased, the quality of her sexual experiences has greatly improved. The patient also has seen changes in her husband that she appreciates; for example, he more frequently invites her out to dinner.

2. She no longer feels impatient and critical with her children. She feels that she handles them more sensitively.

3. She is much more confident and assertive at work. Recently she has assumed leadership responsibilities that would have been impossible a few years ago.

4. Her relationship with her mother has improved. While her mother is still difficult to have around, the patient is more empathic about her difficulties and consequently more tolerant. She also is able to confront her mother about behavior the patient finds irritating.

It has been suggested that an important index of structural change resulting from dynamic therapy is a shift in the patient's fantasies and dreams. In this case, a dramatic shift in the structure of a recurrent dream had precipitated the call for a follow-up appointment. The original recurrent dream involved her yearning to have a rapprochement with the older man she had been involved with around the time of her father's death. In the latest occurrence of this dream, the patient had the sense that this man was seeking a rapprochement, but she had declined, feeling for the first time that she was emotionally disengaging from the relationship. It is noteworthy that this dream occurred during the anniversary month of her father's death. The therapist suggested that one meaning of the dream might be her continued work on disengaging from the old yearning to have a rapprochement with her father and her increasing desire to become closer to the important figures in her current life (her husband). The patient was delighted with this idea and also suggested that the dream might reflect her sense of increasing autonomy from her mother.

The therapist suggested that from another perspective the dream might also represent her increasing confidence in her ability to continue the work of therapy on her own. The patient was less sure about this. She expressed her continuing ambivalence over whether to restart therapy, and openly, and jokingly, pressed the therapist for encouragement to come back. She further indicated that she did not want the therapist to encourage this, because if she decided to contact him again, she wished this to be her own choice.

The patient complained of frequent physical problems over the past few months and wondered if she were somatizing her emotional conflicts. Acknowledging this possibility, the therapist also noted that emotional tension and recurrent physical symptoms were her characteristic responses to realistic stress. Nevertheless, they agreed that the patient might decide at some point to reenter therapy to explore this issue further.

In sum, the patient's spontaneous follow-up appointment offered an opportunity to assess her progress following therapy. There were ample indications of positive changes in the patient's self-concept, relationships with others, freedom in expressing feelings, and mastery of maladaptive relationship predispositions. Furthermore, the dream provided more direct evidence of a possible shift in her intrapsychic state, in the direction of greater mastery over an old but previously unresolved mourning of lost opportunities for a wished-for closer relationship with her dead father. The conclusion can be drawn that at least for ten months following termination this patient had achieved a scope and depth of change that would be considered impressive for any psychotherapy regardless of its length.

Postscript

Since conducting this therapy, we have, in the light of further reflection, come to adopt a somewhat stricter stand on time limits. Specifically, we believe it is desirable to establish time limits at the beginning of therapy and rigorously adhere to them. As the topic of termination is dealt with in therapy, the therapist should, gently but firmly, insist that the patient take a break from therapy for at least six months to a year. As in the preceding case history, we see no harm in granting two or three additional sessions but there should be no ambiguity about the necessity of exposing the patient to the pain of separation and its aftermath. In the final analysis, separation must be *experienced*—it cannot be adequately worked through while therapy continues. Obviously, we do not contend that all, or even the majority of problems in living can be satisfactorily resolved in 25 hours of psychotherapy; however, it appears preferable to reassess the status six months or a year after termination than for the therapist to extend the therapy contrary to the initial stipulation. On the other hand, if it is the therapist's considered judgment at the beginning that the likelihood of significant progress within 25 hours is slight, treatment recommendations should be made to fit that set of circumstances. We realize that such judgments are exceedingly difficult to make, and we do not entirely agree with Wolberg's (1980) recommendation that short-term therapy should *always* be tried. Although there exists as yet insufficient evidence on the degree of therapeutic change that can reasonably be expected in 25 hours of therapy conducted along the lines described in this book, this kind of therapy should no longer be viewed, as it once was, as minor or second best.

Chapter 9

Termination

The Psychology of Termination

Irrespective of whether therapy is short term or long term, termination represents one of the most critical challenges to the therapist. Depending on the management of this issue, therapy may turn out to be a success or a failure.

Many young therapists are insufficiently aware of the criticial importance of termination. For one reason, the problem appears to receive insufficient attention in many training programs; for another, many young therapists entering the profession have been spared the experience of separation and loss. Even if they have undergone such experiences, the affect is typically repressed and thus is not available for therapeutic work. Finally, many therapies conducted by graduate students or residents fail to confront the problem because the relationship is often terminated for fortuitous reasons; for example, the trainee's rotation on a particular service ends, the patients, who are not infrequently students themselves, leave at the end of a semester or academic year, and so on. In short, the full psychological implications of termination have rarely been confronted by young therapists. Nor is this failing restricted to this group; in our experience, even seasoned therapists who conduct intensive, open-ended psychoanalytic psychotherapy may underestimate the signal importance of dealing effectively with termination. We believe the problem cannot be overestimated.

An adequate appreciation of its emotional significance can only be obtained if one succeeds in reviving within oneself the world of the child whose survival—both in a biological and psychological sense—literally depends on the reliable and trustworthy presence of a nurturant caretaker. The panic that overtakes a child who may be lost in a crowd—in a department store, at a sports event, or at a beach—provides a small sample of what abandonment means from the child's perspective. Bowlby's (1980) studies are among the most significant and insightful contributions to this topic. Death of a parent during infancy and childhood, divorce, birth of a sibling, severe illnesses, operations, and prolonged separations are among the traumas that may have an incisive and lasting impact on an individual's personality.

We agree with the proposition that a central purpose of psychodynamic psychotherapy is to help the patient come to terms with previous separations and object losses, whether these be emotional or actual. Accordingly, one may say that many patients enter psychotherapy because they failed to resolve reactions to earlier traumas or losses. Symptoms and complaints often embody a plea to return to earlier lost objects with whom the patient has unfinished business. The patient unconsciously wishes to reinstate the earlier relationship, perpetuate it, and/or bring it to a more satisfactory resolution. Just as physical disease justifies a person in seeking out a physician, so mental symptoms and difficulties provide a (more or less) socially acceptable rationale for entering psychotherapy. The psychotherapist comes to symbolize the lost connections of this ambivalence. Therapy succeeds if the therapist becomes a better object than the object of one's childhood. The therapist gratifies certain fundamental wishes (dependency) which the parent-object did not adequately gratify, and in many other respects provides a more reasonable, rational, and benign model for identification.

Nonetheless, and perhaps precisely for that reason, the patient does not readily relinquish the new object, and will often cling to the therapist with considerable tenacity. Unresolved dependency is a particularly serious hazard in long-term intensive psychotherapy but it is also an issue when therapy is time limited. Indeed, the issue must be confronted sooner and perhaps more poignantly in the shorter forms of therapy. If the therapeutic relationship has been highly ambivalent—a fairly common occurrence in patients who have chronic difficulties in forming and maintaining intimate relationships—termination may be even more difficult. In any event, termination evokes memories of earlier separations and the painful affects— grief, rage, devaluation of the love object—associated with the earlier traumas. Mann's (1973:36) discussion of the problem is particularly perceptive:

> It is absolutely incumbent upon the therapist to deal directly with the reaction to termination in all its painful aspects and affects if he expects to help the patient come to some vividly affective understanding of the now inappropriate nature of his early unconscious conflict. More than that, active and appropriate management of the termination will allow the patient to internalize the therapist as a replacement or substitute for the earlier ambivalent object. *This time the internalization will be more positive (never totally so), less anger laden and less guilt laden, thereby making separation a genuine maturational event.* Since anger, rage, guilt, and their accompaniments of frustration and fear are the potent factors that prevent positive internalization and mature separation, it is these that must not be overlooked in this phase of the time-limited therapy.

Although the clinical picture may take many different forms, the following central features may be discerned: (1) The patient has formed a positive relationship to the therapist and has benefited from the joint therapeutic work. He or she values the new object and wishes to retain (possess) it. (2) This wish to perpetuate the relationship gives rise to controlling tendencies; that is, by attempting to hold onto the love object, the patient seeks to prevent separation and loss. Patients will unwittingly employ the gamut of techniques for averting painful separation experiences. For example, they may bring up "new" problems that "urgently" require solutions; there may be a recurrence of the symptoms and problems that brought them to therapy; they will attempt to cling to the therapist by venting hostility and blame on him or her; and they may attempt to master the problems "actively" by leaving therapy before the actual termination date has been reached. (3) When such attempts fail, as they inevitably will (since the therapist cannot adequately satisfy the patient's wishes for emotional closeness and he or she necessarily emerges as a separate person), the patient will feel frustrated and enraged. (4) As therapy proceeds and as the preceding sequence is worked through, the patient becomes better able to tolerate separation and loss.

By a process which is of pivotal importance but still poorly understood, the patient learns to internalize the generally positive image of the therapist, thereby freeing himself or herself from the neurotic attachment. As many writers have noted, this process never succeeds perfectly. Nonetheless, the process of replacing early (maladaptive) identifications with new (more adaptive) ones is psychotherapy's unique achievement. If we adequately understood how identifications can be loosened and replaced, we would have solved the basic problem of how intrapsychic change is brought about. Toward this end, internalization is not the only route but it is undoubtedly one of the crucial ones. At present, we do know that consistent focus on the transactions between therapist and patient will, in many cases, lead to beneficial intrapsychic change. Since the character of the identifications—their formation, retention, and progression—varies enormously from person to person, it is extremely difficult to formulate general principles of how the process can be accelerated. As Sullivan (1953), Maslow (1962), and many other therapists have pointed out, the best a therapist can do is to help create optimal conditions for personality growth. In Sullivan's terms, this is done by removing to the greatest extent possible the obstacles impeding growth, and for the rest to trust to the impressive human strivings for better solutions of conflicts. A clinical case will illustrate these points:

Mrs. G had made considerable progress in resolving a long-standing conflict with her mother; she had made strides in becoming more assertive and in accepting her femininity; and her relationship with her husband had likewise improved. In various subtle ways she signaled her realization that therapy really was no longer the lifeline it had been and that she was gradually getting ready to terminate it. Operationally, it was clear both to her and her (male) therapist that the problems she now brought to therapy were less pressing; and she had found it easier to deal with occasional separations (due to the therapist's vacations and the like); and there was markedly greater harmony and less conflict both in her relationship with the therapist and with other persons who were significant in her life. Not unexpectedly, this state of affairs posed a threat because it inexorably confronted her with the issue of termination.

When the therapist stated more directly what the patient had been hinting at, namely her thoughts and feelings about termination, she reacted in rather predictable fashion: She became angry at the therapist for his alleged desire "to push me out"; she felt that she had been an unsatisfactory patient and that therefore the therapist wished to get rid of her; she indicated that she needed more time with the therapist; in other words, *she* wanted to set the termination date when she was ready.

As on one or two previous occasions, the therapist noted that he had done no more than paraphrase the patient's own thoughts, that termination was indeed a critical issue that had to be faced and worked through, that it was in the patient's interest to do so, that *we* (emphasis on the therapeutic alliance!) needed to accept the fact that part of her was intent upon perpetuating the relationship, and that, indeed, therapy could not and should not last forever. The therapist also pointed to the patient's very considerable strengths and accomplishments which she recurrently tended to denigrate, perhaps in order to perpetuate a parent-child relationship about which she felt considerable ambivalence. The dilemma, the therapist explained, was something like this: If she came to fully accept herself as the effective and competent adult she was, she would lose the relationship with the therapist. She felt the therapist would "boot me out." (Note the aggressive element here: She did not feel that she had outgrown or was in the process of outgrowing the relationship but rather that she was being rejected.) Therefore, in order to maintain the relationship, she was compelled to see herself as weak, ineffectual, needy, replete with problems. This assured continued access to the therapist and the relationship. Consequently progress in therapy made her anxious, and the lack of progress was, paradoxically, reassuring. The problem was eventually worked through.

In this case, the problem was relatively easy and straightforward because the therapy had gone well and had been characterized by a good therapeutic alliance. The therapist, for his part, had grown fond of the patient and respected her. In addition, her tendency to idealize the therapist, relate to him as daddy's little girl, and her sexual appeal were by no means trivial factors. Note also that the problem of termination, like other problems in therapy, is a *mutual* concern. A therapist who may experience strong ambivalence toward a patient may secretly welcome the prospect of terminating but feel guilty about pursuing a realistic therapeutic objective. In this case, whether or not treatment ends when planned, the decision may not be based on the patient's best interests. In another case, the therapist may derive considerable gratification (perhaps both realistically and neurotically) from work with a patient and may therefore wish to prolong the relationship. If the therapeutic relationship had been a good one, the therapist may be genuinely sorry to lose a patient who has become emotionally meaningful. Thus the therapist may be reluctant to explore and work through the patient's feelings about separation, postpone the event (if the therapy is time unlimited), be too ready to offer a second block of time-limited therapy, and the like. Losing a patient may evoke memories of the therapist's own losses and the manner in which he or she has mastered (or failed to master) them. As in other therapeutic situations, it may be difficult to differentiate between the patient's problems and those of the therapist.

Time limits that are set at the beginning of therapy and of which the patient is recurrently reminded provide a stimulus for serious therapeutic work. The patient realizes that time is at a premium, that he or she should get on with the job, and that the end is always in sight. Thus, time limits tend to stem powerful regressive trends. A similar pull is exerted by the relative infrequency of sessions (once a week), the therapist's greater participatory "activity" (as opposed to the classical analyst's relatively remote stance), and his or her disinclination to pursue byways that may be interesting but whose relevance to the major tasks of therapy are unclear. Thus there tends to be fostered a realization that we are here to accomplish certain goals and we had better waste no time. The danger here may be one of frenzied activity and pushiness that may synergize (rather than counteract) certain characterological trends that are part of the patient's difficulties.

Therapy that operates with time limits must give the patient opportunity to enjoy the moment without feeling driven, as many people have been by parents, teachers, and other taskmasters. In keeping with basic values inherent in western civilization and contemporary society's thrust toward efficiency, time-limited therapy may be experienced by many patients as another instance of the pressure for achievement, productivity, and competition. On the other hand, there is the continual danger that a therapist who conveys the message that there are other and perhaps more important values in life (for example, that contemplation is not synonymous with laziness and indeed quite compatible with mental health) may be experienced as not doing anything. By the same token, a therapist who "merely" listens may be unfavorably contrasted with one who has a great deal of verbal output. If one interpretation is good, perhaps three are better! The young therapist, in particular, tends to assume a straight-line relationship between his or her verbal activity and the extent of the therapeutic change. However, if, as we have seen, identification with the therapist is a major goal, there may be no easy or magic way to hasten the progress. But there may be many ways of retarding it; for example, by excessive and tenacious verbal activity on the therapist's part.

In sum, the patient-therapist relationship in TLDP, as well as in other forms of dynamic therapy, can become a replica of earlier relationships. As a patient contemplates termination, the old problems surrounding this issue will be replayed and enacted with the therapist. In the final analysis, termination, separation, and death are the bedrock of human existence, for which psychotherapy, whether it is time limited or unlimited can offer no cure. The best it can do is to alleviate unnecessary suffering rooted in childhood traumas, and through a constructive experience in living, strengthen the patient's self-trust and capacities to master life, including relationships with significant others. That, we believe, is not a trivial accomplishment.

Guidelines for Termination

We have attempted to show that the termination phase of TLDP has issues uniquely its own, and yet cannot be isolated from the concerns that have been the focus of attention throughout the treatment. Thus, the overriding recommendation for dealing with termination is to continue implementing the technical approach throughout the course of TLDP, bearing in mind the unique stresses generated by termination on patient *and* therapist.

What has been written about the technical management of termination in long-term psychoanalytic therapy clearly indicates little consensus about procedures for drawing treatment to a close (Firestein 1978). The literature on short-term dynamic therapy offers more agreement but notable differences remain. For example, Sifneos (1979) and Davanloo (1978, 1980) do not specify termination dates or specific numbers of sessions, while Malan (1976a) and Mann (1973) do set calendar dates for termination. To the best of our knowledge, there is no convincing clinical or empirical evidence that favors one or the other approach. However, there is general agreement among short-term therapists that making the patient aware at the outset of limits to the duration of treatment does heighten the attention of both patient and therapist to the tasks at hand. It appears that Parkinson's Law applies to psychotherapy as well as to other uses of time (Appelbaum 1972).

We are in agreement with other advocates of short-term therapy that if a termination date is set this should be done early in treatment. Whether this end point is stated as a specific number of sessions or as a calendar date is a matter of personal preference, although we acknowledge Malan's (1976a) warning that setting the termination date by sessions leaves the therapist vulnerable to the problem of determining criteria for making up sessions missed by the patient. We prefer to set a termination date, because without this agreed-upon structure the therapist is more susceptible to avoiding the stress inherent in ending by prolonging treatment and thereby obscuring termination issues.

We strongly advocate that the time limits be set *after* a therapeutic focus has at least begun to be outlined by the participants, because the introduction of a focus is more likely to provide the patient with a belief that there are circumscribed goals that can be achieved in the available time. Once the treatment is underway, the therapist should assume that the issue of a finite length is *always* an influence even if it is not in focus at any given moment. Therefore, the therapist should continually remain alert for evidence of the patient's reactions to the time limits and bring them to the patient's attention. The therapist always attempts to make sense of the patient's communications in terms of the therapeutic focus. This is true as well of references to termination, which the therapist attempts to weave into an understanding of the central issues that occupy their attention throughout the treatment. Some patients react to the reality of termination from the outset, while others seem unconcerned for long periods of time. In any event, it is never an issue to be ignored, and as with other concerns of the patient, the empathic therapist will determine the judicious moment for identifying the issue of termination as a concern of the patient. As we have discussed before, therapists' abilities to handle termination issues, at any point during the course of therapy, are primarily a function of their success at understanding and mastering their own feelings on the subject.

Chapter 10

Research Considerations

A BOOK in any scientific discipline is inevitably a product of its time. In various combinations, it reflects contemporary thinking, cumulative knowledge, and the idiosyncrasies of its authors. In this chapter we shall attempt to trace major influences that have shaped our work. Our greatest debt, of course, remains to Sigmund Freud whose contributions have revolutionized modern psychology which indelibly bears his imprint. Despite advances in psychoanalysis and the emergence of numerous competing systems, basic psychoanalytic principles and concepts (transference, resistance, the impact of unconscious beliefs and fantasies on human behavior, and the importance of symbols and their transformations) have continued to exert a profound influence on therapeutic practice, particularly in the United States and Western Europe.

While modern psychotherapy (of which classical psychoanalysis is considered a subclass) is about one hundred years old, psychotherapy research is of much more recent vintage (dating roughly from the 1940s). It is often asserted that research in psychotherapy has exerted relatively little influence on practice, but this trend is gradually being reversed. Ideally, there should be a reciprocal relationship between the two, such that research results lead to modifications of therapeutic practice, which are again subjected to scrutiny by research, with this sequence being repeated. Thus, researchers and therapists might engage in the kind of action research which Kurt Lewin (Marrow 1969) envisaged many years ago. While progress along these lines has been slow, we hope that this volume is a step in the direction of unifying research and practice. Our formulations have been significantly influenced by the results of our research as well as our clinical experience. Beyond that, we have begun to investigate the effects of a training program based on the principles and techniques described in this book. Our allegiance to clinical practice *and* research remains, and we continue to be engaged in both disciplines. For scientific progress to occur, we believe that the two must increasingly complement each other. In order to delineate the more immediate ancestry of our formulations we shall refer to the clinical investigations which the Vanderbilt Psychotherapy Research Team has pursued since approximately 1970 under the direction of the senior author. However, before doing so, we shall clarify our view of psychotherapy and the context within which the Vanderbilt project emerged.

A Working Definition of Psychotherapy

Depending on one's theoretical orientation and philosophical leanings, psychotherapy is seen by some as a psychosocial treatment, by others as a special form of education (Freud coined the term *after-education*), and by still others as a means of promoting personality growth and self-actualization—to cite but a few divergent views. Along with a growing number of colleagues, we are taking the position that psychotherapy is an interpersonal process designed to bring about modifications of feelings, cognitions, attitudes, and behavior which have proven troublesome to the person seeking help from a trained professional. There remains considerable disagreement as to whether and to what extent psychotherapy differs from other human relationships in which one person tries to help another; however, as ordinarily understood, the modern psychotherapist is a professional person who has acquired special skills.

Since psychotherapy is often described as a treatment, and since medical terminology (patient, diagnosis, etiology, and so on.) has traditionally been used, the analogy of a physician ministering to a passive patient readily springs to mind. In our view, psychoanalytic psychotherapy bears only a superficial resemblance to this model. Instead, we conceive of psychotherapy as a collaborative endeavor or a partnership, in which the patient, almost from the beginning, is expected to play an active part. This means that patients must gradually become more autonomous, more self-directing, and more responsible for their feelings, beliefs, and actions. In order to feel better about themselves and their relationships with others, they must learn to make changes within themselves (and in their environment) that permit them to feel and act differently. The process of therapy is not designed to apply external pressure but to help patients assume a more active role in living their lives.

In this sense, psychotherapy is a learning process and the role of the therapist is analogous to that of a teacher or mentor. Psychotherapy is based on the assumption that feelings, cognitions, attitudes, and behavior are the product of one's life experiences; that is, they have been learned. If something has been learned, modification of previous learning can occur. Where learning is impossible (for example, as a result of genetic or biochemical factors), psychotherapy has little to offer. Similarly, if the disturbance is solely due to factors in a person's social milieu (poverty, oppression, imprisonment) or if patients do not desire change on their own (a situation often associated with referral by a court, school system, and so on), psychotherapy encounters great difficulties. Thus psychotherapy works best if patients desire change of their own accord and are motivated to work toward it; if the environment in which they live tolerates the possibility of change; and if the inner obstacles to learning (defenses and rigidities of character) are not insurmountable.

We are especially committed to the goal of individuation; that is, helping people to become, to the greatest extent possible, individuals in their own right, persons who have outgrown or who are struggling to outgrow the shackles of childhood dependency. To the extent that the person becomes more independent, he or she should be better able to form, maintain, and enjoy interpersonal relationships on an adult level and become capable of greater interpersonal intimacy. Our model of psychotherapy and its instrumentation is geared to the greatest possible approximation of these objectives even when there remains a hiatus between the ideal and its realization. This is true whether therapy is short term or whether it is extended over a long period of time.

Specific versus Nonspecific Factors in Psychotherapy

Techniques are of course the core and raison d'être of modern psychotherapy and, as previously noted, are usually anchored in a theory of psychopathology or maladaptive learning. Psychoanalysis has stressed the interpretation of resistances and transference phenomena as the principal curative factor, contrasting these operations with the "suggestions" of earlier hypnotists. Behavior therapy, to cite another example, has developed its own armamentarium of techniques, such as systematic desensitization, modeling, aversive and operant conditioning, training in self-regulation and self-control. In general, the proponents of all systems of psychotherapy credit their successes to more or less specific operations which are usually claimed to be uniquely effective. A corollary of this proposition is that a therapist is a professional who must receive systematic training in the application of the recommended techniques.

So far, it has not been possible to show that one technique is clearly superior to another, even under reasonably controlled conditions (Luborsky, Singer, and Luborsky 1975; Sloane, Staples, Cristol, Yorkston, and Whipple 1975). The commonly accepted finding that approximately two-thirds of neurotic patients who enter outpatient psychotherapy of whatever description show noticeable improvement likewise reinforces a skeptical attitude concerning the unique effectiveness of particular techniques. Finally, it often turns out that initial claims for a new technique cannot be sustained when the accumulating evidence is critically examined. The latter, for example, appears to be true of systematic desensitization in the treatment of phobias.

An alternative hypothesis has been advanced (Frank 1973) which asserts that psychotherapeutic change is predominantly a function of factors common to all therapeutic approaches. These factors are brought to bear in the human relationship between the patient and the healer. The proponents of this hypothesis hold that a person, defined by himself or herself or others as a patient, suffers from demoralization and a sense of hopelessness. Consequently, any benign human influence is likely to boost the patient's morale, which in turn is registered as improvement. Primary ingredients of these common nonspecific factors include: understanding, respect, interest, encouragement, acceptance, forgiveness—in short, the kinds of human qualities that since time immemorial have been considered effective in buoying the human spirit.

Frank identifies another important common factor in all psychotherapies; that is, their tendency to operate in terms of a conceptual scheme and associated procedures which are thought to be beneficial. While the contents of the schemes and the procedures differ among therapies, they have common morale-building functions. They combat the patient's demoralization by providing an explanation, acceptable to both patient and therapist, for hitherto inexplicable feelings and behavior. This process serves to remove the mystery from the patient's suffering and eventually to supplant it with hope.

Frank's formulation implies that training in and enthusiasm for a special theory and method may increase the effectiveness of therapists, in contrast to nonprofessional helpers who may lack belief in a coherent system or rationale.* This hypothesis also underscores the continuity between faith healers, shamans, and modern psychotherapists. While the latter may operate on the basis of highly sophisticated scientific theories (by contemporary standards), the function of these theories may intrinsically be no different from the most primitive rationale undergirding a healer's efforts. In both instances techniques of whatever description are inseparable from the therapist's belief system, which in successful therapy is accepted and integrated by the patient. Some patients of course may be more receptive to, and thus more likely to benefit from, the therapist's manipulations than others.

Rogers (1957), from a different perspective, regards a set of "facilitative conditions" (accurate empathy, genuineness, and unconditional positive regard) as necessary and sufficient conditions for beneficial therapeutic change. Thus, both Rogers and Frank deemphasize the effectiveness of therapeutic techniques per se, and they elevate relationship factors to a position of preeminence.

Although the hypothesis of nonspecific factors may be correct, it is still possible that some technical operations may be superior to others with particular patients, particular problems, and under particular circumstances (Strupp 1973). Such claims are made, for example, by therapists who are interested in the treatment of sexual dysfunctions (Kaplan 1974) and by behavior therapists who have tackled a wide range of behavior disorders. As yet, many of these claims are untested, and a great deal of research needs to be done to document that specific techniques are uniquely effective.

In any event, it is clear that the problem has important ramifications for research and practice. For example, if further evidence can be adduced that techniques contribute less to good therapy outcomes than has been claimed, greater effort might have to be expended in selecting and training therapists who are able to provide the nonspecific factors mentioned earlier. We also need far more information about the kinds of therapeutic

---

*On the other hand, a nonprofessional therapist may have a rationale, albeit commonsensical. For example, a college professor who functioned as an alternative therapist in the Vanderbilt project tended to insist that his patients (anxious, depressed, and withdrawn male college students) suffered from "girl problems." He used this rationale quite effectively in his therapeutic interviews.

services that may be safely performed by individuals with relatively little formal training (paraprofessionals) as well as the limits set by their lack of comprehensive training. In any case, there may be definite limitations to what techniques per se can accomplish (Frank 1974), limits that are set both by patient characteristics and therapist qualities, including level of training.

The controversy of specific versus nonspecific factors was one of the issues that occupied the attention of Bergin and Strupp (1972) who, toward the end of the 1960s, were commissioned by the National Institute of Mental Health to explore the frontiers of psychotherapy research. In the course of this inquiry a number of studies were sketched which might significantly extend existing knowledge. The specific-nonspecific hypothesis appealed particularly to Strupp who began to undertake pilot work in the early 1970s and subsequently carried out what came to be known as the Vanderbilt I study.

The Vanderbilt I Study and Its Lessons

Design

If one conceives of the therapeutic influence as being composed of specific (technique) and nonspecific (interpersonal) factors, therapeutic outcomes may largely reflect their joint contribution. Thus, one might try to maximize the specific (technical) factors in one experimental group while contrasting it with another in which the contribution of technical factors is presumably less. If one could further assume that the nonspecific (interpersonal) factors were approximately equal in both groups, any differences in outcome favoring the first group would, in a preliminary way, shed light on the extent to which specific factors might uniquely contribute to treatment outcomes.

To execute such a study it was necessary to select appropriate therapist groups, define a reasonably homogeneous patient population, and institute experimental controls that would permit meaningful comparisons. With respect to therapists, a small group ($N = 5$) of trained therapists with considerable professional experience (mean of eighteen years) were selected. This group was contrasted with a group of college professors who had no formal training in psychotherapy. They were chosen on the basis of their ability to interact comfortably with college students with personal problems who appeared to seek them out for counsel. It was subsequently established that the two groups were roughly equivalent in terms of non-specific factors; that is, members of both groups were empathic, understanding, and interested in their clients.

The patient population consisted of male college students who suffered from anxiety, depression, and social withdrawal of clinical proportions. Both professional therapists and college professors met with patients individually on a twice-a-week basis, up to 25 hours. The character of the therapy was not specific except that it was restricted to verbal exchanges. For the rest, therapists were free to follow their usual procedures. Patients were informed that they were being assigned to a person who, in the judgment of the project staff, might help them with their problems.

All patients (approximately fifteen in each group) were carefully assessed by independent clinicians before entering therapy, at termination, and one year thereafter. Clinicians, patients, and therapists also completed a battery of instruments at stated intervals. Special procedures were followed for two control groups. All assessment and therapy sessions were recorded either on audio or videotape. A detailed discussion of design, procedures, and results may be found in Strupp and Hadley (1979).

The two treatment groups demonstrated greater improvement than the control groups; however, patients undergoing psychotherapy with college professors showed, on the average, qualitatively as much improvement as did patients treated by experienced professional therapists. While both treatment groups achieved therapeutic gains in terms of *mean* changes on a variety of measures, there was considerable variability in the outcome of individual dyads, with some patients experiencing marked therapeutic benefits whereas others remained virtually unchanged and a few showed deterioration. The overall group comparisons tended to obscure the important combinations of patient and therapist variables that gave rise to particular relationships and to specific therapeutic outcomes. Therefore, additional investigations were undertaken to explore the determinants of these differential changes.

The variability in the outcome across individual dyads allowed systematic comparisons to be made between "high changers" (successful outcomes) and "low changers" (negative or no change cases) treated by the same therapist (Strupp 1980a, 1980b, 1980c, 1980d).* Aided by the extensive statistical data available on all patients, these comparisons entailed intensive clinical study of the patient-therapist interaction throughout the

---

*One of these comparisons (Strupp 1980d) is presented later in this chapter.

entire course of treatment. A second series of studies was aimed at analyses of salient patient characteristics and process dimensions across all cases (Gomes-Schwartz 1978; Hartley and Strupp 1983; Sachs 1983; Waterhouse 1979). These investigations explored the contribution of antecedent patient variables to the subsequent process and outcome of treatment, as well as the relationship between various aspects of the patient-therapist interaction and therapeutic change.

Major findings of central significance for our subsequent research and the rationale of this book include the following:

1. Neither professional therapists nor college professors were notably effective in treating patients with more pervasive personality problems. On the other hand, professional therapists were most effective with patients showing the following characteristics: high motivation for psychotherapy; ability to form a good therapeutic relationship (working alliance) early in treatment; and relative absence of long-standing maladaptive patterns of relating. The latter were defined by such qualities as pronounced hostility, pervasive mistrust, negativism, inflexibility, and antisocial or asocial tendencies. The foregoing is not meant to imply that professional therapists were most effective with the least disturbed patients. Rather, these therapists were particularly effective with patients whose personality resources and capacity for collaboration allowed them to take maximal advantage of the kind of relationship and traditional techniques proffered by the therapists. These findings are in general agreement with the literature (Luborsky, Chandler, Auerbach, Cohen, and Bachrach 1971), perhaps most notably with the results of the Menninger Project (Kernberg, Burstein, Coyne, Appelbaum, Horwitz, and Voth 1972).

2. The quality of the therapeutic relationship, established early in the interaction, proved to be an important predictor of outcome in this time-limited context. In particular, therapy tended to be successful if by the third session the patient felt accepted, understood, and liked by the therapist (Waterhouse 1979). Conversely, premature termination or failure tended to result if these conditions were not met early in treatment. In addition, preliminary evidence indicated that reasonably accurate predictions of process and outcome can be made from initial interviews, specifically in terms of judgments relating to the patient's motivation for therapy (Keithly, Samples, and Strupp 1980) and quality of interpersonal relationships (Moras 1979). Stated differently, there was no evidence that an initially negative or highly ambivalent patient-therapist relationship was significantly modified in the course of the therapy under study. Furthermore, the patients' perceptions of the therapeutic relationship were found

to remain fairly stable throughout therapy and to the follow-up period.

3. The quality of the therapeutic relationship appeared to depend heavily on the patient's ability to relate comfortably and productively to the therapist in the context of a traditional therapeutic framework. This capacity, in turn, seemed to be a function of the patient's personality resources and suitability for time-limited therapy (see 1 above). In short, there was compelling evidence that the quality of the patient-therapist relationship was significantly, although not entirely, determined by the patient variables.

4. There was no evidence that professional therapists adapted their therapeutic approach or techniques to the specific characteristics and needs of individual patients. Instead, the kind of relationship they offered and the techniques they employed were relatively invariant. Similarly, therapists did not tailor their techniques in specific ways to the resolution of target symptoms, nor did they formulate specific therapeutic goals of their own.

5. Therapists, in general, had little success in confronting or resolving the markedly negative reactions characteristic of the more difficult patients in the project. Instead, they tended to react negatively and countertherapeutically to a patient's hostility, mistrust, inflexibility, and pervasive resistances, thereby perhaps reinforcing the patient's poor self-image and related difficulties. The result of such interactions tended to be (a) negative attitudes on the part of the patient toward the therapist and therapy; (b) premature termination; and/or (c) a poor therapeutic outcome (no change or negative change).

We came to view these results as having significant implications for research and clinical practice:

Patient Selection

Patients with substantial personality resources, high levels of motivation for therapy, relatively circumscribed problems, and the capacity to work productively within a traditional therapeutic framework are likely to show the greatest and the most rapid improvement. From the therapist's standpoint, these persons generally constitute the most desirable and rewarding patients. When viewed from the broader perspective of the needs of society and the future development of psychotherapy, however, they are the least problematic cases.

By contrast, patients falling short of optimal suitability for short-term approaches (according to the criteria mentioned earlier) represent by far the largest segment of the patient population. Paradoxically, while these individuals are in the greatest need of professional services, they are also the ones who have been most neglected by mental health professionals (Rabkin 1977). This judgment applies with particular force to short-term dynamic psychotherapy which has traditionally focused on the selection and treatment of the most promising candidates (Butcher and Koss 1978). (It is noteworthy in this regard that the extensive contemporary literature dealing with borderline conditions and narcissistic personality disorders is almost entirely devoted to long-term intensive therapy [Giovacchini 1979; Kernberg 1975; Kohut 1971; by contrast, see Binder 1979].)

Conclusion 1. In order for psychotherapy to meet more adequately the needs of patients as well as society, it is essential to focus attention upon patients who have typically been rejected as suitable candidates for short-term psychotherapy and to explore systematically the extent to which such patients can be treated more effectively by a well-defined, time-limited approach.

Patient Assessment

Considering the complexity of the human personality, it is perhaps not surprising that even when assessment procedures are designed to select a homogeneous group of patients, the resulting samples are likely to include individuals who differ widely on a number of dimensions considered critical to their suitability for time-limited psychotherapy. For example, in the Vanderbilt Project the initial patient selection was based on significant elevations (T ≥ 60) of scales 2 (Depression), 7 (Psychasthenia), and 0 (Social Introversion) of the Minnesota Multiphasic Personality Inventory (MMPI). Although we did not insist that all patients be "pure" 2-7-0s, marked variability was observed in the subsamples that met this criterion. It emerged that patients showed wide variations in terms of character structure, ranging from mild neurotic disturbances in a relatively well-functioning personality organization to severe obsessionals, character disorders, and even a few borderline conditions.

In light of our findings and those of others (Davanloo 1978, 1980; Malan 1976a, 1979; Sifneos 1972, 1979), additional criteria of crucial significance for treatment planning should include the following: severity of characterological disturbances (negativism, pervasive mistrust, rigidity); degree of impairment in coping ability; quality of past interpersonal relationships; motivation for change; and presence of central conflictual issues that allow for the establishment of a dynamic focus. Despite the importance of these qualities to the determination of a patient's suitability for a particular treatment approach, such careful assessments are typically not made in clinical practice.

Conclusion 2. Psychological assessments must be sharpened to include: (a) evaluations of the patient's character structure; (b) estimation of the quality of the patient's participation in time-limited psychotherapy in terms of the criteria that have been identified as important prognostic indicators; and (c) reformulation of patients' presenting complaints in terms of central issues or themes which lend themselves to focused therapeutic interventions. In order to effect more specific treatment planning, these determinations must become an integral part of the assessment process. Through this step, a closer link will be forged between diagnosis, formulation of therapeutic goals, techniques, and outcomes.

Therapeutic Operations

As shown by our analyses of patient-therapist interactions, therapists tended to use a broad-gauged approach aimed at helping patients achieve insight into certain aspects of their current difficulties. Except for the fact that the treatment was time limited, psychodynamically trained therapists typically followed the analytic model of long-term intensive psychotherapy. Accordingly, they adopted a passive-expectant stance, left the initiative for introducing topics to the patient, and largely confined their activity to clarifications and interpretations of conflictual patterns. Therapists tended to provide relatively little warmth and support, did not focus on the specific problems identified at the beginning of treatment, rarely acquainted patients with the nature of the therapeutic process, and infrequently confronted patients' negative personal reactions. In sum, the therapists' approach tended to be relatively invariant and patients were expected, without significant effort on the therapist's part, to feel comfortable with and respond favorably to the requirements of this therapeutic framework. It should be noted that, with relatively few exceptions, this approach reflects the model followed in most training centers for psychotherapists and psychiatrists, despite the fact that the majority of patients are unable to take optimal advantage of this regimen. Furthermore, as shown by the research results, the absence of a good "fit" between pertinent patient characteristics and the therapist's framework frequently leads to an impasse early in treatment, such as poor therapeutic alliance, premature termination, and/or poor outcome.

Of particular significance to the course and outcome of treatment were therapists' negative personal reactions to patients whose resistance took the form of anger, hostility, negativism, and pervasive mistrust. In view of these findings, we believe that systematic efforts must be made to help therapists deal with these problems.

Conclusion 3. In order to realize the full potential of short-term dynamic psychotherapy, therapists should receive specialized training, with particular emphasis on the following elements:

a. Techniques should be optimally geared to the achievement of reasonably specific therapeutic objectives identified early in the course of treatment. Crucial here is the definition of a central issue, dynamic focus, or theme.

b. The therapeutic situation should be designed to meet the unique needs of the individual patient, as opposed to the tacit assumption that the patient conforms to the therapist's notions of an "ideal" therapeutic framework. Techniques should be applied flexibly, sensitively, and in ways maximally meaningful to the patient.

c. Steps should be taken to foster a good therapeutic relationship (working alliance) from the beginning of therapy, thus enhancing the patient's active participation and creating a sense of collaboration and partnership.

d. Negative transference reactions should be actively confronted at the earliest possible time.

e. Concerted efforts should be made to help therapists deal with negative personal reactions which are characteristically engendered by most patients manifesting hostility, anger, negativism, rigidity, and similar resistances.

f. While time-limited psychotherapy poses particular challenges to all therapists (especially demands for greater activity and directiveness), they should resist the temptation to persuade the patient to accept a particular solution, impose their values, and in other respects diminish the patient's striving for freedom and autonomy.

g. Rather than viewing psychotherapy predominantly as a set of technical operations applied in a vacuum, therapists must be sensitive to the importance of the human elements in all therapeutic encounters. In other words, unless the therapist takes an interest in the patient as a person and succeeds in communicating this interest and commitment, psychotherapy becomes a caricature of a good human relationship (the ultimate negative effect!).

h. Closely related to the foregoing, therapists should keep in mind that all good therapeutic experiences lead to increments in the patient's self-acceptance and self-respect; consequently, continual care must be taken to promote such experiences and to guard against interventions that might have opposite effects.

The foregoing findings and their implications are part of the empirical and conceptual foundation for the therapeutic approach described in the book.

Finally, there are several reasons for our reluctance to conclude, on the basis of the Vanderbilt I study, that specific (technique) factors are of little consequence in psychotherapy and that the weight of the therapeutic influence is carried by nonspecific (interpersonal or relationship) factors: (1) in clinical research which typically involves comparisons of small groups, statistically significant differences are exceedingly difficult to obtain; (2) the nature of the patient population, the relative brevity of therapy, the relatively narrow band of patients and therapists, as well as the crudeness of the outcome measures may have further militated against the ability to demonstrate significant differences between professional therapists and college professors; (3) failure to disprove the null hypothesis is not tantamount to proving it; in other words, the results should not be interpreted as having shown that there are *no* differences between professional therapists and college professors. Taking these considerations together with the results of the process studies, we believe it is premature to conclude, as some critics have done, (1) that psychotherapeutic techniques are unimportant, and (2) that therefore there is little justification for thorough training of therapists.

Last but not least, we have come to doubt whether it is possible, by means of the design used, to partition the influence of specific and nonspecific factors. Anyone engaged in therapeutic conversations uses techniques, but it is highly questionable whether the skills of the professional therapist can be isolated in the manner originally proposed. The evidence showed that kindly college professors can be of therapeutic help to certain patients under the highly specific circumstances of research when patients are carefully selected and assessed; when the untutored counselors (in this case, college professors) are themselves a select group and can readily identify with their clients (in this case, college students); and perhaps most important, when the therapeutic outcome is judged by the global and highly imprecise measures that are the only ones available to the researcher today. In short, more intensive and fine-grained analyses of the kind referred to earlier disclosed a different picture. In particular, the patient's amenability to the kind of therapy under study was shown to be an important determinant of outcome. Perhaps it should have occasioned no surprise that those patients who had the greatest assets fared best, as they did with the professional therapists. Conversely, when these conditions were not met, the results were less impressive regardless of the qualifications of the practitioner. A medical treatment, too, may be most successful when the patient is young, cooperative, and there are no complications. Assessments of outcome must take these factors into account. For all these reasons we believe that the Vanderbilt I study does not inpugn the professional therapists' expertise and that the basic question remains essentially unresolved.

A Comparison of a Patient Pair from the Vanderbilt Psychotherapy Project

As a further illustration of our attempts to build bridges between controlled research and clinical practice, we shall present a comparison between patient pairs treated by the same therapist in the course of the Vanderbilt Psychotherapy Project. One of the patients, whom we shall call Ernest, seemed to achieve lasting benefits whereas the other, Bryan, was essentially a therapeutic failure. The reasons for these divergent outcomes will be traced through antecedent patient characteristics and the nature of the evolving therapeutic alliance; the issue of matching therapists and patients; the necessity of adapting one's therapeutic approach to the patient's character style; and the overriding importance of countertransference problems.

Overview

The two men whose therapy will be compared were both undergraduates, who entered the project in a state of moderate clinical disturbance (anxiety, depression, and social withdrawal), and both were seen in twice-a-week therapy by a senior psychiatrist (Dr. L) whose background included formal psychoanalytic training. Ernest, who was seen for 27 sessions, emerged as a success case on most measures. Bryan terminated therapy after 8 sessions, and while he reported some subjective improvement, neither the therapist's assessment nor the objective measures corroborated these changes. One year after entering therapy Ernest had maintained his therapeutic gains. No follow-up data could be obtained on Bryan. Scores for the two patients on two instruments of objective measures, the MMPI and the Global Change scale, are given in tables 10.1 and 10.2.

Target Complaints

Following extensive intake interviews conducted by an experienced clinician, patients were asked to formulate three problem areas in which they sought change. The severity of each target problem was then rated by the patient on a scale ranging from 13 (could not be worse) to 1 (no

TABLE 10.1

Minnesota Multiphasic Personality Inventory Scores on Three Subscales at Three Times

| Patient; Time | Subscales | | | |
	Depression	Psych-asthenia	Social Introversion	Sum of Difference
Ernest				
Intake	84	79	68	. . .
Termination	48	64	51	68
Follow-up	51	62	50	0
Bryan				
Intake	72	75	77	. . .
Termination	70	79	72	3
Follow-up*	. . .	. . .	. . .	. . .

*No data available.

TABLE 10.2

*Global Change Scores Rated by Patient, Independent Clinician, and Therapist**

| Patient; Time | Scores | | | |
	Patient	Clinician	Therapist	Sum of Difference
Ernest				
Termination	4	3	4	11
Follow-up	4	3	. . .	. . .
Bryan				
Termination	1	0	−1	0
Follow-up**	. . .	. . .	. . .	. . .

*Scores are rated on a scale of 5 (high) to −5 (low).
**No data available.

difficulty). Ratings obtained again at termination and follow-up are given in table 10.3. The data reflect clear differences between the two patients, although, as might be expected, the congruence of patient's, clinician's, and therapist's ratings was not perfect.

Patients' Perceptions

Following the third therapy session, patients were asked to rate their attitude toward the therapist and the therapeutic process on a modified version of the Barrett-Lennard Relationship Inventory. The following discrepancies appeared on the 16-item rating form:

1. Ernest: (a) My counselor seems genuinely interested in helping me.

   Bryan: (b) I get the feeling that I am just another student to him.

4.* Ernest: (a) My counselor seems to *really* understand what I am saying and feeling.

   Bryan: (b) I'm not sure he *really* understands me and what I'm feeling.

5. Ernest: (a) My counselor seems to do his share of the talking and takes an active part in our conversations.

   Bryan: (b) He wants me to do all of the talking and remains rather passive himself.

7. Ernest: (a) My counselor seems willing to give me suggestions and advice.

   Bryan: (b) He usually avoids answering my questions and wants me to do all of the deciding.

8. Ernest: (a) My counselor usually lets me know what he thinks or feels.

   Bryan: (b) I'm never sure what my counselor really thinks or feels.

9. Ernest: (a) My counselor seems quite natural and informal in our relationship.

   Bryan: (b) My counselor seems rather stiff, formal, and professional.

10. Ernest: (a) My counselor seems comfortable and at ease in our relationship.

    Bryan: (b) He seems a little nervous and uncomfortable talking with me.

11. Ernest: (a) I enjoy talking with my counselor and feel at ease.

    Bryan: (b) I'm rather uncomfortable talking with my counselor.

*Items showing nonsignificant differences are omitted.

TABLE 10.3

Ratings of Target Problems *

Problem	Ratings Intake	Termination	Follow-up
Ernest			
To be better at meeting people			
Patient	10	5	4
Clinician	8	5	8
Therapist	7	3	. . .
To say and do things, rather than repressing them			
Patient	7	2	3
Clinician	9	7	9
Therapist	8	3	. . .
To feel free to have casual relationships, especially with women			
Patient	6	4	1
Clinician	6	6	8
Therapist	6	2	. . .
Bryan			
To be able to be honest and not worry about it; to get rid of emotional inhibitions			
Patient	13	5	. . .
Clinician	12	8	. . .
Therapist	8	8	. . .
Apathy and lack of enthusiasm; to develop interest and ability to enjoy life			
Patient	13	5	. . .
Clinician	11	11	. . .
Therapist	7	6	. . .
To have confidence in decision making; to decide life-style and future direction			
Patient	9	3	. . .
Clinician	11	8	. . .
Therapist	5	8	. . .

*Ratings were made on a scale of 13 (could not be worse) to 1 (no difficulty). As Bryan terminated therapy early, no follow-up data were available. The therapist did not see either patient in a follow-up session, and so no ratings are available in this category.

13. Ernest: (a) I feel that my counselor likes me.
    Bryan: (b) I'm not sure whether or not he likes me.
14. Ernest: (a) My counselor seems quite warm and easy to relate to.
    Bryan: (b) My counselor seems rather cool and distant.
16. Ernest: (a) I feel free and open with my counselor and feel I can tell him anything.

TABLE 10.4

Patient-Therapist Interaction Ratings *

Items	Ernest	Bryan
Patient Items		
10. Worked through particular problem	3.5	1
11. Logical and organized in expressing thoughts and feelings	3.5	1
21. Depressed	2	4
23. Frustrated	1.5	4
26. Deferential	1.5	3
27. Defensive	1.5	3
Therapist Items		
32. Showed warmth and friendliness toward patient	2.5	1
33. Helped patient feel accepted in relationship	3	1
34. Supported patient's self-esteem, confidence, and building hope	3	1
35. Shared empathically in what patient was experiencing	3	1
36. Actively encouraged patient to express feelings and concerns freely	3	1
37. Tried to get better understanding of patient, of what was really going on	3.5	1
38. Helped patient recognize feelings	3.5	1
39. Helped patient understand reasons behind rections	3.5	1
40. Encouraged depth rather than shallowness	4	1
43. Kept patient focused on therapy-related topics	4	1.5
46. Encouraged patient to change and to try new ways of dealing with self and others	3	1
49. Assumed role of expert	3.5	1.5

*Ratings on scale of 1 (not at all) to 5 (a great deal). Items are numbered according to Vanderbilt Psychotherapy Process Scale. Copies of the scale and an accompaning manual are available from Dr. Hans Strupp, Dept. of Psychology, Vanderbilt University.

Bryan: (b) My counselor does not make it easier for me to talk about things I find difficult to talk about.

At termination, some of these differences had disappeared, but divergent responses to items 1, 5, 8, 9, 11, and 14 at both times suggested that Ernest had maintained very positive feelings toward the therapist, whereas Bryan's feelings were negative, indicating that he had felt uncomfortable in the therapeutic relationship. Genuineness of the therapist's interest, ease of communication, and the patient's sense of comfort, being liked, and being warmly responded to by the therapist emerged as important areas of divergence.

Process Ratings

Following a procedure described earlier in a previous publication (Gomes-Schwartz 1978), two independent raters assessed the patient-therapist interaction on the basis of videotaped recordings of the third interview. Ratings of patient and therapist behaviors were made on a scale ranging from 1 (not at all) to 5 (a great deal); items showing discrepancies of 1.5 or more scale points among raters are listed in table 10.4.

It is apparent that the clinical raters viewed Ernest as less depressed, frustrated, deferential, and defensive than Bryan, and more actively engaged in therapeutic work on his problems. With respect to the therapist's behavior, the ratings by external clinical observers paralleled the patients' perceptions just reported.

These data clearly suggest that Ernest had established a satisfying and productive working relationship with Dr. L in the course of the first three sessions, whereas there were marked difficulties in the relationship between Bryan and Dr. L.

Comparisons: Histories and Response to Therapy

Ernest

Ernest was an eighteen-year-old sophomore who entered therapy in response to a letter sent to random samples of undergraduate students announcing the availability of a counseling program designed to help anxious, depressed, and shy male students. Ernest identified shyness and discomfort in social settings as his major problem. On the surface, his first two years in college had been fairly unremarkable—his academic performance was satisfactory and he felt comfortable with fellow students. Toward the end of his sophomore year he had become emotionally involved with a girl in a relationship he described as "heavy." It lasted a few months but broke up for reasons that were not readily apparent. Following the separation he was "really depressed," but eventually he felt better and resumed dating. Nevertheless, some difficulties persisted. His career plans were as yet unformed, although he had chosen a major area of study.

Born in a large midwestern city, Ernest had grown up in a western state, where the family continued to live. Ernest's father owned a business and wanted Ernest to follow in his footsteps. A sister, three years younger, was a sophomore in high school. The two had never been close, which was somewhat distressing to Ernest.

The parents were characterized as "both basically reasonable people," and they seemed to get along well. Ernest described his father as a very strong person, and this view struck him as incompatible with the fact that on one occasion his father had sought psychiatric help. Ernest himself had been taken to a psychiatrist when he was about ten years old, apparently because he was nervous and tense. He saw the psychiatrist for only 3 sessions, during which it was determined that the problem was "my mother's fault." He did not view his current problems as particularly pressing or severe but felt that he might benefit from some professional help. This seemed to be a realistic assessment.

Ernest described his mother as a "calm person . . . a typical mother . . . she worries a lot." Ernest had a theory that his history of tenseness was related to the fact that his parents never used physical punishment and instead "ruled by guilt." As a result, Ernest never got into mischief, and both he and his sister were "perfect children in our parents' eyes." Apart from some childhood allergies that he had largely outgrown, Ernest was in good health. He had a close childhood friend, of whom he was still fond, although the latter attended a distant college.

Course of Therapy

From the beginning, Ernest took an active role and seemed to have little difficulty in relating to the therapist. He was articulate in describing experiences and expressing his feelings. This permitted the therapist to function in his accustomed role of an expectant listener who asked facilitative questions and occasionally interpreted a theme. Dr. L's general approach to therapy followed the traditional psychoanalytic model, particularly in its emphasis on therapeutic neutrality and the achievement of insight through interpretations.

As the therapy unfolded, Ernest detailed certain attitudes and traits he disliked in himself. For instance, he criticized himself (echoing his mother's criticisms of him) for being selfish, engaging in daydreaming, being insufficiently attentive to the other person in conversations, and having become less open and trusting as a result of his disappointing love relationship. The latter was described as a triangle in which "I sorta felt like I got burned." Having been hurt, he had withdrawn and harbored some grievances. Comparing himself to his late great-grandfather (and other people) whom he idealized, he was painfully aware of his own shortcomings and his failure to live up to these models.

A series of dreams, reported in the 3d hour, led to the identification of a central conflict. Ernest dreamed, as he had recurrently, that he was falling into water, driving a car into water, or driving backwards over hills and eventually falling into a lake where he began to drown before waking up. Ernest's associations with the theme of losing control clarified the struggle between his wish to rebel against his parents and to be the obedient, compliant son. The problem was complicated by the fact that his parents, as he put it, "sent double messages": for example, if he stayed home they accused him of being antisocial, but if he went out they made him feel guilty for not spending enough time at home. In a similar vein, the father was described as almost antireligious during Ernest's childhood; however, in the more recent past the parents had strongly urged Ernest to date girls of his own faith. As Dr. L pointed out, Ernest had a conflict as to whether his actions expressed his own desires or whether they were fueled by rebellion against parental authority. He also attempted to draw a distinction between Ernest's striving for self-assertion and what his mother termed *selfishness.* In sum, Ernest struggled to break away from the ties of his childhood and to gain his independence. What stood in the way were his fears of competitiveness and aggression, as well as his wishes for dependency and approval. Added to these were the uncertainties of living in a complex and often irrational world.

The vacillation of late adolescence also expressed itself in Ernest's inability (or unwillingness) to make commitments and engage in sustained effort, for instance in dealing with women and choosing a career. The disappointment in his earlier love relationship had further contributed to a self-protective withdrawal.

Perhaps partly as a result of the wish to please authority figures (a tendency Dr. L on one occasion interpreted in relation to himself) but also as a reflection of his striving for growth, Ernest's behavior in therapy was characterized by hard work and a genuine commitment to the therapeutic task. In this effort he found Dr. L an equally serious and committed collaborator. The latter, while maintaining an attitude of strict neutrality from which pampering or control was notably absent, was clearly committed to helping Ernest master his problems in the tacitly agreed-upon analytic manner. Ernest, for his part, seemed to respond positively to this approach and was able to proceed without much prompting or encouragement. Throughout therapy he took the initiative in talking about his difficulties. These accounts were sometimes followed by long pauses, but at other times when the situation seemed to warrant it, the therapist identified a theme or advanced a concise interpretation that might take the form of a summary. Small talk was completely absent, and both participants appeared to proceed on the assumption that there was a job to be done, that time was limited, and that the best way to further the enterprise was to stick to the task. Although Ernest was persistently struggling, his affect was always controlled (as was that of Dr. L).

Recurrent themes for Ernest were concerns about making the right impression in social situations, lack of self-confidence, inability to be himself, the conflict between wishing to be accepted as a member of a peer group versus becoming an independent adult capable of assertiveness and self-expression, fear of criticism, wish for approbation and praise, inhibitions in approaching women, fear of failure and humiliation, the wish to compete and prove himself versus the search for security and comfort. A dream about midway through therapy vividly described Ernest's dilemma:

> I was home and I was running away from home. In order to run away I had to go through barbed-wire fences and finally I got outside and I was running along. Before I got very far, there was my father standing there with two German shepherds. I decided to go back.
>
> I guess my thoughts during the dream were that after my father caught me and I went back, I just accepted it and figured this was the way it was supposed to be anyway. . . . There was one little thing in the dream that seems to always happen to me: in running away I was about to jump out the window when I remembered some little stupid thing I had to do. I went back and took care of it. Then I went out the window but just as I was going out the window my father saw me but I still kept on going. That seems to happen a lot. Whenever I daydream or fantasize I always seem to . . . I just can't seem to have a totally free, "no-strings-

attached" daydream on any subject. There's always some complication involved. I'm always thinking of the things I have to do and I just can't go ahead and do something right off the bat.

In time, Ernest became aware of his contradictory goals and began to report changes in his attitude. In particular, he gained insight into the fact that he played an active part in maintaining the image of the obedient son. However, he also came to appreciate that he had the capacity to change in the direction of greater independence and autonomy. The following is a typical example of the therapeutic interchange from that session:

P: It's strange that lots of times I come in here and start talking about a problem and when I leave I feel good and lots of times the problem seems to have already gotten somewhat better. After I talk about it and get it out of my system I'm not as uptight about it. I've started talking to people again. I've felt a lot better since then. If I didn't work so hard at what to say and just let things come naturally, it would probably be better.

T: Not press so hard?

P: Right. Unfortunately, lots of times I'm trying to make a good impression and that causes me to start thinking about what I should say. I've never been one to do things spontaneously. I remember in high school I would speak out spontaneously with my opinion on something and then other people would give their opinions and they would be different from mine and I would feel bad. So I would backtrack and adjust my opinion.

T: Almost as if you were trying to keep yourself blended in.

P: I think that in junior high I never really had a group of friends that I belonged to, I got to high school and I found this group of people I could become a part of, and down underneath I thought if I wasn't like them and I didn't have the same opinions then I would no longer be a part of the group. Like I had to conform. I really think the consequence of that was I was a part of the group but I really lost a lot of my identity.

T: In other words, you were giving up your individuality in the interest of conforming and being accepted.

The thrust of Dr. L's interpretations is illustrated by the following example:

T: The pattern that you're describing is one that basically started at home with your father and mother. That is, you were the kind of person they wanted you to be and they in turn would provide for you and like you and accept you and do things for you. Then you carry this kind of picture into your situation with other people. But the thing that troubled you all along was that you had some feeling that it meant foregoing being yourself, being what others wanted rather than being what you were.

The themes of dependence versus independence, passivity versus activity, conformity versus spontaneity, taking responsibility versus shrinking into a shell, living in the past versus anticipating the future remained in focus throughout therapy and were examined from various perspectives. The working through led to the identification of character patterns at the level of present-day reality, with negligible excursions into the past. There was no doubt that Ernest gained insight into some important aspects of his conflicts. He described his sessions with Dr. L as one of his most worthwhile experiences, and he verbalized his growing realization that "I have to do things for myself." As therapy ended, he was still struggling, yet as he put it:

P: My attitude toward myself is a lot better. I think the big thing is that I plan to be myself and let people know who I am . . . that I'm not just a conglomeration of everybody around me.

His collaboration with Dr. L, too, was tinged by his wish to please authority figures, a tendency that was partly responsible for the good therapeutic alliance as well as the favorable outcome. Whether this deep-seated disposition was resolved in any significant way must remain an open question. Dr. L, commenting about Ernest's therapy some time after termination, noted that he had some struggle with countertransference feelings:

T: He reminded me of the young men that I associated with back in my college days [on an earlier occasion he had said that the patient reminded him of his own youth]. And, you know, that was a long time ago. For today, Ernest was pretty square. You don't see this kind very much around our campus. You have to go to [a bible college] to see this kind. He was a rather intense young man with almost overly high moral standards and scruples.

He was, in a way, almost too good. And I think his problem with his parents was that he had too great a need to be the good boy and to please them. He belonged back about four decades. He was out of place.

He went on to say that he remembered less about this patient than the others he had seen as part of the project (although he was the most recent one). He attributed this vagueness to the fact that there was nothing "central" about him except that he was a good boy. He felt that Ernest needed to accept his hostility better and to become less concerned about pleasing and keeping everyone happy:

T: He was probably one of those who could not separate assertiveness from aggression. . . . I remember he came very faithfully, and we worked on things. He performed in therapy as he performed in life —faithfully, conscientiously, and ingratiatingly.

In sum, it was apparent that Dr. L could easily identify with this patient and probably grew more fond of him than the objectivity of his comments might suggest.

Bryan

Bryan, an eighteen-year-old sophomore, also became a patient in the project by responding to the letter sent to random samples of the male student body. He gave as his reason for applying:

P: *I was chosen in the random selection,* so I decided to go through with it. I have things that bother me and although I have tried and failed previously to relieve any of the strain that I may or may not feel by talking to a trained counselor, I felt it would be nice to talk again (Bryan had previously had two sessions with a counselor). Talking is fun especially when it is me about whom I speak. I am egocentrical and what bothers *me* is my main concern. I enjoy talking about problems I have in my relation with other animals of all types even though (sic) I gain nothing but enjoyment from the experience. (Note the patient's ambivalence about seeking help, especially his repudiation of personal responsibility for the decision.)

Bryan was born in a northeastern state. The parents, both of whom were office workers, had been divorced when Bryan was in the second grade, and subsequently Bryan had lived with his mother. In addition to a younger sister, Bryan had an older brother. His performance in college had been poor. After much hesitation he had recently selected a major but remained vague about his career plans. During his childhood the family had moved frequently. He stated: "You learn to drop friendships pretty quickly. I mean I've always been pretty good at dropping things. That's another reason why I think you don't really care about people, because it's easy to forget about people."

At the end of the assessment interview, the clinician noted, "Needs to develop insight into extreme hostility and develop more effective ways of dealing with it." He rated Bryan's motivation for therapy as "moderate," considered him "somewhat attractive" for therapy, but admitted that he moderately disliked the patient.

Following the first therapy hour, Dr. L rated the patient as "somewhat motivated" for psychotherapy but considered his attractiveness for therapy as "very slight," noting that he was "lacking in verbal richness." He described his personal reaction as "neutral," commenting, "What appears to be a typical adolescent struggle may cover a borderline state."

A significant feature of Bryan's therapy was its brevity and the frequency of missed appointments. His first missed hour was the 3d session. He failed to appear, although the research coordinator had seen him in the building shortly before the scheduled hour. In keeping with the project plan, the therapist had set up appointments on a twice-a-week basis but had difficulties in adhering to this arrangement because of his travel schedule. Nonetheless, interviews were scheduled at least on a once-a-week basis. At one point there was a gap of about six weeks, partly due to the Christmas recess. Following several instances of no show, the research coordinator attempted to get in touch with the student, and she noted that he usually apologized in his "incoherent fashion." Eventually she inquired whether there was some problem with Bryan's feelings toward the therapist. Bryan denied this, explaining that he missed so many things. According to a note in the file, the therapist had raised the same question with the patient, but since this part of the conversation was not preserved on tape, it is not known how the patient responded. In any case, he assured the research coordinator that he really liked to come and that he was learning "new things." At a later date, Dr. L commented to the research coordinator that every time he made an interpretation that was at all threatening, Bryan would miss one or two sessions.

Following the 3d therapy hour, Bryan indicated on one of the forms administered by the project staff that, given a choice, he would have preferred a different therapist. His reasons were as follows:

P: My present therapist is slow—not in his ability to size up a situation but just overall . . . I spoke to a counselor over the summer and he was more like a little league coach—vivarant [vibrant] and quick—someone I could relate to more—more of a chum type, but also knowledgeable . . . chummy and not experienced would be as unsatisfactory as my present condition.

At termination, Bryan was more direct: "A slight dissatisfaction with my counselor led me to avoid periods . . . and the scheduling of periods. . . . Time became a problem as I became involved in more activities (he had begun to attend an evening trade school).

In short, over the two-and-one-half- to three-month period during which therapy sessions were scheduled, the problem of missed hours was not resolved, and therapy came to a premature end following the eighth session. Although the project staff made repeated attempts to reach the patient, we were hesitant to pressure him into continuing. Bryan did appear for the termination interview with the clinician but failed to respond to requests for a follow-up interview (he had since left the university). Subsequently it was learned that he had enlisted in the military service, and three years later he responded affirmatively to a letter request for permission to use the therapy tapes for teaching purposes.

The termination interview was scheduled because Bryan declined further therapy with Dr. L, asserting that their respective schedules were posing too many difficulties. Acting on his impression, recorded in the notes, that Bryan was a "pretty sick guy," the clinician urged him to continue counseling with someone else. Bryan expressed a mild interest but was taken aback by the suggestion. Nevertheless, he agreed, and the project staff made appropriate arrangements. He saw a counselor (an advanced graduate student in psychology) for a few sessions at the Counseling Center, but since Bryan had been formally terminated by the project, no details became available.

Course of Therapy

From the beginning, Bryan had difficulty articulating the nature of his problems. He spoke in vague terms about not caring sufficiently for people, wanting to be more honest with himself, and experiencing a sense of estrangement from self and others. These feelings appreared to have a long history, and it emerged that his mother had urged him for some time to seek professional help: "She always thought I was mad. . . . She said, 'your're crazy or something,' . . . she has always said that I did erratic things, threatened to commit me and things like that." Examples of "erratic things" were Bryan's driving cars into ditches, beating his younger brother, smoking marijuana, and experimenting with various drugs.

Asked to reflect on his childhood and his current life, he said, "It's hard to grasp," and he added poignantly, almost as an aside, "I am just lost, really." He spoke about his lack of involvement, incessant self-observations, and self-recriminations, all of which seriously interfered with spontaneity. Assuredly, he was a troubled young man.

From the outset Dr. L pursued an exploratory approach in the context of his customary expectant stance. He did so in an objective and dispassionate manner. While his sustained attention probably provided a certain amount of support, he expressed little warmth or empathy (perhaps as a form of counterhostility). In retrospect, it appeared that this approach intensified the patient's anxiety without contributing to the formation of a good working alliance.

The 3d session followed a missed appointment, for which Bryan offered apologies. Following a lengthy and diffuse sequence involving difficulties Bryan experienced with male peers, the therapist interpreted: "I was wondering if the whole thing running through this might be some question on your part as to how much you are wanted . . . how much you are a burden and a drain." Perhaps experiencing the comment as criticism, Bryan responded with a childhood memory in which he was scolded by his grandmother. She had said, "You don't love your mother." He also felt rejected by his father, who disapproved of his choice of a major area of study. Dr. L raised the question of whether a similar struggle might be going on between the patient and the therapist. Bryan agreed.

> T: Well, I wonder if what you're saying is that you constantly struggle with the feeling of being unwanted and a need to get yourself wanted. And you work very hard at producing whatever you think will make you wanted. . . . The question is whether what you produce comes out of your need to learn more about yourself or the need for me to accept you. As you go through this, there seems to be quite a struggle with a need to feel wanted.

Bryan observed that he had never thought of it in that way—he had always thought of his problem as one of wanting to be liked. Dr. L said that the two go together but stressed the former. Following this exchange, the hour ended abruptly, and the patient did not keep his appointments for the next two weeks.

A recurrent theme was Bryan's angry impulses, which at times took the form of murderous wishes directed particularly against his mother and his younger brother. A dramatic incident (which seemed to become fixed in the therapist's memory) concerned Bryan's driving someone else's car into a ditch and finding it "hilarious." Nonetheless, he was troubled by this "sadistic pleasure." Dr. L interpreted these impulses in terms of Bryan's envy of his younger brother ("some feeling of not getting what's coming to you . . . [thus] you delight in destroying other people's things"). Indeed, there was evidence that the younger brother had been preferred, and Dr. L's interpretation was undoubtedly correct. However, it did not seem to be responsive to the patient's anxiety conflict. Bryan responded:

P: How can you get away from something like that? It's going to follow you all the rest of your life. . . . You constantly continue to destroy other people's things because you have this resentment toward something so long ago.

T: Well, it's important while we're talking about it for you to know what you're doing. That may do something for your ability to cope with it. . . . The basic question that we're addressing ourselves to is, Where does it begin, and whom you are angry at and why?

A traumatic sequence of events related to the parents' separation when the patient was about age four, which was also the time of his brother's birth. Bryan remembered crying when the divorce became final several years later. Dr. L attempted to pinpoint the origin of Bryan's anger at the time of his brother's birth. When Bryan had arguments with his mother, she would say, "You're just like your father," which in turn had the effect of rejecting the patient's masculine identification. Yet Bryan also tried to live up to his image of the "ideal" father.

During the next to the last hour, Bryan was able to recognize some "nice things" in himself as well as the fact "I've always been very down on myself." He spoke with considerable feeling about his loneliness and loss, as well as his struggle to find relatedness and freedom. The therapist's interpretations, offered sparingly, were aimed at the early family conflicts and sibling rivalry. On several occasions, interpretations were followed by long pauses, whereupon the patient would turn to a peripheral topic. These shifts appeared to be indications of his feeling inadequately understood and supported by the therapist. (This statement is significant for its questioning of the therapist's empathic ability.) As the hour ended, Bryan confided that he had to search for topics and that he found the patient role demeaning. Still, he assured Dr. L that he had learned some useful things (the desire to be wanted and the origin of his anger in terms of rivalry with his brother).

In what turned out to be the final session, the interchange proceeded largely on an intellectual level. Bryan's heart did not seem to be in the relationship and his statements seemed routine and mechanical. The therapist for his part offered a few interpretations but they were made in a rather detached manner and did not seem to strike a responsive chord. It was apparent that the participants no longer had anything meaningful to say to each other.

At termination, the therapist's ratings on motivation for therapy and attractiveness as a patient were somewhat lower than they had been at the beginning; however, he still described his personal attitude as neutral, adding "not intense in either direction." He agreed with the clinician that there was a problem with underlying hostility "which may become disabling or lead to destructive behavior." Concerning the reasons for termination he stated, "Not clear to me, but from the beginning there was evidence of limited motivation (slept through and failed to keep third appointment)."

Approximately two years after therapy, the following observations were elicited from the therapist:

> Bryan was one patient who didn't follow through on his therapy, although I had hoped he would because he certainly needed help and was the sickest of the bunch I saw. This young man was very sadistic. He got great glee out of banging up cars—especially not his own—and doing other rather hostile acts with much merriment. There seemed to be a struggle that he was going through based on feelings toward a younger sibling. I was afraid that if this young man didn't get help he might act out this sadism in a fairly destructive way. Yet he had good potential. He had been pushed into therapy by outside circumstances— I think largely by his mother. He would come for a while, disappear, and then come back again.
>
> He looked sicker as time went on. Some material came out . . . he didn't tell me early about some of the more horrendous things that caused great merriment in him.

Asked about his diagnostic impressions of Bryan, Dr. L responded:

Well, I don't know. I would have seen it not so much as an ego defect in him as I would have seen it as a serious problem in living . . . a kind of patterning created as a result of early experiences . . . that were causing great difficulty with the handling of hostility.

Pursuing the inquiry, Dr. L was asked whether he had viewed Bryan as a borderline patient. He responded:

Well, that was what I was debating when you asked me. Indeed there is that possibility. As I reflect back, I don't think he was a borderline patient, but I wouldn't rule it out.

The interviewer wondered what kind of therapy Dr. L would have regarded as optimal. He responded:

If he had been willing to stay, I would have proceeded with a psychoanalytically oriented therapy, watching very closely his responses to interpretations . . . and dealing with things a bit more gingerly than I would with some other patients.

Dr. L denied the interviewer's surmise that Bryan was apparently not one of his favorite patients, stating that he was likable. He elaborated:

This man evoked almost a kind of compassion because he was a terribly sick guy and had huge problems that were extremely frightening to him, and I think should have been frightening. I would hope that as he grew a little older and developed a little more ego strength or ego experience he might then be able to get into some kind of dynamic therapy.

Dr. L felt that the problem in therapy was not so much the absence of a good "fit" between patient and therapist but rather that the patient came to therapy:

. . .without being fully committed to doing something, that he was being pushed from the outside rather than being pulled by something internal; and, second, that the nature of what he was struggling with was very frightening so that even getting the toe in the water was painful and difficult. I think he was really running away.

He reiterated that he considered Bryan a very sick young man who needed very careful, painstaking, long therapy.

Comment

The following comparison provides further corroboration of points made in several articles (Strupp 1980a, 1980b, 1980c):

Given the "average expectable" atmosphere created by a person functioning in the therapeutic role, that is, a person who is basically empathic and benign, the key determinants of a particular therapeutic outcome are traceable to characteristics of the *patient* that have been described: If the patient is a person who by virtue of his past life experience is capable of human *relatedness* and therefore amenable to learning mediated within that context, the outcome, even though the individual may have suffered traumas, reverses, and other vicissitudes, is likely to be positive. . . . If on the other hand his early life experiences have been so destructive that human relatedness has failed to acquire a markedly positive valence and elaborate neurotic and characterological malformations have created massive barriers to intimacy (and therefore to "therapeutic learning"), chances are that psychotherapy either results in failure or at best in very modest gains. The therapist's ability to provide a nurturant environment and to curb countertransference reactions undoubtedly plays an important part, as does his expertise in facilitating therapeutic learning (e.g., skills in eroding neurotic barriers against human relatedness). Thus, in the final analysis, the outcome of psychotherapy will be largely determined by the balance of these forces entering into and determining the patient-therapist interaction (Strupp 1980d, p. 953).

Of the patients described here, it is abundantly clear that Ernest (the high changer) had many of the characteristics that have traditionally been associated with a good prognosis for short-term dynamic psychotherapy, such as motivation, a history of good interpersonal relationships, focal conflict, psychological-mindedness—in short, a relatively "intact ego" (Freud, *S.E.* 1937/1963). By contrast, Bryan (the low changer) was a poor candidate by all these criteria. Thus, Ernest was readily able to become engaged in a productive therapeutic working alliance with Dr. L, whereas Bryan was unable to do so.

The preceding points place heavy emphases on patients' character makeup, the nature and depth of their disturbance, and their ability to become productively involved in psychotherapy. These criteria are essentially identical to those traditionally considered crucial in assessing a patient's suitability for psychoanalysis (Bachrach and Leaff 1978). However, it is also important to stress that with both patients, the therapist employed a standard therapeutic approach structured along traditional psychoanalytic lines. Ernest experienced this interpersonal context as congenial, whereas to Bryan it remained foreign. In other words, the therapist conducted therapy in terms of *his* predilections, and the patient was faced with the necessity of working within the therapist's framework. One patient was able to do so; the other wasn't. Does this mean that patients like Bryan are unsuitable for psychotherapy, or merely for psychotherapy of a certain kind? It is certainly plausible that patients like Bryan should not be considered reasonable candidates for time-limited forms of dynamic psychotherapy. Indeed, workers like Malan (1976*a*), Sifneos (1972), Davanloo (1978), and Mann (1973) would undoubtedly rule them out. However, it is also possible that approaches putting greater technical emphasis on analyzing the patient-therapist interactions might provide some form of therapeutic help for these difficult patients even when circumstances dictate time limitations. As is well known, the Bryans of the world constitute a far larger segment of the total patient pool than the Ernests, and the challenge to the mental health professions is to provide more efficient and effective services to those individuals who have too long been neglected.

Further, one should not lose sight of the serious toll exacted by faulty patient-therapist matches. In Ernest's case there was a sense of mutual satisfaction, whereas Bryan's termination was surrounded by feelings of profound frustration on the part of both participants. It is easy to see that any therapist would find patients like Ernest a pleasure to work with. However, as therapists we have not adequately faced up to the negative reactions engendered in us by patients who bring to our offices the products of their unhappy life experiences.

Thus, major deterrents to the formation of a good working alliance are not only the patient's characterological distortions and maladaptive defenses but, at least equally important, the therapist's personal reactions. Traditionally these reactions have been considered under the heading of countertransference. It is becoming increasingly clear, however, that this conception is too narrow. The plain fact is that any therapist, indeed any human being, cannot remain immune from negative (angry) reactions to the suppressed and repressed rage regularly encountered in patients with moderate to severe disturbances. As soon as one enters the inner world of such a person through a therapeutic relationship, one is faced with the inescapable necessity of dealing with one's own response to the patient's tendency to make the therapist a partner in his difficulties via the transference. In the Vanderbilt Project, therapists—even highly experienced ones and those who had undergone a personal analysis—tended to respond to such patients with counterhostility that not uncommonly took the form of coldness, distancing, and other forms of rejection. Needless to say, to the patient such responses become self-fulfilling prophecies leading to a dissolution of the therapeutic relationship, early termination, and poor outcome. In this study we failed to encounter a single instance in which a difficult patient's hostility and negativism were successfully confronted or resolved. Admittedly, this may be due to peculiarities of the therapist sample and the brevity of therapy; however, a more likely possibility is that therapists' negative responses to difficult patients were far more common and far more intractable than has been generally recognized. (For a similar conclusion, based on a review of the research literature, see the article by Luborsky and Spence 1978.) Some years ago, Strupp (1960) adduced preliminary evidence on this topic through an analogue study.

It would lead too far afield at this point to discuss the implications of this finding for therapist selection, training, and therapeutic management. In recent years these difficulties have been discussed with reference to borderline patients. The problem, however, is by no means restricted to the most severely disturbed patients, nor is it an isolated or transient difficulty that "well-analyzed" therapists have fully mastered. To be sure, self-understanding, self-acceptance, and discussions with colleagues may go a long way toward aiding the therapist in coping with the problem. But in the final analysis we are dealing with a ubiquitous human tendency that represents perhaps the single most important obstacle to successful psychotherapy, thus meriting much greater attention than it has been accorded. (For an insightful discussion, see also Vaillant, 1977.)

Summary

The challenge for the field is (1) to devise therapeutic approaches that are more efficient and practical for patients who fall outside the range of suitability for traditional short-term psychotherapy (at times this seems like a contradiction in terms), and (2) to deal with inherent limitations in the therapist's human equipment, which far transcend thorough training and personal analysis.

Chapter 11

Epilogue

IN THIS VOLUME we have presented a design for a form of time-limited psychotherapy based on psychodynamic principles. The typical length of one-to-one therapy is 25 hours (more or less), with 45- to 50-minute sessions scheduled at weekly intervals. Thus, TLDP usually extends over a period of approximately six months. There is no consensus regarding how a time limit should be arranged. Some therapists (Malan, 1976a; Mann 1973) recommend that a calendar date be set that demarcates the outside limit of sessions, while others (Davanloo 1980; Sifneos 1979) propose a more ambiguous end point. It is our impression that neither approach has been proven therapeutically superior. We have a slight preference for offering about 25 hours and setting a specific termination date.

What, if anything, is unique about TLDP? How does it differ from other forms of time-limited dynamic psychotherapy as well as from psychoanalytic psychotherapy as commonly practiced? Let us reiterate distinctive features of TLDP and contrast them with more common open-ended approaches:

1. Assessment

a. The short-term therapists have explicitly taken the position that diagnostic labels and dynamic formulations are not as relevant to an assessment of suitability as are those personality dimensions (ability and willingness to explore feelings) that are essential for the patient's collaboration in the therapeutic tasks. This position is also relevant for the assessment of suitability in long-term work. Even if long-term work is being considered, assessing relevant ego dimensions provides highly useful information about the difficulties that are likely to be encountered in therapy. This information may also provide guidelines for adapting the therapist's approach to deal with the patient's specific ego strengths and weaknesses.

b. A dynamic focus, as described in this book, is formulated at a level of inference that offers working guidelines for the problems at hand, rather than in terms of generalizations that may have a theoretical elegance but lack practical implications for immediate work. Our lower-level inferences and interpersonal emphasis offer a means of establishing empathic rapport with a patient. This is useful in the critical opening phase of a therapy, regardless of the length of therapy.

c. The use of trial interpretations aids in assessing the patient's suitability and in adapting the technical approach to the needs of the patient, regardless of the length of therapy.

2. Dynamic Focus

The articulation of a focus that identifies and demarcates the working area characterizes TLDP. Such a focus may also be useful in long-term therapy since it determines the most salient issue or theme to which the therapist should pay closest attention. Regardless of the ultimate length of therapy, it should begin with an affective theme that is salient and accessible. The process of finding a focus, as we conceptualize it, helps to determine the best place to start. Attempting to maintain a therapy focus, regardless of the length of therapy, also conduces to therapist discipline in attending to the most relevant and affectively charged theme(s). This attention to what is most important emotionally to the patient is critical for keeping a therapy on track regardless of its length. Attention to an organizing theme should be maintained within sessions and across sessions.

3. Therapist's Alertness

Time-limited therapy may appear to place a greater premium on alertness than other forms, although we do not wish to create the image of a therapist whose vigilance is that of a bird of prey. More accurately, we would like to reduce to a minimum the number of lost sessions which every therapist is familiar with; that is, hours in which, perhaps as a result of the patient's resistance, little seems to happen. In long-term work, as a result of nonexistent time pressures the therapist may be in greater danger of becoming a victim of passivity or lethargy. This may be true particularly with patients whose resistances are characterized, to varying degrees, by emotional aloofness. In turn, this may create a chronic, if subtle, state of boredom (masked as patience) in the therapist. We propose that each session be viewed as a minitherapy, with palpable progress as its aim. If no progress can be discerned, the therapist should scrutinize the process more intensely.

4. Maintaining "Tension"

Related to the foregoing is the maintenance of a state of tension, which reflects the motivation of both participants to remain *actively* involved in the therapeutic work, as well as reflecting a progressive therapeutic process. In long-term therapy there is a continual danger of the patient's becoming profoundly dependent on the therapist and the ritualistic aspects of therapy (Alexander and French 1946). Concurrently, the therapist may become lulled by these ritualistic features. In time-limited therapy a productive tension is fostered by the time constraints of therapy. In long-term work, this tension must be generated by the therapist's quiet but insistent *attitude* that every session should count. As each session unfolds, the therapist should assess whether something of therapeutic value appears to transpire. If not, the therapist should attempt to identify the source of resistance.

5. Termination

There is a tendency for long-term therapy to stagnate or to end in unplanned fashion. Even if termination is planned, it is sometimes not treated as a regular phase of treatment, characterized by unique issues as well as by the recrudescence of the themes that have characterized the entire treatment. Regardless of how termination is approached, it should be considered a necessary process that must be understood and examined. This issue has been highlighted in other forms of time-limited therapy. Regardless of the length of therapy, termination must be examined with reference to (a) separation and loss, and (b) the meanings of separation and loss within the context of the current as well as the enduring affective themes of the particular therapy.

Clearly, TLDP shares elements with all forms of therapy based on psychodynamic principles. Thus we do not claim to have added yet another therapeutic modality to the many existing ones. Instead, we have drawn on elements that we considered most useful in other approaches. Throughout, we have striven for clarity and clinical meaningfulness. Beyond TLDP's debt to the brief dynamic psychotherapies, we have noted its links to contemporary thinking in psychoanalytic psychotherapy. Most of the advances in the latter domain have not been related to time-limited psychotherapy, although in our view, they are fully compatible with it. Indeed, we maintain that any first-rate form of psychotherapy aimed at character change (therapies ranging from modern-day psychoanalysis to psychoanalytically oriented intensive psychotherapy) would greatly benefit from systematic application of the principles and procedures set forth in this book. In short, time limits do not define the modus operandi of TLDP; they merely direct the therapist's attention to the need for formulating reasonably specific goals, and through constant alertness to transference and countertransference phenomena, working systematically toward their approximation. The design of TLDP urges the therapist to assume a particular stance and to chart the journey that will be undertaken with the patient. Depending on various conditions (the chronicity of the patient's difficulties, his or her motivation to work in therapy, pervasiveness of neurotic patterns, available time, money, and so on), the journey may be brief or extended. But in any event, concerted effort should be made to identify a goal, to chart a course, to become aware of the obstacles likely to impede progress, and to estimate the arrival time. Thus, the therapist is urged to think clearly about the therapeutic undertaking.

The foregoing steps, we believe, will spell significant progress in the field of psychotherapy. The objective is to ascertain as clearly as possible what can be done under particular circumstances and how it might best be done. Furthermore, by attending to the passage of time, both patient and therapist are more likely to stay focused on the task.

The goal of therapy, time limited or otherwise, must take account of the patients' current difficulties in living and the extent to which these interfere with their capacity for enjoyment and productivity (Freud's famous epigram: *Lieben und arbeiten*). There are no hard and fast rules for judging what is needed or desired in a particular case. With some individuals, the current problem may be narrowly circumscribed; with others, serious neurotic difficulties may pervade many facets of their lives. Often, regardless of the severity of the problem and the patient's adaptation, there are practical reasons (time, finances, geographical distance) that dictate compromises. These factors must be carefully weighed, and this assessment should be made as early as possible. As therapy proceeds, it may develop that a seemingly simple problem has broader ramifications or it is more deeply rooted than had been anticipated. The converse may also be true. The single best predictor, by the available evidence, is encompassed by the patients' past success in living, the quality of their adaptation to life, and their ego resources.

There can be no doubt that those individuals whose ability to cope has been demonstrated in the past are far better candidates for any form of psychotherapy than patients whose persistent failures in living are a function of their neurotic problems. The psychotherapist cannot and should not be expected to work miracles and should never pretend or imply that this is possible. Instead, the therapist's potential successes are usually commensurate with the available raw material. In this respect, psychotherapy is no different from a medical treatment which may be uniquely effective provided the patient is generally healthy, there are no complications, and the patient is optimally cooperative. Conversely, as impediments increase, the probabilities of success decline. These factors are beyond the control of the psychotherapist who should not be held responsible for an inability to override them. Freud addressed these issues in his writings on psychoanalytic therapy. Although his stance in one of his last papers (Freud 1937, S.E., 23) is rather pessimistic, his points are well taken. To this day, the psychotherapeutic enterprise has been greatly hindered by the field's collective inability to arrive at more realistic assessments of what is possible under particular circumstances.

By the same token, the recognition of adverse factors provides no blanket excuse for personal and technical deficiencies in the therapist. There may be some exceptional individuals who can function effectively in the therapeutic role without prior tutoring. On the whole, however, the field recognizes the necessity of providing aspirants with intensive and prolonged training. The therapist's basic skill consists of the ability to help a patient come to terms with neurotic problems without becoming embroiled as a coactor in the patient's unwitting scenarios. To this end, therapists must acquire a clear picture of their role and function, the goals they are trying to pursue with a particular patient, and the technical steps considered most conducive to the achievement of these goals. (In the Vanderbilt I study, untutored but carefully selected college professors were clearly able to be of therapeutic help to certain patients but the professors freely admitted that their efforts generally lacked direction and often they "ran out of material.")

Therapists, having received training in TLDP, should become more fully aware of their role and functions as therapists, acquiring a clear sense of direction. The identification of a dynamic focus forces therapists to keep in mind a destination and a broad outline of the territory to be traversed. This should be the case whether the therapists are practicing time-limited therapy or analytic therapy extending over longer periods of time. In either event, although TLDP-trained therapists do not "push" the patient, they firmly guide the course of therapy.

This orientation is radically different from the ambitious but vague goals traditionally postulated by psychoanalysis—making the unconscious conscious, reconstructing the past, lifting childhood repressions, and the like. Instead, emphasis rests squarely on the patient's current life, the manner in which he or she relates to significant others in the here-and-now, including the therapist, and the extent to which unresolved problems from the past exert a disturbing influence on the present-day adaptation. By this reasoning, insight that fails to modify the patient's contemporary functioning—self-concept, feelings, and actions—is valueless; and analysis for the sake of analysis (without evidence that therapy improves the patient's coping ability and mastery) is not a legitimate goal. In short, for structural change to be meaningful it must have operational counterparts that are clearly discernible by the patient, the therapist, and (usually) by significant others in the patient's present life.

The design of TLDP is meant to instill an attitude of realism and rationality in the therapist. He or she must come to realize that some forms of psychopathology (like the crippling effects of poliomyelitis) are irreversible; others may be deeply ingrained but with intensive and prolonged effort may yield to empathic and skillful intervention; still others, depending on the factors we have mentioned, may be quite amenable to time-limited therapy. We understand as yet too little about the process of therapeutic change to make accurate predictions about the kind of therapeutic work that may be required in a given case and the forces in the patient and the environment that may accelerate or obstruct the therapist's effort. Some workers in the short-term area unfortunately continue to hold out the hope—which is always avidly seized upon by a public wishing for magical solutions—that time-limited therapy can offer unique or inexpensive answers to the perennial problems facing psychotherapy. Our clinical experience and cumulative research results tell us that this is improbable. The achievements that are possible in psychotherapy are usually commensurate with the amount and quality of therapeutic work, modulated by the nature and extent of the problems to which it is addressed.

The potential contribution of TLDP, as we see it, is to be found in its emphasis on sharpening the therapist's thinking and therapeutic practices. This attitude is closely related to that of the researcher who is dedicated to the goal of greater precision in describing and understanding the phenomena in the therapeutic domain. Thus, whether we practice time-limited or time-unlimited psychotherapy, we should strive for increasing clarity of what we are doing, what we are trying to do, and how we might expedite the achievement of our goals. This approach entails a concomitant appreciation of what cannot be done and why it cannot be done. Efforts in this direction need not transform therapy into a mechanical task or deprive it of its artistic and aesthetic components. Like painters or composers, psychotherapists should view their craft as a highly disciplined enterprise. While many of the patient's and the therapist's mental processes may remain obscure and unspecifiable, it is the striving for clarity and self-awareness that ultimately differentiates the activities of the skilled therapist from those of the intuitive mental healer.

Assessment of Outcomes

In this spirit, the psychotherapist practicing TLDP, or, for that matter, any other treatment modality, cannot escape the issue of treatment effectiveness. Has the therapy helped? In what respects has it helped? Are the changes lasting? Would some other form of therapy have produced different results? These are but a few questions that must be addressed from both a clinical and research perspective.

It is apparent that the problem of outcome touches on many facets of human life, and conceptions of mental health and illness cannot be considered apart from problems of philosophy, ethics, religion, and public policy. Inescapably we deal with human existence and humanity's place in the world, and ultimately we must confront questions of *value* (Strupp and Hadley 1977). In the end, someone must make a judgment that a person's concern with duty is a virtue or a symptom of compulsiveness; that a decrement of 10 points on a depression scale is clinically significant; that in one case we accept a patient's judgment that he or she feels better whereas in another we set it aside, calling it flight into health, reaction formation, and so forth. These decisions can only be made by reference to the values society assigns to feelings, attitudes, and actions. These values are also inherent in conceptions of mental health and illness as well as in clinical judgments based on one of these models.

One of the great stumbling blocks in psychotherapy research and practice has been a failure to realize the importance of values. While researchers have rightfully dealt with technical and methodological issues and made considerable gains in clarifying them, objective assessments and measurements have remained imperfect and imprecise. For example, it is a common finding (Garfield, Prager, and Bergin 1971) that there is only moderate correlation of outcome assessments by patients, peers, independent clinicians, and therapists. One may attribute this to the imperfection of the instruments and the fallibility of raters, but one should also be aware of the fact that raters bring different perspectives to bear and that the relative lack of correlation partially results from legitimate divergences in their vantage points.

Freud (1916-1917; *S.E., 16*) already saw the outcome issue as a practical one, and this may well be the best way to treat it. When all is said and done, there may be commonsense agreement on what constitutes a mentally healthy, nonneurotic person. Knight (1941) postulated three major rubrics for considering therapeutic change which still seem eminently reasonable: (1) disappearance of presenting symptoms; (2) real improvement in mental functioning; and (3) improved reality adjustment. Most therapists and researchers, while they may disagree on criteria and operations for assessing these changes, would concur that therapeutic success should be demonstrable in the person's (1) feeling state (well-being); (2) social functioning (performance); and (3) personality organization (structure). The first is clearly the individual's subjective perspective; the second is that of society, including prevailing standards of conduct and "normality"; the third is the perspective of mental health professionals whose technical concepts (ego strength, impulse control) partake of information and standards derived from the preceding sources but which are ostensibly scientific, objective, and value free. As Strupp and Hadley (1977) have shown, few therapists or researchers have recognized the problem or taken the implications seriously. Therapists continue to assess treatment outcomes on the basis of global clinical impressions whereas researchers have assumed that quantitative indices can be interpreted as if they were thermometer readings; instead, values influence and suffuse every judgment of outcome.

The foregoing considerations have important practical implications. For example, with increasing frequency insurance companies require practitioners to evaluate the outcome of treatment for which the patient or the therapist is being compensated. It is predictable that greater specificity than a check mark on an insurance form to show that the patient has improved will be demanded in the future. There are similar concerns, often mandated by law, relating to evaluations of the effectiveness of a community mental health center or a therapy program. Both among the public and mental health professionals there continues to exist considerable lack of clarity about the outcomes that may be expected from psychotherapy and how to describe and evaluate them.

Research activity in the area of therapy outcomes has been voluminous and sustained. In the years since Eysenck (1952) charged that psychotherapy produces no greater changes in emotionally disturbed individuals than naturally occurring life experiences, researchers and clinicians alike have felt compelled to answer the challenge. Analyzing and synthesizing the data from twenty-five years of research on the efficacy of psychotherapy, Luborsky, Singer, and Luborsky (1975) concluded that most forms of pyschotherapy produce changes in a substantial proportion of patients— changes that are typically greater than those achieved by control patients who did not receive therapy. Other reviewers (Bergin and Lambert 1978; Meltzoff and Kornreich 1970) have reached similar conclusions. In another thorough analysis, Smith, Glass, and Miller (1980) demonstrated that across all types of therapy, patients, and outcome criteria, the average patient is better off than 75 percent of untreated individuals. The preponderance of the evidence, it has become clear, does not support Eysenck's pessimistic conclusion (for a fuller discussion, see Strupp 1978).

What can be said about the results of short-term therapy? Since the briefer forms of psychotherapy have been developed to deal with more sharply circumscribed problems and more specific patient populations, one might expect to see more solid research evidence than in the general literature on psychotherapy. The briefer forms, too, are less difficult to investigate than the unlimited ones. Unfortunately, as Butcher and Koss (1978) document in an incisive review of the literature, problems similar to the ones afflicting all therapy outcome studies are equally prevalent in the short-term domain. Deficiencies in sophistication, design, and measurement have been rampant although there has been a gradual improvement in recent years. Most studies of outcomes in short-term therapy, too, have reported substantial improvement rates, but no definite conclusions can be drawn. Suggestive evidence that shorter forms of therapy produce results comparable to those in the longer modalities must likewise be viewed with reservations. Butcher and Koss (1978:760) state: "The major value of brief psychotherapy may be that it helps to accelerate positive change in the patient." At the present state of knowledge, we need more precise data on the kinds of positive changes that are produced, and the types of patients in whom such changes occur (or fail to occur). In addition, we need to become more specific concerning the kinds of therapist interventions that are most conducive to beneficial results.

Research programs of massive proportions are needed in order to achieve these goals. Science being a cumulative enterprise, no single program of research or group of researchers is likely to provide all the answers we need. However, it may be anticipated that future research will yield convergent trends. It is also important to note that in this endeavor practicing therapists and researchers must vigorously collaborate. Thus, refinements in clinical practice and advancement of knowledge must go hand in hand, and advances in one will predictably improve the other. Individual practitioners of TLDP can and should begin to collect data of the kind we called for earlier but they cannot be expected to carry out systematic research. This has become a task for specialists.

The TLDP program which is in progress at Vanderbilt University is an effort to achieve productive interrelationships between training, practice, and research. As described in the preceding chapters, the TLDP approach presented in this volume grew out of the Vanderbilt I study—the analysis of quantitative results as well as the qualitative scrutiny of the patient-therapist interactions that were preserved on tape. We also benefited greatly from the broader clinical, theoretical, and research literature. Every step in the current Vanderbilt II study, to which the TLDP formulations are central, is anchored in specific measurement operations that are expected to bring us several steps closer to the stipulated objectives. For example, we have worked out specific procedures for patient selection (a major goal here will be to compare treatment outcomes of individuals who have varying degrees of suitability for this form of therapy); we have developed techniques for identifying a dynamic focus and tracking it over the course of therapy; we shall develop and apply improved procedures for measuring therapeutic change; and we shall carry out detailed studies of the patient-therapist interactions by means of process measures intended to assess the degree to which a therapist adheres to TLDP principles and techniques. As this research progresses, it may be possible for independent therapists to apply these procedures in their own work.

Therapists' Training and Competence

A perennial shortcoming of psychotherapy research—both time unlimited and short term—has been the failure to specify the nature of the treatment with any degree of accuracy. Instead, it has been common practice to describe the therapy in very broad terms (behavioral, psychodynamic, client-centered), a practice which provides few clues about character or "purity" of the treatment modality. Only in recent years, with the advent of treatment manuals (Beck, Rush, Shaw, and Emery 1978; Klerman, Rounsaville, Chevron, and Weissman 1984; Luborsky 1984) have systematic efforts been made to remedy this problem. Specialized instruments, coordinated with the treatment manuals, now enable researchers to make reasonably objective assessments of the treatment modality under study. Furthermore, if therapists are being trained to apply a particular form of therapy it is now possible to monitor the progress of the training and to ascertain the degree to which trainees are adhering to the treatment model and pertinent technical procedures. As noted earlier, our own group has begun to develop a competency measure—the TLDP Adherence Scale— which serves a comparable purpose. The scale is designed to make appropriate determinations concerning a therapist's practices as they are being applied in therapy with particular patients.

Our current research at Vanderbilt University is designed to study the effects of a specialized TLDP training program. To this end, we are selecting a group of practicing psychotherapists (fully trained psychiatrists and clinical psychologists with several years of postdoctoral experience) who will treat selected patients both before and after the therapists have obtained training in TLDP. Our goal is to compare not only treatment outcomes but to investigate, in detail and depth, the *process* by which these changes are achieved. Central to this effort will be the intensive study of recordings of individual therapy hours.

The TLDP training program itself centers on careful supervision of participating therapists over a period of approximately six months. During this time each therapist will treat a training case under expert supervision. Toward the end of the training, the therapist's skills in TLDP will be assessed. Pilot experience has shown that individual supervision over an extended period of time is the single best approach to communicating TLDP principles and techniques, and encouraging therapists to apply them systematically and skillfully. In our judgment, subject to revision as we accumulate greater experience, trainees should have a reasonable background in general psychodynamic psychotherapy (as is generally provided in dynamically oriented residency programs in psychiatry and doctoral programs in clinical psychology), and a certain amount of professional experience. However, we believe that TLDP principles and techniques may be equally useful in the early stages of graduate or residency training as well as to therapists with more extensive training and experience.

Specifically, our research is guided by the following hypotheses:

1. *TLDP training will influence the manner in which psychodynamic psychotherapists conduct treatment.* In particular, we predict that the effects of training will be demonstrated by: (a) consistent pursuit of a dynamic focus; (b) increased attention to and elucidation of the dynamics of the patient-therapist interaction; (c) greater skill with the patient's enactments of maladaptive interpersonal patterns within therapy; and (d) greater skill in making ap-

propriate use of the therapist's own emotional reactions to the patient.

2. *The process and outcome of TLDP therapy will be different, in a desirable direction, from that of psychodynamic treatment-as-usual.* After TLDP training, therapy should be characterized by: (a) improvments in the quality of the patient-therapist relationship; (b) greater likelihood that a central issue will be mastered and therapy brought to a more successful conclusion; and (c) a decreased tendency on the patient's part to desire or seek further therapy.

3. *TLDP training will extend the range of treatable patients.* Although we hypothesize that, following TLDP training, therapists will achieve greater therapeutic effectiveness with all patients selected for treatment, the greatest relative improvements will occur in patients whose potential for dynamic psychotherapy is considered low. The objective here is to study systematically the range of patients who might benefit from time-limited dynamic psychotherapy and to achieve greater precision in determining the limitations of this form of treatment.

In conclusion, in order to advance psychotherapy both as a field of scientific knowledge as well as an area of disciplined clinical practice, it is essential to gain a clearer scientific understanding of the predisposing factors and psychological processes giving rise to differential treatment outcomes. To this end, it is essential to seek an improved understanding of the contribution of antecedent patient variables, on the one hand, and the contributions of therapist intervention variables, on the other.

Accumulating research as well as clinical knowledge have pointed to the importance of antecedent *patient* variables as critical determinants of treatment outcomes. Concomitantly, there is currently a widespread tendency to devalue psychotherapy treatment outcomes by asserting that they are largely predetermined by the foregoing patient variables (the claim is made that psychotherapy works best with those who need it least, "the rich get richer" phenomenon). Such interpretations allow little room for the therapist's expertise. Indeed, critics of psychotherapy (Gross 1978; Zilbergeld 1983) have questioned whether the therapist's technical knowledge makes a difference. If this were true, training would be expendable. We doubt that there ever can be simple answers to complex questions. We do know, from our own empirical research that the *quality* of the patient-therapist relationship is an important variable contributing to treatment outcomes. While patient variables play an important part, the therapist's contribution is far from trivial. In presenting the TLDP approach in this book and pursuing the research program mentioned above, we are working toward, and are encouraging colleagues to pursue, the kind of specificity which the field of psychotherapy so urgently needs.

References

Alexander, F., and T. M. French. 1946. *Psychoanalytic Therapy: Principles and Applications.* New York: Ronald Press.

Allport, G. W. 1937. *Personality.* New York: Holt, Rinehart & Winston.

Allen, J. 1977. "Ego States and Object Relations." *Bulletin of the Menninger Clinic* 41:522–38.

American Psychiatric Association. 1980. *Diagnostic and Statistical Manual of Mental Disorders.* 3d ed. Washington, D.C.: American Psychiatric Association.

Anchin, J. C., and D. J. Kiesler, eds. 1982. *Handbook of Interpersonal Psychotherapy.* New York: Pergamon Press.

Appelbaum, S. A. 1972. "How Long is Long-term Psychotherapy?" *Bulletin of the Menninger Clinic* 36:651–55.

———. 1981. *Effecting Change in Psychotherapy.* New York: Jason Aronson.

Arlow, J. 1980. "The Genesis of Interpretation." In *Psychoanalytic Explorations of Technique: Discourse on the Theory of Therapy,* edited by H. P. Blum. New York: International Universities Press.

Armstrong, S. 1980. "Dual Focus in Brief Psychodynamic Psychotherapy." *Psychotherapy and Psychosomatics* 33:147–54.

Auerbach, A. H., and L. Luborsky. 1968. "Accuracy of Judgments of Psychotherapy and the Nature of the Good Hour." In *Research in Psychotherapy,* vol. 3, edited by J. M. Shlien. Washington: American Psychological Association.

Bachrach, H. M. , and L. A. Leaff. 1978. "Analyzability': A Systematic Review of the Clinical and Qualitative Literature." *Journal of American Psychoanalytical Association* 26:881–920.

Balint, M., P. Ornstein, and E. Balint. 1972. *Focal Psychotherapy: An Example of Applied Psychoanalysis.* London: Tavistock Publications.

Barten, H. H. 1969. "The Coming of Age of the Brief Psychotherapies." In *Progress in Community Mental Health,* edited by L. Bellak and H. H. Barten. New York: Grune & Stratton.

Bateson, G. 1972. *Steps to an Ecology of Mind.* New York: Ballantine Books, pp. 279–308.

Bateson, G., D. D. Jackson, J. Haley, and J. H. Weakland. 1956. "Toward a Theory of Schizophrenia." *Behavioral Science* 1:251–64.

Beck, A. T. 1976. *Cognitive Therapy and the Emotional Disorders.* New York: International Universities Press.

Beck, A. T., A. J. Rush, B. I. Shaw, and G. Emery. 1978. *Cognitive Therapy of Depression: A Treatment Manual.* Center for Cognitive Therapy, University of Pennsylvania. Typescript.

References

Bellak, L., and L. Small. 1978. *Emergency Psychotherapy and Brief Psychotherapy.* 2d ed. New York: Grune & Stratton.

Bergin, A. E., and M. J. Lambert. 1978 "The Evaluation of Therapeutic Outcomes." In *Handbook of Psychotherapy and Behavior Change: An Empirical Analysis.* 2d ed., edited by S. L. Garfield and A. E. Bergin. New York: John Wiley & Sons.

Bergin, A. E., and H. H. Strupp. 1972. *Changing Frontiers in the Science of Psychotherapy.* Chicago: Aldine-Atherton.

Binder, J. L. 1977. "Modes of Focusing in Psychoanalytic Short-term Therapy." *Psychotherapy: Theory, Research, and Practice 14*(3):232–41.

Binder, J. L. 1979. "Treatment of Narcissistic Problems in Time-limited Psychotherapy." *Psychiatric Quarterly 51:*257–80.

Binder, J. L., and I. Smokler. 1980. "Early Memories: A Technical Aid to Focusing in Brief Psychotherapy." *Psychotherapy: Theory, Research, and Practice 17:*52–62.

Blatt, S. J., and H. S. Erlich. 1982 "Levels of Resistance in the Psychotherapeutic Process." In *Resistance in Psychoanalysis and Behavioral Therapies,* edited by P. Wachtel. New York: Plenum Press.

Blatt, S. J., and H. Lerner, 1983. "The Psychological Assessment of Object Representation." *Journal of Personality Assessment 47*(1):7–28.

Blos, P. 1941. *The Adolescent Personality.* New York: Appleton-Century-Crofts.

Blum, H. P. 1983. "The Position and Value of Extratransference Interpretation." *Journal of the American Psychoanalytic Association 31:*587–613.

Bowlby, J. 1980. *Attachment and Loss,* vol. 3. *Loss, Sadness and Depression.* New York: Basic Books.

Breuer, J., and S. Freud. [1895] 1957. *Studies on Hysteria.* New York: Basic Books.

Brierly, M. 1937. "Affects in Theory and Practice." *International Journal of Psychoanalysis 18:*256–68.

Budman, S. H., ed. 1981. *Forms of Brief Therapy.* New York: Guilford Press.

Budman, S. H., and A. S. Gurman. 1983. "The Practice of Brief Therapy." *Professional Psychology: Research and Practice 14:*277–92.

Butcher, J. N., and M. P. Koss. 1978. "Research on Brief and Crisis-oriented Psychotherapies." In *Handbook of Psychotherapy and Behavior Change: An Empirical Analysis.* 2d ed., edited by S. L. Garfield and A. E. Bergin. New York: John Wiley & Sons.

Carson, R. C., 1969. *Interaction Concepts of Personality.* Chicago: Aldine.

———. 1982. "Self-fulfilling Prophecy, Maladaptive Behavior, and Psychotherapy." In *Handbook of Interpersonal Psychotherapy,* edited by J. C. Anchin and D. J. Kiesler. New York: Pergamon Press.

Castelnuovo-Tedesco, P. 1975. "Brief Psychotherapy." In *American Handbook of Psychiatry.* 2d ed., vol. 5, edited by S. Arieti. New York: Basic Books.

Cohen, A. 1982. *Confrontation Analysis: Theory and Practice.* New York: Grune & Stratton.

Coltrera, J. T. 1980. "Truth from Genetic Illusion: The Transference and the Fate of the Infantile Neurosis." *Psychoanalytic Explorations of Technique,* edited by H. P. Blum. New York: International Universities Press.

Curtis, H. C. 1980. "The Concept of Therapeutic Alliance: Implications for the 'Widening Scope.'" In *Psychoanalytic Explorations of Technique: Discourse on the Theory of Therapy,* edited by H. P. Blum. New York: International Universities Press.

References

Davanloo, H., ed. 1978. *Basic Principles and Techniques in Short-term Dynamic Psychotherapy.* New York: Spectrum.

———., ed. 1980. *Short-term Dynamic Psychotherapy.* New York: Jason Aronson.

Dewald, P. A. 1967. "Therapeutic Evaluation and Potential: The Dynamic Point of View. *Comprehensive Psychiatry 8:*284–98.

———. 1982. "Psychoanalytic Perspective on Resistance." In *Resistance in Psychodynamic and Behavioral Therapies,* edited by P. Wachtel. New York: Plenum Press.

Diesing, P. 1971. *Patterns of Discovery in the Social Sciences.* Chicago: Aldine.

Ekstein, R. 1956. Psychoanalytic Techniques. In *Progress in Clinical Psychology,* vol. 2, edited by D. Bower and L. E. Abt. New York: Grune & Stratton.

Epstein, L., and A. H. Feiner. eds. *Countertransference.* New York: Jason Aronson.

Eysenck, H. J. 1952. "The Effects of Psychotherapy: An Evaluation." *Journal of Consulting Psychology 16:*319–24.

Feiner, A. H. 1979. "Countertransference and the Anxiety of Influence." In *Countertransference,* edited by L. Epstein and A. H. Feiner. New York: Jason Aronson.

Fenichel, O. 1945. *The Psychoanalytic Theory of Neurosis.* New York: W. W. Norton & Co.

Firestein, S. 1978. *Termination in Psychoanalysis.* New York: International Universities Press.

Ferenczi, S., and O. Rank. 1925. *Development of Psychoanalysis.* Translated by C. Newton. New York: Nervous and Mental Disease Publishing Co.

Flegenheimer, W. V. 1982. *Techniques of Brief Psychotherapy.* New York: Jason Aronson.

Foulkes, D. 1978. *The Grammar of Dreams.* New York: Basic Books.

Frank, J. D. 1973. *Persuasion and Healing.* 2d ed. Baltimore, Md.: Johns Hopkins University Press.

———. 1974. "Therapeutic Components of Psychotherapy." *Journal of Nervous and Mental Disease 159:*325–42.

———. 1979. "The Present Status of Outcome Studies." *Journal of Consulting and Clinical Psychology 47:*310–16.

Frank, J. D., R. Hoehn-Saric, S. D. Imber, B. L. Liberman, and A. R. Stone. 1978. *Effective Ingredients of Successful Psychotherapy.* New York: Brunner/Mazel.

Freud, A. 1936. *The Ego and the Mechanisms of Defense.* London: Hogarth Press.

———. 1965. *Normality and Pathology in Childhood.* New York: International Universities Press.

Freud, S. 1905. *On Psychotherapy.* In *Standard Edition, 7:*255–68.

———. 1909. "Notes Upon a Case of Obsessional Neurosis." In *Standard Edition, 10:* 155–249.

———. 1911–1915. *Papers on Technique.* In *Standard Edition, 12:*89–171.

———. 1912. "Recommendations to Physicians Practicing Psycho-Analysis." In *Standard Edition, 12:*109–20.

———. 1916–1917. "Analytic Therapy." In *Standard Edition, 16:*448–63.

———. 1917. "Transference." In *Standard Edition, 16:*431–47.

———. 1918. "Lines of Advance in Psycho-Analytic Therapy." In *Standard Edition, 17:*157–68.

———. 1923. *The Ego and the Id.* In *Standard Edition, 19:*3–66.

———. 1925–1926. *Inhibitions, Symptoms and Anxiety.* In *Standard Edition, 20.*

———. 1937. "Analysis Terminable and Interminable." In *Standard Edition, 23:*216–53.

References

——. 1940. *An Outline of Psycho-Analysis*. In *Standard Edition, 23*.

Fromm-Reichmann, F. 1950. *Principles of Intensive Psychotherapy*. Chicago: University of Chicago Press.

Garfield, S. L., R. A. Prager, and A. E. Bergin. 1971. "Evaluating Outcome in Psychotherapy: A Hardy Perennial." *Journal of Consulting and Clinical Psychology 37:* 320–22.

Gill, M. M. 1976. "Metapsychology is not Psychology." In *Psychology versus Metapsychology: Psychoanalytical Essays in Memory of George S. Klein*, edited by M. M. Gill and P. S. Holzman. *Psychological Issues*, vol. 9, no. 4, monograph 36. New York: International Universities Press.

——. 1979. "The Analysis of the Transference." *Journal of the American Psychoanalytic Association 27:*263–88.

——. 1980. "The Analysis of Transference." *Psychoanalytic Explorations of Technique: Discourse on the Theory of Therapy*, edited by H. P. Blum. New York: International Universities Press.

——. 1982. *Analysis of Transference I: Theory and Technique*. New York: International Universities Press.

Gill, M. M. and I. Hoffman. 1982. "A Method for Studying the Analysis of Aspects of the Patient's Experience of the Relationship in Psychoanalysis and Psychotherapy." *Journal of the American Psychoanalytic Association 30:*137–67.

Gill, M. M., and H. L. Muslin. 1976. "Early Interpretations of Transference." *Journal of American Psychoanalytic Association 24:*779–94.

Giovacchini, P. 1979. *Treatment of Primitive Mental States*. New York: Jason Aronson.

Glover, E. 1955. *The Technique of Psychoanalysis*. New York: International Universities Press.

Gomes-Schwartz, B. 1978. "Effective Ingredients in Psychotherapy: Prediction of Outcome From Process Variables." *Journal of Consulting and Clinical Psychology 46:* 1023–35.

Greenacre, P. 1980. "Certain Technical Problems in the Transference Relationship." In *Psychoanalytic Explorations of Technique: Discourse on the Theory of Therapy*, edited by H. P. Blum. New York: International Universities Press.

Greenson, R. R. 1967. *The Technique and Practice of Psychoanalysis*, vol. 1. New York: International Universities Press.

——. 1965. "The Working Alliance and the Transference Neurosis." *Psychoanalytic Quarterly 34:*155–81.

Greenson, R. R., and M. Wexler. 1969. "The Nontransformation Relationship in the Psychoanalytic Situation." *International Journal of Psychoanalysis 50:* 27–39.

Gross, M. L. 1975. *The Psychological Society*. New York: Random House.

Gross, S. J., and J. O. Miller. 1975. "A Research Strategy for Evaluating the Effectiveness of Psychotherapy." *Psychological Reports 37:* 1011–21.

Gustafson, J. P. 1981. "The Complex Secret of Brief Psychotherapy in the Works of Malan and Balint." In *Forms of Brief Therapy*, edited by S. H. Budman. New York: Guilford Press.

Haley, J. 1973. *Uncommon Therapy. The Psychiatric Techniques of Milton H. Erickson, M. D.* New York: W. W. Norton & Co.

Hartley, D. E., and H. H. Strupp. 1983. "The Therapeutic Alliance: Its Relationship to Outcome in Brief Psychotherapy." In *Empirical Studies of Psychoanalytical Theories, Vol. 1*, edited by J. Masling. Hillsdale, N.J.: The Analytic Press.

References

Havens, L. 1976. *Participant Observation.* New York: Jason Aronson.

Heimann, P. 1950. "On Countertransference." *International Journal of Psychoanalysis 31:* 81–84.

Hill, L. B. 1958. "On Being Rather Than Doing in Psychotherapy." *International Journal of Group Psychotherapy 8:* 115–22.

Hoffman, I. Z. 1983. "The Patient as Interpreter of the Analysis Experience." *Contemporary Psychoanalysis 19:* 389–422.

Horowitz, M. 1979. *States of Mind.* New York: Plenum Press.

Hoyt, M. F. 1980. "Therapist and Patient Actions in 'Good' Psychotherapy Sessions." *Archives of General Psychiatry 37:* 159–61.

Issacharoff, A. 1979. "Barriers to Knowing." In *Countertransference,* edited by L. Epstein and A. H. Feiner. New York: Jason Aronson.

Kanzer, M. 1980. "Developments in Psychoanalytic Technique: A Critical Review of Recent Psychoanalytic Books." In *Psychoanalytic Explorations of Technique: Discourse on the Theory of Therapy,* edited by H. P. Blum. New York: International Universities Press.

Kaplan, H. S. 1974. *The New Sex Therapy. Active Treatment of Sexual Dysfunctions.* New York: Brunner/Mazel.

Keithley, L. J., S. J. Samples, and H. H. Strupp. 1980. "Patient Motivation as a Predictor of Process and Outcome in Psychotherapy." *Psychotherapy and Psychosomatics, 33:* 87–97.

Kernberg, O. F. 1975. *Borderline Conditions and Pathological Narcissism.* New York: Jason Aronson.

———. 1976. *Object Relations Theory and Clinical Psychoanalysis.* New York: Jason Aronson.

———. "Some Implications of Object Relations Theory for Psychoanalytic Technique." In *Psychoanalytic Explorations of Technique: Discourse on the Theory of Therapy,* edited by H. P. Blum. New York: International Universities Press.

Kernberg, O. F., E. D. Burstein, L. Coyne, A. Appelbaum, L. Horowitz, and H. Voth. 1972. "Psychotherapy Research Project." *Bulletin of the Menninger Clinic 36:* 1–275.

Kiesler, D. J. 1966. "Some Myths of Psychotherapy Research and the Search for a Paradigm." *Psychological Bulletin 65:* 110–36.

———. 1982. "Interpersonal Theory for Personality and Psychotherapy." In *Handbook of Interpersonal Psychotherapy,* edited by J. C. Anchin and D. J. Kiesler. New York: Pergamon Press.

Kinston, W., and A. Bentovim. 1981. "Creating a Focus for Brief Marital Therapy." In *Forms of Brief Therapy,* edited by S. H. Budman. New York: Guilford Press, pp. 361–86.

Klebanow, S., ed. 1981. *Changing Concepts in Psychoanalysis.* New York: Gardner Press.

Klerman, G. L., B. Rounsaville, E. Chevron, and M. Weissman. 1984. *Interpersonal Psychotherapy of Depression.* New York: Basic Books.

Klein, G. S. 1976. *Psychoanalytic Theory: An Explanation of Essentials.* New York: International Universities Press.

Knight, R. P. 1941. "Evaluation of the Results of Psychoanalytic Therapy." *American Journal of Psychiatry 98:* 434–46.

Kohut, H. 1971. *The Analysis of the Self.* New York: International Universities Press.

References

Labov, W., and D. Fanshel. 1977. *Therapeutic Discourse: Psychotherapy as Conversation.* New York: Academic Press.

Langs, R. 1976. *The Therapeutic Interaction,* vol. 2. New York: Jason Aronson.

Levenson, E. A. 1972. *The Fallacy of Understanding: An Inquiry into the Changing Structure of Psychoanalysis.* New York: Basic Books.

————. 1982. "Language and Healing." In *Curative Factors in Dynamic Psychotherapy,* edited by S. Slipp. New York: McGraw-Hill.

Lidz, T. 1963. *The Family and Human Adaptation.* New York: International University Press.

Luborsky, L. 1977. "Measuring a Pervasive Psychic Structure in Psychotherapy: The Core Conflictual Relationship Theme." In *Communicative Structures and Psychic Structures,* edited by N. Freedman and S. Grand. New York: Plenum Press.

————. 1984. *Principles of Psychoanalytic Psychotherapy: A Manual for Supportive-Expressive Treatment.* New York: Basic Books.

Luborsky, L., M. Chandler, A. H. Auerbach, J. Cohen, and H. M. Bachrach. 1971. "Factors Influencing the Outcome of Psychotherapy: A Review of the Quantitative Research." *Psychological Bulletin 75:* 145–85.

Luborsky, L., B. Singer, and L. Luborsky. 1975. "Comparative Studies of Psychotherapies: Is it True that 'Everybody has Won and All Must Have Prizes?'" *Archives of General Psychiatry 32:* 995–1008.

Luborsky, L., and D. P. Spence. 1978. "Quantitative Research on Psychoanalytic Therapy." In *Handbook of Psychotherapy and Behavior Change: An Empirical Analysis.* 2d ed., edited by S. L. Garfield and A. E. Bergin. New York: John Wiley & Sons, pp. 331–68.

Macalpine, I. 1950. "The Development of the Transference." *Psychoanalytic Quarterly 19:* 501–39.

Malan, D. H. 1963. *A Study of Brief Psychotherapy.* New York: Plenum Press.

————. 1976a. *The Frontier of Brief Psychotherapy: An Example of the Convergence of Research and Clinical Practice.* New York: Plenum Press.

————. 1976b. *Toward the Validation of Dynamic Psychotherapy: A Replication.* New York: Plenum Press.

————. 1979. *Individual Psychotherapy and the Science of Psychodynamics.* London: Butterworth.

Mann, J. 1973. *Time-limited Psychotherapy.* Cambridge: Harvard University Press.

Mann, J., and R. Goldman. 1982. *A Casebook in Time-limited Psychotherapy.* New York: McGraw-Hill.

Margulies, A., and L. Havens. 1981. "The Initial Encounter: What to Do First." *American Journal of Psychiatry 138:* 421–28.

Marrow, A. J. 1969. *The Practical Theorist. The Life and Work of Kurt Lewin.* New York: Basic Books.

Maslow, A. H. 1962. *Toward a Psychology of Being.* New York: Van Nostrand.

————. 1966. *The Psychology of Science.* New York: Harper & Row.

Mayman, M. 1968. "Early Memories and Character Structure." *Journal of Projective Techniques and Personality Assessment 32:* 303–16.

McGuire, T. G., and L. K. Frisman, 1983. "Reimbursement Policy and Cost-effective Mental Health Care." *American Psychologist 38:* 935–40.

Meltzoff, J., and M. Kornreich. 1970. *Research in Psychotherapy.* New York: Atherton Press.

References

Menninger, K. 1958. *Theory of Psychoanalytic Technique.* New York: Basic Books.

Moeller, M. C. 1977. "Self and Object in Countertransference." *International Journal of Psychoanalysis 58:*365–74.

Moras, K. 1979. "Quality of Interpersonal Relationships and Patient Collaboration in Brief Psychotherapy." Paper presented at the European Conference of the Society for Psychotherapy Research, Oxford, England.

Moras, K., and H. H. Strupp. 1982. "Pre-therapy Interpersonal Relations, a Patient's Alliance, and Outcome in Brief Therapy." *Archives of General Psychiatry 39:* 405–9.

Mortimer, R. L., and W. H. Smith. 1983. "The Use of the Psychological Test Report in Setting the Focus of Psychotherapy." *Journal of Personality Assessment 47:* 134–38.

Neubauer, P. B. 1980. "The Role of Insight in Psychoanalysis." In *Psychoanalytic Explorations of Technique: Discourse on the Theory of Therapy,* edited by H. P. Blum. New York: International Universities Press.

Paolino, T. J. 1981. *Psychoanalytic Psychotherapy: Theory, Technique, Therapeutic Relationship, and Treatability.* New York: Brunner/Mazel.

Pardes, H., and H. A. Pincus. 1981. "Brief Therapy in the Context of National Mental Health." In *Forms of Brief Therapy,* edited by S. H. Budman. New York: Guilford Press.

Peterfreund, E. 1983. *The Process of Psychoanalytic Therapy: Models and Strategies.* New Jersey: Analytic Press.

Polanyi, M. 1966. *The Tacit Dimension.* Garden City, N.Y.: Doubleday.

Rabkin, J. G. 1977. "Therapists' Attitudes Toward Mental Illness and Health." In *Effective Psychotherapy: A Handbook of Research,* edited by A. S. Gurman and A. R. Razin. New York: Pergamon Press.

Racker, H. 1968. *Transference and Countertransference.* New York: International Universities Press.

Rakoff, H. C., H. C. Stauler, and H. B. Redward, eds. 1977. *Psychiatric Diagnosis.* New York: Brunner/Mazel.

Reich, W. 1933. *Character Analysis.* Translated by T. Wocfus. Rangeley, Me.: Orgonics Institute Press.

Rogers, C. R. 1925. "The Necessary and Sufficient Conditions of Therapeutic Personality Change." *Journal of Consulting Psychology 21:* 95–103.

Rycroft, C. 1958. "An Inquiry Into the Function of Work in the Psychoanalytic Situation." *International Journal of Psychoanalysis 39:*408–15.

Ryle, A. 1979. "The Focus in Brief Interpretive Psychotherapy: Dilemmas, Traps, and Snags." *British Journal of Psychiatry 134:*46–54.

Sachs, J. S. 1983. "Negative Factors in Brief Psychotherapy: An Empirical Assessment." *Journal of Consulting and Clinical Psychology 51:*557–64.

Salzman, L. 1968. *The Obsessive Personality: Origins, Dynamics, and Therapy.* New York: Science House.

Sandifer, M., A. Horndern, and L. Green. 1974. "The Psychiatric Interview: The Impact of the First Three Minutes." *American Journal of Psychiatry, 126:*968–73.

Sandler, J. 1976. "Countertransference and Role-responsiveness." *International Review of Psychoanalysis, 3:*43–47.

Sandler, J., C. Dare, and A. Holder. 1970. "Basic Psychoanalytic Concepts: X. Interpretations and Other Interventions." *British Journal of Psychiatry 118:*53–59.

References

Sandler, J. and A. M. Sandler. 1978. "On the Development of Object Relationships and Affects." *International Journal of Psychoanalysis 59:285–96.*

Schacht, T. E. In press. "Toward Operationalizing the Transference: A Research Method for Identifying a Focus in Time-limited Dynamic Psychotherapy." In *Empirical Studies of Psychoanalytic Theory,* vol. 3, edited by J. Masling. Hillsdale, N.J.: Erlbaum/Analytic Press.

Schafer, R., 1976. *A New Language for Psychoanalysis.* New Haven, Conn.: Yale University Press.

———. 1983. *The Analytic Attitude.* New York: Basic Books.

Schaffer, N. D. 1982. "Multidimensional Measures of Therapist Behavior as Predictors of Outcome. *Psychological Bulletin 92:*670–81.

Schank, R. C., and R. Abelson. 1977. *Scripts, Plans, Goals, and Understanding.* Hillsdale, N.J.: Erlbaum.

Schecter, D. 1981. "Attachment, Detachment, and Psychoanalytic Therapy: The Impact of Early Development on the Psychoanalytic Treatment of Adults." In *Changing Concepts in Psychoanalysis,* edited by S. Klebanow. New York: Gardner Press.

Schlesinger, H. 1982. "Resistance as a Process. In *Resistance in Psychodynamic and Behavioral Therapies,* edited by P. Wachtel. New York: Plenum Press.

Shevrin, H., and H. Schectman. 1973. "The Diagnostic Process in Psychiatric Evaluations." *Bulletin of the Menninger Clinic 37:*451–594.

Sherwood, M. 1969. *The Logic of Explanation in Psychoanalysis.* New York: Academic Press.

Sifneos, P. 1972. *Short-term Psychotherapy and Emotional Crisis.* Cambridge, Mass.: Harvard University Press.

———. 1979. *Short-term Dynamic Psychotherapy: Evaluation and Technique.* New York: Plenum Press.

Sloane, R. B., F. R. Staples, A. H. Cristol, N. J. Yorkston, and K. Whipple. 1975. *Psychotherapy versus Behavior Therapy.* Cambridge, Mass.: Harvard University Press.

Small, L. 1979. *The Briefer Psychotherapies.* 2d ed. New York: Brunner/Mazel.

Smith, M. L., G. V. Glass, and T. I. Miller, eds. 1980. *The Benefits of Psychotherapy.* Baltimore, Md.: Johns Hopkins Press.

Spence, D. P. 1982. *Historical Truth and Narrative Truth.* New York: W. W. Norton & Co.

Stierlin, H. 1968. "Short-term versus Long-term Psychotherapy in Light of a General Theory of Human Relationships. *British Journal of Psychiatry 32:*127–35.

Stoller, R. J. 1977. Psychoanalytic Diagnosis. In *Psychiatric Diagnosis,* edited by V. C. Rakoff, H. C. Stancer, and H. B. Kedward. New York: Brunner/Mazel.

Strachey, J. 1958. *Editor's Introduction: Papers on Technique.* In *The Standard Edition of the Complete Psychological Works of Sigmund Freud, 12:* 85–88. London: Hogarth Press.

Strupp, H. H. 1960. "Nature of Psychotherapist's Contribution to Treatment Process: Some Research Results and Speculations." *Archives of General Psychiatry 3:* 219–31.

———. 1960. *Psychotherapists in Action: Explorations of the Therapist's Contribution to the Treatment Process.* New York: Grune & Stratton.

———. 1973. "On the Basic Ingredients of Psychotherapy." *Journal of Consulting and Clinical Psychology 41:* 1–8.

———. 1975. "Psychoanalysis, 'Focal Psychotherapy,' and the Nature of the Therapeutic Influence." *Archives of General Psychiatry 32:*127–35.

———. 1978. "Psychotherapy Research and Practice: An Overview." In *Handbook of Psychotherapy and Behavior Change: An Empirical Analysis.* 2d ed. edited by S. L. Garfield and A. E. Bergin. New York: John Wiley & Sons. pp 3–22.

———. 1980*a.* "Success and Failure in Time-limited Psychotherapy: A Systematic Comparison of Two Cases" (Comparison 1). *Archives of General Psychiatry 37:* 595–603.

———. 1980*b.* "Success and Failure in Time-limited Psychotherapy: A Systematic Comparison of Two Cases" (Comparison 2). *Archives of General Psychiatry 37:* 708–16.

———. 1980*c.* "Success and Failure in Time-limited Psychotherapy: With Special Reference to the Performance of a Lay Counselor" (Comparison 3). *Archives of General Psychiatry 37:* 831–41.

———. 1980*d.* "Success and Failure in Time-limited Psychotherapy: Further Evidence" (Comparison 4). *Archives of General Psychiatry 37:* 947–54.

Strupp, H. H., and A. E. Bergin. 1969. "Some Empirical and Conceptual Bases for Coordinated Research in Psychotherapy." *International Journal of Psychiatry 7:* 18–90.

Strupp, H. H., J. A. Ewing, and J. B. Chassan. 1966. "Toward the Longitudinal Study of the Psychotherapeutic Process." In *Methods of Research in Psychotherapy,* edited by L. A. Gottschalk and A. A. Auerbach. New York: Appleton-Century-Crofts.

Strupp, H. H., and S. W. Hadley. 1977. "A Tripartite Model of Mental Health and Therapeutic Outcomes." *American Psychologist 32:*187–96.

———. 1979. "Specific versus Nonspecific Factors in Psychotherapy: A Controlled Study of Outcome." *Archives of General Psychiatry 36:*1125–36.

Strupp, H. H., S. W. Hadley, and B. Gomes-Schwartz. 1977. *Psychotherapy for Better or Worse: An Analysis of the Problem of Negative Effects.* New York: Jason Aronson.

Sullivan, H. S. 1953. *The Interpersonal Theory of Psychiatry,* New York: W. W. Norton.

———. 1954. *The Psychiatric Interview.* New York: W. W. Norton.

———. 1955. *The Interpersonal Theory of Psychiatry,* edited by H. S. Perry and M. L. Gawel. New York: W. W. Norton & Co.

Thompson, C. 1950. *Psychoanalysis: Evolution and Development.* New York: Hermitage House.

Vaillant, G. E. 1977. *Adaptation to Life.* Boston: Little Brown.

Wachtel, P. 1982. "Vicious Circles: The Self and the Rhetoric of Emerging and Unfolding." *Contemporary Psychoanalysis 18*(2): 259–72.

Wallerstein, R. S. and L. L. Robbins. 1956. "The Psychotherapy Research Project of the Menninger Foundation: Rationale, Method, and Sample Use IV: Concepts." *Bulletin of the Menninger Clinic 20:* 239–62.

Waterhouse, G. J. 1979. "Perceptions of Facilitative Therapeutic Conditions as Predictors of Outcome in Brief Therapy." Paper presented at the European Conference of the Society for Psychotherapy Research, Oxford, England.

Watzlawick, P. 1978. *The Language of Change. Elements of Therapeutic Communication.* New York: Basic Books.

Watzlawick, P., J. H. Weakland, and R. Fisch. 1974. *Change: Principles of Problem Formation and Problem Resolution.* New York: W. W. Norton & Co.

Weiss, J., H. Sampson, and The Mount Zion Psychotherapy Research Group. In

References

press. *The Psychoanalytic Process: Theory, Clinical Observations, and Empirical Research.* New York: Guilford Press.

Wender, P. H. 1968. "Vicious and Virtuous Circles: The Role of Deviation-amplifying Feedback in the Origin and Perpetuation of Behavior." *Psychiatry 31* (4): 309–24.

Witenberg, E. G. 1979. "The Inner Experience of the Psychoanalyst. In *Countertransference,* edited by L. Epstein and A. H. Feiner. New York: Jason Aronson.

Wolberg, L. 1980. *Handbook of Short-term Psychotherapy.* New York: Grune & Stratton.

Yalom, I. 1980. *Existential Psychotherapy.* New York: Basic Books.

Zilbergeld, B. 1983. *The Shrinking of America. Myths of Psychological Change.* Boston: Little Brown.

Name Index

Abelson, R., 69
Alexander, F., *xv,* 10, 11, 25, 66, 141, 304
Allen, J., 34
Allport, G. W., 191
Anchin, J. C., *xv,* 28, 72, 89
Appelbaum, A., 274
Appelbaum, S. A., 104, 265
Arlow, J., 146
Armstrong, S., 65
Auerbach, A. H., 43, 274

Bachrach, H. M., 274, 299
Balint, E., 11, 16, 66, 107
Balint, M., 11, 16, 66, 107
Barten, H. H., 3
Bateson, G., *xv*
Beck, A. T., *xii,* 311
Bellak, L., 6, 65
Bentovim, A., 66
Bergin, A. E., *xii, xv,* 5, 9, 272, 308, 310
Binder, J. L., 65, 90, 276
Blatt, S. J., 90
Blos, P., 66
Blum, H. P., 144, 162
Bowlby, J., 260
Breuer, J., 8, 10, 12
Budman, S. H., 3, 66
Burstein, E. D., 274
Butcher, J. N., 11, 276, 310

Castelnuovo-Tedesco, P., 11
Chandler, M., 274
Chassan, J. B., 43
Chevron, E., *xii,* 311
Cohen, A., 274
Coltrera, J. T., 144
Coyne, L., 274
Cristol, A. H., 270

Dare, C., 164
Davanloo, H., 7, 11, 12, 18–20, 22, 55, 66, 108, 148, 161, 163, 180, 265, 276, 299, 302
Dewald, P. A., 179
Diesing, P., 88

Ekstein, R., 66
Emery, G., *xii,* 311
Epstein, L., 141, 148
Erikson, E., 28
Ewing, J. A., 43
Eysenck, H. J., 310

Fanshel, D., 80
Feiner, A. H., 141, 148
Fenichel, O., *xi*
Ferenczi, S., 10, 25
Firestein, S., 265
Fisch, R., *xv*
Flegenheimer, W. V., 7, 66
Foulkes, D., 90
Frank, J. D., 41, 139, 270–72
French, T. M., *xv,* 10, 11, 25, 66, 141, 304
Freud, A., 52, 180
Freud, S., *xi,* 8–10, 12, 32–34, 135, 140, 143, 145, 155, 177, 180, 191, 192, 267, 268, 299, 305, 306, 309
Frisman, L. K., 4*n*
Fromm-Reichmann, F., 41, 47, 139

Garfield, S. L., 308
Gill, M. M., *xv,* 26, 65, 67, 91, 135, 138, 141, 144–46, 149, 157, 162, 163, 186
Giovacchini, P., 276
Glass, G. V., 5, 310
Glover, E., *xiii*
Goldman, R., 7, 11, 14–16, 22, 66
Gomes-Schwartz, B., 139, 166, 274, 285

Name Index

Green, L., 59n
Greenacre, P., 144, 146, 147
Greenson, R. R., xii, 22, 148
Gross, M. L., 313
Gurman, A. S., 3

Hadley, S. W., 139, 166, 273, 308, 309
Haley, J., xv
Hartley, D. E., 274
Havens, L., 88, 141
Heisenberg, W., 141
Hill, L. B., 41
Hoffman, I., 65, 67, 186
Hoffman, I. Z., 137, 138, 141, 142, 145
Holder, A., 164
Horndern, A., 59n
Horney, K., 28, 144
Horowitz, L., 274
Hoyt, M. F., 43

Kaplan, H. S., 271
Keithley, L. J., 274
Kernberg, O. F., xv, 141, 147, 274, 276
Kiesler, D. J., xii, xv, 28, 72, 89
Kinston, W., 66
Klein, G. S., xv, 26
Klerman, G. L., xii, 311
Knight, R. P., 309
Kohut, H., 47, 276
Kornreich, M., 5, 310
Koss, M. P., 11, 276, 310

Labov, W., 80
Lambert, M. J., xv, 5, 310
Langs, R., 190
Leaff, L. A., 299
Lerner, H., 90
Levenson, E. A., 141, 149
Lewin, K., 268
Lidz, T., 29
Luborsky, L., xii, 5, 43, 66, 67, 270, 274, 300, 310, 311

Macalpine, I., 140
Malan, D. H., 7, 11, 12, 16–20, 22, 43n, 55, 56, 66, 79, 148, 161, 163, 190, 265, 276, 299, 302
Mann, J., 7, 11, 12, 14–16, 20, 22, 66, 147, 261, 265, 299, 302
Margulies, A., 141
Marrow, A. J., 268

Maslow, A. H., 262
Mayman, M., 53, 90
McGuire, T. G., 4n
Meltzoff, J., 5, 310
Menninger, K., xi
Miller, T. I., 5, 310
Moras, K., 274
Mortimer, R. L., 96, 97
Muslin, H. L., 149

Neubauer, P. B., 163

Ornstein, P., 11, 16, 66, 107

Pardes, H., 3
Peterfreund, E., 68, 108, 166–68
Pincus, H. A., 3
Polanyi, M., 170
Prager, R. A., 308

Rabkin, J. G., 276
Racker, H., 66, 141, 147, 148
Rangell, L., 144
Rank, O., 10, 25
Reich, W., 180
Robbins, L. L., 66
Rogers, C. R., 47, 139, 271
Rounsaville, B., xii, 311
Rush, A. J., xii, 311
Ryle, A., 66, 67

Sachs, J. S., 274
Salzman, L., 177
Samples, S. J., 274
Sampson, H., 149
Sandifer, M., 59n
Sandler, A. M., 34, 36, 148, 164
Sandler, J., 34, 36
Schacht, T. E., 67, 76
Schafer, R., xv, 23, 24, 26, 61n, 69, 71, 138, 141, 144, 155, 180, 181
Schank, R. C., 69
Schecter, D., 45
Schectman, H., 52, 64
Schlesinger, H., 181
Shaw, B. I., xii, 311
Sherwood, M., 69
Shevrin, H., 52, 64
Sifneos, P., 7, 11–15, 17, 18–20, 55, 66, 108, 147, 161, 163, 265, 276, 299

326

Name Index

Singer, B., 5, 270, 310
Sloane, R. B., 270
Small, L., 3, 6, 11, 65, 161
Smith, M. L., 5, 310
Smith, W. H., 96, 97
Smokler, I., 66, 90
Spence, D. P., 25, 69, 75, 104, 105, 166, 175, 300
Staples, F. R., 270
Strachey, J., xi
Strupp, H. H., xii, 9, 43, 59n, 139, 150, 166, 271–74, 298, 300, 308–10
Sullivan, H. S., xv, 28, 31, 51, 141, 167, 262

Thompson, C., 9

Vaillant, G. E., 301
Voth, H., 274

Wachtel, P., 72
Wallerstein, R. S., 66
Waterhouse, G. J., 274
Watzlawick, P., xv
Weakland, J. H., xv
Weiss, J., 149
Weissman, M., xii, 311
Wender, P. H., 72
Wexler, M., 22
Whipple, K., 270
Wolberg, L., 55, 56, 258

Yalom, I., 68
Yorkston, N. J., 270

Zilbergeld, B., 313

Subject Index

Action patterns, 174

Affective disorders, 113

Affective experiences, 31; in case history, 200, 201, 206, 235, 238, 239; resistance and, 187–88; in termination, 261

Affects: context of, 157–58; repressed, 8

Aggressive fantasies, 30, 32

Alcoholism, 57

Alertness of therapist, 303–4

Anachronistic relationship predispositions, 142

Anger: patient's, 154; therapist's, 150–53, 155

Anxiety: castration, 71; in childhood, 32; chronic, 30; death, 68; evoked by therapy, 191–92; at exploration of focal topics, 109; interventions producing, 187; provocation of, 108; warding off of, 209

"Archaic superego," 34

Assessment, 51–64, 302–3; in case history, 196; clinical illustration of, 110–34; dynamic focus and, 103; example of, 55–56; guidelines for, 56–61; interview outline for, 61–63; by Montreal group, 19; of outcomes, 308–11; process of, 51–55; by Tavistock group, 17; in Vanderbilt I study, 273, 276–77

Autonomous functioning: increasing patient's, 107; interferences with, *xiv*

Aversive conditioning, 270

Barrett-Lennard Relationship Inventory, 282

Behavior therapy, 171*n,* 271; technique in, 270

Borderline conditions, 9, 26, 276; therapist selection for treatment of, 300

Case histories, 194–258; affective experiences in, 200, 201, 206, 235, 238, 239; background of, 195–96; childhood recol-

lections in, 202, 203, 205, 219–21, 225, 226, 231, 233, 248–49; corrective emotional experience in, 206; countertransference in, 228, 230, 231; dreams in, 221, 227, 236, 240, 245, 255–57; expectations in, 206, 221, 222, 227, 232–33, 237, 255; focal theme of, 199, 203–6, 208, 211, 213, 214, 221, 225, 227, 231, 232, 236, 237, 240, 242, 252; follow-up to, 255–57; resistance in, 209, 216; of Tavistock group, 18; termination in, 237–41, 244–47, 249–55, 257; therapeutic alliance in, 217, 234, 249; therapeutic relationship in, 199, 202, 203, 205–8, 214, 217, 218, 223–25, 230, 232–36, 239, 240, 245, 247, 255; T/P links in, 223–25; transactions in, 215, 231, 235, 238; from Vanderbilt I study, comparison of, 285–98

Castration anxiety, 71

Cause and effect, linear models of, 72–73, 75

"Central issue," 66

Change, motivation for, 13, 58, 276

Character armor, 19

Character disorders, 276

Character structure, changes in, 12

Characterological disturbances, severity of, 276

Childhood: conflicts rooted in, 8, 10, 21–23, 25, 144; interpersonal relationships in, 29–32; recollections of, in case histories, 202, 203, 205, 219–21, 225, 226, 231, 233, 248–49, 294; separation experiences in, 260

Cognitive restructuring, 171

Colitis, 6

Conditioning techniques, 270

Conflict: actions expressing, 70–71; approach-avoidance, 56; in assessment process, 54, 55, 57, 62; in case histories, 287, 290; childhood, 8, 10, 21–23, 25, 144; collaborative examination of, 221; discrepancies of process and content indicating, 92; in dynamic focus, 22; enactment in therapeutic relationship of, 26; exposure of, behavioral change and, 192;

in free association, 168; guidelines for understanding, 143–59; identification of, 174; interpretation and, 165; model of manifestations in therapeutic situation of, 23; Montreal group on, 19; in narrative presentation, 24; obstacles to therapy produced by, *see* Resistance; parent-child constellation and, 173; present experience of, 10–11; resources for coping with, 159; in short-term anxiety-provoking psychotherapy, 13; Tavistock group on, 16–18; about termination, 240, 247, 261, 262; in time-limited psychotherapy, 15

Confrontation, 67–68; least possible, principle of, 107, 108; resistance and, 180–81

Content, interpersonal, 90–94

Control, neurotic struggle for, 154

Coping ability, 159; degree of impairment of, 276

Core conflict, 22, 144

"Core conflictual relationship theme," 66

"Core neurotic conflict," 66

Corrective emotional experience, 11, 45, 141; in case history, 206

Cost-effectiveness, 3

Countertransference, *xiv,* 23, 139, 140, 142; ability to curb, 298; alertness to, 305; in assessment process, 54; in case histories, 228, 230, 231, 290–91; in clinical illustration, 120; interpersonal process and, 91; Montreal group on, 20; in object relations theory, 141; research on, 280, 300; resistance and, 188; in short-term anxiety-provoking psychotherapy, 13; technical role of, 146–55; in time-limited psychotherapy, 16

Crisis intervention techniques, 6

Cyclical psychodynamic patterns, 72–74, 103; salience and, 95, 97

Death anxiety, 68

Defenses, 32; Montreal group on, 19; *see also* Resistance

Dependency issues, 260

Desensitization, systematic, 270

Destructive acting out, 57

Developmental deficits, 29

Diagnosis, 51, 52, 64; in clinical illustration, 127; *see also* Assessment

Diagnostic and Statistical Manual of Mental Disorders (DSM-III), 113

Double binds, 49, 139

Dreams: childhood conflicts in, 30–31; in clinical illustration of assessment, 132, 134; in case histories, 221, 227, 236, 237, 240, 245, 255–57, 287, 288; expectations

in, 93; interpersonal content of, 90; therapeutic relationship and, 161–62

Drug addiction, 57

Drug therapy, 5

Dynamic focus, 21, 22, 65–109, 303, 306; alternative framework for, 24; assessment and, 52, 56, 61; case illustrations of, 77–78, 82–88, 94–95, 102, 199, 203–6, 208, 211, 213, 214, 221, 225, 227, 231, 232, 236, 237, 240, 242, 252; central conflictual issues and, 276; clinical illustration of development of, 110–34; completed, working with, 103–9; conceptual foundations of, 67–75; construction of, 78–80; defining characteristics of, 70–75; flexibility of therapist and, 170–76; format of, 76–77; formulation of, 98–102; free association and, 167; gathering interpersonal information for, 80–98; setting of time limits and, 265–66; as structure for interpersonal narratives, 68–70; themes related to, 155; training and, 312; transference and, 146

Dysthymic disorder, 113, 127

Ego: attempt to master old traumatic events by, 22; defensive organization of, *xiv,* 180; observing, 39, 131, 154

Ego functions, 25, 100; assessment of, 303; in short-term anxiety-provoking psychotherapy, 13; Tavistock group on, 17; in time-limited psychotherapy, 15

Ego psychology, 180

Electroconvulsive therapy, 57

Emotional discomfort, 57

Empathy: communication of, 201; countertransference and, 148–49; dynamic focus and, 108; failure of, 188, 192, 228–29; free association and, 168, 169; in interpretations, 165; listening with, *xiv,* 41, 46–50; patient's response to, 216; reestablishment of, 231; research on, 273; termination and, 266

Enculturation, 29

Enmeshment, 149, 150

Entrapment, 43, 192

Expectations, 92–93; in case history, 206, 221, 222, 227, 232–33, 237, 255; interpretive stance and, 138; of significant others, 148; transference, 141, 145

"False solutions," 190

Fantasies, 31; childhood, 32; curative, 106; in object relations theory, 34; physical symptoms and, 198; about relationship

Fantasies *(continued)*
  with therapist, 42; resistance and, 183; sexual, 237; about termination, 245, 251, 254; unconscious, 30, 38
Feelings: willingness to examine, 57; *see also* Affective experience; Affects
Flexibility of therapist, 169–79
Focal psychotherapy, 66
Focus: Montreal group on, 19; Tavistock group on, 17, 18; in time-limited psychotherapy, 15; *see also* Dynamic focus
Free association, 9, 81, 168–69
"Free floating responsiveness," 36
Functional autonomy, 191

General systems theory, *xv*, 191
Genetic reconstructions, 13–14
Genetic transference interpretations, 13, 14, 18, 22, 161, 163, 180; *see also* T/P links
Global Change scale, 281
Grief reaction, 154
Grieving process in termination, 252–53

Health-care delivery, changing structure of, 3
Helplessness, sense of, 30
Historical reconstructions, 24–26, 74–75, 163
History taking, 52–53; interpretive linking and, 164
Homosexuality, 57
Honesty, 49
Hospitalization, 57
Human actions in dynamic focus, 70–72
Hypnosis, 8, 9
Hysteria, 8

Idealization of therapist, 49, 171, 263
Identification, 93; in childhood, 29; with therapist, 29, 260–62, 264
Imitation, 92, 93
Individuation, 269
"Indwelling," 170
Inertia, 190–92
Infantile neurosis, 9, 10; as core conflict, 22
Infantile sexuality, 8
Inpatient psychotherapy, 4
Insight, 24–25, 163, 165; in case history, 290
Instincts, 22
Internal object relationships, 35
Interpersonal relationships, 28–39; assessment process and, 55, 56, 59–60, 62–63, 276; childhood experience and, 29–32; in clinical illustration, 113–15; gathering

information on, 80–98; inability to form, *xiv;* interpretive links to, 163–64, 167; mature, capacity for, 57–58; narratives of, *see* Narratives; object relations theory on, 34–35; patient–therapist, *see* Therapeutic relationship; psychotherapeutic model and, 36–39; reality orientation in, 32–33; reciprocal patterns in, 191; skills of therapist in, 170; Sullivan's theory of, *xiv;* and working definition of psychotherapy, 268–69; *see also* Transactions
Interpretations, *xv;* of action patterns, 174; active stance in making, 10; in case histories, 203, 212, 287–90, 292, 294–96; early in therapy, 199; of feelings about termination, 254; flexibility and, 171–72, 179; genetic, *see* Genetic transference interpretations; inappropriate, 106; intellectualized, 188; linked to outside relationships, 163–64; of material outside therapeutic relationship, 161; Montreal group on, 19; in psychoanalytic technique, 269–70; of patient's questions, 206; reasons to avoid, 156; in short-term anxiety-provoking psychotherapy, 13–14; Tavistock group on, 17, 18; technique of, 164–68; of themes, 157; of therapeutic relationship, 159–60; in time-limited therapy, 12; in time-limited psychotherapy, 16; timing of, 162, 175; of T/P links, 25; trial, 55, 120–22, 126, 127, 303
Interventions: in case history, 225–27; flexibility and, 170–76; guidelines for, 159–79; reasons to avoid, 156; resistance and, 183, 186–87; timing of, 104; trial, 21; *see also* Confrontations; Interpretations
Interview: clinical example of, 111–34; outline for conducting, 61–63
Intimacy: achievement of, 38; avoidance of, 32; internal object relationships and, 35; primitive forms of, 34; therapeutic stance and, 49; threat of, 56
Intrapsychic change, 262

Least possible confrontation, principle of, 107, 108
Life disruptions, assessment of, 62
Life stories, *see* Narratives
Linear models, 72–73, 75
Listening, 41, 45–50; empathic, 46–50, 168, 169; respect and, 45–46
London Clinic of Psycho-Analysis, 57
Long-term psychotherapy, 4–6, 11*n;* alertness in, 303; analytic model of, 277; application of principles of, 23; for borderline conditions and narcissistic personality disorders, 276; dependency is-

sues in, 260; organizing tendencies in, 65; patient selection for, 303; resistances in, 180; ritualistic aspects of, 304; termination of, 259, 265, 304

Loss, 15–16; assessment of, 62; *see also* Separation

Memories: in clinical illustration, 131–32, 134; interpersonal content of, 90; reconstruction of, 53, 75; *see also* Childhood, recollections of

Menninger Project, 274

Mental health and illness, conceptions of, 308

Metacommunication, 89

Metapsychology, *xv*, 26; dynamic focus and, 22; hydraulic interpretations of, 72–73

Minnesota Multiphasic Personality Inventory (MMPI), 276, 281

"Misalliance cures," 190

Modeling, 93, 270

Montreal group, 18–20

Morale building, 270

Motivation for change, 13, 58, 276

Mount Zion Psychotherapy Group, 149

Mourning reactions, 6

Narcissistic personality disorders, 276

Narratives, 23, 24; case example of, 77–78; categories of information required for, 76–77; dynamic focus as structure for, 68–70; formulation of, 98, 99; historical, 75; human actions in, 70–72; organization of information in, 211; overextension of, 104; residual ambiguity of, 105; themes of, 155; transactional, 72, 80–94

National Institute of Mental Health, 272; Collaborative Study of Depression, *xiii*

Negative transference, 278

Neo-Freudians, 26, 28

Neuroses: childhood origins of, 29; infantile, 9, 10; transference, 143–44

Nuclear conflict, 66, 144

Nurture, 29

Object relations theory, *xv*, 26, 34–35; transference and countertransference in, 141, 146–47

Object representations, 36, 147

Objects, 200; losses of, 260; *see also* Significant others

Observing ego, 39, 141, 154

Obsessional symptoms, 57; severe, 276

Obsessive-compulsive personality disorder, 176

Oedipal conflicts: focus on, 66; in short-term anxiety-provoking psychotherapy, 13, 14; in time-limited psychotherapy, 15

Operant conditioning, 270

Outcome: assessment of, 280, 308–11; measures of, 279; poor, 275, 277; predictions of, 274; therapeutic alliance and, 36; variability in, 273–74

Panic attacks, 6

Patience, 48

Patient selection, 6, 21, 23, 24; assessment and, 52, 55–58, 63; formulation of focus and, 99–100; Montreal group on, 19; for short-term anxiety-provoking psychotherapy, 13, 14; by Tavistock group, 17; for time-limited psychotherapy, 15, 16; training and, 313; for Vanderbilt I study, 275–76

Patient-therapist relationship, *see* Therapeutic relationship

Personality function, assessment of, 57–58

Personality structure: in childhood, 29; object relations and, 34; patient selection on basis of, 24

Personality theories, 78

Phobias, 9, 57; confrontation of situation provoking, 192; systematic desensitization in treatment of, 270

Preoedipal conflicts, 15

Presenting problem, 62; in clinical illustration, 111, 114, 124, 127

Process, interpersonal, 90–94; ratings of, 284, 285

Projection, 33; of transference, 23

Projective tests, 92

Provocative behavior of patients, 149–50; in case history, 222

Psychoanalysis, 4, 6; assessment in, 299; cognitive therapy and, 171*n*; concept of resistance in, 179–81; continued influence of, 267; free association in, 169; history of, 8–11; interpretation in, 166–67; technique in, 269–70; traditional goals of, 307

Psychoses, childhood origins of, 29

Psychological testing, 90

Psychotherapy: specific versus nonspecific factors in, 269–72; working definition of, 268–69

Punitive role, avoidance of, 50

Reality testing, 47

Regression, 264

"Reinforcement history," 191
Repetition compulsion, 22, 191; in counter-transference, 147
Repression, 8, 29
Research, 267–301; on outcomes, 309–10; and specific versus nonspecific factors in psychotherapy, 269–72; treatment modalities and, 211–13; working definition of psychotherapy for, 268–69. *See also* Vanderbilt I study
"Residual trauma," 66
Resistances, *xiv,* 32, 179–90; alertness of therapist to, 304; analysis of, 9; case examples of, 182–88, 209, 216; in clinical illustration, 118–20, 126; concept of, 179–81; definition of, 181–83; diversionary, 107; iatrogenic, 54; identification of, 183–86; interpretation of, 12, 270; management of, 186–88; Montreal group on, 19; negative reactions of therapists to, 277, 278; Tavistock group on, 17; of therapist, 188–90; of trial interpretations, 55–56
Respect for patient, 45–46; flexibility and, 170
Restructuring, 179*n;* cognitive, 171
Rigidity, avoidance of, 49
Rituals, avoidance of, 49
Role assignments, 48

Salience, transactional, 94–98
Scenarios, enactment of, 38
Scripts, 69
Seductive behavior of patients, 150, 185–86
Selection of patients, *see* Patient selection
Selective attention and selective neglect, 107–8
Self-destructive acting out, 57
Self-esteem: childhood injuries to, 31; deficiencies in, *xiv;* interpretations and, 166; therapeutic stance to strengthen, 48; of therapist, 189
Self-identity, 29
Self-image, countertransference and, 54
Self-observation, capacity for, 33; *see also* Observing ego
Self-regulation, training in, 270
Self-representations, 36, 147
Sequence analysis, 93
Separations, 15–16, 260; termination and, 261, 263, 264, 304
Sexual dysfunctions, treatment of, 271
Sexual fantasies, 30, 32
Short-term anxiety-provoking psychotherapy (STAPP), 12–14
Significant others, *xiii,* 29, 173, 175, 265; anger at, 176, 178; in childhood, 29–31; emphasis on current relationships with,

307; in enactment of unrealistic scenarios, 38; need to control, 154; reciprocal behavior patterns of, 191; resistance and, 186; therapist as, 42, 137, 145, 148, 171
Socialization, 29
Stress reactions, 100
Suicide attempts, 57
Superego: "archaic," 34; hypertrophied, 176–79
Supervision, 312
Symbolic productions, interpersonal content of, 90
Symptoms, *xv;* relief of, 12
Systematic desensitization, 270
Systems theory, *xv,* 191

Target complaints, 281–82; rating of, 283
Tavistock group, 11, 16–18, 20
Technique, 135–93; errors in, 192–93; examination of therapeutic relationship in, 159–60; flexibility of, 169–79; of free association, 168–69; goals of, 140–43; of interpretation, 164–68; for interpretive links to outside relationships, 163–64; of interventions, 159–79; obstacles to progress and, 179–93; research on, 269–72, 274, 275, 277–79; role of countertransference in, 146–55; role of transference in, 143–46; themes of sessions and, 155–59; therapeutic process and, 136–40; therapeutic relationship in, 140–43; therapeutic stance and, 135; for use of material outside therapeutic relationship, 160–62
Tension, productive, 304
Termination, 11, 21, 259–66, 304–5; in case histories, 237–41, 244–47, 249–55, 257, 293, 296, 299; and failure to examine therapeutic relationship, 190; guidelines for, 265–66; illustration of, 262–63; Montreal group on, 20; premature, 274, 275, 277; psychology of, 259–65; setting date for, 302; of short-term anxiety-provoking psychotherapy, 14; Tavistock group on, 17; of time-limited psychotherapy, 15, 16
Themes of sessions, 43, 47; technical aspects of, 155–59
Therapeutic alliance, 39, 140; ambivalence of, 154–55; in case history, 217, 234, 249; deterrents to formation of, 300; essential ingredients of, 36; flexibility and, 170–76; poor, 277; research on, 274; resistance and, 188, 190; response to patient's questions and, 197; termination and, 262, 263; trust and, 33
Therapeutic relationship, *xiv;* ambivalence

in, 260, 263; assessment process and, 51–
55, 58–61, 63; in case history, 199, 202,
203, 205–8, 214, 217, 218, 223–25, 230,
232–36, 239, 240, 245, 247, 255; in clinical illustration, 120, 123; coercive approach to, 108; consequences of failure
to examine, 190–92; enactment of focal
pattern in, 105, 107; examination of,
159–60; expectations in, 93; as factor
common to all technical approaches, 270;
fearful anticipation of, 55; functional
salience in, 95, 96; historic significance of
transactions in, 75; human quality of,
139; interpersonal process in, 91; learning in, 35; patient's perception of, 282–
85; ratings of, 284, 285; research on, 273–
75, 278; resistance and, 181–84, 186, 188,
189; sense of safety in, 109; in short-term
anxiety-provoking psychotherapy, 13,
14; Tavistock group on, 17; technical
focus on, xv, 140–43; termination and,
261, 264; themes in, 156–57; in time-
limited psychotherapy, 16; training and,
312–13; use of material outside, 160–62
Therapeutic stance, 40–50; empathy in, 46–
50; flexibility and, 173; interpretations
and, 166; respect for patient in, 45–46;
technique and, 135
Time-limited psychotherapy, 14–16
Timing of interventions, 104; interpretive
links to outside relationships, 163–64
TLDP Adherence Scale, 312
T/P links, 22–25, 163–64; in case history,
223–25; see also Genetic transference interpretations
Training, xi, xiii, xvii, 29n; analytic model in,
277; investigation of results of, 268; in
long-term psychotherapy, 6; necessity
of, 306; research on, 311–13; for short-
term dynamic therapy, 278–79; specific
versus nonspecific factors and, 270–72;
termination and, 259
Transactions, xiv, 29, 34; analysis of, 144; in
assessment process, 56; in case history,
215, 231, 235, 238; in clinical illustration,
115, 120, 127; in construction of focus, 79;
emphasis on, 68–69; flexibility and, 178;
functional salience of, 94–98; historic and
current significance of, 74–75; identifications and, 262; interpretation of, 165;
narratives of, 72; outside therapeutic relationship, 161; patient's construal of
meanings of, 204; process and content of,
90–94; resistance and, 181, 189; seeking,
80–94; self- and object images activated
in, 35, 148; sequences of, 93–94; themes
of, 43, 155–58; in therapeutic process,
136; in therapeutic relationship, 140–43
Transference, xiv, xv, 36, 139, 140; action

component of, 142; affective experience
of conflictual behavior in, 163; alertness
to, 305; analysis of, 9, 21; in clinical illustration, 120, 121; "corrective emotional
experience" and, 141; definition of, 145;
"disguised allusions" to, 157, 162; dynamic focus and, 54; expression of conflicts in, 10; flexibility and, 172; historical
reconstructions and, 25; implications of
patient's questions for, 197; in interpersonal terms, 35; interpretation of, 12,
270, and see Genetic transference interpretations; intertwining of countertransference and, 148–49; Montreal group on,
19; negative, 278; and organizing tendencies of therapy, 65; patient's expectations
in, 11, 207; projection of, 23; and recall of
past, 75; re-experience of childhood conflict in, 10, 21, 22; resistance and, 180,
182–83, 186–88; in short-term anxiety-
provoking psychotherapy, 13–14; Tavistock group on, 18; technical role of, 143–
46; in time-limited psychotherapy, 15, 16
Transference neurosis, 143–44
Transference-parent links, see T/P links
"Transference predisposition," 66
Treatment manuals, 311–12
Trial interpretations, 21, 55, 303; clinical
illustration of, 119–22, 126, 127
Trust, 33, 57; patient's questions and building of, 197

Unconscious instincts, 22

Values, 308–9
Vanderbilt I study, 150, 196, 271n, 272–
301, 306, 311; assessment procedures in,
276–77; case histories from, 285–98;
comparison of patient pair from, 280–85;
design of, 272–75; patient selection for,
275–76; process ratings in, 284, 285; therapeutic operations in, 277–79
Vanderbilt II study, 311
Vanderbilt Psychotherapy Process Scale,
284
Vanderbilt University Psychotherapy Research Group, xiii, 7, 26, 268, 311, 312
Vicious circles, 73, 144

"Wild analysis," xi
Working alliance, see Therapeutic alliance
Working through, 10; in case history, 290